SCRIPTURAL TRACES:
CRITICAL PERSPECTIVES ON THE RECEPTION
AND INFLUENCE OF THE BIBLE

6

Editors
Claudia V. Camp, Texas Christian University
W. J. Lyons, University of Bristol
Andrew Mein, University of Cambridge

Published under

LIBRARY OF HEBREW BIBLE/
OLD TESTAMENT STUDIES

615

Formerly Journal for the Study of the Old Testament Supplement Series

Editors
Claudia V. Camp, Texas Christian University
Andrew Mein, University of Cambridge

Founding Editors
David J. A. Clines, Philip R. Davies and David M. Gunn

Editorial Board
Alan Cooper, John Goldingay, Robert P. Gordon,
Norman K. Gottwald, James E. Harding, John Jarick, Carol Meyers,
Carolyn J. Sharp, Daniel L. Smith-Christopher,
Francesca Stavrakopoulou, James W. Watts

Reception History and Biblical Studies

Theory and Practice

Edited by
Emma England
and
William John Lyons

t&tclark
LONDON • NEW YORK • OXFORD • NEW DELHI • SYDNEY

T&T CLARK
Bloomsbury Publishing Plc
50 Bedford Square, London, WC1B 3DP, UK
1385 Broadway, New York, NY 10018, USA

BLOOMSBURY, T&T CLARK and the T&T Clark logo are
trademarks of Bloomsbury Publishing Plc

First published in Great Britain 2015
Paperback edition first published 2018

Copyright © Emma England and William John Lyons, 2015

Emma England and William John Lyons have asserted their rights under the Copyright,
Designs and Patents Act, 1988, to be identified as Editors of this work.

All rights reserved. No part of this publication may be reproduced or
transmitted in any form or by any means, electronic or mechanical,
including photocopying, recording, or any information storage or
retrieval system, without prior permission in writing from the publishers.

Bloomsbury Publishing Plc does not have any control over, or responsibility for,
any third-party websites referred to or in this book. All internet addresses given
in this book were correct at the time of going to press. The author and publisher
regret any inconvenience caused if addresses have changed or sites have ceased
to exist, but can accept no responsibility for any such changes.

A catalogue record for this book is available from the British Library.

ISBN: HB: 978-0-56766-008-4
PB: 978-0-56767-246-9
ePDF: 978-0-56766-009-1
ePub: 978-0-56766-010-7

A catalog record for this book is available from the Library of Congress.

Series: Scriptural Traces, 6
Series: Library of Hebrew Bible/Old Testament Studies, 615

Typeset by RefineCatch Limited, Bungay, Suffolk

To find out more about our authors and books visit
www.bloomsbury.com and sign up for our newsletters.

Contents

Acknowledgements vii
List of Contributors viii

Part 1 Introduction

1   Explorations in the Reception of the Bible   *Emma England and William John Lyons*   3

Part 2 Reception History, Historical-Criticism and Biblical Studies

2   Biblical Studies on Holiday? A Personal View of Reception History   *Susan Gillingham*   17

3   What is Reception History, and What Happens to You if You Do It?   *James E. Harding*   31

4   The End of Reception History, a Grand Narrative for Biblical Studies and the Neoliberal Bible   *James G. Crossley*   45

5   Visitors, Gatekeepers and Receptionists: Reflections on the Shape of Biblical Studies and the Role of Reception History   *Jonathan Morgan*   61

Part 3 Conceptualizing Reception History

6   The Head of John and its Reception or How to Conceptualize 'Reception History'   *Caroline Vander Stichele*   79

7   What Can a Text Do? Reception History as an Ethology of the Biblical Text   *Brennan Breed*   95

8   The End of Biblical Interpretation – the Beginning of Reception History? Reading the Bible in the Spaces of Literature   *Samuel Tongue*   111

9   Reception History of the Bible: Prospects of a New Frontier in African Biblical Studies   *Masiiwa Ragies Gunda*   125

Part 4 Practical Implications, Difficulties and Solutions

10 Unlikely Bedfellows: Lenin, Calvin and Nick Cave *Roland Boer* 141

11 Tracing Patmos Through the Centuries *Ian Boxall* 155

12 Digital Humanities and Reception History; or the Joys and Horrors of Databases *Emma England* 169

13 Layers of Reception of Jephthah's Daughter (Judges 11) Among the AmaNazaretha: From the Early 1900s to Today *Gerald O. West* 185

Part 5 Bible, Reception and Popular Music

14 The Story of Leonard Cohen's 'Who by Fire', a Prayer in the Cairo Genizah, Babylonian Astrology and Related Rabbinical Texts *Helen R. Jacobus* 201

15 'Time to cut him down to size?' A Critical Examination of Depeche Mode's Alternative 'John of Patmos' *William John Lyons* 219

16 'God', 'God Part II' and 'God Part III': Exploring the Anxiety of Influence in John Lennon, U2 and Larry Norman *Michael J. Gilmour* 231

17 High, Low and In-between: Reception History and the Sociology of Religion and Popular Music *Ibrahim Abraham* 241

Bibliography 255
Index 277

Acknowledgements

This book originated in two sessions of the 'Biblical World and Its Reception' research group at the Society of Biblical Literature International/European Association of Biblical Studies Annual Meeting, held at the University of Amsterdam, in July 2012. We are grateful to the presenters and the participants in those sessions for their valuable contributions to what can only to be seen as an ongoing discussion. About half of the volume's essays came from elsewhere, however, and we would like to say thank you to those contributors who were happy to lend their ideas and experience to this exploration of reception history. The book was coaxed through its birthing with help from James Crossley and Andrew Mein, but most especially Miriam Cantwell at Bloomsbury whose patience, most particularly in our most critical of decisions – the book cover – was unerring. Grateful thanks are also offered to Paul King, Josh Pawaar and Merv Honeywood for their care and attention at the copy-editing and proof stages. It is all very much appreciated.

Personally Emma England would like to thank her husband Robert Nieuwenhuijs, sister Laura England, brother-in-law Matt Smith and friends Joan Saunders and Anne Kustritz, all of whom were particularly present in the final months of the preparation of this book. Their willingness to eat unhealthy amounts of cake will always be appreciated.

John Lyons would like to thank Jonathan Campbell, Jorunn Økland, and Bella Sandwell for writing the introductions to the previous edited volumes in which he has been involved; he now knows what they went through. For their valuable and inspirational support in his struggles with the meaning and significance of reception history, he would like to record his thanks to David Gunn and Chris Rowland. They have long trodden this path at no little cost to themselves. May their vindication not be too long in coming! Finally, thanks for their support and forbearance go to his wife, Katie, and to his daughters, Hannah and Megan, who have begun to suspect, he thinks, that their father is really some kind of cyborg, being permanently attached to a computer of some kind. He hopes it is not true, but fears that it may be.

List of Contributors

Ibrahim Abraham
Ibrahim Abraham is a postdoctoral researcher in the discipline of social and cultural anthropology at the University of Helsinki, currently studying Christian music and youth culture in South Africa with the support of the Academy of Finland. Ibrahim received his PhD in sociology from the University of Bristol in 2012 for a study of the global Christian punk subculture. He has published articles on various aspects of the relationship between contemporary religion, society and culture in journals including *The Bible and Critical Theory*, *Contemporary Islam* and the *International Journal of Children's Spirituality*.

Roland Boer
Apart from voyages by ship and cycling as long and as far as he can, Roland Boer is Professor of Literary Theory at Renmin University of China, Beijing, and Research Professor at the University of Newcastle, Australia. Among numerous publications, the most recent are *Idols of Nations* (with Christina Petterson, Fortress 2014), *Marxist Criticism of the Hebrew Bible* (Continuum 2014) and *In the Vale of Tears* (Brill and Haymarket 2014).

Ian Boxall
Ian Boxall is Associate Professor of New Testament at the Catholic University of America, Washington DC. His recent publications include *Patmos in the Reception History of the Apocalypse* (2013) and *Discovering Matthew* (2014).

Brennan Breed
Brennan Breed is Assistant Professor of Old Testament at Columbia Theological Seminary, and works in the fields of Wisdom literature, Hebrew poetry, visual art, and biblical reception history. His first monograph, *Nomadic Text: A Theory of Biblical Reception History*, was published in 2014, and he is currently co-authoring a reception historical commentary on Qohelet with C. Davis Hankins for Eerdmans' Illuminations series.

James G. Crossley
James Crossley is Professor of Bible, Culture and Politics at the University of Sheffield. He is the author of numerous articles and books including *Jesus in an Age*

of *Neoliberalism: Quests, Scholarship and Ideology* (2012) and *Harnessing Chaos: The Bible in English Political Discourse since 1968* (2014).

Emma England
Emma England is a Guest Researcher at the University of Amsterdam specialising in the intersections between the Bible and Popular Culture. Her publications include work in children's Bibles and comics. She is currently researching transmediality and the Bible, and the Bible in science fiction and fantasy television. She is co-editing special issues of *Transformative Works and Cultures* and *Foundation: The International Review of Science Fiction*.

Susan Gillingham
Sue Gillingham is Fellow and Tutor in Theology at Worcester College, and Reader in Old Testament in the University of Oxford. She has published several books on the Psalms, including the first volume of a reception history analysis of the entire Psalter, *Psalms through the Centuries* (2008) and *A Journey of Two Psalms: The Reception of Psalms 1 and 2 in Jewish and Christian Tradition* (2014).

Michael J. Gilmour
Michael J. Gilmour teaches New Testament and English literature at Providence University College, Canada. He is the author of *The Gospel According to Bob Dylan: The Old, Old Story for Modern Times* (2011) and *Eden's Other Residents: The Bible and Animals* (2014).

Masiiwa Ragies Gunda
Masiiwa Ragies Gunda is a consultant on Religion, Gender and Sexuality and a specialist in Transformative Biblical Studies and lecturer in Old Testament Studies and Biblical Hebrew at ZEGU, Zimbabwe. He has published on the use of the Bible in African Christianity including his PhD Thesis, *The Bible and Homosexuality in Zimbabwe* (2010) and 'Prediction and Power: Prophets and Prophecy in the Old Testament and Zimbabwean Christianity', *Exchange* 41/4 (2012) 335–51.

James E. Harding
James E. Harding is Senior Lecturer in Hebrew Bible/Old Testament Studies at the University of Otago, priest in the Anglican Diocese of Dunedin, and author of *The Love of David and Jonathan: Ideology, Text, Reception* (Sheffield: Equinox Publishing, 2012).

Helen R. Jacobus
Helen R. Jacobus (PhD University of Manchester, 2014) is currently a hon. Research Associate at University College London, Department of Hebrew and Jewish Studies. Her revised thesis is published as a monograph, *Zodiac Calendars in the*

Dead Sea Scrolls and their Reception: Ancient Astronomy and Astrology in Early Judaism (Brill, 2014), forthcoming. She received the Sean Dever Award (2011) for her article, 'A Jewish Zodiac Calendar at Qumran?', in C. Hempel (ed.), *The Dead Sea Scrolls: Texts and Contexts.* (Brill, 2010).

William John Lyons
John Lyons is Reader in Biblical Interpretation at the University of Bristol. His recent publications include *Joseph of Arimathea: A Study in Reception History* (2014); (with I. Sandwell (eds)), *Delivering the Word: Preaching and Exegesis in the Western Christian Tradition* (2012), and (with J. Økland (eds)), *The Way the World Ends? The Apocalypse of John in Culture and Ideology* (2009).

Jonathan Morgan
Jon Morgan is Lecturer in Religion and History at the University of Chester. His publications include 'Sacrifice in Leviticus: Eco-Friendly Ritual or Unholy Waste?', in David Horrell et al (eds), *Ecological Hermeneutics: Biblical, Historical, and Theological Perspectives*, (London: T&T Clark, 2010), 32–45; and 'Transgressing, Puking, Covenanting: The Character of Land in Leviticus', *Theology*, Vol. CXII (2009), 172–80.

Samuel Tongue
Samuel Tongue (Ph.D. Glasgow University, 2012) is Associate Teacher and Researcher at the University of Glasgow. His monograph *Between Biblical Criticism and Poetic Rewriting: Interpretative Struggles over Genesis 32:22–32* is published by Brill (2014). He is also co-editor (with A.K.M. Adam) of *Looking Through a Glass Bible: Postdisciplinary Biblical Interpretations from the Glasgow School* (2014).

Caroline Vander Stichele
Caroline Vander Stichele is *Universitair Docent* (Lecturer) in Religious Studies at the University of Amsterdam. Her recent publications include (with H. S. Pyper (eds)), *Text, Image, and Otherness in Children's Bibles: What Is in the Picture?* (2012) and (with T. Penner (eds)), *Contextualizing Gender in Early Christian Discourse: Thinking Beyond Thecla* (2009)

Gerald O. West
Gerald West teaches Old Testament/Hebrew Bible and African Biblical Hermeneutics in the School of Religion, Philosophy, and Classics in the University of KwaZulu-Natal, South Africa and works extensively with the Ujamaa Centre for Community Development and Research. Among his recent publications are (with H. de Wit (eds)) *African and European Readers of the Bible in Dialogue: In Quest of a Shared Meaning* (Leiden: E. J. Brill, 2008); (ed.) *Reading Other-Wise: Socially Engaged Biblical Scholars Reading with Their Local Communities (Semeia Studies* 62), Atlanta and Leiden: SBL and E. J. Brill, 2007); and *The Academy of the Poor: Towards a Dialogical Reading of the Bible* (Pietermaritzburg: Cluster Publications, 2003).

Part One

Introduction

1

Explorations in the Reception of the Bible

Emma England and William John Lyons

Introduction

Studying the reception of the Bible is – or could easily be – a garden of delights allowing us to expand the discipline of biblical studies to embrace a much wider world of biblical interpretation. All manner of study objects could be included, whether popular, technical, artistic, hubristic, or ridiculous; virtually everything the biblical materials touch would be open to scholarly investigation. Such research is spreading, like a global case of guerrilla gardening, with small rebellious groups sowing its seeds. At the same time, biblical studies as a discipline has effectively become a discipline of bonsai tree cultivation, leaving little of its narrow remit untouched and with much repeated ad nauseam. As academia is threatened with increasing budget cuts, the loss of individual posts and departmental closures, some, including the editors of this volume, wonder how long such a narrowly focused discipline can survive at anything approaching its current size without significant change.[1]

---

[1] Roland Boer argues in *Rescuing the Bible* (Oxford: Blackwell Publishing, 2007) that unless change happens in biblical studies the only people left studying and working within the discipline will be conservative groups (both politically and religiously). He proposes a new alliance called the Worldly Left, between the religious left and the secular left in order to save the discipline so that it can continue to educate and combat the effects of the conservative groups (the editors of this volume represent both groups in this proposed alliance). Boer makes his argument using reception history (albeit not clearly identified as such), with examples of the influence of the Bible on political events. Hector Avalos in his *The End of Biblical Studies* (Amherst: Prometheus Books, 2007) goes further by arguing that biblical studies should end because it is a religious exercise and exists to maintain religiosity and the value of the Bible. He does so while paying little attention to the growth of cultural and reception studies in the discipline, or in its potential to change the discipline. For other views on the future of the discipline see Michael V. Fox, 'Biblical Scholarship and Faith-Based Bible Study', *Society of Biblical Literature Forum*. 22/02/2006 to 04/05/2006, http://www.sbl-site.org/publications/article.aspx?articleId=490; Stephen D. Moore and Yvonne Sherwood, *The Invention of the Biblical Scholar: A Critical Manifesto*. (Minneapolis: Fortress Press, 2011); Caroline Vander Stichele, Is Doña Quixote Fighting Windmills? Gendering New Testament Studies in the Netherlands. 01/2013, http://www.lectio.unibe.ch/13_1/vander_stichele_caroline_is_dona_quixote_fighting_windmills.html; W. J. Lyons, 'Hope for a Troubled Discipline? Contributions to New Testament Studies from Reception History', *Journal for the Study of the New Testament* 33 (2010), 207–20; and the multiple essays in Roland Boer and F. Segovia's edited volume, *The Future of the Biblical Past: Envisioning Biblical Studies on a Global Key* (Atlanta, GA: Society of Biblical Literature, 2012).

The irony is that these evaluations are taking place at the same time that there is a deepening and ongoing academic interest in the Bible[2] and its reception[3] elsewhere. Increasingly, such discussions are taking place outside of the confines of biblical studies.[4] This has further diluted what might already have been considered a feeble effort on the part of biblical scholarship to understand broader questions about the Bible, including those pertaining to biblical literacy, cultural appropriations and recreations of biblical texts. With people from other fields exploring our own specialism (and teaching the subject), biblical studies needs to find a way to defend itself and maintain its foothold if it wishes to remain relevant to – and financially viable within – the academic community. To prove our (financial) worth we need to build connections with our colleagues outside of biblical studies and to do this we need to offer the specializations that they cannot. We think the best way of doing this is through a concerted effort to build the strength, reputation and practices of reception studies of the Bible within the current guild.

In order to do this, scholars need to address a few important areas. First we need to openly acknowledge, without prejudice, when something we are working

---

[2] The title of the series in which this volume appears – 'Scriptural Traces' – demonstrates that terms other than 'Bible' are also possible. 'Scripture' (and its adjectival variants) has the advantage of being applicable to the pre-biblical occasions of reception. It also has its objectors, however, especially those who find it has more conservative, religious, and Christian connotations than the term 'Bible' (which nonetheless has its own cultural baggage). Another possibility, 'sacred texts', benefits from more easily including – and encouraging the study of – those materials outside the Protestant Bible, such as the Deutero-canonical works, the Qumran Scrolls and Pseudepigrapha. Despite these options, the complexities of labelling the materials currently explored within biblical studies mean that the term 'Bible' seems worth retaining pragmatically for general disciplinary usage, not least because of its common currency. One should be careful not to use it too prescriptively, however.

[3] Terms currently being offered to designate the kind of study encouraged here include the German terms, *Wirkungsgeschichte* and *Rezeptionsgeschichte*, harking back to H.-G. Gadamer and its subsequent development by H. R. Jauss, with those terms being translated into English equivalents such as the 'history of effects' or 'reception history', 'reception criticism', 'reception studies', 'reception theory', 'biblical reception' or 'reception of the Bible', 'cultural history', and in two essays in this volume, that of Caroline Vander Stichele, 'cultural impact', and that of Brennan Breed, 'ethology of the Bible' respectively. Each proposed label, its proponents argue, has its benefits, and each has been criticized in turn as being potentially misleading and unhelpful. It is also clear that such studies long predate any of these terms (cf., e.g., the sixteenth-century provenance described by N. Klancher, 'A Genealogy of Reception History', *Biblical Interpretation* 21 (2013), 99–129). Regardless of either the current useful insights or the undoubted weaknesses that are brought into the discussion by each of these terms, however, we remain unconvinced that any of them will eventually provide a universally accepted catch-all label for the kind of work we wish to encourage. It is our view that eventually the work that we describe here will simply be known as biblical studies and that any current term applied is useful only in so far as it promotes the work envisaged. The popularity of the term reception history, favoured here, is therefore of use for now primarily because of its ubiquity, we would argue, and not for its explanatory power.

[4] Cf. Piero Boitani, *The Bible and its Rewritings* (Translated by Anita Weston; Oxford: OUP, 1999); Alain Badiou, *Saint Paul: The Foundation of Universalism* (Translated by Ray Brassier; Stanford: Stanford University Press, 2003); Slavoj Žižek, *The Puppet and the Dwarf: The Perverse Core of Christianity* (Cambridge: The MIT Press, 2003); Mieke Bal, *Loving Yusuf: Conceptual Travels from Present to Past* (Chicago: The University of Chicago Press, 2008).

on is reception history. It should be the norm for biblical scholars to be able to discuss and refer to their own work in such terms without it being automatically considered a lesser task. Second, there need to be more foundational, entry level texts, to make it easier for students (and the curious scholar) to pick up a book and understand what reception history is from the contents. Third, there needs to be historic reflection upon the definition, name, subject matter and methodologies as they relate to the study of reception of the Bible. This is true both for the tried and tested and for the potential and unknown. And, so, we have this volume which, through a number of discrete but inter-related signposts, suggests some answers to questions such as: Who should carry out biblical reception studies and within what disciplinary framework(s)? What parameters should form the basis of any attempt to describe and encompass such a topic of study? What should the study of the reception of the Bible be called? What does the term 'Bible' even mean? Should 'reception', 'impact' and 'use' of a text be differentiated? Is the reception of a given text only a one-way street?

The diverse essays in this book offer scholarly considerations on theoretical ideas that may be used to underpin our study of the reception of the Bible, reflections on particular issues or problems that have already arisen, and snapshots of what has already been achieved in specific studies. Offered from within a variety of different scholarly contexts, these essays are intended to provide a broad range of examples of theoretical and practical interactions between text, context and audience, and thus to encourage further scholarly consideration of this exciting area of study. What this volume does not do is claim to definitively outline the range of methodologies to be used in studies of the reception of the Bible or limit the boundaries of such an area of study. In fact, its editors are convinced that there is no single methodology suitable for competent reception studies and the methodologies that currently exist are still in their infancy. The approaches offered in this book are therefore just a fraction of the available possibilities, but they are all, in their different ways, potentially groundbreaking and eye-opening.

Ultimately, these essays are intended to continue and encourage a multi-faceted discussion about the purpose, usefulness and framing of both biblical studies and the reception of the Bible. This volume's primary purpose is therefore as an invitation to embrace expansion, diversity and change in the academic study of the Bible. It is intended not only for the already converted biblical scholar (or her students), but also – if not more so – for those readers who currently work only in traditional areas of biblical studies (or indeed in other relevant disciplines) to encourage them to transcend their boundaries. This volume is therefore enthusiastically aimed at scholars who are attracted to the ideas and practices of studying the reception of the Bible, but who currently shy away from it, or maybe do not even know where to start.

Reshaping boundaries

The chapters in this book implicitly characterize the reception history of the Bible as a form of enquiry that is essentially defined by two discrete features. The first is the general subject matter; the series of 'events' generated by the historical journey/ies of the biblical texts down through the centuries. It will not be enough to show and tell examples of the Bible appearing in different locations, however; we need to analyse the use, impact and influence of these appearances. The second is the inherent limitation given to it because of the complications attached to researching evidence that has survived, but with various levels of success, within the multitudinous streams of a two-millennia-plus long journey down through history. The tensions created by these two features not only demand and generate creative ways of tackling discrete questions about the biblical materials, they also require scholars to work out what questions need to be asked in the first place. Uncovering these questions is one of the greatest challenges faced by reception historians. There can be no simple series of enquiries because it is not possible to ask identical questions of each and every biblical text, or of each and every occasion of biblical use or impact. Even the availability of specific types of information changes; information that enables us to ask a question of a certain text, a certain context and a certain audience, and feel confident of having produced a satisfactory and plausible answer may simply be unavailable elsewhere. While we will be able to develop common questions that apply in a large number of situations, it is the partial and happenstance nature of the work produced within reception history that will mark the future development of the approach, and indeed a discipline of biblical studies dominated by it.

It is the case that the diversity of the material and questions scholars are forced to consider often lie in areas where the expertise required is not currently part of the biblical scholar's training: art, politics, the media, popular culture, philosophy, economics, cultural studies and so on. Since expertise in numerous fields, sub-disciplines and disciplines is beyond the capacity of most individuals to acquire, other options are required. This may include replacing some of the methods currently studied as part of the biblical scholar's training (e.g. advanced language skills, archaeology, ancient history) with other interdisciplinary skills, and perhaps also introducing more disciplinary cross-fertilization and collaborative work. In the shorter term, however, we expect to find more dilettante wanderers, who have somewhat heroically left their academic comfort zone behind them, even if for only a little while. It is these wanderers who will encourage the growth of the field and, quite frankly, how can one fail to be excited by such a prospect?

To entice more wanderers into experiencing some of the joys of reception history, the essays in this volume are placed in four (somewhat arbitrary) groups, beginning with the broad and becoming narrower in theme: 1) Reception history, historical-criticism and biblical studies; 2) Conceptualizing reception history; 3)

Practical implications, difficulties and solutions; and 4) Bible, reception and popular music. Most, if not all, of the articles overlap the categories but by making the decision to guide the reader in this way we hope to have highlighted the greatest strengths of the articles for the purposes of challenging the discipline.

Reception history, historical-criticism and biblical studies

Challenging the idea that biblical studies is an easily identifiable and static discipline based on a single idea of the 'Bible', the four articles in this part all defend the place of reception history in the discipline of biblical studies. None of the approaches suggested are mutually exclusive and none of them erase the need for traditional historical-critical scholarship. Rather they argue for a discipline where all scholars are encouraged and creativity is a welcome asset, for the benefit of individuals and the discipline as a whole.

For Susan Gillingham a chance overheard description of reception history as 'biblical studies on holiday' is the jumping off point for a positive appropriation of the slur. Holidaying involves changes of perspectives as different cultures are encountered, previous priorities are challenged and new projects are generated. The metaphor of the 'department store' offers a way of categorizing the discipline's recent history, with new areas added increasing its methodological diversity to the extent that even defining what 'it' is has become difficult. Focusing on the psalms, Gillingham offers examples which illustrate the critical role that reception history could play in future. Consideration of certain criticisms – its lack of theoretical underpinning, and its tendencies to description, subjectivity and eccentricity – are followed by a call for scholarly collaboration.

In his contribution, James E. Harding questions both the identity and the coherence of Biblical Studies as a discipline in light of the emergence of reception history, challenging the idea that there is even a single, identifiable 'biblical text' with which biblical scholars are concerned. This, together with the competing theological and ideological positions that determine the approaches biblical scholars take, renders Biblical Studies unstable. Moreover, reception history shows that both the questions biblical scholars ask, and the fluid biblical texts themselves, are part of the reception history of the Bible. The (inter)disciplinary complexity of Biblical Studies, conceived in reception-historical terms, presents enormous challenges, as it is impossible for individual scholars to hold all of the competencies required. Thus collaborative research is necessary, but this raises questions about where, among the disciplines of modern academia, reception history of the Bible really belongs. In the end, Harding asserts that there are profound ethical reasons to place reception history at the heart of what biblical scholars do.

Engaging with recent attempts to restrict biblical studies' disciplinary boundaries, James Crossley rejects the idea of confining the label of 'biblical scholar' to those with the skill-set of traditional biblical studies. He goes on to argue that fragmentation and divisiveness within the discipline hinder the continued existence of a Bible-based discipline within either Theology and Religious Studies (THRS) departments or, more significantly, within the wider humanities. Instead, a coherent unified discipline is required to convince academics elsewhere of their need for dedicated biblical studies and of their lack without it. The discipline needs to present itself as working with questions about the origins, development, survival and transmission of the Bible as well as its ability to attract, create indifference, or repel those who encounter it. The significance of the discipline's potential contribution to the humanities is demonstrated by outlining the impact of the Liberal Bible.

In the final article in this section Jonathan Morgan uses William John Lyons' 'Hope for a Troubled Discipline?' as a jumping off point. Morgan argues that reception historians should stop apologizing and justifying their work. Instead they should be steadfast in their approaches and forceful in the diversity of their objects of research. Locating Lyons' article in ongoing debates about the core purpose and methods of biblical studies, Morgan asserts that Lyons is one of the scholars who threaten historical-critical practitioners by suggesting they re-label their work as reception history. Such an approach is unlikely, but if the approach were adopted reception history would then be understood in terms of historical-critical scholarship, and it is these scholars who are so frequently the gatekeepers of the discipline. As gatekeepers they keep the gates narrow but it is reception historians who, by working collaboratively and with non-biblical texts, expand the field and stand the best chances of keeping the discipline alive in a difficult landscape.

Conceptualizing reception history

While most of the articles in this volume briefly touch upon the definition of reception history, the articles in this section go a stage further. They conceptualize the area of research, exploring how it should be understood while questioning its purpose. Diverse in their theoretical approaches, the articles are complementary and can be seen to build a unified understanding, placing reception history in a framework balancing social, political, religious, cultural, intellectual and aesthetic changes.

Using the narrative of the beheading of John the Baptist as an example, Caroline Vander Stichele conceptualizes reception history using 'intertextuality' (Jonathan Culler), 'pre-posterous history' (Mieke Bal) and 'rhizomorphous systems' (Gilles Deleuze with Felix Guattari). Intertextuality is a concept that shows the connections between texts while uncovering origins and making codes intelligible. Pre-posterous history highlights the interconnections of multiple forms of visual and written texts across history in a multi-directional manner so earlier texts are also interpreted and understood through later texts. Rhizomorphous systems are root networks interconnected in complex ever-growing webs thereby connecting history with the present and future and expanding opportunities for discussion in all areas of creativity including music and the Internet. The cultural impact of the Bible is Vander Stichele's focus as she uses Giovanni di Paolo's paintings of John the Baptist and their connections to literature, art history and the Internet to explore the heuristic usefulness of her concepts.

In Brennan Breed's essay the power of metaphors in shaping scholarly behaviour is critiqued with regard to Daniel 7. Eschewing traditional images like 'anchorage', the 'pristine' (in an 'original text' sense) and 'etiology' (in an 'original context' sense), he offers the notion of ethology, drawn from the work of Gilles Deleuze. Ethology is a view of animal behaviour 'which emphasizes the range of a species' potential action' in response to the problems – or 'problematic field' – posed to it by complex, challenging and ever-changing environments. Uninterested in genetic essence or in previous historically demonstrated activity, ethology understands animals – and hence by way of analogy, biblical texts – 'by means of what they actually do'. Reception history as ethology goes beyond a simple echoing of the traditional discipline's questions in different times and places, and seeks to understand larger questions about how 'the problematic field of particular biblical texts changes through time and space in response to surrounding environments'.

Calling for an approach to biblical texts and interpretation as fragmentary, Samuel Tongue engages with Jacques Berlinerblau and Timothy Beal while providing an analysis of Yehuda Amichai's poetic rewriting of Jacob and the Angel. Berlinerblau calls for a secular aesthetic that challenges the theological paradigm of much biblical scholarship. Yet, Tongue notes, aesthetics is not so readily separated into the secular and religious. Furthermore, we must not forget that biblical texts, and their retellings, are imbued with an authority that needs to be addressed. The dual aesthetic of secular and religious is explored through an analysis of Amichai's poem, which leads to a discussion of Beal's reconstruction of reception history as part of a broader religious studies. In such a location the balance and conflict between secular and religious, that biblical reception historians work with, provide a perfect place to practise their art.

Conceptualizing reception history through politics, Masiiwa Ragies Gunda argues for its critical significance in African biblical studies. Gunda demonstrates how the heightened status of the Bible leads to its influence over socio-political situations. The reception historian's goal is therefore not to justify, ignore, or otherwise be an apologist for biblical texts but to highlight, analyse and discuss them as they are and have been appropriated and understood in practice. This is not without its challenges as scholars must avoid superficiality, appropriating and colonizing cultures that are not their own, and recognize that the Bible means different things at different times in different communities. To demonstrate his point Gunda offers a reading of interpretations of Sodom and Gomorrah in Zimbabwe, where the Bible was introduced by Christian missionaries. Through an autobiographical account Gunda explores how songs shaped by this colonialist history dominated biblical interpretation and how they have been replaced with anti-sodomy readings.

Practical implications, difficulties and solutions

Reception history pushes the boundaries of biblical studies by actively working with alternative subject areas and in many instances using methods from outside of the traditional arenas of the discipline. Each of the following articles represents an exploration of new types of material for biblical studies and different methods and/or approaches. Not all of the practices will be suitable for everyone, whether through lack of time or simply lack of necessity, but the purpose of these articles is to demonstrate that there is, and should not be, a 'one size fits all' approach. What we need is to tap into our inventiveness and ingenuity to achieve the goals our texts deserve.

In Roland Boer's essay, the personal benefits of – and also some of the difficulties arising within – reception history are made plain. Traditionally, biblical scholars have dealt with a restricted canon of material, comprising biblical texts, secondary literature and, perhaps, the occasional pre-third century CE author. For Boer, however, the study material is much broader with flexible limits stretching way beyond an individual scholar's ability to master. Rather than knuckling down to conquering a small piece of history, Boer instead enjoys the 'erotics' of the opportunity set before him, to (literally) wander the road wherever it leads, viewing the internal logic of his discipline as one which leads out of itself into the world, a world on which the biblical scholar's skills have considerable purchase. Boer bids us to adopt such a view and to do likewise. His reflections on (only) a few of his interests, the corpuses of the reformer, John Calvin, the political revolutionary, V. I. Lenin, and the song-writer, Nick Cave, help lead the way.

For Ian Boxall, the 'journey' metaphor proves a useful way into reflecting upon the five years that he has spent tapping into the 'divergent journeys', the 'guide books', of Apocalypse of John interpreters. Boxall's expected 'guide books' – works by the great scholars of traditional biblical studies – raised self-exploratory questions about his own skill-set as he embarked on an 'anything goes' study of the geographical setting of John's visionary experience. To anyone willing to follow, however, Boxall offers reassurances by acknowledging the provisional nature of studying such a historically contingent topic and by noting the rich amounts of surviving material on which to build a satisfying study of the reception of 'Patmos' and of its various aspects.

Emma England outlines her solution to the question 'how should scholars analyse a large corpus while minimizing anecdotes and potentially misguided generalizations?' Her answer was to develop a digital humanities project, a database to enable quantitative and qualitative analysis of the flood story retold for children and published in England between 1837 and 2006. Noting that digital technologies have already impacted on biblical studies, she defines three types of such research: programs that aid textual analysis; (biblio-)blogging; and least developed, 'multimodal humanities', an area in which 'scholarly tools, databases, networked writing and peer-to-peer commentary' are utilized to enable new forms of analysis. England details the five-stage process – corpus selection, design and pilot, evaluate and finalize, data entry, data analysis – that led to the creation of a database able to compare both images and texts and containing a detailed breakdown of the story elements in almost three hundred works.

Arguing that analysis of African usage of the Bible today must include discussion of the hermeneutics of how Africans have transacted with the Bible in relation to colonialism, Gerald West discusses the works of Isaiah Shembe, founder of the AmaNazaretha community in the early 1900s. Shembe rejected missionary Christianity but used and interpreted their Bible. West analyses Shembe's appropriation of Jephthah's Daughter in his liturgy and the rules of the community including the behaviour of the community's female virgins. Demonstrating the complexity of textual afterlives, West presents and analyses Carole Muller's etic response to Shembe's appropriation of Jephthah and Nkosinathi Sithole's emic response to Shembe, Muller and West's own work. The layers of reception offer different interpretations of the texts, their usage, and their relationship to (post-)colonialist changes and theological developments in South Africa.

Bible, reception and popular music

'Bible, Reception and Popular Music' takes the previous sections to their logical conclusion by demonstrating four approaches to analysing the reception of popular music, thereby providing an opportunity to begin to compare the number of topics and techniques available to scholars. Even when discussing similar material, these articles show that with a little imagination, patience and an open-mindedness to follow the path where it leads, we can glean new insights into appropriations of biblical texts.

Tracing the history of Leonard Cohen's song 'Who by Fire', Helen R. Jacobus discusses the connections between a prayer in the Cairo Genizah, Babylonian astrology, the Bible and related rabbinic texts. 'Who by Fire' is a rewriting of the *Unetaneh toqef*, a Jewish prayer recited in Synagogues at Yom Kippur and Rosh Hashanah. It repeatedly asks 'who will die from?' with each line adding a different way to die. Jacobus begins by comparing the differences between the song and the prayer and continues by actively demonstrating the unusual directions that can come from following the reception trail as she rediscovers an eleventh-century Cairo Genizah version of the prayer and connects both versions to the Jerusalem Talmud, Babylonian Talmud, Rabbi Eleazar and Genesis Rabba. Among the connections are commentaries on how individuals can change their astrological fate through repentance, prayer and charity. This degree of intertextuality leads Jacobus to note the similarities between the *Unetaneh toqef* and a late Babylonian astrological tablet (AO 6483), which also asks how people will die, thereby suggesting that the prayer may have an astrological history.

Analysing Depeche Mode's 'John the Revelator', William John Lyons asks to what extent these songs can be considered an actualization of Revelation in as much as they, in conjunction with the biblical text, provide a way of understanding the interpreters and/or prompt related 'visions'. Situating the lyrics in the song among the works of contemporary biblical scholars, Lyons argues that the song leads to an analysis of John of Patmos as a controlling and oppressive tyrant who steals the words of others, notably Ezekiel, while preventing them from being heard. This analysis is placed within the framework provided by lyricist Martin Gore's own publicly stated theistic beliefs and provides a harsh commentary on John the Revelator's/John of Patmos's God. The song can therefore be seen as an actualization of Martin Gore's public persona and his agenda as a call for a new gospel.

For Michael Gilmour, the concept of an 'anxiety of influence' offered by Harold Bloom suggests a critical way to interrogate three songs written by John Lennon, U2 and Larry Norman ('God', 'God Part II' and 'God Part III' respectively). Bloom suggests that strong poets (songwriters) 'choose their vocation because some earlier writer grips their imagination but their relationship with that predecessor is ambivalent, analogous to what Freud observes in the Oedipal relation of son to father'. 'Admiration, hate, and envy' erupt as later writers strive heroically to create a space for their works; failures are consigned to oblivion. For U2 and Larry Norman, their songs are explicit responses to Lennon, but this affectionate tribute is mixed with anxious competition; as Gilmour puts it, 'they too want their chance, to make the people dance'. Changing deployments of 'belief' language and differing attitudes to rock music illustrate the shift from Lennon's cynicism about religion, through U2's creative, unresolved engagement, to Norman's confessionalism in service to a conservative faith.

For Ibrahim Abraham, the focus of his contribution is the nascent state of the study of the Bible's reception in popular music. Recent studies have done some things well, he contends, but exhibit limitations framed by three 'problems': the privileging of production over consumption; the privileging of subjective readings over engagement with real listeners in secularizing societies; and approaching popular music as a 'text' with a true meaning available upon a close historicized reading. Moving beyond these limitations, he suggests, involves contextualizing popular music within its actual social setting using tools drawn from the sociology of religion. This enables the scholar to ask questions beyond those which merely analyse biblical allusions, questions about identity, culture, origins and impact.

Through a shared a sense of enthusiasm for biblical reception history, these articles all question and challenge the reader to try new things. They ask us to reconsider what it is we do, whether we have never (consciously) tried to tackle reception history or whether that is our primary focus. The articles do not permit us, as scholars, to continue trimming the bonsai tree or, indeed, to start a new bonsai tree. Rather, we should, explore and experiment together, engaging our enthusiasm and finding ways to increase our significance within biblical studies, for the benefit of not only our discipline, but also those outside it, for the 'Bible' is a cultural text. It belongs to everyone, it affects – or has affected – everyone (directly or indirectly), and only through the analysis of the (ab)use, influence and impact of it can we truly do justice to the Bible as a collection of texts, to the individuals and communities affected by it, and to ourselves.

Part Two

Reception History, Historical-Criticism and Biblical Studies

2

Biblical Studies on Holiday? A Personal View of Reception History

Susan Gillingham
University of Oxford

The holiday metaphor

I recently heard 'reception history' referred to as 'biblical studies on holiday'. I am not sure who originally said this, but it seems to me that such an observation is an ideal way to start to reflect on reception history as a relatively new arrival to the discipline of biblical studies. I do not think this was how it was intended, but it could of course be a commendation rather than criticism. Let me start with this way of reading it, anyway.

Much, of course, depends on how one sees a 'holiday'. For someone who loves travel, 'holiday' is what makes sense of the rest of life. You begin to gain a total change of perspective through encountering a new culture, a new language, a different history. Gradually you acquire a different set of priorities: things which really mattered 'back there' seem to be not quite as urgent or pressing as you have time to focus on different opportunities – perhaps in art, or music or literature. And you can return with new projects which might complement the older, more familiar ones.

So the metaphor of a 'holiday' might work well in defining reception history in relation to biblical studies. It offers a change of *perspective* because its encounter with so many cultures through time and space means that the framework of interpretation is much broader. It certainly provides a challenge to a traditional set of *priorities* which has evolved in historical and literary studies of the Bible over the last two centuries. And it also offers new *projects* to biblical studies, not least in bringing in other humanities disciplines such as music, art and literature, and cultural and ecclesiastical history. So the 'holiday' metaphor is a good one. In fact reception history could be one of the best travel guides biblical studies could use.

Defining biblical studies

If much depends upon how one sees a holiday, much also depends on how one sees *biblical studies*. My own perspective is that biblical studies, as an academic discipline, has really gone through the mill since I studied it as an undergraduate in the late 1960s and early 1970s. When I started, there was still some confidence about what we were doing and how it might produce some assured results: Gerhard von Rad's *Theology of the Old Testament* and Martin Noth's theory of the amphictyony could still be cited without too much apology. But by the time I had finished it was clear that several new methodological questions were being asked, for which there were no clear answers. I remember how, throughout the 1970s, historical criticism underwent enormous fragmentation, so that one was never really clear whether one should read a biblical text by first applying textual criticism, or form criticism, or source criticism, or tradition criticism, or redaction criticism or, later still, canon criticism. At that time biblical studies seemed to me to be rather like a huge department store, where it became increasingly difficult to know which 'floor' of critical enquiry one should start with first. My own interests were in tradition criticism, and I did my MA thesis on assessing Wolfhart Pannenberg's theory that Old Testament History comprised in the main 'the history of the transmission of traditions'. So to follow the analogy of the department store I suppose at that time I started near the top floor first.

But by the late 1970s and early 1980s new emphases were coming to the fore. Partly as a result of the questions asked by, for example, feminist interpreters and social scientists and liberation theologians, rhetorical criticism, in its various forms, both theoretical and more pragmatic, became a crucial methodology for asking about the meaning of the text: this took the emphasis away from initial questions about the 'text in context' to questions about the 'reader in context'. By the mid-1980s this gave rise to a whole range of other methodological approaches, not least a fresh understanding of the Bible as literature – not just as good ancient literature, but as literature capable of being understood by the use of more contemporary literary techniques which could be applied both to biblical prose and to biblical poetry. This huge variety of methodological approaches to biblical studies has multiplied and fragmented up to the present day. And depending on what you say and how you say it you can so easily get pigeon-holed; I have been called everything from a post-modernist to a covert evangelical.

This autobiographical account of biblical studies has been interpreted only through the eyes of the 'academy'. If we added to this a version of biblical studies as understood in the church or the synagogue, or through the non-specialist secular judgements of the media, it would become even more difficult to define precisely what 'biblical studies' is and does. If I were being very pessimistic, I might argue that biblical studies could certainly do with a holiday; it needs fresh perspectives, a reassessment of its priorities and a consideration of new projects.

Defining reception history

Whether we perceive reception history positively or negatively is closely related to our perception of biblical studies; whether we define the latter discipline according to those particular methodologies which 'work' for us, or whether we have a sufficiently open view of it to include approaches other than those we usually espouse. So there are some who see reception history as escapism, lacking 'rigour' in the way they would define that term in their own specialism, and there are others who view reception history as an inevitable consequence of the last forty years' evolution within the discipline and so welcome its presence. It is clear that I belong to the latter category. I see it as very much part of the academy of biblical studies rather than an unwelcome intruder. I would claim this on two counts.

First, I would argue that it is reception *history*. Some aspects of it are closely related to the historical concerns of biblical studies. To use an analogy of an archaeological dig, reception history allows us to see there are many more levels in our historical understanding of the text than the purportedly 'top' level which in the 1980s I might have labelled as 'canon criticism'. Because it is interested in cultural history and the influence of a particular text in a particular culture, 'history of culture' is a vitally important dimension which is added on to the more traditional understanding of the 'history of the text'. Reception history encourages a dialogue between these two elements: what holds this dialogue together is a perspective which is *historical*. Some scholars work from the reception of text in a particular period of history *backwards* to the earlier history of the text in its biblical setting; others work from the history of the text in its biblical setting *forwards* to the reception of the text in a cultural setting. I usually do the latter. The sort of specifically textual work I do, focussing on individual psalms, means it is actually easier for me to start as far back as possible, with the text in its ancient context and then move forwards, chronologically speaking.[1] So (again using the analogy of the archaeological dig) another significant level would be the reception of the text in its early translation; a further level would involve assessing the occurrences of the psalm in the literature of the Second Temple Period (including of course, where relevant, Qumran); and other levels, further and further upwards, would be the consideration of later Jewish interpretations through Midrashim and the Targums and later Christian reconstructions through the Church Fathers and the Glosses. So this is the historical approach with a much broader remit; even though precise answers cannot be given, continual questions have to be asked about the origins not just about the text in its ancient setting but about the text in the cultural

---

[1] By this I am not implying that the closer to the 'original' one attempts to work, the closer to the 'truth' one gets. Mine is more to do with a practical methodological process; it is easier to start at the beginning of a story than to take it up halfway through.

settings of later interpreters.² Discerning the levels in the text this way applies mainly to the more *exegetical* aspects of reception history, but just as ancient texts have contexts, 'receptors' of ancient texts have contexts as well, and this is what makes this project both challenging and stimulating. Let me illustrate this in just three ways from some work that I did recently on Psalm 137.

One obvious example is that in order to assess the later (Jewish) Greek translations and Aramaic paraphrases, or the later (Christian) Latin translations and even the Elizabethan English renderings of this Psalm, I have to gain some knowledge of the sound and sense of the psalm and to be aware of the problematic words or phrases in the Hebrew which lie at the base, directly or indirectly, of all translation. So this is why I personally think it is important to *start* with the Hebrew text. Secondly, I cannot fully understand the differences between later Jewish readings, which tend to read Psalm 137 as a complete 'poetic narrative', and later Christian readings, which are more predisposed to isolate and allegorize individual verses, unless I have some view myself about the overall structure of the psalm that each tradition is using; so again I need to have some understanding of the possible composition of the text in its earlier setting. Thirdly, I cannot appreciate the various receptions of Psalm 137 as a lament for a lost homeland, whether by Diaspora Jews in Persia or Greece or Rome or even thirteenth-century Italy, or by Christians suffering disenfranchisement in seventeenth- and eighteenth-century England and America, without coming to some view, however provisional, about whether its ancient setting is about the Babylonian exile or just after it, because this is what has consistently motivated these later imitations and commentaries. So, in my view, each new layer is part of an increasingly rich and complex discourse with the *past*. A sense of cultural history is vital; but in my view this begins with 'the beginning', assuming it might then inform some appreciation of how and why Jewish and Christian responses throughout that history diverge. This, then, is how I personally engage with the exegetical reception of the text at different stages in Jewish and Christian cultural history. It is, in part, a *historical* project.³

The second reason for accommodating reception history into the discipline of biblical studies is that it is *reception* history. This means it belongs as much to the more recent rhetorical and reader-response methods used in biblical studies as it does to the variety of more traditional historical methods referred to earlier. It has often been termed *Wirkungsgeschichte*; the history of the *influence* or the *impact* of

---

[2] I shall say something later about how this relates to the 'History of Interpretation', although it should be clear that I see a close relationship between the two disciplines. As for the historical bias in this discipline, Christopher Rowland makes a good point when he argues (of the Blackwell Bible Commentary Series) that '...the historical-critical exegesis is included as part of *Wirkungsgeschichte* rather than as a primary datum to which matters of *Wirkungsgeschichte* can be added' (See http://bbibcomm.net/files/rowland2004.pdf, p. 1).

[3] See Susan Gillingham, 'The Reception of Psalm 137 in Jewish and Christian Traditions', in Susan Gillingham (ed.), *Conflict and Convergence. Proceedings of the Oxford Conference on Jewish and Christian Approaches to the Psalms* (Oxford: OUP, 2012).

a text, acknowledging that the way a text is received and interpreted in a later period will probably be very different from the way it was received in its earlier context. Think, for example, of the way in which the psalms are so easily read by Christians as prayers or prophecies of Jesus Christ; what David Frost, in translating the Psalms in the mid-1960s, has rather graphically called 'pious fibs'.[4] So although its perspective is historical, its way of reading takes for granted that the meaning of the text is something brought to it through the responses of later readers in different cultural contexts. Sometimes this might mean not so much a bland acceptance of an earlier meaning, but a resistance to it, offering appropriate criticism of that earlier meaning in the light of its impact at a later stage in the process.

However, although reception history finds its *metier* alongside many of these more recent approaches, it again has a much broader purview. I offer just one example. *Reception* history is not only about the text as given and interpreted in words, but it is also about its reception of the text *beyond* the medium of words, especially, where the Psalms are concerned, in visual art, in liturgical enactment and in musical performance. But it is always the text – in my case, a particular psalm – which is at the centre of both the verbal and non-verbal reception; when the text itself disappears from sight and we realize we are working more on the reception of the interpreters than the reception of the text, in my view, something has begun to go awry.

Again let me use Psalm 137 as an example of this, for I would argue that there are several different ways in which one can 'see' and 'hear' this psalm. The first is, quite simply, looking at and listening to the language and structure of the text in its most literal sense, as a corpus of words. The words may be in Hebrew, or Greek, or Latin, or Aramaic: but they are words, imitating and representing the words they are translating or paraphrasing, subtly shifting and changing the meanings throughout the passage of time. These may also be words created through the Hebrew poetry of disenfranchised *paytanim*, or words in many European languages in the laments of Holocaust survivors, or they may be words of metrical psalms, or imitations of psalms composed by political dissidents, both Catholic and Protestant, in sixteenth-century England: in each of these examples the shifts and changes in the meaning of this psalm are much more clear. At this more literary level we have to learn to be 'good readers', asking why this word or phrase has been emphasized and not another, why this poetic rhythm has been chosen and not another, and so on.

However, 'seeing' and 'hearing' pertains to more than just the transference of Psalm 137 from one verbal medium into another. It also involves, for example, 'seeing' through visual reception, and 'hearing' through musical reception. If I want to appreciate Psalm 137 visually – for example in the sketchy brown line drawings

---

[4] See David Frost, *Making the Liturgical Psalter. The Morpeth Lectures 1980* (Bramcote, Notts: Grove Books, 1981), pp. 10–25.

in the ninth-century Utrecht Psalter, or in the starker contemporary black and white images in the art forms of Arthur Wragg, or in the more subtle representations of Roger Wagner or Michael Jessing – I have to learn how to 'look' and 'see' and 'perceive' how the text works beyond the medium of words alone. Similarly, if I want to understand the iconography of Psalm 137 in the Jewish Parma Psalter where the image of weeping carefully follows the Hebrew על and precedes נהרות, or observe it in the great wall mosaic in the Knesset by Marc Chagall, I again have to learn how to 'look' and 'see' and 'perceive' how the text works beyond the medium of words alone. And if I want to appreciate Psalm 137 in Philip de Monte's 'Super flumine Babylonis' or William Byrd's response in 'Quomode cantabimus' from Elizabethan England, or in Giuseppe Verdi's *Nabucco* in nineteenth-century Italy, I have to learn how to 'listen' and 'hear' and 'understand'. Similarly if I want to appreciate the psalm in the seventeenth-century Jewish melismatic chanting by Salomone Rossi of Mantua, or in the protest songs of the Rastafarians popularized by Boney Em and the Melodians and Sinead O'Connor, I have again to learn how to 'listen' and 'hear' and 'understand', and each time this is very different from how I would respond when using textual exegesis.[5] *Reception history* allows us to engage with the text, but at many different and often unexpected levels.

So although reception history studies might sometimes sit uncomfortably in the domain of biblical studies, especially when the latter is defined predominantly by particular historical and literary concerns, this, I contend, is its home base. Its presence is, at times, uncomfortable for the status quo; it challenges historical critical methods when they are too exclusively focussed on just the *ancient* meaning, and it asks equally awkward questions of more recent 'readerly' methods when they are too confined by the *words* of the text and its subsequent literary impact as the only resource for meaning.[6]

Responding to the critics

Nevertheless, there have been some quite reasonable criticisms of reception history as a legitimate way of assessing the biblical text. I shall look at just four of them.

One of the most insistent criticisms is that reception history lacks any real theoretical theological underpinning. There have been two ways of responding to this. One is found in works which have sought to provide just this, at least in an introductory way: John Sawyer's account on the Blackwell Bible Commentary

---

[5] See Susan Gillingham, 'Seeing and Hearing Psalm 137' in Kristinn Ólason, et al (eds), *Mótun menningar. Shaping Culture. FS Gunnlaugur A. Jónsson* (Reykjavík: Hið íslenska Bókmenntafélag 2012), pp. 91–108.

[6] This account is not different from the way in which Christopher Rowland defends the significance of reception history, although his perspective is longer, reaching back to the Enlightenment, and he argues for the right balance between properly understood 'diachronic' and 'synchronic' approaches (C. Rowland in http://bbibcomm.net/files/rowland2004.pdf p. 3).

website and Jonathan Roberts' introductory chapter in *The Oxford Handbook of the Reception History of the Bible* are cases in point. Sawyer traces the terminology of *Rezeptionsaesthetik* back to the Konstanz School of literary studies in the 1960s, developed by Hans Robert Jauss in his work on the relationship between the aesthetics of reception and *Wirkungsgeschichte*; Jauss's work on the multiple meanings resonant in the one text has some correspondences, Sawyer argues, with the work of Stanley Fish in the 1980s.[7] Roberts takes a similar line: he traces the foundations of the discipline to the philosophical hermeneutics of Jauss's *Doktorvater*, Hans-Georg Gadamer, particularly in his model of the dialogical relationship between the past and the present, and argues that the first publications applying this to biblical studies emerge in Germany by New Testament scholars such as Ulrich Luz in the 1960s.[8]

A related but more measured response to this criticism is to state that it is too premature to synthesize the results of such a vast and burgeoning discipline; as Christopher Rowland has argued, it still needs more time to develop before any further hermeneutical models can be discussed with confidence.[9] I would argue that this view still holds (it dates from 2004). For example, the hermeneutical models proposed by Gadamer and Luz do not take into sufficient account the need to assess both Christian *and Jewish* receptions of the text, a task which is essential for anyone working on the Psalms. This more cautious approach is not unique. I can think of several other disciplines within biblical studies which also have not accounted for their presence in an explicit way, and, perhaps worse, disciplines where the discourse is so convoluted it is difficult to find a way out of the maze. So even if the criticism of reception history for not yet creating its own rationale is legitimate, it is unfair to accuse it of this failure exceptionally and at this point in time. More reflection is required to explain better the origins and purpose of this discipline. What I believe is happening at present within this relatively new mode of study is that its focus is more on the 'how', in terms of consolidating its methods and reflecting on the purpose of its methods, and so at this point in time is less on the 'why'. It is in many ways still a pragmatic discipline, assessing the *performative* nature and the practical *impact* of biblical texts: at least, this is my own perspective, from working on the reception history of the Psalms. Reflections on good practice

---

[7] See John Sawyer in http://bbibcomm.net/files/sawyer2004.pdf, pp. 1–2, referring to Hans Robert Jauss's *Towards an Aesthetic of Reception* (trans T. Bahti, Minneapolis: University of Minnesota 1982), and the seminal work by Stanley E. Fish, *Is There a Text in this Class? The Authority of Interpretive Communities* (Harvard: Harvard University Press, 1980).

[8] See Jonathan Roberts, 'Introduction' in Michael Lieb et al (eds), *The Oxford Handbook of the Reception History of the Bible* (Oxford: Oxford University Press, 2011), pp. 1–8. The same point is made by Mary Chiltern Callaway in her 'What's the Use of Reception History?'. See http://bbibcomm.net/files/callaway2004.pdf, pp. 2–5.

[9] See Christopher Rowland: 'The task of *Wirkungsgeschichte* at the present juncture requires, I think, that we refuse to move too quickly to hermeneutical models or theological syntheses. I'm really worried that we shall short-circuit the historical mapping exercise of the history of interpretation otherwise.' (http://bbibcomm.net/files/rowland2004.pdf p. 4).

have begun, and others are bound to follow, and criticisms on bad practice will undoubtedly continue to be offered by those from outside.[10] But the theoretical underpinning is part of a process; it will happen, and is happening, but coherence in a relatively new discipline, and reflections on that coherence, take time to evolve.[11] But in my view this is one of the most important challenges reception history has to face.

A second criticism in some ways is related to the first and is perhaps more serious because it is in part redeemable. This censures the discipline because of its tendency to be too *descriptive*. I can certainly understand how this happens. Usually one needs to draw together such a vast amount of data, often over a long period of time, so that by the end of the process – which usually results in collating multiple responses to one single text – one is apt to lose sight of any clear hermeneutical key. There are many examples in print of what might be termed 'anthology without a purpose'. Usually one wants to ask after reading or hearing such papers, 'So what?' I would argue that if the exercise is little other than the assembling of information, one should probably avoid publishing it.

Yet, I contend, this somewhat 'flat' descriptive approach can be minimized by applying more focus, both in method and purpose. This is particularly possible in works which start with the text (in my case a psalm, and usually a short one at that) and work forwards, chronologically, in tracing some of its reception history. Initially one can gain a better focus by concentrating on just a few commentators and a defined period of history, where it is then possible to look more analytically at, for example, different Jewish and Christian modes of reception. A similar focus can be achieved by looking at one specific medium again over a prescribed period of time, perhaps with reference to ninth- and tenth-century illuminated manuscripts, or to sixteenth-century music for the royal court, or through contemporary music or film, to offer but three examples. Several publications, going back as far as the early 1990s, show the increased interest in reception history, and these include many examples in art, literature, music and film.[12]

---

[10] For example, Roland Boer (http://bbibcomm.net/).
[11] Roberts for example points to the 'multiplicity and diversity' of the papers in *The Oxford Handbook of the Reception History of the Bible*: '...the material is hermeneutically stimulating precisely because it will not coalesce. The more history of reception of the Bible one reads, the clearer it becomes that the human importance of the Bible does *not* lie in a single foundational meaning that, by dint of scholarly effort, may finally be revealed.' (p. 8).
[12] See for example Paul Morris and Deborah Sawyer (eds.) *A Walk in the Garden. Biblical, Iconographical and Literary Images of Eden* (Sheffield: JSOT Press, 1992); John F. A. Sawyer, *The Fifth Gospel. Isaiah in the History of Christianity* (Cambridge: Cambridge University Press, 1996); Margaret Stocker, *Judith, Sexual Warrior: Women and Power in Western Culture* (New Haven: Yale University Press, 1998); Yvonne Sherwood, *A Biblical Text and Its Afterlives: The Survival of Jonah in Western Culture* (Cambridge: Cambridge University Press, 2000); Bernhard Lang, *Joseph in Egypt: A Cultural Icon from Grotius to Goethe* (New Haven: Yale University Press, 2009); Andrew Mein and Paul Joyce (eds.), *After Ezekiel: Essays on the Reception of a Difficult Prophet* (London and New York: T & T Clark International, 2010); and John Byron, *Cain and Abel in Text and Tradition: Jewish and Christian Interpretations of the First Sibling Rivalry* (Leiden: Brill, 2011).

Another way of achieving analysis rather than plain description could be to start the other way round, and critically assess how one or two individuals (or indeed, communities) have used one particular biblical text or a group of texts: for example, Cheryl Exum's work on the Bible in literature, music, art and film; Martin O'Kane and John Morgan-Guy's volume on biblical art in Wales; Chris Rowland's work on Blake and the Bible, especially the book of Job; Deborah Rooke's account of Handel's use of biblical texts in his *Oratorio Libretti*; Aaron Rosen on Marc Chagall's stained glass windows of the Psalms; and Bill Goodman's work on the use of different psalms by U2.[13] Of those who work with a more pragmatic and social-political emphasis in *Wirkungsgeschichte*, Christopher Rowland's work is probably the best known.[14] The purpose is to establish a dialogue between the text and, in this case, visual or musical modes of reception; in my view, the problem of being over-descriptive only takes over when that dialogue dries up, for then all one hears is a description of the reception; the issue of the impact of the text is lost, and this is an example not so much of biblical studies on holiday as on a quick sightseeing tour.

A third criticism is perhaps more justified. This concerns the 'particularity' and 'selectivity' of reception history studies, and hence the problem of subjectivity on the part of anyone working in this field. I certainly find that the more I work on reception history, the more I am aware that I am an interpreter 'frozen' in a particular time and place and culture. So my perception is that of a western, English, white, middle-aged woman who also happens to be an Anglican Lay Reader. So although up to the first millennium I try to keep my eye on Christian and Jewish traditions, not only in the West but also in the East, increasingly my focus has to move westwards, and then to Western Europe, and then to the English-speaking world. I produced a series of maps at the beginning of each chapter in my *Psalms through the Centuries*, and these illustrate, alas, the increasingly parochial vision of the project; starting with the ancient Near East and moving through the Mediterranean, gradually working up northern France, with an eye to Germany and Italy and Spain, and then, by the seventeenth century, other than a brief glance towards America, remaining increasingly fixed on 'Britain'.[15] Reception history

---

[13] For example, Cheryl Exum, *Retellings: The Bible in Literature, Music, Art and Film* (Leiden: Brill Academic Publishers 2007); Martin O'Kane and John Morgan-Guy (eds.), *Biblical Art from Wales* (Sheffield: Sheffield Phoenix Press, 2010); Christopher Rowland, *Blake and the Bible* (New Haven: Yale University Press, 2011); Deborah Rooke *Handel's Israelite Oratorio Libretti: Sacred Drama and Biblical Exegesis* (Oxford: Oxford University Press, 2012); Aaron Rosen, 'True Lights. Seeing the Psalms through Chagall's Church Windows', in Susan Gillingham (ed.), *Conflict and Convergence. Proceedings of the Oxford Conference on Jewish and Christian Approaches to the Psalms* (Oxford: OUP, 2013); Bill Goodman, *Relegere* 2/1 (2012) (http://www.relegere.org/index.php/relegere/article/view/483). A number of other examples (including John Hedley Brooke on Samuel Wilberforce and Thomas Huxley and Genesis, Emma Mason on William Blake's Illustrations of Job, Jeremy Holtom on Gandhi's use of the Sermon on the Mount) can be found in *The Oxford Handbook of the Reception History of the Bible*, pp. 397–412, 460–75 and 542–56 respectively).

[14] See for example Christopher Rowland and Jonathan Roberts, *The Bible for Sinners. Interpretation in the Present Time* (London: SPCK, 2008).

[15] See Susan Gillingham, *Psalms through the Centuries, Volume One* (Oxford: Wiley-Blackwell 2008), pp. 6, 48, 78, 132, 193, 243.

may have a broad remit, but the paradox is that any one individual collating and interpreting the material has to make difficult choices as to what to use. The processing of the data thus requires making informed but nevertheless *subjective* choices about what to include and what to exclude. Yet this 'incarnational' aspect can be found, in different degrees, in most other fields of biblical studies as well; I think here of biblical archaeology, of social scientific analyses, of ancient Near Eastern comparative studies, and even of exegetical commentaries. So the problem is not exceptional: it is just that reception history, because of its breadth and scope, sometimes highlights this limitation particularly clearly.[16] So, the problem of being 'subjective' is inescapable. Reception history, like all other disciplines within biblical studies, is constrained by culture, gender, race and personal history.

A fourth criticism levelled against reception history is its tendency towards isolated (and indeed sometimes eccentric) individualism. This is particularly pertinent when one is working in a relatively new area where there are fewer sympathetic and experienced colleagues. I know all too well how one person attempting to draw together many different issues of reception, often over a long period of time, can be a recipe for disaster. I think of a closely related discipline, 'history of interpretation', where sometimes these are publications by a team of experts and sometimes these are works by one individual.[17] Take, for example, Magno Saebø's lengthy edited volumes, *Hebrew Bible Old Testament. The History of Its Interpretation*, or Alan Hauser and Duane Watson's shorter editions, *A History of Biblical Interpretation*, or the one-volume *Cambridge Companion to Biblical Interpretation*, edited by John Barton; compare this with Graf Reventlow's single-authored four-volume publication, *Epochen der Bibelauslegung*, translated into English between 2009 and 2010 as *A History of Biblical Interpretation*.[18] It is true

---

[16] This is the position taken by Mary Callaway in her 'What's the Use of Reception History?' (http://bbibcomm.net/files/callaway2004.pdf, p. 9). Sawyer discusses this issue in a different way: noting that opponents of Reception History accuse the proponents of subjectivity, his defense for the discipline is in relation not so much to the scholar/interpreter as to the meaning found in a text. Following the argument of Fish, that a text does not exist until someone reads it, and that the text when read does not have one meaning but the many meanings brought to it (rather than arising from it) by readers of many different interpretive communities, Sawyer contends that both objective analysis and objective results are impossible goals (http://bbibcomm.net/files/sawyer2004.pdf, pp. 2–3).

[17] Callaway, http://bbibcomm.net/files/callaway2004.pdf, pp. 13–14, notes that the differences between History of Interpretation and Reception History is that the former takes a more exegetical and theological approach, and the latter approaches the subject more anthropologically and sociologically with a different concern about the impact of the text within a period of cultural history. But the two disciplines are undoubtedly closely related.

[18] See Magno Saebø (ed.) *Hebrew Bible Old Testament. The History of Its Interpretation, I/1: Antiquity*, (Göttingen, Vandenhoeck & Ruprecht, 1996); I/2: *The Middle Ages* (Göttingen, Vandenhoeck & Ruprecht, 2000); II: *From the Renaissance to the Enlightenment* (Göttingen, Vandenhoeck & Ruprecht, 2008); Alan J. Hauser and Duane F. Watson (eds.) *A History of Biblical Interpretation. Volume 1. The Ancient Period*, (Grand Rapids, MI: William B. Eerdmans Publishing Company, 2003); *Volume 2, The Medieval through Reformation Periods* (Grand Rapids, MI: William B. Eerdmans Publishing Company, 2009); John Barton (ed.), *The Cambridge Companion to Biblical Interpretation* (Cambridge: CUP 1998); and Henning Graf Reventlow, *Epochen der Bibelauslegung* (Bände 1–4) (München: Verlag C. H. Beck oHG, 1990–2001), Trans. Leo G. Perdue and James O. Duke, *History of Biblical Interpretation* (4 Volumes) (Atlanta, GA: SBL 2009–10).

that an edited work can result in a project lasting for many years, so that one loses a good deal of continuity, but such a work can also achieve the breadth and depth which one individual even as skilled and informed as Reventlow could never do; the individual is inevitably less able to achieve the depth and breadth of a multi-authored edited work. What applies in works on the 'History of Interpretation' also applies to publications on reception history; for example, although the de Gruyter project is ambitiously intending to publish some thirty volumes from 2009 to 2018, publishing some three volumes a year, it is clearly going to be an exceptionally thorough job, with over thirty editors working in five different divisions.[19] By contrast, the projects undertaken by writers contracted into the Wiley-Blackwell Bible Commentary Series are hampered by being a single- (or sometimes two-) authored work, and so the depth and breadth they can really achieve is limited. However, I would still argue that the benefit of working in this one-authored way is that it provides cohesion and continuity and consistency.[20]

The importance of collaboration

It may seem strange to end a response to these four criticisms on a rather negative note, for this could be represented as undermining everything which the Wiley-Blackwell Reception History Commentary Series is trying to do. But I have deliberately emphasized this at the end as I believe that this weakness can in fact be turned into a most significant advantage, namely, reception history's potential for collaboration.

Again I speak personally, but it seems that it is precisely out of this sort of individual isolation that one also recognizes the need for scholarly support and advice (and e-mail communication and the provision of so much Internet access now helps enormously to this end). Collaboration works at many different levels. First, it can involve graduate research assistants who can retrieve material, collate the data electronically and produce a viable database; I find I now can turn to any one psalm and retrieve an enormous amount of material, both online and in filed hard copies, most of which has been assembled not by me but by those who have worked for me, some of them over a long period of time.[21] Secondly, collaboration also includes turning to the many resources found within the wider academic

---

[19] See http://www.degruyter.com/ebr for details of the extent of this project.
[20] The details of the series can be found on http://bbibcomm.net and http://www.blackwellpublishing.com/seriesbyseries.asp?ref=BC and, focusing on the Old Testament, include publications by David G. Gunn, *Judges through the Centuries* (2004); Eric S. Christianson, *Ecclesiastes through the Centuries* (2006); and Jo Carruthers, *Esther through the Centuries* (2007). As well as the Wiley-Blackwell Commentary Series, John F. A. Sawyer's *A Concise Dictionary of the Bible and its Reception* (Louisville, KY: Westminster John Knox Press, 2009) is a commendable example of a 'one-person' achievement in and is arguably the first ever dictionary on Reception History.
[21] I am particularly indebted to Holly Morse in this respect.

community. I offer just one example. I am completing at the moment a monograph on the reception history of Psalms 1, 2 and 1–2, which ranges from the Second Temple Period up to the present day, and which looks at both Jewish and Christian receptions of these psalms, separately and together; I first compare and contrast different types and results of exegesis, then assess the different liturgical innovations, and manuscript illuminations, and literary imitations, and musical compositions, and finally modern translations and contemporary artistic representations.

Setting aside the obvious need to be selective and to apply clear methods and always to keep the text in view, there is no way I can presume competence in every medium and certainly not through every historical period. So when I am concerned about whether I have understood properly the use of Psalm 1 (and possibly Psalm 2) in 4QFlorigelium at Qumran, I can ask (and have asked!) George Brooke in Manchester, or Peter Flint in Toronto, or Michael Wolter in Bonn. And when it comes to issues of the Septuagint translation, or New Testament readings (where Psalm 1 actually never appears but where Psalm 2 is frequently used) or the Church Fathers, or Medieval or Reformation Commentators, there are many colleagues in the wider 'academy' to whom I can now turn for help. Similarly when it comes to writing about Christian illuminated manuscripts, or medieval Jewish exegesis, or the liturgical or political or musical use of these psalms, there are now several different colleagues to whom I dare turn for advice about pursuing resources and understanding them as well as I can. Sometimes it seems like a great jigsaw puzzle, with individuals helping to place the smaller (and larger) pieces along on a very large table, with my job being to try to assemble it into a coherent, albeit multi-faceted whole.

There is another way in which collaboration can be made effective. This is by way of brief, perhaps two-day, conferences where several papers are presented on the reception of just one biblical text or one biblical character or theme through a multiple number of media over a lengthy period of history. If these can be turned around into a publication of conference papers within, say eighteen months, this is a vital way of demonstrating how a more corporate form of collaboration works. One seminal example is a conference on the Jewish and Christian reception of the Psalms by Harold Attridge and Margaret Fassler, at Yale, some ten years ago.[22] Another, on the reception of the Decalogue, was organized by Dominik Markl and took place in Oxford at Trinity College, from 16 April to 18 April 2012: this was a multi-faceted project which still had a clear focus, and it is in the process of being turned into an edited work.[23]

---

[22] H. W. Attridge and M. E. Fassler, *Psalms in Community: Jewish and Christian Textual, Liturgical and Artistic Traditions* (Atlanta: SBL, 2003).

[23] Another outlet is of course the Society for Biblical Literature international meetings. And yet another way is the publication of material in journals and periodicals: on this count, the new reception history journal, *Biblical Reception*, edited by Cheryl Exum and David Clines, is most welcome. It covers art, literature, film, popular culture, as well as the history of interpretation; the first issue is due in November 2012.

Reception history also offers a model of collaboration between the academic community and other communities which have a different remit. To the outsider, biblical studies in the academy can sometimes seem to be an introverted discipline, and if it is to be respected in the outside world it needs to find as many ways as possible of crossing that divide. My own experience – and I do not think this is simply because I work on the Psalms – is that reception history offers a 'bridge' between academic and confessing communities, perhaps on diocesan retreats or parish days away. There are similar opportunities for fostering dialogue between Christian and Jewish aspects of reception of various biblical texts, perhaps through the Council of Christians and Jews or debates in local synagogues or at conferences held by The British Association for Jewish Studies. I am less adept than many at doing this, but if reception history is about the *impact* and the *influence* and the *performance* of biblical texts in all aspects of human history, then this element seems to me a vital part of the collaborative process. So to my mind, collaboration within and outside the discipline is the greatest contribution studies in reception history can make to biblical studies.[24]

Doing reception history critically

I want to conclude with a reminder that we all do reception history in one way or another, whether it is by reading a text through the eyes of a nineteenth-century German commentator or trying to understand a text through the fieldwork of a biblical archaeologist. What has taken place over the last two decades is in part a way of expanding and making further sense of what we are doing whenever we receive the text through a third hand, and indeed, of making sense of what others have done before us. The key issue is that we have to be properly critical in what we do, and reception history must also rise to this challenge. I end therefore with a pertinent observation from John Barton in his *The Nature of Biblical Criticism*. Barton is discussing the 'plain sense meaning' of Psalm 84, noting that it has further layers and textures beyond its own literal meaning. He concludes:

> The plain sense can well contain within itself possibilities for finding layers of meaning well beyond the literal, and biblical critics need no more be under a self-denying ordinance that would rule this out than are their colleagues in the

---

[24] Taking a much wider framework of reference, it is also important to note the work which has been done comparing First World and Third World receptions of biblical texts: one seminal example would be *The Global Bible Commentary* (Nashville, TN: Abingdon Press, 2004), edited by Daniel M. Patte. This is a model of reception history 'in the present tense', showing how the diverse social and economic contexts of readers can expose both the oppressive and liberating dynamics of biblical texts, and thus illustrating how reception history must also be an active process as well as a receptive one, offering a *critical* analysis of biblical texts rather than a bland acceptance of them.

study of other branches of literature. To acknowledge this is far from making biblical study a free-for-all… There is responsible criticism, and there is irresponsible criticism, and knowing the difference is part of the skill of the good critic.[25]

This chapter evolved out of a paper given to The Society for Old Testament Study Summer Meeting at Manchester University on 17 July 2012.

---

[25] John Barton, *The Nature of Biblical Criticism* (Louisville, KY and London: Westminster John Knox Press, 2007), p. 116.

3

What is Reception History, and What Happens to You if You Do It?

James E. Harding
University of Otago

There is no such thing as Biblical Studies... is there?

In my recent book *The Love of David and Jonathan*, I made the rather bold claim that 'there is no such thing as Biblical Studies.'[1] My reasons for making this claim had a great deal to do with reception history. For if the reception history of the biblical texts, within and outside both the academy and communities of faith, demonstrates anything, it is that there is nothing obvious or natural about the questions biblical scholars ask, or the methods they use in trying to answer them.

This is merely one aspect of a crisis in the identity of Biblical Studies that has been growing in intensity in recent decades. For example, in their recent book *The Meaning of the Bible*, Douglas Knight and Amy-Jill Levine remark, '...given that biblical studies is itself a multi-faceted discipline — it draws from literature and sociology, legal theory and archaeology, ethics and psychology, and anything else that might give insight into the text — different studies will emphasize different approaches.'[2] As uncontroversial as this claim may seem, it nevertheless points to two unspoken, yet problematic assumptions: that it is *a single discipline* that is multi-faceted, and that the single fundamental purpose of biblical study is to give insight *into an identifiable text*, the meaning of which is ultimately retrievable. All sorts of questions flow from this: on what grounds can we speak of a single discipline? Where is the boundary, say, between Classics and Biblical Studies for scholars working on the reception of biblical narratives in the works of Josephus,[3]

---

[1] James E. Harding, *The Love of David and Jonathan: Ideology, Text, Reception* (BibleWorld; Sheffield: Equinox Publishing, 2013), 405.
[2] Douglas A. Knight and Amy-Jill Levine, *The Meaning of the Bible: What the Jewish Scriptures and Christian Old Testament Can Teach Us* (New York: HarperCollins, 2011), xviii.
[3] Arguably works such as the recent commentaries on the *Antiquitates Judaicae* are example of biblical reception history, yet at the same time their focus is on the works of Josephus in their own right. See e.g. Louis Feldman, *Flavius Josephus: Judean Antiquities 1-4* (Leiden: Brill, 2004); Christopher T. Begg, *Flavius Josephus: Judean Antiquities 5-7* (Leiden: Brill, 2005); Christopher T. Begg and Paul Spilsbury, *Judean Antiquities 8-10* (Leiden: Brill, 2005).

or between Biblical Studies and Assyriology or Hittitology for scholars trying to contextualize biblical covenants and treaties historically?[4] Is the coherence of the discipline a matter of a single text into which biblical scholars are seeking to provide insight, or a matter of the methods we use, or the assumptions we bring to the text?[5] Is there a single goal of a biblical scholar's work that is to be sought *within* a text? Is it meaningful to talk about a single 'text' at all, and if not, what does that say about the possibility of 'Biblical' Studies as a discipline? Does Biblical Studies exist to call the very nature of textuality into question, with particular reference to one, highly influential (in some contexts), set of written traditions?

While the increasing methodological plurality of Biblical Studies, together with the rise of postmodern approaches to the biblical texts, has called the identity of the discipline into question, the recent burgeoning of reception-historical studies has helped to intensify this crisis of identity.[6] I intend in this essay to pick up on a dimension of the recent debate between James Crossley and Larry Hurtado in *Relegere*,[7] but also to draw some insights out of my own recent work on the David and Jonathan narrative,[8] and on the narrative of Josiah's reform.[9]

---

[4] See now Kenneth A. Kitchen and Paul J. N. Lawrence, *Treaty, Law and Covenant in the Ancient Near East* (3 vols; Wiesbaden: Harrassowitz Verlag, 2012). The authors have some rather sharp, and frankly not entirely fair, remarks to make about the consequences of biblical scholars' alleged ignorance of external evidence (see e.g. *Treaty, Law and Covenant*, 3:259–61).

[5] Fr Seraphim Rose's work on the early chapters of Genesis (*Genesis, Creation, and Early Man: The Orthodox Christian Vision* (2nd edn; ed. Hieromonk Damascene; Platina, CA: St Herman of Alaska Brotherhood, 2011)) is certainly an attempt to give insight into the biblical text, and its survey of the teachings of the Church Fathers can be read as a form of reception history, but could it be recognized as 'Biblical Studies' in the way that Walter Moberly's *The Theology of the Book of Genesis* (Cambridge: Cambridge University Press, 2009) might? They are both geared towards offering theological insight into the biblical text in a manner that an atheist scholar of the same text could not, yet their respective responses to modern biblical scholarship are incommensurable.

[6] Other recent works have approached this sort of question rather differently, and I will not engage them directly here, as I want to focus on what *reception history* specifically might be saying about the discipline. For a rather pessimistic view, see Hector Avalos, *The End of Biblical Studies* (Amherst, NY: Prometheus Books, 2007); more constructively, see George Aichele, Peter Miscall, and Richard Walsh, 'An Elephant in the Room: Historical-Critical and Postmodern Interpretations of the Bible', *Journal of Biblical Literature* 128 (2009): 383–404; William John Lyons, 'Hope for a Troubled Discipline? Contributions to New Testament Studies from Reception History', *Journal for the Study of the New Testament* 33 (2010): 207–20; Stephen D. Moore and Yvonne Sherwood, *The Invention of the Biblical Scholar: A Critical Manifesto* (Minneapolis: Fortress, 2011). Taking a global view of the state of the field, see now Roland Boer and Fernando Segovia (eds.), *The Future of the Biblical Past: Envisioning Biblical Studies on a Global Key* (Atlanta, GA: Society of Biblical Literature, 2012).

[7] James G. Crossley, 'An Immodest Proposal for Biblical Studies', *Relegere: Studies in Religion and Reception* 2 (2012): 153–77; Larry W. Hurtado, 'On Diversity, Competence, and Coherence in New Testament Studies: A Modest Response to Crossley's "Immodest Proposal"', *Relegere: Studies in Religion and Reception* 2 (2012): 353–64.

[8] James E. Harding, 'David and Jonathan between Athens and Jerusalem', *Relegere: Studies in Religion and Reception* 1 (2011): 37–92; *The Love of David and Jonathan*, esp. chapters 4 and 5.

[9] 2 Kings 22–23; par. 2 Chronicles 34–35. My recent paper in the Ideology, Culture, and Translation Group of the Society of Biblical Literature Annual Meeting (Chicago, November 17, 2012) — '"[W]e the Cornyshe Men... utterly refuse thys newe Englyshe": Josiah's Reform, the Western Rebellion, and the Ideology of Uniformity'— focused on the reception and effect of the narrative of Josiah's reform in connection with the Edwardine Reformation in mid-sixteenth-century England.

Hurtado recognizes the importance of the problem of justifying the continuing place of Biblical Studies in secular academia,[10] offering not only intellectual but practical reasons for the existence of New Testament Studies as a discrete discipline:

> I think that to justify the place of 'New Testament Studies' or 'biblical studies' in today's universities it will be all the more important to demonstrate a coherent field of study, even a discipline. There is a danger if biblical studies becomes essentially an *entrepôt* where data, ideas and approaches from other fields are acquired and applied. We had better have some goods of our own to offer, some identifiable contribution to Humanities scholarship in particular that cannot easily be made in other disciplines... I think it will be important to show what particular kind of expertise biblical scholars bring to the study of the biblical texts, enabling analysis of these texts and related matters that will not likely be done as well in other disciplines, such as history, literature departments, sociology, anthropology, cultural studies, film studies, etc.[11]

This expertise is bound to a certain coherence Hurtado regards as connecting the field together, a coherence found in a focus on the texts of the New Testament themselves in their original historical contexts, and in a set of competencies proper to their study, in particular an ability to read with skill at least ancient Greek and Hebrew (and perhaps Latin), and the major modern languages, principally French and German, in which scholarly research on the New Testament is undertaken.[12]

If this is where coherence lies in 'New Testament Studies', there is a basic question to be asked. Hurtado seems to treat 'New Testament Studies' and 'Biblical Studies' as if they were the same, or at least the same kind of thing. But this assumption is itself fundamentally bound up with the reception history of the Bible. It is largely because Western Europe, particularly in the wake of the Reformation, inherited a certain kind of bible, that the discipline of Biblical Studies developed the way it did. But scholarship on the Old Testament or Hebrew Bible

---

[10] As do Lyons ('Hope for a Troubled Discipline?', 216–17) and Crossley ('Immodest Proposal', 165–66, 170–7). See also Hurtado's earlier 'New Testament Studies at the Turn of the Millennium: Questions for the Discipline', *Scottish Journal of Theology* 52 (1999): 158–78 (esp. pp. 158–63), which takes this problem as its point of departure. Interestingly, both Hurtado and Crossley would seem to agree that the critical study of the New Testament should be 'among the university subjects vital to humane learning' (Hurtado, 'New Testament Studies', 163, which Crossley cites in 'Immodest Proposal', 165–6): the point of difference is in what actually constitute the boundaries of such study. For Crossley, this has much to do with the fact that 'understanding [the Bible's] reception and influence is a significant task for understanding humanity' ('Immodest Proposal', 164), by virtue of the place of the Bible in the shaping of Western culture, and so reception history moves to the very heart of the field.

[11] Hurtado, 'On Diversity, Competence, and Coherence in New Testament Studies', 364.

[12] See also Hurtado's blog post 'Tools of the Trade', September 4, 2011 (http://larryhurtado.wordpress.com/2011/09/04/tools-of-the-trade/ [accessed 30 November 2012]), which provoked some lively though not always entirely constructive discussion in the blogosphere, and provided the foil for Crossley's 'Immodest Proposal'.

has evolved somewhat differently to scholarship on the New Testament. Students of the Hebrew Bible in its ancient contexts would seem to need a different range of linguistic competence, to begin with. In addition to the rather obvious — to me[13] — fact that skills in Hebrew, Aramaic, and arguably other ancient Semitic languages such as Akkadian and Ugaritic could be said to constitute the core competence of a scholar of the Hebrew Bible, certain branches of the study of the Hebrew Bible would seem to require at least Modern Hebrew as well as French and German. Furthermore, Hebrew Bible and New Testament, not to mention the associated literature of late Second Temple Judaism, are approached and studied in different ways in Jewish, Christian, and other contexts. Can we then speak of a single discipline 'Biblical Studies'?

There is a certain methodological coherence to John Barton's vision of a biblical criticism that, using the appropriate linguistic tools, homes in on 'what the text actually says.'[14] But that would still beg the question whether there needs to be not only methodological coherence (which is where historical-critical and postmodern approaches part company), but a single, clearly definable, universally agreed upon subject matter (which is where reception history throws a spanner in the works). The globalization of Biblical Studies adds extra dimensions to the potential incoherence of the discipline by radically decentring it,[15] at the same time as exposing both the ideological underpinning of all methods and approaches developed and sanctioned in the West, and the implication of the biblical texts themselves in imperialism and colonialism, and their effects.

The place of reception history in New Testament Studies is a key point of disagreement between Hurtado and Crossley. Crossley sees understanding the reception and influence of the Bible as fundamental to understanding humanity,[16] and thus as a fundamental part of what should constitute Biblical Studies in the contemporary academy. It is not something scholars do when they are done with the serious work of historical-critical exegesis — it is a core part of the biblical scholar's task. Hurtado criticizes Crossley for misunderstanding his take on reception history, and rejects outright the idea that reception history should be regarded as marginal to Biblical Studies. Yet for Hurtado, reception history is still

---

[13] It is true that not all institutions require students and budding scholars of these texts to have the same range of linguistic and literary competence, and it is here that my training as an historical critic seems desperate to rein in my desire to see the widest range of competencies and specialisms as possible collected under the umbrella of Biblical Studies.

[14] John Barton, *The Nature of Biblical Criticism* (Louisville, KY: Westminster John Knox, 2007), 6.

[15] Cf. Boer and Segovia, *The Future of the Biblical Past*.

[16] I am sure Crossley does not intend this, but the way he frames the matter risks reinscribing the hegemony of the West by seeing 'understanding *all humanity*' as the goal of studying 'the most high-profile literary collection *in Western culture* (and *perhaps beyond*)' ('Immodest Proposal', 164, italics mine). This is mitigated somewhat by Crossley's discussion of 'Internationalism' ('Immodest Proposal', 167-70). Here Crossley rightly problematizes the way that essentializing certain kinds of historical-critical project as the core business of Biblical Studies contributes to the ongoing marginalization of approaches that did not emerge in western academia.

to be done *in addition to*, not *as a core part of* the New Testament scholar's work.[17] When New Testament scholars do reception history, they should bring to it their specific competence *precisely as historically and philologically-oriented scholars*, whose main object of research is the texts of the New Testament in their historical context. The reception of these texts is secondary, not in terms of importance, but in terms of the order of doing things. The texts come first, their reception comes second. But can a distinction between first and second stages in interpretation, that is, between the study of the texts *in their original historical contexts* and their *subsequent history of reception* actually be maintained?[18] And why should the former be essentialized as *the* point of coherence for the discipline?

There is a troubling irony in the relation between the kind of scholarship Hurtado advocates as basic to New Testament Studies, and the reception history of biblical texts, one that Hurtado,[19] and myself,[20] have both touched on. That is: *biblical scholarship is itself part of the reception history of the biblical texts*. The ways in which we carve up Biblical Studies are arbitrary. The questions we ask, and the methods and approaches we use, are themselves part of the reception history of the texts we study. Given this, it is surely equally arbitrary to make a fundamental distinction between accounts of the history of scholarly research on the biblical texts on the one hand (i.e. *Auslegungsgeschichte*, often a prelude to yet more historical-critical research), and the study of their reception in art, literature, music, and popular culture on the other (i.e. *Rezeptionsgeschichte in sensu stricto*). It would seem that, given the historical contingency of the way the various branches of Biblical Studies have developed, to regard the former alone as serious biblical scholarship, and the latter as what scholars do when they are on holiday, would be a difficult position to defend coherently. And when we are on holiday, is there any qualitative difference between studying the use of the Book of Revelation by Johnny Cash or Depeche Mode on the one hand, and the use of the Book of Samuel by Carl Nielsen or Arthur Honegger on the other?

The real elephant in the room here is that a knowledge of how modern Biblical Studies in Western Europe during the Enlightenment evolved shows that *it could all have been otherwise*. The questions that guide biblical criticism emerged under particular circumstances in particular historical contexts. They arguably tell us more about biblical critics than they do about the directions Biblical Studies should take. This is not a call for plurality or relativism: it is simply to state a basic

---

[17] Hurtado, 'On Diversity, Competence, and Coherence in New Testament Studies', 361-2.
[18] Lyons says no, and I largely agree ('Hope for a Troubled Discipline?', 214-16). He offers a brilliantly succinct definition of reception history, which is more or less implied by some of my comments on the David and Jonathan narrative below: 'Reception history aims to understand the interaction between a text, a context and an audience's response' ('Hope for a Troubled Discipline?', 213).
[19] Hurtado, 'On Diversity, Competence and Coherence in New Testament Studies', 362 (building on Lyons, 'Hope for a Troubled Discipline?').
[20] Harding, *The Love of David and Jonathan*, 404-5 (see n. 1 above).

implication of the historical situatedness of the questions we ask, the texts we receive and study, and the methods we use.[21]

Do biblical texts have intrinsic qualities?

There is also another aspect of Hurtado's case. Having made a claim for the coherence of New Testament Studies as a discipline, he goes on to add that, 'In any case, I think that the New Testament writings have intrinsic qualities and a distinctive significance that fully justify serious and direct engagement with them, and with their subsequent reception as well.'[22] This claim could be taken several ways. What are the intrinsic qualities of the texts, and what is their distinctive significance? How does one go about defining what are the intrinsic qualities of texts that make them particularly worthy of study (and make the funding of such study worthwhile)? Is the intrinsic quality of, say, Luke's Gospel or the Epistle to the Hebrews of the same order as the intrinsic quality of the Epistle of Jude, or the Book of Revelation? Or in the Hebrew Bible, is the intrinsic quality of the Book of Job of the same order as that of the Book of Esther, or Ezra-Nehemiah (as a scholar who dabbles in Job occasionally I would like to scream 'No!' at this point)? And what about their distinctive significance: is this a matter of *Religionsgeschichte*, of their place in the evolution of Judaism and Christianity as phenomena of human religious history? Is it a matter of their broader cultural impact? Or is it tied to their status as authoritative texts for adherents of those traditions?

Here we rub up against a key problem for the identity of Biblical Studies as a discipline. We can claim that the biblical texts are of immense religio-historical, or political, or cultural significance, and thus worthy of study. We can also claim that they are of intrinsic *theological* significance, somehow witnesses to God's revealed Word, however we might construe this. But is it possible for us to have it both ways, or does Biblical Studies at this point fail to exhibit *ideological* coherence, and thus fail to exhibit integrity as a discipline? This is particularly critical in relation to the formation of those preparing for ordination, especially in contexts like Otago and Edinburgh, where students can acquire linguistic and critical skills in the study of the biblical texts as part of their training for ministry, but in 'secular' universities. It may be difficult to see how secular and confessional approaches to the biblical texts can meaningfully be said to be part of the same discipline, given that there is a key contradiction between their respective sources of authority. Perhaps, though,

---

[21] Other fields and disciplines are no less contingent, which might go some way towards mitigating the problem of defending the place of Biblical Studies in the academy by appeal to its nature and coherence.

[22] Hurtado, 'On Diversity, Competence, and Coherence in New Testament Studies', 363.

we could recognize the biblical texts as the site of a fundamental conflict of intellectual authority within the Humanities, one which is at the very heart of the intellectual history of the West, and with which responsible intellectuals within the Humanities — in western academia, at least — are bound to struggle.

Where exactly does reception history fit into this? In respect of the problem posed by the tension between secular and confessional approaches to the biblical texts, one crucial issue is the extent to which reception history and theological hermeneutics belong together. If they do belong together, is this a branch of Biblical Studies, or does it belong in some other part of Theology, assuming that Biblical Studies can be separated from Theology at all? Consider two 'biblical scholars': on the one hand, a committed Christian exegete concerned with reading Scripture with the Church Fathers in order to contribute to the edification of the Church, who is studying Gregory of Nyssa's homilies on the Song of Songs (in Greek, of course)[23] for this purpose, and a reception historian who *happens* to be a Christian, who is studying these homilies to better understand how the Song of Songs has been read and interpreted as a document of the human imagination. Are they doing the same kind of thing?[24] Presumably not. The (in)coherence of the discipline here seems to have more to do with the subjective formation and attitude of the interpreter, and with the particular questions one desires to ask of the texts, than it does with some objective dimension of the discipline.

Can we distinguish text and reception?

So the relationship between reception history and theological hermeneutics is a complex one. But what about the relationship between the study of a text and the study of its reception? Can a firm distinction between the two be maintained? In the case of a work such as the Book of Samuel, both internal evidence that the work is composite, and the quasi-external evidence of the manuscript tradition, from Qumran to the Lucianic recension and beyond, show that it is difficult to determine what the text of the book is. This yields some peculiar results. For example, the major commentaries on 1 and 2 Samuel by P. Kyle McCarter are based on McCarter's thorough and brilliant analysis of the witnesses to the text, not on a

---

[23] See now Richard A. Norris (trans.), *Gregory of Nyssa: Homilies on the Song of Songs* (Writings from the Greco-Roman World 13; Atlanta, GA: Society of Biblical Literature, 2012).

[24] Anthony Thiselton's commentary on 1 and 2 Thessalonians (*1 & 2 Thessalonians: Through the Centuries* (Blackwell Bible Commentaries; Chichester: Wiley-Blackwell, 2011)) is a good example of the fuzzy boundary between reception history and theological hermeneutics, and also highlights the fact that the various volumes in the Blackwell Bible Commentaries series may not really be doing the same kind of thing, in spite of the fact that they are all, in some sense, reception-historical in orientation. Perhaps what they call into question is the very nature of commentary as a scholarly activity.

single textual tradition, and are thus arguably not commentaries on the biblical text at all; they are commentaries on one scholar's erudite *reconstruction* of the text.[25] More to the point, they highlight the extent to which there is no single textual basis to be separated from its reception in the first place: we are dealing with a text that developed over time, within and between manuscript traditions in Hebrew and Greek. As is now abundantly clear to anyone who has studied the 'biblical' manuscripts from Qumran, the biblical 'text' contains the beginnings of the history of its own reception. Text and reception are inseparable.[26]

There is a very basic reason for this. Literary — and theological —texts imply the existence of readers, and before the advent of printing they imply the existence of tradents. Authors cannot with any exactitude anticipate the direction their texts will take in the hands of those who receive what they have written. Perhaps the first task of the reception historian is to explain what it is about the text that made it possible for its reception to have taken the course that it did, and here I must side with Hurtado in acknowledging the importance of a thorough competence in the relevant ancient languages.[27] In my recent study of the David and Jonathan narrative, I tried to show that the work is, while neither random nor chaotic, nonetheless not only composite and fluid, but more or less open to a range of different construals,[28] and it is in the myriad attempts to close down this textual openness that the history of its reception, including the various translations into Greek, Aramaic, Syriac and Latin, resides. But in order to show this, it is necessary to have both the linguistic skills and the critical acumen to trace, and explain, the process.

There are two problems here, one practical and the other theoretical. The practical problem is that no single scholar can hope to master the entire history of reception of any more than a very small segment of the biblical tradition. Different branches of this field require different competencies. How many biblical scholars, for example, have the skills in Church Slavonic and Russian, and the expertise in Russian literature, to do real justice to the use of biblical and related traditions in *The Brothers Karamazov*? How many have the skills in Welsh, and the expertise in Welsh religious history, to deal with biblical echoes and allusions in the work of Ann Griffiths? But the infinity of the field of reception history, which is due in large part to the infinity of language itself, is not really a problem when seen

---

[25] See P. Kyle McCarter, *I Samuel: A New Translation with Introduction and Commentary* (AB 8; New York: Doubleday, 1980); *II Samuel: A New Translation with Introduction and Commentary* (AB 9; New York: Doubleday, 1984).

[26] Lyons makes a similar point in redefining historical criticism in reception-historical terms, suggesting that redaction criticism, for example, is a form of reception history ('Hope for a Troubled Discipline?', 213).

[27] Might this mitigate my old-fashioned attachment to philology, confessed in n. 13 above?

[28] See esp. Harding, *The Love of David and Jonathan*, 122–73. I owe the idea of the 'open' work primarily to the theoretical studies of Umberto Eco.

in light of the fact that some areas of biblical criticism are sinking under their own weight, while others are passed over in apparently blissful ignorance.[29] How much more is there, really, to be said about the phrase πίστις Χριστοῦ? Probably a lot, actually, which points to the fact that using historical-critical tools to grasp what some text or other originally meant is only one aspect of the way the scholarly task is embodied: there are complex ideological reasons why we scholars feel drawn to ask some questions and not others, reasons of which we are not necessarily aware.

The vastness of reception history as a project means that it cannot be other than collaborative, and this offers a serious challenge to the implicit individualism of other forms of biblical scholarship, in which monographs and sole-authored articles and essays have such prestige, and form the basis for measuring an individual academic's value in exercises such as PBRF.[30] But the vastness of reception history also points to the sheer fecundity of the biblical texts, due not only to their polyvalence at the point where text and readers meet, but to the array of contexts through which they have been transmitted, and in which they have been read. The very attempt to master all of this is futile, but this in itself is significant: it tells us something about the nature of the text as it interacts with generations of readers in an ultimately untraceable range of different contexts, and about how the text is transformed and reconfigured in the process. It tells us a great deal also about the process of reading, whether within or without the transparent walls of the academy, and about the infinity of language, all of which tells us more about what it means to be *human*.

The theoretical problem is to do with the extent to which we can distinguish reception *history* from reception *criticism*. What exactly is it that we are meant to be doing? Is our task a theoretical one, of explaining how and why a given text provokes the responses it does from its readers, in light of theories about the interactions of texts and readers? Or is our task archival, tracing the accumulation of uses of biblical texts in religious traditions (Judaism, Christianity, Islam), in art, music, literature, and so on?[31] How might these tasks overlap?[32] They surely do, since a reception-historical archive cannot be ideologically neutral, and critical acumen is essential to explaining not only how reception history

---

[29] The example of this cited by Lyons, which can be understood in reception-historical terms, is the fact that there is a 27th edition of the Nestle-Aland Greek New Testament (there is now a 28th!), yet no critical edition of Chrysostom's homilies on 1 Corinthians ('Hope for a Troubled Discipline?', 216 n. 13).

[30] I.e., Performance-Based Research Funding, the equivalent in the New Zealand context to the REF in the UK.

[31] De Gruyter's colossal *Encyclopedia of the Bible and Its Reception* (*EBR*) appears largely dedicated to this task.

[32] I have attempted to do both in chapters 3 and 4 of *The Love of David and Jonathan*, and to a lesser extent in my short entries on David and Jonathan in vol. 6 of the *EBR* (Berlin: de Gruyter, 2013).

functions semiotically, but how it is ideologically implicated. But are there methods appropriate to reception-historical research, as there are usually considered to be in other branches of Biblical Studies, methods that pin down meanings and control texts and their uses, or is reception history inherently resistant to methodology, and in some way ludic, even anarchic, in character?

Where does reception history belong?

Another aspect of the issue at hand is where reception history belongs. For if reception history highlights the inability of methodology to subject texts to its control, it also, surely, highlights the impossibility of imprisoning the biblical texts within the walls of a single, fixed, discipline. Hurtado's view seems to be that reception history is something biblical scholars might attend to when they have done the more basic business of historically and philologically-oriented exegesis, and that practitioners of other disciplines might contribute to the study of biblical reception history from their particular fields. At any rate, there are *discrete disciplines* out of which the biblical texts can be studied, one of which — Biblical Studies — in some sense owns the right to offer the first interpretation.

Who, then, owns the right to interpret this passage, from E. M. Forster's novel *Maurice*?

> The boy had always been a scholar, awake to the printed word, and the horrors the Bible evoked for him were to be laid by Plato. Never could he forget his emotion at first reading the *Phaedrus*. He saw there his malady described exquisitely, calmly, as a passion which we can direct, like any other, towards good or bad. Here was no invitation to licence. He could not believe his good fortune at first—thought there must be some misunderstanding and that he and Plato were thinking of different things. Then he saw that the temperate pagan really did comprehend him, and, slipping past the Bible rather than opposing it, was offering a new guide for life. 'To make the most of what I have.' Not to crush it down, not vainly to wish that it was something else, but to cultivate it in such ways as will not vex either God or man.
>
> He was obliged however to throw over Christianity. Those who base their conduct upon what they are rather than upon what they ought to be, always must throw it over in the end, and besides, between Clive's temperament and that religion there is a secular feud. No clear-headed man can combine them. The temperament, to quote the legal formula, is 'not to be mentioned among Christians,' and a legend tells that all who shared it died on the morning of the Nativity. Clive regretted this. He came of a family of lawyers and squires, good and able men for the most part, and he did not wish to depart from their

tradition. He wished Christianity would compromise with him a little and searched the Scriptures for support. There was David and Jonathan; there was even the 'disciple that Jesus loved.' But the Church's interpretation was against him; he could not find any rest for his soul in her without crippling it, and withdrew higher into the classics yearly.[33]

This passage is part of the reception histories of the David and Jonathan narrative, and of the love of Jesus and the Beloved Disciple in the Fourth Gospel. It is not only part of their histories of *reception*, but also of the *effective* history of the Bible in general, which, particularly by virtue of the afterlife of the narrative of the destruction of Sodom and Gomorrah, is fundamental to the genealogy of homophobia, and to the creation of the self-condemning same-sex oriented subject. But this passage is also part of the reception history of the dialogues of Plato, and of the effective history of the ancient divides between Jew and Greek, pagan and Christian. Does *Maurice* belong, then, to the biblical scholar, the classicist, the scholar of early-twentieth-century English fiction, or to the historian of sexuality?

One might argue that the biblical scholar's task begins with the text in its historical context, and can then proceed to an engagement with the history of reception. In this scenario, *Maurice* belongs to the scholar of early-twentieth-century English literature first and foremost, and only secondarily to the scholar of the Bible. I think, however, that the situation is far more complex than this. First, *Maurice* highlights a point at which several fields and disciplines overlap, and thereby highlights the artificiality of the lines that divide those disciplines from one another. Second, passages such as this raise the question of how the questions modern biblical scholars ask have been shaped. What I tried to show in *The Love of David and Jonathan* was that the relationship between David and Jonathan in the Book of Samuel was part of the process by which the modern idea of the homosexual came into existence in the late-nineteenth and early-twentieth centuries. This construct, the 'homosexual', has more recently been turned back on the biblical text, and scholars have begun to ask whether David and Jonathan were homosexual lovers. My point is that even historically-oriented approaches to exegesis are shaped by the contexts in which such research is undertaken. *All* the questions scholars ask are reception-historically conditioned, and are thus themselves part of the reception history of the biblical texts. Indeed, it is this that keeps biblical scholarship going: were it not the case that scholars desire an answer to particular questions, conditioned in complex ways by the contexts in which they are asked, there would be no need for biblical scholarship of any sort in the first place.

---

[33] Forster, E. M., *Maurice* (ed. P. N. Furbank; introduction and notes by D. Leavitt; London: Penguin, 2005; 1st edn, London: Edward Arnold, 1971), 59–60. Although not published until after Forster's death, the novel was written in 1913–1914.

Reception history and the ethics of interpretation

At this point one might be tempted to throw up one's arms in despair at the futility of scholarship that is merely chasing its own tail (or hunting for the woozle), but I think a more compelling case can be made that reception history might, in fact, have a profoundly ethical orientation, because it confronts us with the effects of biblical texts as they are received throughout history. Biblical texts have the *effects* they do in particular contexts because of the way they have been *received* by particular readers and interpretive communities.[34] The effect of the reception of biblical texts on the invention of both homophobia and homosexuality would be one example, but I wish to draw on another example here, namely one brief moment in the reception history of the narrative of Josiah's reform.

The narrative of Josiah's reform (2 Kings 22–23; par. 2 Chronicles 34–35) was a major biblical resource for evangelical polemic in the mid-sixteenth century, on account of its reference to the rediscovery of an authoritative, written religious text, purporting to contain the Word of God, that became the basis for the reform of what its detractors regarded as a corrupt religion cluttered with images and implicated in treason. It was used by Thomas Cranmer in reference to evangelically-oriented reform during the reign of Henry VIII,[35] but particularly in reference to Edward VI,[36] the connection between the boy kings Edward VI and Josiah becoming a staple of evangelical historiography by the time of the 1570 edition of John Foxe's *Actes and Monuments*.[37] This is well recognized by historians of the period,[38] but to my knowledge has yet to be fully engaged by biblical scholars. This is despite the fact that the kinds of ideological forces that shaped the narrative in 2 Kings have a great deal in common with those that gave impetus to evangelical

---

[34] It should be clear from this that I regard over-fine distinctions between *Rezeptionsgeschichte* and *Wirkungsgeschichte* as splitting hairs: they can be distinguished theoretically (e.g. Christina Petterson's review of Judith Kovacs and Christopher Rowland, *Revelation: The Apocalypse of Jesus Christ* in *The Bible and Critical Theory* 2.1 (2006), 7.1–7.4), but they are really two sides of the same coin.

[35] Thomas Cranmer, 'v. Of good woorkes', in *Certayne Sermons, or homelies, appoynted by the kynges Maiestie, to be declared and redde, by all persones, Vicars, or Curates, euery Sondaye in their churches, where they haue Cure* (London: Printed by Richard Grafton, July 31, 1547). This sermon dates to the July of the first year of Edward's reign, and looks back on Henry's reign with approbation in respect of religious reform.

[36] Esp. Cranmer's speech at Edward's coronation on February 20, 1547. This speech was printed in Robert Ware, *The Second Part of Foxes and Firebrands: or, a Specimen of the Danger and Harmony of Popery and Separation* (Dublin: Printed by Jos. Ray, for Jos. Howes, to be sold by Awnsham Churchill, 1682), 2–9, and attributed there to Cranmer. This is the basis for the edition in *Miscellaneous Writings and Letters of Thomas Cranmer, Archbishop of Canterbury, Martyr, 1556* (ed. J. E. Cox for the Parker Society; Cambridge: Cambridge University Press, 1846), 126–7.

[37] Foxe, *Actes and Monuments*, 1570 edition, 9:1521–2; 1576 edition, 9:1281–2; 1583 edition, 9:1318–19. See *The Unabridged Acts and Monuments online* or *TAMO* (HRI Online Publications, Sheffield, 2011). Available from: http://www.johnfoxe.org [accessed 1 December 2012].

[38] See e.g. Margaret Aston, *The King's Bedpost: Reformation and Iconography in a Tudor Group Portrait* (Cambridge: Cambridge University Press, 1993); Diarmaid MacCulloch, *Tudor Church Militant: Edward VI and the Protestant Reformation* (London: Penguin, 1999), 14, 35, 57–104.

reform, the link being, of course, the biblical text. The rich symbolic imaginary of medieval Catholic devotion was swept away in favour of, and under the impetus of, the vernacular Christian Bible.[39] Among the effects of this was the imposition of both religious and linguistic uniformity,[40] an imposition that contributed to both the proliferation of religious violence in the sixteenth and seventeenth centuries, and, arguably, to the rise of biblical fundamentalism.[41]

This is key territory for the biblical scholar, because it not only draws attention to the reception and effect of a biblical text, but highlights a moment in the history of Western Europe that forms part of the complex historical background of the rise of biblical scholarship. Furthermore, the centrality of the reading of the Bible in the vernacular that is so much at the heart of Reformation piety is part of what has made the Bible such an immensely important element in the formation of modern Western culture, which both Hurtado and Crossley recognize as a very good reason for having Biblical Studies in secular academia. Of course, the provinciality of this moment in English religious history highlights my location as a *Western*, indeed an *English*, biblical scholar who might have a mind to focus on such relative obscurities. But this leaves a universe of room for an infinite proliferation of other locations in which the reception and effective histories of the biblical texts can be shown to be fundamental to how Biblical Studies could be framing its agendas.

Conclusion

Where does this leave us? It seems to me that it is not possible convincingly to limit Biblical Studies in such a way as to give philological research priority over whatever else a biblical scholar might do, and neither a single subject matter nor a single method or group of methods can be said to be more essentially Biblical Studies than others. That it might look that way to a casual observer is no more than an accident of history. The same must be said with respect to the confessional

---

[39] For deeply contrasting views on this, see Eamon Duffy, *The Stripping of the Altars: Traditional Religion in England c. 1400–c. 1580* (2nd ed.; New Haven and London: Yale University Press, 2005) and *The Voices of Morebath: Reformation and Rebellion in an English Village* (New Haven: Yale University Press, 2001), *versus* David Daniell in *The Bible in English: Its History and Influence* (New Haven: Yale University Press, 2003).

[40] Among the often cited effects of the Prayer Book Rebellion, sparked in part by the imposition of Cranmer's English Book of Common Prayer through the Act of Uniformity in 1549, is not simply the suppression of Latin as a liturgical language, but the demise of Cornish. See e.g. Ken George, 'Cornish,' in *The Celtic Languages* (ed. M. J. Ball and J. Fife; London: Routledge, 1993), 410–468 (pp. 413–414); Brian Murdoch, *Cornish Literature* (Cambridge: D. S. Brewer, 1993), 15.

[41] This case has been made by James Simpson in *Burning to Read: English Fundamentalism and its Reformation Opponents* (Cambridge, MA: Belknap, 2007), who aims to overturn the idea that the ability to read the Bible in the vernacular was inevitably a move in the direction of freedom and liberalism. In this he is directly opposing the sort of evangelical position taken by Daniell, *The Bible in English* (n. 39 above).

framework with which one begins: neither a confessional nor a non-confessional approach is more characteristic of Biblical Studies than the other. There are good ethical reasons, however, for an approach to Biblical Studies that accounts, in as much detail as possible, for how biblical texts shape the ways in which particular cultures have come to think, and that requires a vast collaborative effort from scholars from an unlimited variety of backgrounds, contexts and competencies. Such an effort will be of incalculable value in the ongoing moral formation of the societies in which biblical scholars have the luxury of practicing their art.[42]

---

[42] I write this on the day after Margaret Thatcher's death. Thatcher is said to have once responded to a student who told her she was studying Norse literature: 'What a luxury!' (Josh White, 'Students must now choose between learning and earning,' *New Statesman* [June 5, 2011], http://www.newstatesman.com/education/2011/06/students-university-learning, [accessed 9 April 2013]). The obscurities we academics study may have the appearance of luxury but they are part of an exercise of the mind that, I suggest, has immense ethical value. This should transcend both our internal squabbles over how to define our discipline, and our external stress over proving our economic value.

4

The End of Reception History, a Grand Narrative for Biblical Studies and the Neoliberal Bible

James G. Crossley

It is well-known in the gossipy circles of Biblical Studies, occasionally breaking through to conference panels and discussions, that what we commonly call 'reception history' (more often than not understood as post-antiquity uses of the Bible and biblical texts) is often demoted or even ridiculed by scholars for whom 'serious' history seems to end in 200 CE. As some of the cattier remarks would have it, reception history is supposed to be an 'easy' option, and the more pop cultural aspects especially so. Of course, we are not really supposed to respond to unpublished gossip and witty scholarly aphorisms. However, this discussion is largely being undertaken under the radar of published work and does have a bearing on the assumptions of what the field of Biblical Studies ought to be. For a start, it seems an absurdity to be able to assume a measurement of how 'easy' or 'hard' a given period of history is to study. If we wanted to study Persian period Judah, knowledge of Hebrew, Aramaic, German, English, archaeology, etc. might be most obviously important. If we wanted to study the role of biblical texts in contemporary Hollywood films, knowledge of critical theory, cinema studies, cultural studies, modern American history, etc. might be most obviously important. Both examples would require dedication and hard work and I must admit to being at a loss to measure which is inherently 'more difficult'. It is, of course, no surprise that there are scholars who like to inform us, even if implicitly, just how clever they are but it seems to me that bragging about being smarter based on studying a different period of history is a most peculiar way to view history, society and intellectual development.

Naturally, not all biblical scholars take up such a position. Another criticism of 'reception history' of the sort that might look at receptions of the Bible in contemporary culture is that it is valuable in its own right but not really to be included in the discipline or field of Biblical Studies, or at least not among its core skills. Compare also the comments made by Steve Walton in the published version of his inaugural lecture on New Testament studies: 'Reading later interpreters of the New Testament is, I repeat, a valuable exercise, but it should not be mistaken for New Testament study – it should be seen, instead, as a sub-section of Cultural Studies or (within the broad discipline of theology) historical theology.'[1] This line of thinking becomes problematic for, among other things, reasons of simple pragmatism. The annual Society of Biblical Literature (SBL) meeting has numerous sessions and papers relating to the reception of the Bible, as have localized conferences from the Society of Old Testament Study to the Oceania Biblical Studies Association. Relatively new journals (e.g. *Relegere, The Bible and Critical Theory, Biblical Reception, Postscripts*, and *Biblical Interpretation*) are dedicated to areas related to reception and now traditional journals (e.g. *New Testament Studies, Journal of Biblical Literature*) are entertaining submissions based on reception history. As this should obviously imply, there are more and more scholars who are associated with the field of Biblical Studies working in the general area of reception and so reception history is now embedded in the field whether we like it or not.

But sheer pragmatism is hardly the most edifying argument in favour of the justification of the importance of the reception of the Bible in the field of Biblical Studies. And, if we remain at the level of pragmatism, there would be no reason why we should have departments of Biblical Studies, or justify Biblical Studies within departments of Religious Studies and Theology; such scholars could presumably function within the narratives of other fields and disciplines such as Literary Studies, Cultural Studies or History. What can be done, however, is to give some coherency to what we know as 'reception history' and, by implication, Biblical Studies as a whole.[2] Biblical scholars all know that the Bible has been relentlessly used in the history of ideas and historical change, from comic books to opera, from

---

[1] S. Walton, 'What Is Progress in New Testament Studies?', *Exp. Tim.* 124 (2013), pp. 209–26 (215–16). It is not entirely clear if Walton is limiting this assessment to a specifically Christian study or the critical study in the universities (he attempts to address both) but presumably the reference to Cultural Studies implies university study at least is in mind here. See also the discussion in L. Hurtado, 'Tools of the Trade', *Larry Hurtado's Blog* [September 4, 2011], http://larryhurtado.wordpress.com/2011/09/04/tools-of-the-trade/; J. Crossley, 'Languages, Humanities and a New Testament PhD', *Sheffield Biblical Studies* [September 7, 2011], http://sheffieldbiblicalstudies.wordpress.com/2011/09/07/languages-humanities-ntphd/; L. Hurtado, 'Tools of the Trade ... Encore', *Larry Hurtado's Blog* [September 5, 2011], http://larryhurtado.wordpress.com/2011/09/05/tools-of-the-trade-encore/; L. Hurtado, 'Languages, Theories, Approaches', *Larry Hurtado's Blog* [September 8, 2011], http://larryhurtado.wordpress.com/2011/09/08/languages-theories-approaches/; J. Crossley, 'More on Widening the Definition of NT Studies', *Sheffield Biblical Studies* (September 8, 2011), http://sheffieldbiblicalstudies.wordpress.com/2011/09/08/more-on-widening-the-definition-of-nt-studies/. For related discussion on seemingly contradictory trends in the field see G. Aichele, P. Miscall and R. Walsh, 'An Elephant in the Room: Historical-Critical and Postmodern Interpretations of the Bible', *JBL* 128 (2009), pp. 383–404.

[2] J. G. Crossley, 'An Immodest Proposal for Biblical Studies', *Relegere* (2011), pp. 95–116 attempts to provide an approach to biblical studies which incorporates the ancient and the modern uses of the Bible and biblical texts into a coherent narrative for the field. The response by Hurtado seems to me simply to repeat the primacy of ancient texts in ancient contexts and ancient languages as the *primary* focus of Biblical Studies. See L. W. Hurtado, 'On Diversity, Competence and Coherence in New Testament Studies: A Modest Response to Crossley's "Immodest Proposal"', *Relegere* 2 (2012), pp. 353–64.

the English Civil War to the obsession with Paul in Philosophy and Critical Theory. It is a matter of some urgency for biblical scholars to persuade those colleagues in the Arts and Humanities who have no idea what we do that any understanding of the history of ideas and historical change is sorely lacking if it does not understand the involvement of the Bible and biblical texts. We cannot justify the importance of Biblical Studies by making that stale argument that the Bible is hugely important for people today and then keep studying the ancient contexts alone. There are indeed powerful defences to be made of the importance of studying ancient texts in ancient contexts but if we want to justify Biblical Studies by the contemporary relevance of the Bible then it might reasonably be expected that we explain *why* it is still relevant in the ways that it is.

This sort of thinking begins to give the field its coherency, or suggests what *could* give the field its coherency, by bringing these seemingly diverse strands together into a narrative of how and why 'the Bible' originated, how and why 'the Bible' developed and survived, how and why biblical texts got to the multiple places where they are today, how and why people have felt the need to engage with biblical texts, and how and why there is loathing, despising and indifference.[3] In thinking in such terms, Biblical Studies can provide a not insignificant contribution to our understanding of human history and society. Indeed, as Timothy Beal has suggested, reception history should turn its attention more to the cultural production of scripture as a means of interpreting culture more widely and thus further bringing Biblical Studies more firmly into the humanities and social sciences.[4]

In doing this we can see why those conventionally labelled 'historical critics' and those conventionally labelled 'reception historians' are obviously as important as each other in contributing to the narrative of the origins, use and influence of the Bible. But by thinking holistically, one clear ramification is that we should join those who want to do away with, or at least critique, the term 'reception history' (as conventionally understood),[5] though by the same logic we should also do away with the label 'historical criticism' if understood in a conventionally limited sense. When we think in terms of the origins, development and use of the Bible and biblical texts, we no longer need to make the distinction between (for instance) 'historical criticism' and 'reception history' because, not only is everything

---

[3] In some ways, this sort of thinking underpins Burton Mack's ambitious project on the Christian Myth, from the earliest Christian groups through the generation of a dominant imperial myth to the ongoing power of the myth in American culture. A recent, and in my view most important, instalment of Mack's project is B. Mack, *Christian Mentality: The Entanglements of Power, Violence, and Fear* (London: Equinox, 2011).

[4] T. Beal, 'Reception History and Beyond: Toward the Cultural History of Scriptures', *Bib. Int.* 19 (2011), pp. 357–72.

[5] E.g. W. J. Lyons, 'Hope for a Troubled Discipline? Contributions to New Testament Studies from Reception History', *JSNT* 33 (2010), pp. 207–20; R. Boer, 'Against "Reception History"', *Bible and Interpretation* (May, 2011), http://www.bibleinterp.com/opeds/boe358008.shtml

reception in some form, but everything is, obviously, history.[6] If historical critics use a range of methods to understand history, culture and society then 'historical criticism' clearly does not end (for instance) at the second century CE. In fact, the binary categories, 'historical criticism' and 'reception history', only perpetuate the idea that there is something inherently important, or indeed superior, about that period we conventionally label 'biblical'. The boundary between The Original Biblical Period (sometimes with the addition of Patristic reception), on the one hand, and The Rest of History, on the other, is little more than a reinscription of Reformation-inspired categories of time.[7]

Much work has, of course, already been carried out on the origins and generation of the biblical texts and the canonization processes, even if greater attention still needs to be paid to more materialist explanations of Christian origins at least. Experts on pre-modern history will be able to give explanations of different interpretative trends and histories with more authority and detail than I will ever be able to do but clearly Christendom, Christianity and Judaism made survival of biblical texts possible in general terms. But for the rest of this essay, I want to turn the chronological pattern upside down, as it were, and look at the role of the present. Of course, this is, to some extent, an arbitrary decision. However, as Peter Thompson argued in his defence of the importance of the Arts and Humanities, much of humanity has been about seeking patterns out of chaos, establishing the multiple contingent events that got us to where we are and possibly where we might be going, and unravelling the assumptions of the end point.[8] And in this spirit, I want to turn to some big picture explanations to unravel the 'common sense' (in the Gramscian sense) assumptions about, and the survival of, biblical texts in more contemporary history. Moreover, reliance on the importance of Judaism and Christianity, synagogues and churches, at least in basic forms of ideological dominance can no longer be *the* overwhelmingly dominant part of our explanations. Of course, even if Christianity does not have the imperial power it once did, it is clear that one crucial means of the survival of biblical texts up to the present has been through churches and investigations of which will likewise produce a range of different interpretative traditions. But it is also significant that

---

[6] Recall the famous opening words of F. Jameson, *The Political Unconscious: Narrative as a Socially Symbolic Act* (Ithaca: Cornell University Press, 1981), p. ix: 'Always historicize!'

[7] I owe this point to Chris Rowland. Compare Walton's argument on reception history: There is undoubted value in reading what earlier interpreters have found in Scripture ... Classic protestant Christian biblical interpretation ... follows the Renaissance principle of *ad fontes*—back to the sources. The revival of study of the Bible as the primary source of Christian faith—and that in Hebrew and Greek—was a key driver of the Christian renewal movement we know as the Reformation ... Christian interpreters of the New Testament will want to maintain the vital distinction between the New Testament and what others say about the New Testament, for in a Christian context, the New Testament carries a weight of importance which interpretations of it do not. (Walton, 'What is Progress in New Testament Studies?', *Exp. Tim.* 124 (2013), pp. 214–16).

[8] A podcast, including Peter Thompson's lecture, is available at http://uecho.shef.ac.uk:8080/ess/echo/presentation/2490a955-7c12-4b64-bf31-c2a4e8c65bd8/media.mp3

the Bible and biblical texts continue to survive in less obvious contexts which we label (problematically) 'secular'. With this in mind, I want to give some general explanations for how the Bible and biblical texts continue to survive with particular reference to our era of liberal democracy and postmodern capitalism. What follows is not, of course, the only explanation for understanding the survival of the Bible and biblical texts but a generalizing explanation which will hopefully illustrate just some of the ways in which we might begin to develop a more rounded narrative for the field of Biblical Studies.

The Liberal Bible and the Cultural Bible: The Bible Decaffeinated

The Bible's continued survival in Western cultural contexts has involved coming to terms with secularism, nationalism and global capitalism. This has produced a major interpretative tradition which Yvonne Sherwood has labelled the 'Liberal Bible'.[9] It is important not to confuse different types of liberalism here. The Liberal Bible does not automatically mean a Bible which supports, for instance, a range of sexualities (though it might) but rather a Bible more supportive of the Western liberal democratic tradition more generally. Thus, Sherwood shows that the Liberal Bible is supportive of freedom of conscience, rights, justice, law and consensus, and its impact has produced the mistaken assumption that the Bible is the foundation of Western democracies, or at least complements Western democratic thought, thereby masking the modern origins of this major strand of biblical interpretation in sixteenth- and seventeenth-century Europe.

A clear illustration of this tradition is found in a speech by the British Prime Minister David Cameron at the close of the 400th anniversary of the King James Bible where he described Christianity and the Bible in terms of the following values, most of which are not really entertained in the Bible: 'human rights and equality...our constitutional monarchy and parliamentary democracy...the first forms of welfare provision...language and culture...the foundations for protest and for the evolution of our freedom and democracy ... the irrepressible foundation for equality and human rights a foundation that has seen the Bible at the forefront of the emergence of democracy, the abolition of slavery and the emancipation of women ...'.[10] We can also see the importance of the Liberal Bible in American politics, particularly since the late 1970s, thanks to the work of Jacques Berlinerblau.[11] According to Berlinerblau, figures such as Bill Clinton,

---

[9] Y. Sherwood, 'Bush's Bible as a Liberal Bible (Strange though that Might Seem)', *Postscripts* 2 (2006), pp. 47–58.

[10] D. Cameron, 'Prime Minister's King James Bible Speech (December 16)', *Number 10 Downing Street* (2011), http://www.number10.gov.uk/news/king-james-bible/

[11] J. Berlinerblau, *Thumpin' It: The Use and Abuse of the Bible in Today's Presidential Politics* (Louisville: WJK, 2008).

George W. Bush and Barack Obama are 'successful' users of the Bible because, unlike 'unsuccessful' users of the Bible (e.g. John Kerry, Joe Lieberman) they are not only perceived to be 'credible' believers but also manage to keep their biblical references and allusions sparse, measured, sufficiently vague and supportive of positive things like freedom, inclusivity and care for others. This allows such uses of the Bible to be picked up by the believer without automatically putting off those voters more nervous about anything 'too religious'.

The Liberal Bible can be found in any number of contemporary cultural contexts working in ways which advocate separation from the state as much as those uses in support of it. One example might be the use of the Bible in the understanding of 'religion' in the contemporary British press.[12] Favoured phrases are *love thy neighbour* and *render unto Caesar*. A typical example might be Dominic Lawson who claimed that Pope Benedict is 'un-political' and 'has no interest in inserting the Catholic Church into the political process.' This is because the Pope apparently inherited his worldview from Jesus who declared 'that the temporal and spiritual worlds should be entirely separate'. To support this claim Lawson gives the biblical proof text: 'Render unto Caesar the things that are Caesar's and unto God the things that are God's.'[13] What we have here is the Bible being used to support the typical privatization of 'religion' which is, as Russell McCutcheon put it, 'firmly entrenched in the well-established liberal tradition of distinguishing the relatively apolitical freedom "to believe" from the obviously political freedom to behave, organize, and oppose. It is none other than the rhetorical distinction between private and public ... that makes possible both the internalization of dissent and conformity of practice'.[14] The history of those practices commonly constructed as 'religious' in relation to public versus private, state versus church and so on has not been entirely comfortable, from the distinction between the 'spiritual' and the 'temporal' realms growing out of the Protestant Reformation to the liberal toleration of religion and the apparent separation of Church and State in America. Despite the rhetoric of stark distinction, in practice the relationship regularly overlaps and intersects.[15] But it is this simplifying construction that can allow the Bible to be presented as palatable and non-threatening whilst all sorts of power games continue beneath the surface.

---

[12] J. G. Crossley and J. Harrison, 'The Mediation of the Distinction of "Religion" and "Politics" by the UK Press on the Occasion of Pope Benedict XVI's State Visit to the UK (2010)', *Political Theology* (forthcoming 2015).

[13] D. Lawson, 'Pope Benedict ... an apology', *Independent* (September 21, 2010). http://www.independent.co.uk/opinion/commentators/dominic-lawson/dominic-lawson-pope-benedict-an-apology-2084788.html

[14] R. T. McCutcheon, *Religion and the Domestication of Dissent: or, How to live in a less than perfect nation* (London & Oakville: Equinox, 2005), p. 62.

[15] For a detailed history, deconstruction and analysis of the rhetorical distinction between 'religion' and 'state' from early modern Europe and as a product of modernity see C. Martin, *Masking Hegemony: A Genealogy of Liberalism, Religion and the Private Sphere* (London and Oakville: Equinox, 2010), pp. 33–57.

To add to our labels, we might even alternatively nickname the Liberal Bible, 'the Decaffeinated Bible'. Here I have in mind Slavoj Žižek's summary of his discussion of contemporary capitalism with reference to the limited toleration of liberal multiculturalism: 'On today's market, we find a series of products deprived of their malignant property: coffee without caffeine, cream without fat, beer without alcohol...'.[16] In terms of the contemporary survival of the Bible, this might be the removal of anything deemed too 'religious' or problematic for contemporary manifestations of liberalism. Contemporary manifestations of Decaffeinated Bible owe much to the long tradition of the Cultural Bible or the Enlightenment Bible, where the Bible is deemed a vital part of 'our' cultural heritage – much like Shakespeare or Milton – and is to be respected as such.[17]

For instance, in sending out King James Version (KJV) Bibles to English schools in 2012, the UK Education Secretary Michael Gove may well describe this particular Bible's influence on 'our culture … history, language, literature and democracy' (and any other area it may or may not have had any influence on),[18] but we should not expect him to praise the actions of Joshua, the vision of Revelation, the smashing of babies' heads against rocks, the labelling of Gentiles 'dogs', fasting, condemning the rich to Hades, weeping and gnashing of teeth, or the numerous sexually peculiar tales. Nor should we expect Gove to endorse the use of the KJV in the conversion of heathens and the colonized, in dealing with heretics appropriately, or in establishing the pros and cons of consubstantiation and transubstantiation. Curiously, this is close to the logic of Richard Dawkins. Dawkins is, of course, much more vocal about the problematic contents of the Bible, and would even want our children to see them for what they really are, but once we get beyond such problems we get nothing less than the Cultural Bible: 'A native speaker of English who has never read a word of the King James Bible is verging on the barbarian'.[19]

To help explain the ongoing relevance of the Cultural Bible for contemporary liberal and capitalist contexts, we might again turn to Žižek here who sees 'culture'

---

[16] S. Žižek, *The Puppet and the Dwarf: The Perverse Core of Christianity* (Cambridge, MA: MIT Press, 2003), 96.

[17] J. Sheehan, *The Enlightenment Bible: Translation, Scholarship, Culture* (Princeton, NJ: Princeton University Press, 2004); S. D. Moore and Y. Sherwood. 2011. *The Invention of the Biblical Scholar: A Critical Manifesto* (Minneapolis: Fortress, 2011), pp. 46–81

[18] Quoted in BBC, 'Schools get King James Bible to mark 400th anniversary', *BBC News* [15 May 2012]. http://www.bbc.co.uk/news/education-18073996

[19] R. Dawkins, 'Why I want all our children to read the King James Bible', *Observer* (May 19, 2012). As Dawkins put it in his famous book, *The God Delusion*: 'I must admit that even I am a little taken aback at the biblical ignorance commonly displayed by people educated in more recent decades than I was … The King James Bible of 1611 – the Authorized Version – includes passages of outstanding literary merit in its own right … But the main reason the English Bible needs to be part of our education is that it is a major sourcebook for literary culture … Surely ignorance of the Bible is bound to impoverish one's appreciation of English literature … We can give up belief in God while not losing touch with a treasured heritage'. See R. Dawkins, *The God Delusion* (London: Bantham Press, 2006), pp. 340–1, 343, 344.

emerging as 'the central life-world category'. What this means is that when we deal with the topic of religion, people do not necessarily 'really believe' today but rather 'just follow (some) religious rituals and mores as part of respect for the "lifestyle" of the community to which we belong'. As Žižek suggests (and with clear relevance for the KJV-as-heritage argument):

> 'I don't really believe in it, it's just part of my culture' effectively seems to be the predominant mode of the disavowed/displaced belief characteristic of our times. What is a cultural lifestyle, if not the fact that, although we do not believe in Santa Claus, there is a Christmas tree in every house, and even in public places, every December? ... 'culture' is the name for all those things we practice without really believing in them, without 'taking them seriously' ... Today, we ultimately perceive as a threat to culture those who live their culture immediately, those who lack a distance toward it. Recall the outrage when, two years ago, the Taliban forces in Afghanistan destroyed the ancient Buddhist statues at Bamiyan: although none of us enlightened Westerners believe in the divinity of the Buddha, we were outraged because the Taliban Muslims did not show the appropriate respect for the 'cultural heritage' of their own country and the entire world. Instead of believing through the other, like all people of culture, they really believed in their own religion, and thus had no great sensitivity toward the cultural value of the monuments of other religions—to them, the Buddha statues were just fake idols, not 'cultural treasures'.[20]

'Belief in' the content may not matter for the Cultural Bible to be maintained, any more than actually being too concerned with any extensive reading of the contents for whatever purposes. It is simply accepting the importance of the object – the Bible – that is important, with a few key phrases and figures to be likewise remembered. This takes us to what we might label the Neoliberal Bible.

The Neoliberal Bible

Looking at the uses of language from the KJV in the contemporary British media, R. S. Sugirtharajah argued that 'From the use of these quotations it is sometimes difficult to assess whether the sacred text of Christians is held in veneration or being mocked ... one is often baffled as to whether the Sacred Word is held in reverence or taken for its comic value'.[21] This bafflement is perhaps even more significant than Sugirtharajah suggests (and there are plenty more examples from the contemporary press) because playful, comic, mocking and ironic language can

---

[20] Žižek, *The Puppet and the Dwarf*, pp. 7–8.
[21] R. S. Sugirtharajah, 'Loitering with Intent: Biblical Texts in Public Places', *Bib. Int.* 11 (2001), pp. 567–78 (572–73).

be significant in perpetuating relevance and ideology.²² Compare one example from the *Guardian* given by Sugirtharajah on the 'ritualized form of football results aired after the matches' which manages to maintain the KJV's cultural capital through playfulness and witty quasi-intellectual allusion:

> And these are the kings of the land whom Joshua and the children of Israel smote beyond Jordan westwards . . .
> King of Jericho, one; the king of Ai, which is beside Beth-el, one.
> The king of Jerusalem, one, the king of Hebron, one;
> The king of Jarmuth, one; the king of Lachish, one;
> The king of Eglon, one; the king of Gezer, one.
> The king of Debir, one; the king of Geder, one.²³

But Sugirtharajah adds a telling 'postcolonial postscript': 'The founding totem of the western world has now ended up in the popular press as "an erratic" and "an eccentric" cultural artifact sans religious authority or theological clout'.²⁴ But in accepting such eccentricities as evidence of decline, it may be that Sugirtharajah has missed the crucial point: the KJV *should* have lost its theological clout and religious authority as traditionally understood. The KJV and the Bible more generally still serve nationalism but now survive by bowing down at the altar of the dominant ideology of our time: liberal capitalist democracy.

Developing this with reference to more contemporary manifestations of capitalism, we might add that we now also have one label which may even bring all the above labels together for our times: the Neoliberal Bible. Some general comments on neoliberalism might help. Neoliberalism advocates individual property rights and free trade, promotes the private sector over the public sector, supports deregulation of the market, challenges traditional manifestations of state power, urges virtually every aspect of human existence to be brought into the market, encourages individual responsibility, downplays systemic problems as a cause of individual failure, and emphasizes the importance of the market for the common good, human freedom, elimination of poverty and creation of wealth.²⁵ Neoliberalism has been the dominant ideological position in the West since the 1970s, replacing the previous Fordist-Keynesian consensus. Of course, in reality, 'pure' neoliberalism does not really happen and state interventionism has hardly

---

²² S. Žižek, *The Sublime Object of Ideology* (London and New York: Verso, 1989); J. G. Crossley, *Jesus in an Age of Neoliberalism: Quests, Scholarship, Ideology* (Sheffield: Equinox, 2012), pp. 32–4.
²³ Sugirtharajah, 'Loitering with Intent', p. 570, quoting Matthew Engel, 'Dark Angel', *Guardian*. Sugirtharajah was unable to supply the date of the Guardian article but estimates that it is from the 'middle 1990s'.
²⁴ Sugirtharajah, 'Loitering with Intent', p. 577.
²⁵ Crossley, *Jesus in an Age of Neoliberalism*, pp. 21–37. For full discussions of neoliberalism see e.g. D. Harvey, *A Brief History of Neoliberalism* (Oxford: Oxford University Press, 2005); D. Plehwe, B. J. A. Walpen, G. Neunhoffer (eds.), *Neoliberal Hegemony: A Global Critique* (London: Routledge, 2007); P. Mirowski and D. Plehwe (eds.) *The Road from Mont Pelerin: The Making of the Neoliberal Thought Collective* (Cambridge, MA: Harvard University Press, 2009).

withered. But the *ideal*, with increasingly higher degrees of implementation, has been dominant and has become manifest in forms of high profile advocates or implementers, such as Thatcher, Reagan, Blair and Cameron.

David Harvey can even write about 'the neoliberalism of culture'[26] and he, along with Jameson and others have shown the links between late capitalism, or neoliberalism, and postmodernity,[27] all with the accompanying challenges to traditional concepts of truth and metanarratives and greater emphasis on diversity, indeterminacy, instability, kitsch, playfulness, eclecticism, derivation, and a certain de-centeredness.[28] Assisted by the rise of mass media and communications, the instant image and PR have become more prominent than ever before. Perhaps paradoxically, however, we find nationalism, jingoism, imperialism and war taken up by neoliberal states to promote or provoke, directly or indirectly, neoliberalism (think of the Falklands or the Iraq wars), or indeed as a reaction to the globalizing tendencies of neoliberalism.[29] This tension between non-intervention and state intervention partly explains why neoconservatism has come to the fore in the past decade. Neoconservatism has not only provided vigorous support for neoliberal economics but has positively revelled in the possibilities of militarization, authoritarianism and threats to the order (whether real or otherwise).

Perhaps there are few better examples of what we might now label the Neoliberal Bible than the republishing and repackaging (usually by Zondervan) of existing Bibles (often the New International Version (NIV) in various packages) for niche audiences and identities, and in the case of military Bibles, intersecting with nationalism and (multiple) identity politics. These include: *Playful Puppies Bible; Curious Kittens Bible; The Holy Bible: Stock Car Racing Edition; True Images: The Teen Bible for Girls; Revolution: The Bible for Teen Guys; The Word on the Street; Couples' Devotional Bible; Engaged Couples' Bible; Life Journey Bible; The Soldiers' Bible* and so on. Clearly image is crucial for the Neoliberal Bible. In a related way, Katie Edwards has shown that the Bible in advertising only needs a split-second image to convey a range of 'common sense' meanings. For instance, a standard advert with an Eve-type figure tempted by an apple can convey a set of assumptions about consumerist desire and constructions of gender, whilst an advert with the England footballer Wayne Rooney in Messianic pose and with blood-red St

---

[26] Harvey, *Neoliberalism*, p. 47. Cf. F. Jameson, *Postmodernism, or, The Cultural Logic of Late Capitalism* (London and New York, 1991), pp. 261, 263, 265–6, 278.

[27] E.g. D. Harvey, *The Condition of Postmodernity* (Oxford: Blackwell, 1989); Jameson, *Postmodernism*; P. Anderson, *The Origins of Postmodernity* (London and New York: Verso, 1998).

[28] T. Eagleton, *The Illusions of Postmodernism* (Oxford: Blackwell, 1996), p. vii.

[29] See e.g. Jameson, *Postmodernism*, p. 5; Harvey, *Neoliberalism*, pp. 64–86; N. Klein, *The Shock Doctrine: The Rise of Disaster Capitalism* (London: Allen Lane, 2007), pp. 136–40; W. Brown, 'American Nightmare: Neoconservatism, Neoliberalism, and De-democratization', *Political Theory* 34 (2006), pp. 690–714.

George's cross (the English flag) painted across his body shows the intersection of (among other things) branding, masculinity and nationalism.[30] This intersection of image, masculinity, nationalism and multiple manifestations of the Bible not only illustrates the tensions at work in globalizing capitalism, but also just how embedded the Bible is in contemporary capitalism's relentless quest for more markets and how it replicates itself in a seemingly endless range of contexts.[31]

In this postmodern world of instant imaging the content might be thought to be largely irrelevant.[32] To some extent this is true. An excellent example with little concern for the content of the Bible is the ongoing survival of the King James Bible. We might be forgiven for thinking that the KJV had its best days behind it by the twentieth century. Its language was too archaic for congregations, better Greek manuscripts had been discovered, the British Empire was in decline, and the relentless Bible translations have not ceased. But it has survived, and not just as a picturesque artifact or a Christening gift. It is also the language of the KJV that has allowed it to survive. The distinctive 'KJV language' has relentlessly involved the removal or downplaying of anything perceived to be too 'religious'. David Crystal provides a wide range of famous phrases from the KJV (or King James 'sounding' phrases), from low and high culture, including those which have had a 'permanent influence on the development of the English language' (*Let there be light, My brother's keeper, Begat, Bread alone, Heal thyself* and so on).[33] He shows that idioms are adapted, often with comical intent, with all sorts of unexpected language play (e.g. *Am I my brothel's keeper?*). All these points are central to his analysis of the extent to which KJV idioms have 'permeated genres of modern spoken or written English', such as, for instance, marketing, journalism, sport, theatre, punk music, computing and so on. Likewise, one of the key reasons for survival of idioms (and not necessarily in the same form found in the King James Bible) is a range of phonetic properties, such as iambic rhythms and rhyme, or indeed words which lend themselves to rhyme and thus adaptation.[34] Crystal simultaneously points out that there is little evidence for lexical innovation and grammatical innovation and so, in this sense, the KJV is little more than a book of witty or useful idioms.

---

[30] K. Edwards, *Ad Men and Eve: The Bible and Advertising* (Sheffield: Sheffield Phoenix Press, 2012); K. Edwards, *The Messiah Wears Prada: Functions of Christ-imagery in Contemporary Popular Culture* (Sheffield: Sheffield Phoenix Press, Forthcoming).

[31] There are clear similarities with memetic readings of biblical survival and Hugh Pyper's suggestion that the multiple manifestations of biblical books, versions, and translations etc. have generated the Bible's own survival. See H. S. Pyper, *An Unsuitable Book: The Bible as Scandalous Text* (Sheffield: Sheffield Phoenix Press, 2006).

[32] See now H. S. Pyper, *The Unchained Bible: Cultural Appropriations of Biblical Texts* (T&T Clark, 2012), e.g. pp. 157–64.

[33] D. Crystal, *Begat: The King James Bible and the English Language* (Oxford: Oxford University Press, 2010), p. 2.

[34] Crystal, *Begat*, e.g. pp. 75, 85, 261.

One result from the analysis of this collection of idioms is that 'the items discussed in this [Crystal's] book are not quotations: they are everyday expressions used by speakers and writers of modern English, most of whom will have no religious motivation for their use'.[35] One phenomenon which has particularly lent itself to the ongoing survival of biblical texts and cultural allusions, with little concern for any 'religious' motivation and owing something to the tradition of the Cultural Bible and the Liberal Bible, has been pop music.[36] Indeed, the significance of avoiding 'religious' connotations in pop music has not been lost on even Christian musicians who are attempting to perpetuate biblical language. Deane Galbraith, for instance, shows how U2 – effectively an evangelical Christian band with Christian lyrics and plenty of biblical references – were able to hide their Christianizing biblical allusions in subcultural contexts in America, the UK and Ireland which were heavily antipathetic towards Christianity. They could do this with ambiguous lyrics and positioning themselves in line with political issues important within 80s and 90s subcultures (e.g. anti-racism, equality).[37] Here only the initiated 'get' the references and its popular portrayal survives seemingly deprived of its evangelical or Christian meaning.

Another important recent example of the survival of biblical language in pop music is John Lyons' work on the reception of Johnny Cash's reception of Revelation, in particular, and biblical language, more generally in his famous song 'When the Man Comes Around'. While of course Cash's Christian interpretation continues in overtly Christian contexts, its reception also continues in a range of subcultures. As Lyons shows, 'When the Man Comes Around' turns up in a variety of broadly 'apocalyptic' contexts in YouTube clips about, for example, World War I, nuclear explosions, September 11, and the Kennedy assassination. It can turn up in support of a seemingly contradictory range of politicians or political position, with Jesus often removed from the reception. The song is even integral to the Zombie film, *Dawn of the Dead*, now necessarily stripped of the necessary hope in the Cash song. The reception of the reception, aided and abetted by the ever growing social media, spreads out, replicates, mimics, changes, modifies, and seemingly with no end in sight.[38]

For whatever reasons, Johnny Cash has cultural capital perhaps not typical for Christians and he and his image have been taken up in a variety of 'secular' contexts which would ordinarily be distanced from Christianity. And yet, as Lyons shows,

---

[35] Crystal, *Begat*, p. 257.
[36] E.g. J. G. Crossley, 'For EveryManc a Religion: Uses of Biblical and Religious Language in the Manchester Music Scene, 1976–1994', *Bib. Int.* 19 (2011), pp. 151–80.
[37] D. Galbraith, 'Drawing Our Fish in the Sand: Secret Biblical Allusions in the Music of U2', *Bib. Int.* 19 (2011), pp. 181–222.
[38] W. J. Lyons, 'The Apocalypse according to Johnny Cash: Examining the "Effect" of the Book of Revelation on a Contemporary Apocalyptic Writer', in W. J. Lyons and J. Økland (eds.), *The Way the World Ends? The Apocalypse of John in Culture and Ideology* (Sheffield: Sheffield Phoenix Press, 2009), pp. 95–122.

Cash's Christianity, despite all Cash's personal intentions and prominence in certain Christian circles, is not typically brought to the fore in such contexts. We might add a striking example from Cash which highlights the importance of his particularly postmodern cultural 'cool' deprived of meaning and integral to the perpetuation and the survival of biblical texts: the use of Cash's 'Ain't No Grave' by the WWE for The Undertaker's entrance music at the wrestling extravaganza, *Wrestlemania* 27. 'Ain't No Grave' is a song which has the following straightforward endorsement of bodily resurrection at end times with clear biblical or quasi-biblical references, including trumpets, angels and meeting Jesus in the air, as well as explicit Christian interpretation:

There ain't no grave can hold my body down
When I hear that trumpet sound I'm gonna rise right out of the ground
...
I see a band of angels and they're coming after me
Ain't no grave can hold my body down
...
Well, look down yonder Gabriel, put your feet on the land and sea
But Gabriel don't you blow your trumpet 'til you hear it from me
...
Well, meet me Jesus, meet me. Meet me in the middle of the air
And if these wings don't fail me I will meet you anywhere
...
Well, meet me mother and father, meet me down the river road
And momma you know that I'll be there when I check in my load
Ain't no grave can hold my body down

By contrast, The Undertaker has, throughout his twenty-plus year career in WWE, largely worked with the gimmick of 'The Deadman', a black-clad demonic figure who has a submission move called 'Hell's Gate', finishing manoeuvre called 'The Tombstone', and is known for a Dracula-style 'resurrection', even after the heaviest of beatings.[39] While there are obvious points of contact concerning death and resurrection, the Christianizing sentiment has been removed from Cash's evangelical song or even turned on its head by the slow moving cadaver that is The Undertaker whose twenty-year unbeaten *Wrestlemania* streak was only ended in 2014 but during the streak was visibly aging as he was reduced to wrestling one match per year. Picking up on Cash's cultural capital and draining any significant evangelical meaning and marketing Cash's image and song as almost cool for cool's sake, The Undertaker can remain one of the most popular wrestlers of all-time precisely because of his dark, anti-clean cut image which has long stood in sharp

---

[39] H.S. Pyper, 'Wrestling the Bible', *SBL Forum* (July 2006), http://sbl-site.org/Article.aspx?ArticleID=569

distinction to superstar wrestlers such as a John Cena and a much younger Hulk Hogan. He is, I would suggest, the epitome of postmodern 'cool' and thus highlighting another important aspect of the transmission of the Bible and biblical texts, a phenomenon known, of course, from non-biblical postmodern receptions elsewhere in popular culture.[40]

The Bible therefore survives. Whether the audiences pick up on the biblical resonances is another question but emptying the evangelical meaning at least suggests that foregrounding biblical allusions remains a vague concern at best. Whether this sort of example allows the biblical texts to survive into the future remains to be seen. Like the KJV idioms, such snapshots could be replicated and be mimicked thereby finding more and more users, whether users or audiences know they are transmitting and perpetuating biblical texts or not.[41] Alternatively, such uses could be dead markets and this could be the beginning of the end for the importance of the Bible. But that will require a future retrospective (from biblical scholars, no doubt).

Conclusion

My focus has been on some (and only some) generalizing contexts at play within contemporary Western capitalism as a means to understanding how the Bible and biblical texts have spread, survived and continue to survive. In doing so, this simultaneously establishes some, and only some, of the major contemporary interpretative traditions guiding the work carried out by conventional biblical scholars and consumers of pop culture alike.[42] There are, of course, countless research topics to be carried out in order to support, critique, or replace this narrative. There have also been research topics which explain the reception and continuation of the Bible and biblical texts in a range of non-Western contexts. Collectively, these can be brought together, or at least brought into dialogue, to produce further an even more internationalist explanation for the origins, development and survival of the Bible and biblical texts. It seems to me, at least, that a field with a distinctive object of study like the Bible can be both as globally wide-ranging as Literary Studies or History yet retain a precise focus or narrative thread. This will mean that we should probably be working towards dropping the

---

[40] One example: Austin Fisher has shown how postmodern cinema (e.g. Tarantino, Rodriguez) picks up on 'cool' pop cultural stylistics of the Italian westerns while the heavy emphasis on violence has removed the political nature of violence in the Italian westerns and brought it into the world of playful referencing drained of its ideological significance. See A. Fisher, *Radical Frontiers in the Spaghetti Western: Politics, Violence and Popular Italian Cinema* (London and New York: I.B. Tauris, 2011), pp. 193–201.

[41] Again, memetics might be another appropriate analogy here.

[42] Crossley, *Jesus in an Age of Neoliberalism*.

labels 'historical criticism' and 'reception history' and simply calling the field something as general and revolutionary as (for instance) Biblical Studies. Otherwise (and I appreciate some people do not mind this) Biblical Studies will continue to remain a sometimes troubled subset of Religious Studies and Theology when it could be so much more.

5

Visitors, Gatekeepers and Receptionists: Reflections on the Shape of Biblical Studies and the Role of Reception History

Jonathan Morgan
University of Chester

Introduction

Do not be historians who ignore the passing, or underestimate the power, of time. The true goal of the historian is to strive to speak the wisdoms of the world's pasts to its future. Those who select an era and, veiling one of Janus's faces, attempt to seal it off and explore it only according its own contexts (as if such a thing were possible), are not historians, but rather a curious sort of antiquarians. Such an approach fits a person only to spend an absent life 'in the field', to curate an unpopular museum, or to teach at a rarefied British University – although thinking about it, such activities perhaps constitute one vocation rather than three.

Those are the words of Mr Giddens, my A-level history lecturer, offered as part of a farewell lecture he delivered in the final class, and I remember them lying so heavily on my ears that I swiftly noted them down (sometime in May 2000). Although a man of fine learning and an excellent tutor, Mr Giddens was not an academic in the strictest sense, and certainly not a biblical scholar, and I can almost hear a sceptical reader smirking at what they might see as an appeal to his authority. I include these words, however, not primarily as a witness to superior expertise, but as an example of something that I once found, and continue to find, resonant with my experience and inspirational.

Given this slice of autobiographical contextualization, it will probably generate scant surprise if I note that I have never found biblical studies' traditional historical-critical method particularly attractive, nor the widespread, conservative appeals to and arguments from its all-sufficiency even remotely satisfying. Furthermore, I, like many others, feel that the hour is coming, and is now here, when frank discussion concerning its conceptual and practical weaknesses must bring an end to its persistent yet increasingly hollow and damaging hegemony.

This chapter emerged from a discussion of John Lyons' recent proposition regarding the potential role of reception history within a reordered discipline.[1] I have a considerable amount of sympathy for the argument laid out in that article, and engage it here very much on collegial rather than adversarial grounds. By means of contextualizing its argument within the larger discussion of which it was a part, and then bringing it to bear on another recent conversation concerning the 'proper' boundaries of biblical studies, I aim both to highlight some potential weaknesses of Lyons' proposition and to carve out space nearby for some alternate ideas concerning the most fruitful role for reception history in the biblical studies of the future.

Biblical reception history is very much an evolving and multidimensional field (to which this volume attests), and, as such, it is perhaps worth including a note concerning my conception of the key notions and principles involved. As I understand it, reception history combines various insights and methods drawn from philosophical hermeneutics,[2] reception theory[3] (which is closely associated with both reader-response criticism[4] and audience theory[5]) and certain literary-influenced trends in historiography and the philosophy of history.[6] As such, reception history focusses on the history of meanings that have been associated with a particular event, or, in this case, text. We might, therefore, think of the reception historian as attending to multiple sites of meaning: the text (including the recognition that it is itself the product of a history of interpretation); the

---

[1] Lyons, W. John, 'Hope for a Troubled Discipline? Contributions to New Testament Studies from Reception History', *JSNT* 33 (2), 2010, 207–20.

[2] Heidegger, Martin, *Being and Time* (trans. Macquarrie and Robinson), Oxford: Blackwell, (1962); Gadamer, Hans-Georg, *Truth and Method*, (trans. Weinsheimer and Marshall), 2nd edition, London: Sheed and Ward, (1989); Ricoeur, Paul, *The Conflicts of Interpretation: Essays in Hermeneutics*, (trans. Domingo *et al*), Evanston, IL: Northwestern University Press, (1974); Hoy, David, *The Critical Circle: Literature, History, and Philosophical Hermeneutics*, Berkeley, CA: University of California Press, (1978); Thiselton, Anthony C., *Hermeneutics: An Introduction*, Grand Rapids, MI: Eerdmans, (2009).

[3] See Iser, Wolfgang, *The Act of Reading: A Theory of Aesthetic Response*, Baltimore, MD: Johns Hopkins University Press, (1978); Jauss, Hans Robert, *Towards An Aesthetic of Reception*, (trans. Bahti), Minneapolis: University of Minnesota Press, (1982); Holub, Robert C., *Reception Theory: A Critical Introduction*, London & New York, NY: Methuen, (1984).

[4] See Tompkins, Jane P., (ed.) *Reader-Response Criticism: From Formalism to Post-Structuralism*, Baltimore, MD: Johns Hopkins University Press, (1980); Suleiman, Susan R. and Inge Crosman (eds), *The Reader in the Text: Essay on Audience and Interpretation*, Princeton, NJ: Princeton University Press, (1980); Freund, Elizabeth, *The Return of the Reader: Reader-Response Criticism*, London & New York, NY: Methuen, (1987).

[5] See Hall, Stuart, 'Encoding/decoding', in Hall, Stuart, *et al* (eds), *Culture, Media, Language: Working Papers in Cultural Studies, 1972–79*, London: Hutchinson, (1980) 128–38; Allen, Robert C., 'From Exhibition to Reception: Reflections on the Audience in Film History', *Screen*, Vol. 31, No. 4, (1990), 347–56; Staiger, Janet, *Interpreting Films: Studies in the Historical Reception of American Cinema*, Princeton, NJ: Princeton University Press, (1992).

[6] See Carr, Edward H., *What Is History?* Cambridge: CUP, (1961); White, Hayden, *Metahistory: The Historical Imagination in Nineteenth-Century Europe*, Baltimore, MD: Johns Hopkins University, (1973); White, Hayden, 'Interpretation in History', *New Literary History*, Vol. 4, No. 2, (1973); Thompson, Martyn P., 'Reception Theory and the Interpretation of Historical Meaning', *History and Theory*, Vol. 32, No. 3, (1993) 248–72.

history of the interpretation of the text; and the ongoing interpretation of the text and its history as witnessed by their work. Reception historical work may focus on interpretations from a particular period (e.g. medieval commentaries on the book of Job) or attempt to assess trends from across the entire sweep of the history of a text's interpretation. However, in both cases, the location of the reception historian in relation to the text and their own context, and their choices with regard to which sites have been privileged and which interpretations emphasized, are seen as operative in the ongoing process of reception.

For the reasons set out above, it is important both to distinguish between the *subjects* of reception historical inquiry and its *products*, and also to perceive the interconnectedness of these two aspects. As Jonathan Roberts has emphasized,

> [t]he reception of the Bible comprises every single act or word of interpretation of that book (or books) over the course of three millennia ... Reception *history*, however, is a different matter. That is usually – although not always – a scholarly enterprise, consisting of selecting and collating shards of that infinite wealth of reception material in accordance with the particular interests of the historian concerned, and giving them a narrative frame. In other words, to get from the plenitude of *reception* to the finitude of *reception history* requires that historians of reception – like any others – envisage parameters: in particular, when reflecting on the history or responses to the Bible, *whose* responses do they deem to be of importance? That is the first, practical, question, and the second, which cannot be disentangled from it, is its theoretical counterpart: how is the choice of material to be justified, and to what end is it being marshalled? These questions are, as it were, the exegetical and hermeneutical faces of reception history, and it is the special character of reception history that they are thought of as interdependent facets of the same whole.[7] (Emphasis in original.)

No other medicine[8]

In an instructive and inspired *JSNT* article from 2010 entitled *Hope For A Troubled Discipline?*, John Lyons argues for what seems to be somewhere between a *coup d'état* and a public relations exercise in which historical criticism is *clothed* or *re-labelled* (to use two of his own metaphors) *in* or *with* the terminology and methodological framework of reception history. This vision of the transformation of terminology is set within the context of a claim that certain historical-critical

---

[7] Roberts, Jonathan, 'Introduction', in Lieb, Michael, *et al* (eds), *The Oxford Handbook of the Reception History of the Bible*, Oxford: OUP, (2011) 1.
[8] This is an allusion to Act III, Scene I of *Measure for Measure* – 'The miserable have no other medicine./ But only hope.' (III, i, 1224–5), Gibbons, Brian (ed.), *Measure for Measure*, Cambridge: CUP, (1991) 128.

methodologies are 'forms of reception history'[9], whether or not historical critics recognize that fact.

While I am in sympathy with Lyons' general aim ('[the] broadening of the discipline'[10]), and am in considerable agreement with his assessment of the critical issues currently confronting biblical studies, elements of his proposal strike me as problematic and potentially counterproductive. This chapter explores my concerns regarding Lyons' argument, sets out another perspective on the current 'lie of the land' within biblical studies, and offers an alternative proposal concerning the most constructive role that reception history might play in shaping its future.

The argument presented by Lyons is set against a backdrop of the juxtaposition of historical criticism with various other interpretive approaches grouped together under the heading 'postmodern'. He inherits this context from a previous discussion, one initiated by a 2009 *JBL* article by George Aichele, Peter Miscall and Richard Walsh,[11] in which the two aforementioned groups within biblical studies are portrayed as both utterly entrenched and seemingly all-inclusive, and an appeal is made for inter-methodological dialogue.

In a thoroughly predictable (and thus surely avoidable) way, Aichele *et al*'s (problematic) account of a sharply divided discipline, their rather narrow portrait of historical criticism, and their attempt to re-contextualize it (along with postmodern approaches) as a specific kind of 'mythmaking', gave rise to a contemptuous 'rejoinder' from the historical critic John Van Seters.[12] In his reply, published a few months later in *JHS*, Van Seters takes understandable exception to Aichele *et al*'s 'outlandish caricature'[13] of the historical critic as the modern, objective (and yet somehow also Romantic) idealist on a(n) (implicitly) theologically motivated quest for the holy grail of tangible truth. Likewise, he objects to the vague and non-methodological nature of Aichele *et al*'s definition of postmodern approaches, and to their rather poorly-conceived analogy concerning parallel constructed mythologies. Van Seters' response to these perceived weaknesses functions not only as an answer to, but also a dismissal of, Aichele *et al*'s curiously couched call for dialogue.

Regardless of any sympathy one might have with the general shape of Van Seters' complaint, unfortunately, the limited scope of his knowledge of, and prior engagement with, the conceptions and concerns of postmodernism, seems fairly clear. On the basis of an achingly unsophisticated and outmoded appeal to the *simple* or *usual* definition of 'myth', Van Seters (seemingly wilfully) refuses to

---

[9] Lyons, 'Hope for . . .', 213.
[10] Lyons, 'Hope for . . .', 207.
[11] Aichele, George, Peter Miscall and Richard Walsh, 'An Elephant in the Room: Historical-Critical and Postmodern Interpretations of the Bible', *JBL* 128, (2009) 383–404.
[12] Van Seters, John, 'A Response To G. Aichele, P. Miscall and R. Walsh, 'An Elephant in the Room: Historical-Critical and the Postmodern Interpretations of the Bible', *JHS* 9: 26, (2009), http://www.jhsonline.org/Articles/article_128.pdf [all websites cited were last accessed 7 January 2013].
[13] Van Seters, 'A Response . . .', 4.

recognize that Aichele *et al*'s application of the term to the traits of historical criticism is not intended as pejorative, but in their eyes constitutes a positive. Moreover, in his naïve and rather scientistic insistence that the elements they call 'mythical' effectively derive from an importation of ideology equivalent to 'researcher error' (of a sort that a perfectly purified historical-critical method would transcend)[14] there seems to be evidence that the interlocutors are – to borrow from Shaw's famous quip – divided by a common discipline. Or, perhaps they do not even share that point of commonality, a notion that is expanded below.

Whilst rejecting the call for substantial inter-methodological discussion, Van Seters builds his juxtaposition of historical-critical and postmodern approaches (at least in part) on the claim that the former is a methodology whereas the latter is not. Picking up on a phrase employed by Aichele *et al*, he states that:

> historical-critical and postmodernist approaches are not symmetrical partners for a conversation. The former are tantamount to a methodology, the latter 'is characterized by diversity in both method and content' (p. 384) and therefore, it is not a method at all. Instead it represents a wide array of attitudes or stances that a scholar/reader may choose to take towards a text in the process of interpreting it.

It is worth noting in passing that, in this, Van Seters is at odds with James Barr, who insisted that historical criticism was also rightly conceptualized not as a single method, but a loosely bound range of methods that could properly be at odds with each other.[15]

In discussing the brief and rather unfruitful exchange constituted by the two articles, Lyons notes that Van Seters perhaps best demonstrates his particularly high conception of what was once called 'higher criticism' when he asserts that:

> [t]he vast changes that have come about in historical studies in general and biblical historical criticism in particular, as they have in modern science, owe nothing to postmodernism and everything to its own hermeneutic of suspicion. It is for this reason that most historical critics do not feel obliged to spend time plowing through vast quantities of the postmodern literature and adopting a new 'scholarly' jargon in order to attempt a dialogue.[16]

This statement contains several interesting and revealing elements. One such element is the clear link in Van Seters' thinking between historical criticism and scientific enquiry. This connection is made even more explicit elsewhere in the paper, where he states that 'liberal theology has tried to accommodate itself to the

---

[14] Van Seters, 'A Response . . .', 3–4.
[15] See Barr, James, *History and Ideology in the Old Testament*, Oxford: OUP, (2000) 32–58, and Collins, John J., *The Bible After Babel: Historical Criticism in a Postmodern Age*, Grand Rapids: MI, Wm. B. Eerdmans, (2005) 4.
[16] Van Seters, 'A Response . . .', 7, quoted in part in Lyons, 'Hope for A Troubled Discipline?', 210.

reality of modern science and the results of historical criticism,'[17] and plainer still thereafter, where he asserts that:

> [t]here is no post-scientific/*wissenschaftlich* or post-historic era, and we engage in such fantasies at our peril. Contrary to the (implied) assertion that contemporary historians claim to be 'in possession of the Truth,' (p. 401) and that it is only postmodernists that give up this claim, nothing could be a greater distortion of what *science and historical criticism* is all about.[18] (Emphasis my own.)

As the flipside to these explicit links between historical criticism and science, we might also detect an implicit link in Van Seters' thinking between postmodern interpretation and literature. While the proximity of 'postmodern' and 'literature' in Van Seters' description of what the historical critic does not feel obliged to plough through might well be non-rhetorical (or at least not consciously rhetorical), his subsequent assertion that he would struggle to distinguish between a work of postmodern biblical criticism and a novel is extremely revealing.[19] Indeed, it is the adumbration of the 'proper' distinction between a work of literature and a piece of biblical criticism that exercises him for much of the latter half of the article. Moreover, his rather juvenile employment of inverted commas surrounding 'scholarly' when used in connection with postmodern approaches drives the message home. It is pretty clear that for Van Seters historical criticism squarely occupies, and more or less fills, the legitimate, 'scholarly' ground in biblical studies, and, as such, its proponents simply need not waste time engaging postmodern approaches, especially given that such exploits have, by his measure, failed to yield anything that historical criticism had not previously and more effectively discovered for itself.

For Lyons, Van Seters' rejoinder both legitimates Aichele *et al*'s description of the entrenched opposition between historical criticism and postmodern approaches, and effectively demonstrates the need for a different way into dialogue. Perhaps, Lyons muses, where Aichele *et al*'s account of parallel mythmaking had apparently failed to provide fruitful grounds, reception history might be able to succeed.

Seemingly setting his stall outside the overly-neat, constructed divide between modernist/historical-critical approaches and postmodernist ones, Lyons suggests that reception history can 'offer something that the postmodernists do not, namely, a way of phrasing their concerns that may provide a productive way into dialogue.'[20] Lyons appears to deconstruct Aichele *et al*'s 'us and them' dichotomy by witnessing to a third position, instantiated by reception history. On closer inspection, however, it is not absolutely clear that this is what his argument achieves. Whilst in one breath Lyons appears to extol the bringing of reception history into the discussion

---

[17] Van Seters, 'A Response...', 6.
[18] Van Seters, 'A Response...', 8–9.
[19] Van Seters, 'A Response...', 9–13.
[20] Lyons, 'Hope for...', 210.

on the basis that its language and methodology might provide more suitable grounds for dialogue, in almost the very next, he suggests that:

> re-labeling historical-critical methodologies with the terminology of reception history should lead to a modification in the historical-critic's self-understanding, offering us a more fruitful way forward than anything offered by the postmodernists.[21]

It seems to me that a historical critic might well want to ask questions about what sort of a dialogue begins by one party being forced to undergo a 'modification'. Or, to put it another way, who are the partners in the dialogue that Lyons envisages taking place once the historical-critical methodologies have undergone this process of 're-labeling'? It turns out, however, that this process is being envisaged by Lyons as a fairly non-invasive procedure on the basis that, as far as he is concerned, historical criticism is already a form of reception history, albeit a narrowly focussed one. It is facing up to the fact that his method is simply one aspect of a wider approach that brings about the required modification to the historical critic's perspective:

> The suggestion that historical-critical methodologies are forms of reception history means that the historical critics will have to partake of that approach's assumptions. The resulting adjustment in self-understanding might give us something to talk about.

Despite setting out to offer alternative grounds that reshape arguments on both sides of the debate, it is fair to say that Lyons' 'suggestion' requires a lot more of the historical critic than the postmodern interpreter. While that imbalance might be justifiable given the disparity between the two sides in terms of both influence within the discipline and apparent openness to discussion, it does have implications in terms of how such a shift might come about. The key weakness, it seems to me, lies in the fact that those who use and defend the language and concept of historical criticism most ardently (and thereby contribute most to its self-understanding) are likely to resist this shift most tenaciously. It might be more realistic, therefore, to say that the outcome Lyons describes would most likely result *only* if it could be convincingly demonstrated that historical criticism *must* be understood as a (narrow) form of reception history. In other words, Lyons' proposal seems to necessitate compulsion, be that by means of logic or perhaps *realpolitik* – the former of which seems unlikely, and the latter undesirable.

In further support of his case, Lyons makes an appeal to Barton and Muddiman's notion of 'chastened historical criticism',[22] seemingly suggesting that if it is open to

---

[21] Lyons, 'Hope for ...', 210.
[22] See Barton, John and John Muddiman (eds), *The Oxford Bible Commentary*, Oxford: OUP, (2001) 1–4; Barton, John, *The Nature of Biblical Criticism*, Louisville, KY: Westminster John Knox, (2007) 1–8, 31–68.

being chastened, it might as well go the whole hog. Highlighting some of the more interesting directions in which he thinks recent work has pointed, and hinting at the limited value of narrow historical-critical approaches in an academic environment in which emphasis is being increasingly shifted onto 'real world' application, Lyons then fleshes out his suggestion that allowing (or rather *insisting*) that historical criticism be subsumed by reception history provides not only better grounds for external dialogue, but also the space required by the methodology's own internal developments. To further support his case, Lyons refers to a 'growing emphasis on audiences within biblical studies',[23] citing a trend in New Testament studies towards reconstructing imagined receiving and producing communities with regard to the Gospels, the Pauline epistles, and indeed Q. While it is not especially clear how Van Seters, as a Hebrew Bible scholar, might have been directly affected by these shifts in New Testament studies, further, briefer observations about the emerging role of audiences in source and form criticism perhaps have more traction. It is, however, with redaction criticism that Lyons sees the closest existing 'fit'.[24]

For those most familiar with his work, however, the irony of the fact that Van Seters has over the last few years been at the forefront of a move within biblical scholarship to question the very legitimacy of rhetorical criticism will be obvious. In fact, in his 2006 volume *The Edited Bible*, Van Seters goes as far as to assert that the biblical editor/redactor is an ossified anachronistic invention of seventeenth-century criticism, and – as if to heap irony upon irony – in place of the notion of the editor/redactor and the processes of redaction, he champions a return to the concept of biblical authors as 'historians' (in the von Radian sense of the term).[25]

If, therefore, hardline historical critics like Van Seters hardly appear to be prime candidates for self-motivated conversion to reception history, perhaps this process can happen from outside the methodology, with historical critics finally coming to recognize themselves as reception historians as a result of how they are treated by others? Certainly Lyons seems to have a somewhat 'removed' context in mind when he states that '[c]lothing historical-critical methodologies with reception history's terminology makes a difference to how practitioners view them'[26] – the clear implication being that the 'practitioners' and those doing the 'clothing' are not the same people. While this seems to me to be a potentially promising avenue, the question perhaps remains as to why a conservative historical critic, like Van Seters – who seems very contented with the self-contained nature and profound influence of historical criticism, and with his belief in its ability to perfect itself over time – should be at all affected by a shift in the language used by an *outside minority* to

---

[23] Lyons, 'Hope for ...', 213.
[24] Lyons, 'Hope for ...', 213.
[25] Van Seters, John, *The Edited Bible: The Curious History of the "Editor" in Biblical Criticism?*, Winona Lake, IN: Eisenbrauns (2006).
[26] Lyons, 'Hope for ...', 214.

describe his approach. To address that concern, I turn now to a survey of the current state of the discipline.

For the gate is narrow[27]

Given that it is largely (or, depending on who you ask, *solely*) constituted by the organization and analysis of philological, archaeological and source-critical data, there is a significant tendency in certain quarters to see historical criticism as *the* historical approach within biblical studies: that is, *the* approach that makes proper use of the scholarly apparatus of the discipline of history. One of the issues, therefore, with rallying and unifying all other approaches against the hegemonic forces of historical criticism is the possibility that, for its defenders, the resultant historical-critical/non-historical-critical dichotomy maps neatly onto an historical/ahistorical (or even historical/anti-historical) divide. We see this kind of logic at work in Van Seters' emphasis on how postmodernism, as he understands it, derives from little more than an 'othering' of modernity (a term which, given the established terms of his discourse, he feels able to elide with historical criticism).[28]

The problematic nature of this blurring of the distinction between historical criticism and historical biblical scholarship *per se* was apparent in the voluminous and multi-faceted online discussion that took place in the autumn of 2011 surrounding what became known in certain circles as 'Hurtadogate'. While it is in no way my intention to rehearse a blow-by-blow account of the several impassioned responses and the multitude of positions expressed by commentators, for the benefit of those not familiar with the posts in question, or the 'biblioblogosphere' in general, I will sketch a rough outline of the episode, which centred on five blog posts written by the historical critic and New Testament scholar Larry Hurtado.[29]

In response to some apparently 'worrying' talk at the 2011 British New Testament Conference regarding the familiarity with and aptitude for Koiné Greek of some British New Testament (NT) PhD candidates, Hurtado proposed a series of blog posts attending to the key 'tools of the trade' of New Testament scholarship. In the first and, as it turned out, only of these posts, Hurtado addressed the essential role of languages, insisting that all NT PhD candidates should be able (and required) to demonstrate (in their vivas) competence in Koiné Greek and Hebrew,

---

[27] cf. Matt. 7.14.
[28] See Van Seters, 'A Response...', 6–7.
[29] Hurtado, L. W., 'Tools of the Trade', http://larryhurtado.wordpress.com/2011/09/04/tools-of-the-trade/; Hurtado, L. W., 'Tools of the Trade...Encore', http://larryhurtado.wordpress.com/2011/09/05/tools-of-the-trade-encore/; Hurtado, L. W., 'Languages, Theories, Approaches', http://larryhurtado.wordpress.com/2011/09/08/languages-theories-approaches/; Hurtado, L. W., 'The UK PhD: Structure and Pressures', http://larryhurtado.wordpress.com/2011/09/10/the-uk-phd-structure-and-pressures/; Hurtado, L. W., 'NT Research Languages: Encore', http://larryhurtado.wordpress.com/2011/09/27/nt-research-languages-encore/.

the basic primary languages of the Bible, as well as English, French and German, the primary languages of biblical scholarship. Although desirable, Latin, Hurtado concluded, was not essential.[30]

It is important to note that whilst Aichele *et al*'s call for dialogue came out of the context of the main meetings of the Society for Biblical Literature – which, despite being always held in the USA, functions as an international forum – the analysis and recommendations in Hurtado's posts explicitly addressed the British context and the question of how PhDs should be examined in British universities. Soon, however, the online discussion took on a more general tone, expanding the purview to address issues relating to the nature of the discipline at large.

In these ensuing comments and counter-posts,[31] lines were drawn between those who largely supported Hurtado's proposals and those who wished to resist and/or test them. In the 'pro-Hurtado' camp, more primary languages were added to further lists on other blogs, and their necessity was expressed in increasingly insistent terms, until the point came at which I discovered that as a Hebrew Bible scholar I apparently needed to know a language which not only could I not read, but of which I had not even heard (although, as it turned out, it was simply the particular name with which I was unfamiliar, rather than the language).[32] For those suspicious of Hurtado's approach, questions clustered around how much leeway there was in terms of projects that utilized methodologies for which original languages were not necessarily relevant, such as those doing reception history focussed on later periods and/or other cultures, and on whether the suggestions regarding the required 'secondary' languages did not simply reflect and reinforce a Western-European bias.

---

[30] Hurtado, 'Tools of the Trade'.

[31] For a flavour of the wider discussion/debate generated by Hurtado's posts see: Crossley, James, 'An Immodest Proposal for Biblical Studies', *Relegere: Studies in Religion and Reception*, Vol. 2, no. 1 (2012) 153–177; Crossley, James, 'Languages, Humanities and a New Testament PhD', http://sheffieldbiblicalstudies.wordpress.com/2011/09/07/languages-humanities-ntphd/; BW16, 'The Victorian Straight-Jacket of 'Subjective' Empiricism in British New Testament Studies', http://bwsixteen.wordpress.com/2011/09/04/the-victorian-straight-jacket-of-subjective-empiricism-in-british-new-testament-studies/; BW16, 'An Objective Queer Marxist Rejoinder to Larry Hurtado's Hegemonic Essentialisms', http://bwsixteen.wordpress.com/2011/09/05/an-objective-queer-marxist-rejoinder-to-larry-hurtados-hegemonic-essentialisms/; Witherington, Ben, 'The Pretenders and the Contenders – NT Studies Doctoral Students', http://www.patheos.com/blogs/bibleandculture/2011/09/04/the-pretenders-and-the-contenders-nt-studies-doctoral-students/; McGrath, James, 'Essential Languages for New Testament Study?', http://www.patheos.com/blogs/exploringourmatrix/2011/09/essential-languages-and-tools-for-new-testament-study.html; West, Jim, 'What Languages Must One Know in order to be Competent in the Field of Biblical Studies?', http://zwingliusredivivus.wordpress.com/2011/09/06/what-languages-must-one-know-in-order-to-be-competent-in-the-field-of-biblical-studies/; Boer, Roland, 'The Closing of Larry Hurtado's Mind', http://stalinsmoustache.wordpress.com/2011/09/09/the-closing-of-larry-hurtados-mind/; Brady, Christian, 'How many languages does it take to get to the center?', http://targuman.org/blog/2011/09/06/how-many-languages-does-it-take-to-get-to-the-center/; Smith, Duane, 'This Isn't Kindergarten', http://www.telecomtally.com/this-isnt-kindergarten/; Smith, Duane, 'The Backyard Of Biblical Studies', http://www.telecomtally.com/the-backyard-of-biblical-studies/.

[32] I had not previously encountered the term 'Eblaitic', but am assured it is the same as Eblaite. See West, 'What Languages Must One Know ...'.

The responses to these two clusters of questions were especially intriguing because of the way they stimulated reflection on and pronouncement concerning the nature of the discipline of biblical studies *in toto* and in particular how it relates to its own history. At times, for example, questions regarding the exclusivity of requisite secondary languages elicited appeals to a kind of canon of legitimate secondary literature, while discussions concerning primary languages revealed concerns that the abandonment of original languages (a proposition that, it is important to state, was never advanced by any of Hurtado *et al*'s detractors) was already constituting the forsaking of the historical project. Not only was a fairly narrow conception of historical criticism defended as *the* historical paradigm in biblical studies, but, in at least one place, the boundaries of historical criticism and those of biblical studies all told were elided when Hurtado, seemingly convinced he was offering both a corrective and a concession, responded to a post by fellow NT scholar James Crossley with the following assertions:

> I would also suggest that there is a difference between gearing up to take part in a discipline and simply pursuing a given research project. So, e.g., one could trace the influence and reception of the Beowulf story in, e.g., modern English-language film and fiction, without acquiring the original language of the poem. But, to my mind, that wouldn't make one a scholar in the field of Beowulf and Norse poetry. Still a scholar, mind you, but not in that field ... James mentions particularly post-colonial approaches in biblical studies, and I note that this is heavily done in English.[33]

The analogy veils the intended implications with the utmost thinness: without an emphasis on original languages and original meaning, for Hurtado the work in question simply could not legitimately consider itself to be biblical studies.

One of the things this discussion has revealed most clearly is the gap between Hurtado's expectations, and those of several who joined the debate in his defence, and the reality of what is actually happening within the discipline. It is fairly clear from his response to the discussion created by his first post that Hurtado was not expecting much, if any, disagreement from other colleagues within the 'guild' – a contention supported by the, now infamous, phrase with which he concluded his first post: 'There are other things that ought to characterize the PhD in the field, but these are essential tools. *I presume that all fellow scholars will agree*'.[34] (Emphasis mine.)

Of course, they did not. In fact, even if we confine our attention just to the British context, it is not at all clear that Hurtado's perspective accurately represents the current state of the discipline. It is true to say that there are several departments where traditional historical-critical approaches are emphasized in

---

[33] Hurtado, 'Languages, Theories, Approaches'.
[34] Hurtado, 'Tools of the Trade'.

both undergraduate and taught-postgraduate programmes; but it is also the case that many offer significant space to non-traditional approaches to biblical texts: literary, reception-historical, feminist, political, ecological, socio-cultural and so on. It is now rare to find a list of plenary papers (let alone short papers) from even the most conservative biblical studies conferences hosted in the UK that does not reflect at least one of these approaches. What is more, it is perhaps worth nothing that of the handful of UK universities that currently offer explicitly biblically focussed undergraduate programmes (as opposed to general courses in theology/divinity or religion/religious studies), at least two make prominent statements in their promotional material about the fact that biblical languages are not compulsory.[35]

Gathering stones[36]

How best, then, to make sense of these two discussions about the nature and scope of the discipline? And what of the most fruitful role for reception history? At the heart of my approach is the notion that these discussions are best contextualized by reference to time as its key conceptual operator. As I see it, conservative historical critics and postmodern interpreters stand at opposite ends of a spectrum with regard to the concept of time, and therefore of what constitutes history.

For the average historical critic, history is, in line with modernist thought, a repository of events, ideas, memories and texts that is accessible to the present by means of an appropriately trained and resourced researcher. The resources are over there, we are over here, so the task is to go over there, see what's what, find out more about why what's what and then come home (or perhaps not). For the postmodernist, however, no such possibility exists. 'History' in postmodern terms is essentially an event within the individual; an encounter between the researcher and 'texts' of various sorts from the past. Because of postmodern conceptions

---

[35] The information page for the Religion, Theology and the Bible programme at the University of Sheffield provides the following information for prospective undergraduates: 'Studying biblical languages isn't compulsory, but if you choose to you can learn Hebrew and Greek with us. We're one of very few departments [sic] offering this opportunity to read the Bible in its original form.' The point that languages are potentially beneficial but entirely optional is reinforced by means of the prominent use on the page of the following quotation from Hannah Welsh: 'You don't have to do biblical languages if you are not interested, but reading biblical texts in their original languages allows you to make your own decisions about how to translate words and not just accept what translators have said.' http://www.sheffield.ac.uk/theology/undergraduate/courses. Likewise, Liverpool Hope University offers prospective undergraduates in Biblical Studies this advice: 'As part of a joint degree, Biblical Studies does not require the study of the biblical languages (if you are interested in undertaking such studies, then our single honours degree in Theology is the course to explore).' http://www.hope.ac.uk/undergraduate/undergraduatecourses/biblicalstudies. [All information correct as of January 2015].

[36] cf. Ecclesiastes 3.5.

of and awareness concerning the impact and reach of linguistics, semantics, psychology, ideology, ontology and a host of other -ologies and -isms, there is no such grand project as History (with a capital aitch) because there is scant firm ground on which reliably to establish the present, let alone the past.

For someone like Van Seters, as he has made clear in his discussion of biblical 'editors', the most serious heresy is that of anachronism – a concept being made to operate outside its 'rightful' place in time.[37] For the postmodern interpreter, however, given that the linear notion of time that lies beneath the modern conception of 'History' effectively functions as a constructed grand narrative about which it is perfectly right to be incredulous, no such taboo exists. The postmodern critic has the freedom to be much more creative: to 'play' with time and to juxtapose texts and interpretations from various periods, reordering or utterly reversing the hermeneutical flow.[38]

Describing the two approaches in these terms might make it possible to imagine a mediatory role for the reception historian. Her approach, after all, is thoroughly 'historical' and, in part, concerned with a standard historical-critical notion of contextualization. However, she also means to apply that concern across a wider period of time, positing many diverse moments of encounter between a text and a context. Returning for a moment to my final A-level history class, we might see a scintilla of truth in Mr Giddens' highly rhetorical distinction between an 'historian' and an 'antiquarian', and perceive that, in her insistence on a thoroughly diachronic approach, the reception historian is perhaps *more* historical (or, at least, interested in more history) than the conservative historical critic and his confined gaze and synchronic tendencies (although this is an argument for another time). Certainly, however, what her work will not allow is for her historical-critical colleagues to claim history as their own – especially given the fact that it would more than likely prove easier for her to consult and work in conjunction with those from her institution's Department of History than it would for them.

Staying with this thought, we might likewise ponder for a moment Mr Giddens' suggestion that certain ways of understanding history fit a person only for certain, very particular vocations – and, furthermore, the extent to which we see space for 'biblical scholar' in his list of jobs for antiquarians.

In one sense, of course, this is a trivial exercise. However, the general warning that one can limit one's ability to work in certain areas and with certain people on

---

[37] The irony being, of course, that many have begun to see a narrow focus on tradition historical criticism as itself thoroughly anachronistic.

[38] This phrase is borrowed from the subtitle (and methodologies) of Larry Kreitzer's series of four books examining Old Testament and New Testament texts alongside elements of their reception in fiction and film – Kreitzer, Larry J., *The Old Testament in Fiction and Film: On Reversing the Hermeneutical Flow*, Sheffield: Sheffield Academic Press, (1993); Kreitzer, Larry J., *The New Testament in Fiction and Film: On Reversing the Hermeneutical Flow*, Sheffield: Sheffield Academic Press, (1993); Kreitzer, Larry J., *Pauline Images in Fiction and Film: On Reversing the Hermeneutical Flow*, Sheffield: Sheffield Academic Press (1999); Kreitzer, Larry J., *Gospel Images in Fiction and Film: On Reversing the Hermeneutical Flow*, New York, NY: Continuum, (2002).

the basis of the approach that one adopts certainly seems apposite in the context of the modern University. In a context where 'impact' beyond the scholarly realm, interdisciplinarity, and integration across departments grouped together in a school have been established (rightly or wrongly) as key normative values, it is tricky to see, for example, with whom someone who has an interest only in the narrowest historical-critical study of the Bible might look to collaborate. While such people are unlikely to find themselves in a school of sciences and recourse to the language of *wissenschaftlich* might therefore be of limited assistance, it is probably also true to say that they might struggle to find members of a history faculty still working with an unadulteratedly modernist method.

Moreover, when it comes to colleagues in English, Philosophy, Liberal Arts, the History of Ideas, Cultural Studies or Modern Languages – all of which are likely candidates to be (for example) part of a School of Arts and/or Humanities – the common ground is likely to be smaller still. Is it not strange, therefore, that in an era of financial pressure and the related need to justify one's own place (and that of one's discipline) in the University, certain biblical scholars seem most concerned about narrowing the gate and keeping tighter control over who may and may not enter the field? It is tempting to suggest that this is one area in which the evidence seems strong that such people are living facing the past.

The sense I get from reading Hurtado's blog posts and Van Seters' article is that as they pause from gazing proudly down the long and noble history of biblical studies and swivel around, they see a similarly long and glorious future rolling out ahead. A related sentiment was apparent in the first session of the 2013 Winter Meeting of the Society for Old Testament Study. In his presidential address,[39] incoming president Eryl Davies devoted a considerable amount of time to a defence of objectivity in biblical studies, or, more accurately, to an attack on its critics. As part of this attack, Davies asserted that, aside from certain valuable insights (which, incidentally, he reproduced in a recent monograph),[40] the collective approach of much feminist biblical scholarship, with, in particular, its obsessions with locatedness, autobiography and suspicion concerning objectivity, will, in the long-run, most likely prove to have been merely a quixotic fad.

In addition to finding Davies' address alarmingly narrow in its scope, woefully outdated in its approach, and, in places, downright offensive in its rhetoric, I also simply could not relate to his seemingly unproblematic vision of a future in which the discipline of biblical studies persists, or even thrives, on the basis of the refinement and purification of its traditional methods. I, like Lyons, am much more inclined to see the discipline as facing or about to face a crisis – a crisis that

---

[39] Davies, Eryl, 'Ideology and Constructions of the 'History of Israel'', presented to the Winter Meeting of the Society for Old Testament Study, Fitzwilliam College, Cambridge, UK, 2 January 2013.
[40] Davies, Eryl, *The Dissenting Reader: Feminist Approaches to the Hebrew Bible*, Aldershot and Burlington, VT: Ashgate, (2003).

it will most likely not survive unless those who wield the most influence over it can come to terms with its true and necessary breadth.

Rather than having to try to force the historical critic to change his nomenclature and broaden his self-understanding, I see the reception historian as being in the favorable position of being able to demonstrate to him that the approach she employs simply creates more possibilities for the kind of creative, interdisciplinary and impactful research that an academic post now requires. In some instances it is possible to see how this approach might well end up (organically) giving rise to a similar realization on behalf of both scholars that their approaches are at certain points usefully adjacent. Likewise, to the postmodern interpreter the historical critic can both demonstrate a critical awareness of the constructed nature of the past, the present and of all discourse, and offer a scheme by which various constructions of the past and present can be fruitfully analysed and described in terms consonant with other historical projects. Neither side need be subsumed, co-opted or repackaged by an external intervention for these small but significant sites of encounter to demonstrate their potential value. To my mind, the foundation that reception history has in the tradition of dialectical philosophy, the combination of its emphasis on process and its inherited suspicion of 'method' (*Methode*),[41] and its dual commitment to close historical analysis and hermeneutical reflection, all point to its suitability for this liminal role. Maybe, then, the third way between compulsion by logic or *realpolitik* is invitation through socialization – an invitation that is addressed to the historical critic and the postmodern interpreter alike.

Conclusions

In an insightful analogy concerning the probable impotence of historical criticism in the face of something like the disastrous 1993 FBI siege of the Branch Davidian compound in Waco, Texas, Lyons brings the issues into sharp focus.[42] With the rhetorical quip '[j]ust how vital would the *Oxford Bible Commentary* have been to the FBI at Waco?',[43] Lyons puts a profound question to all approaches to biblical texts within the modern academy. It is precisely these kinds of scenarios, he suggests, in which reception history could succeed in speaking the wisdom of the world's pasts to its futures, where other approaches have failed. However, alongside Lyons' penetrating question of just how effective an emphasis on *wissenschaftlich* on behalf of those advising the FBI would have been (as opposed to an approach that might have allowed them to 'inhabit Koresh's hermeneutic and exploit its ambiguities'[44]), I cannot help but feel that there is, in his call for the enforced

---

[41] See Gadamer, *Truth and Method*.
[42] Lyons, 'Hope for . . .', 215.
[43] Lyons, 'Hope for . . .', 215.
[44] Lyons, 'Hope for . . .', 215.

transformation of historical criticism, something of an implicit echo of the kind of approach employed by the FBI at Waco.

As I see it, the most effective way for reception history to shape the future of the discipline is to be steadfast in its now well-established contributions to the discipline, at each turn both demonstrating its hermeneutical commitments and stridently affirming its historicity. In so doing, it should illustrate its ability to engage and critique modernist and postmodernist conceptions of history and approaches to interpretation, and to create and sustain fruitful interdisciplinary dialogue. Moreover, in addition to a more effective mediation between opposing positions, I also see the approach sketched out in this chapter as one that enables reception history to retain a key emphasis that might otherwise be left behind. While Lyons' article focusses on the method and message of reception history, I am keen to place an equal stress on the media through which it operates. As Sue Gillingham reminded the 2012 Summer Meeting of the Society for Old Testament Study, one of reception history's most important contributions to biblical scholarship is the way it refuses to allow the written word to define its boundaries.[45] Interpretation of the use of biblical themes and imagery in the visual arts, film, music, dance and many other media is a crucial aspect of the kind of real-world contexts that Lyons and I agree biblical studies must address if it is to continue to function as a viable discipline, and its is my contention that it is from the imagined, dialectical middle constructed in this chapter that it can most fruitfully engage these cultural phenomena.

---

[45] Gillingham, Susan, 'Reception History: Biblical Studies on Holiday?', presented to the Summer Meeting of the Society for Old Testament Study, Hulme Hall, Manchester, 17th July 2012. (See the written version of the paper in this volume).

Part Three

Conceptualizing Reception History

6

The Head of John and its Reception or How to Conceptualize 'Reception History'[1]

Caroline Vander Stichele
Universiteit van Amsterdam

Introduction

In his article 'Reception History and Beyond,' Timothy Beal argues that reception history can in two respects be potentially revolutionary for Biblical Studies. First of all, it has the potential to bridge the divide between historical-critical and literary-critical approaches within Biblical Studies,[2] and second, it also has the potential to stimulate the dialogue between biblical scholars and their colleagues in Religious Studies. Reception history, however, also has its limitations. Beal identifies three such limitations. Two of them are more general, the third more serious and specific for Biblical Studies. The first is the decidedly literary orientation of reception history. It is the scriptural content rather than its materiality and mediality that is focussed upon. A second, related issue is that only limited attention is given to the modes of production and consumption of scriptural texts, but the third, more pressing, problem is the notion of origination underlying the idea of reception. It is the presupposition that there is a fixed point of origin, in this case 'the Bible', which is the source of numerous, subsequent interpretations. However, according to Beal, 'if there is one thing the material history of Bibles makes extremely clear, it is that there is no such *thing* as the Bible, and there never has been.'[3]

These three limitations are sufficient reasons for Beal to want to move beyond reception history toward a cultural history of scriptures. To make such a move possible, in his view three concerns should be taken into account. First of all, 'the

---

[1] Parts of this article were previously presented as papers at the International SBL Meeting in Amsterdam (July 2012) and the Annual Meeting in Chicago (November 2012).

[2] See also John Lyons, 'Hope for a Troubled Discipline? Contributions to New Testament Studies from Reception History', in *JSNT* 33(2010), 207–20.

[3] Timothy Beal, 'Reception History and Beyond: Toward the Cultural History of Scriptures', in *Biblical Interpretation* 19 (2011), 357–72, p. 367.

Bible' and 'biblical' should be understood as discursive objects that are constantly changing. Second, attention should be given to the many material and media incarnations of scripture, and third, scriptural culture is not only about content and its interpretations but also about its form and performance. According to Beal, these concerns imply a radical shift in focus in two respects: on the one hand, 'from hermeneutical reception to cultural production' and on the other, 'from interpreting scripture via culture to interpreting culture, especially religious culture, via scripture.'[4]

Overall, I share Beal's view that reception history is often too narrowly conceived and that a cultural turn is therefore much needed. In many ways my concern in what follows is similar to that of Beal, although I broach the subject from a somewhat different angle. It differs however in one important respect, insofar as I would propose to replace the notion of 'history' with that of 'impact'. The focus then would be on the cultural impact of scriptures rather than on their history, which I consider to be more narrow in scope.[5] In what follows I argue why that is the case.

Conceptualizing reception history

As my starting point I take three concepts that are used to capture processes that take place within 'reception history'. The concepts under discussion are 'intertextuality', 'pre-posterous history' and 'rhizomorphous systems', as developed by Jonathan Culler, Mieke Bal, and Gilles Deleuze with Felix Guattari respectively. In my view these concepts capture different aspects of the dynamics at work in 'reception history' and I illustrate this with examples taken from the story about the beheading of John the Baptist (Matthew 14:1-12, Mark 6:14-29).

Intertextuality and the issue of origins

In his book *The Pursuit of Signs* (1981), literary theorist Jonathan Culler criticizes the tendency to narrow 'intertextuality' down to sources and influences that can be found in any given text. In his view, this approach does not do justice to the encompassing character of this concept, which also includes 'anonymous discursive practices, codes whose origins are lost, that make possible the signifying practices

---

[4] Beal, 'Reception History and Beyond', 371.
[5] The term 'impact' is used in different disciplines and refers to the potential effects certain conditions or actions may have on, for instance, the environment, health, the social or economic situation, etc. See for instance the definition of 'health impact' by the World Health Organization at: http://www.who.int/hia/about/glos/en/index1.html. Similarly, the term could be used in Biblical Studies to assess the impact Bibles/scriptures have on cultures.

of later texts.'[6] Culler admits that such a wide definition is hard to work with in practice and that therefore some form of restriction is necessary in order to make it operational. Restrictions, however, are far from innocent, he warns, because they undermine the general meaning of the concept. The danger he sees is that 'one either falls into source study of a traditional and positivistic kind (which is what the concept was designed to transcend) or else ends by naming particular texts as the pre-texts on grounds of interpretive convenience.'[7]

In order to transcend the limitations of these approaches, Culler states, multiple strategies and different focusses are needed. An alternative approach he himself suggests is to use a linguistic model and explore the *logical* and *pragmatic* presuppositions embedded in a text. *Logical* presuppositions are the presuppositions of a sentence. They form what Culler calls 'a modest intertextuality',[8] because they relate sentences to other sentences which they presuppose. Together they constitute an intertextual space, a pre-text of any given text. This type of intertextuality is very limited in that it stays close to the text, but it makes one aware of how each text creates its own pre-text.

Let me illustrate this with three examples taken from the story about the beheading of John the Baptist. First, in Mark 6:14, we read: 'King Herod heard of it, for Jesus' name had become known.' This sentence presupposes the existence of a character called 'a king' (βασιλεύς) and in particular one named Herod. That he heard something (ἤκουσεν), presupposes that something had been told, and the fact that Jesus' name had become known, presupposes that there was a time when Jesus was still unknown. The second example is the statement in verse 17 that Herodias was 'his brother Philip's wife', which presupposes that Herod had a brother named Philip, and that this brother had married a woman named Herodias. Finally, the statement in verse 24: 'She went out and said to her mother, 'What should I ask for?' presumes the existence of a daughter and the presence of her mother in a different place (ἐξελθοῦσα). These are all logical presuppositions, insofar as they can be inferred from the sentences themselves.

The second type of presupposition that Culler mentions are called *pragmatic* presuppositions. They relate a speech-act such as 'warn', 'command' and 'promise' to a particular context that is presupposed. Let me use an example here from the parallel story in Matthew 14. In verse 7 Herod promises (ὡμολόγησεν) to grant the daughter of Herodias whatever she might ask. This statement pragmatically presupposes a contextual motive for Herod to make such a promise and that there is a person to which he addresses this promise, who knows how to interpret this particular utterance. Another example is the command Herod gives in verses 9–10

---

[6] Jonathan Culler, *The Pursuit of Signs. Semiotics, Literature, Deconstruction* (London: Routledge, 2001), 114.
[7] Culler, *Pursuit of Signs*, 121.
[8] Culler, *Pursuit of Signs*, 124.

to have John beheaded. This presupposes he gives this command to someone who understands both *that* he is expected to do something and *what* he is expected to do.

Culler sees a connection between this second type of linguistic presupposition and literature, insofar as conventions make it possible to interpret particular speech-acts as commands or promises, while literary conventions, such as issues of genre, make it possible, for instance, to interpret the text about the beheading of John as a story and more specifically as a flashback in the larger narrative about Jesus, which explains why Herod thinks that John the Baptist has been raised (Mark 6:16; Matthew 14:2). What these linguistic and literary forms of intertextuality have in common, is that no points of origin, no sources can be traced. We can, for instance, no longer determine the 'first story ever told' or trace back the first occurrence of the word 'king' in English. As Culler notes 'it is part of the structure of discursive conventions to be cut off from origins.'[9]

In Biblical Studies, however, intertextuality is often used in its more narrow sense, as referring to sources, citations and allusions. The promise that Herod makes in Mark 6:23 to give the girl 'even half of his kingdom' is, for example, often interpreted as an intertextual link with the book Esther where Ahasuerus makes the same promise to Esther several times (5:3.6; 7:2), but as Culler points out, there is more to intertextuality than the establishment of such intertextual relationships.

In my view a broader understanding of intertextuality also opens up a space for the exploration of connections between texts that share the same cultural reservoir in a more fluid way. For instance, the *Cambridge Idioms Dictionary* gives as explanation for the expression 'someone's head on a plate/platter': 'if you want someone's head on a plate, you are very angry with them and want them to be punished' and gives the following example: 'The director was furious at what had happened and wanted Watt's head on a platter.'[10] The expression is perfectly intelligible, even for a reader who is unaware that it goes back to the biblical story of the beheading of John. The relationship between the two is there, but it is fluid, insofar as the expression is in a way cut off from its origin.

When it comes to the use of intertextuality as a concept to capture processes taking place in the context of 'reception history', Culler's approach may, however, still be too limited, first of all, because he only deals with textual material and second, because he focusses on what given texts presuppose, what prior codes make them intelligible. In my view the concepts used by Bal and by Deleuze and Guattari can broaden the perspective.

---

[9] Culler, *Pursuit of Signs*, 113.
[10] *Cambridge Idioms Dictionary*, Cambridge University Press, 2nd edn 2006. At: http://idioms.thefreedictionary.com/head+on+a+plate.

Pre-posterous histories

In her book *Quoting Caravaggio: Contemporary Art, Preposterous History*, literary theorist Mieke Bal discusses the way in which contemporary art relates to the art of the past, in this case Baroque Art, with Caravaggio serving as eminent example.[11] In the introduction to that volume Bal develops two concepts that are of interest to us here. One is the notion of 'preposterous history', the other the concept of 'quotation'. As far as the latter is concerned, Bal points to the fact that quotations (the reference of one work to another) play a role in both iconography and intertextuality and thus connect two disciplines, more specifically art history and literary source studies, with each other. In her view, these two disciplines have three important features in common.

The first – and this sounds familiar in light of Culler's analysis – is that they consider the historical precedent as a source of the later work in which it is used. Bal proposes to problematize this idea of the precedent as origin by considering the later work as an active intervention in the earlier work, rather than as a passive recipient. The second feature relates to the place where meaning is located. Instead of trying to pin down the meaning of a sign or motif, as is often done in traditional approaches, Bal suggests 'to trace the process of meaning-production over time (in both directions: present/past and past/present) as an open, dynamic process, rather than to map the results of that process.'[12] The third feature has to do with the textual nature of intertextual allusions, in that iconography often refers visual motifs back to written texts. Bal mentions classical myths here, but one can also think of biblical stories. Bal proposes to use the notion of 'visual textuality', meaning that when an artist uses elements from earlier works, he or she constructs a new image-as-'text', using textual elements broken away from the earlier work in order to make something new.

The shifts in focus that Bal suggests: 1. Later work as active intervention; 2. Meaning production as process; and 3. Image-as-'text' – imply a new way of dealing with the relationship between past and present, a reversal in the way of doing history, as expressed in her notion of 'preposterous history', meaning that what came chronologically first ('pre-') is considered to be an after-effect ('post-') of its later recycling.[13]

---

[11] Mieke Bal, *Quoting Caravaggio. Contemporary Art, Preposterous History* (Chicago: University of Chicago Press, 1999).

[12] Bal, *Quoting Caravaggio*, 9.

[13] Bal (p.7 n.4) coins the concept after Patricia Parker's 'Preposterous Events' (*Shakespeare Quarterly* 43[1992], 186–213) and quotes T.S. Eliot (on p.1), who notes: 'Whoever has approved this idea of order, of the form of European, of English literature, will not find it preposterous that the past should be altered by the present as much as the present is directed by the past.' Cf. T. S. Eliot, 'Tradition and the Individual Talent', in *The Sacred Wood: Essays on Poetry and Criticism* (1920). Available online at http://www.bartleby.com/index.html). A similar understanding of how later work shapes the interpretation of past works is also expressed by Borges, who notes that 'each writer creates his precursors. His work modifies our conception of the past, as it will modify the future.' Cf. Jorge Luis Borges, *Selected Non-Fictions*, ed. Eliot Weinberger, trans. Esther Allen (New York: Penguin, 1999), 365. With thanks to Richard Walsh for drawing my attention to this parallel in Borges's work.

Similarly, later work also informs the way we read biblical stories. This can, for instance, be illustrated with two photographs from the series, *INRI*, by Bettina Rheims, dating from 1998.[14] The subtitle of both pictures is: 'Herod's Feast. What does Salome ask for? The object of her mother's desire: John's head on a platter.' While this subtitle builds an intertextual link with the gospel story about the beheading of John, it also identifies the daughter as Salome, a name not mentioned in the gospels but in Josephus' *Antiquities* 18.136, and often subsequently used throughout history to identify Herodias' daughter.

However, the link with the past is more complex than that, because Salome's dress, especially in the first picture, also evokes earlier re-interpretations of the story, notably the dance of the seven veils, mentioned by Oscar Wilde in his play *Salomé*, (1893) which was later put to music by Richard Strauss in his opera *Salome* (1905). These later appropriations often shape the way readers preposterously understand the biblical stories, as they tend to 'presume' that the daughter is Salome and her dance is the one with the seven veils.

The second picture, a close up of Salome with the head of John on a platter,[15] 'quotes' earlier representations, in this case paintings representing Salome with the head of John on a platter.[16] The comparison with these numerous, earlier representations makes it possible to go back and forth between them, noticing similarities and differences for instance in dressing, posture, facial expression and age of the different Salomes, allowing one to see the photograph as an active appropriation of the past rather than a passive copy.

Compared with Culler, Bal's approach foregrounds historicity, moves beyond texts to include other artefacts, and has a more dynamic understanding of time as a two-way process rather than a one-way process from text to pre-text. As such her approach expands an understanding of reception history, in which a more passive recipient and one-way process of interpretation (from the past to the present) are presumed. Bal, however, even when moving back and forth between past and present still works with a linear understanding of time. Moreover, her analysis focusses on the relationship between iconography and intertextuality in visual art and literature. As a result, other forms of reinterpretation, such as for instance music, are not taken into consideration.

Rhizomorphous systems

A broader perspective, I think, is made possible by the concept of the 'rhizome' as developed by Deleuze and Guattari. In the first chapter of their book, *A Thousand Plateaus*, originally published in French in 1980, philosopher Gilles Deleuze and

---

[14] Serge Bramley and Bettina Rheims, *INRI* (New York: Monacelli Press, 1999), 72–3.
[15] In the pictures under discussion, Bettina Rheims herself is posing as Salome.
[16] See for instance paintings of Salome by Lucas Cranach the Elder, Bernardini Luini, Titian, Caravaggio, Carlo Dolci, Giacomo Zoboli, and Gustave Moreau (all available online).

psychoanalyst Félix Guattari introduce the image of the rhizome, a subterranean stem which develops roots and offshoots from its nodes. Bamboo and Lily of the Valley, for instance, are plants with such underground rhizomes. Their structure is different from the roots of trees, which are part of a hierarchically organized, segmented structure. According to Deleuze and Guattari 'the tree has dominated Western reality and all of Western thought, from botany to biology and anatomy, but also gnosiology, theology, ontology and all of philosophy.'[17] Arborescent systems are substantially different from rhizomorphous systems, insofar as arborescent systems are centred, and information is transmitted along pre-established paths. Rhizomorphous systems, however, are a-centred and non-hierarchical. Every point in a rhizome is connected with any other point. Rhizomes have multiple entryways, no beginning nor end. Like a map, a rhizome is 'open and connectable in all of its dimensions; it is detachable, reversible, susceptible to constant modification.'[18]

In my view, the concept of the rhizome may be a useful tool to rethink 'reception history' as a dynamic and open-ended process, with multiple entries and exits, rather than linear trajectories. As a result, 'the Bible' is no longer conceived as origin or centre, but as a node from which its history unfolds in multiple directions. This concept of the rhizome also makes it possible to include diverse forms of appropriation, not only texts or visual art, but also film, games, music – you name it. One possible entry point into reception history conceived this way could for instance be the character of Herodias as she appears in nineteenth-century paintings. From there one could follow her trace back to the Bible, or into the twenty-first century, but one could also move from visual art to literature in the same time period, or from France to Italy and from there to Great Britain. One could also explore orientalist elements in these representations and the way in which she is depicted as a *femme fatale*... to name just a few directions in which one could move.

Cultural impact

The concepts of Culler, Bal and Deleuze/Guattari discussed so far thus capture different aspects of the cultural impact of scriptures. Culler's notion of intertextuality draws our attention to the fact that texts participate in the discursive space of a culture, but insofar as his focus is on texts and their relation to the past, his use of the concept has its limitations. In connecting intertextuality with iconography, Bal broadens the perspective to include visual art, while her definition of preposterous history introduces a more dynamic understanding of the

---

[17] Gilles Deleuze and Félix Guattari, *A Thousand Plateaus. Capitalism and Schizophrenia* (London: Continuum, 2004), 20.
[18] Deleuze and Guattari, *Thousand Plateaus*, 13.

relationship between past and present. Finally, the image of the rhizome as used by Deleuze and Guattari further expands our view on the directions in which a 'reception history of the Bible' can be taken, but it also puts into question the adequacy of this way to define what we are doing, what we want to do and how we want to go about it. Its scope is simply too narrow.

Deleuze and Guattari wrote their book a decade before the advent of the Internet, but that could well be the most rhizomorphous system in existence today. Exploring the cultural impact of scriptures would then be comparable to surfing on the Net. Any link is a connection with multiple other ones. Some will be dead-ends, others may lead us too far away, but we can always go back and take off in another direction.

In his earlier work Deleuze already argued that the advent of cinema profoundly transformed our perception of time through the use of montage and that technological innovations thus make it possible for us to think differently.[19] Similarly, I would argue, the use of the Internet has profoundly changed our perception of reality, as it opens up almost limitless possibilities to access material that is far removed from us in both time and space as well as allows the creation of a virtual reality, that only 'exists' online. Internet can also help us think about the cultural impact of scriptures in a more rhizomatic way. The following discussion of the representation of the death of John the Baptist by Giovanni di Paolo (1403–83) serves as a test case.

The head of John and its reception by Giovanni di Paolo[20]

The work of Giovanni di Paolo under discussion here consists of six panels devoted to the life of John the Baptist, three of which represent scenes related to the story about his death. The panels are on display at the Art Institute of Chicago, but can also be 'visited' online.[21] The sixth panel, representing the head of John brought before Herod, is remarkable, because John's head is presented here to Herod rather than Herodias or her daughter as suggested by the biblical texts (Matthew 14:11; Mark 6:27–28) and this happens in the presence of the dancing girl, whose dance, both narratively and logically, precedes the request for John's head (Matthew 14:6; Mark 6:22). To find an answer to the question of why Di Paolo chose to do this I used both traditional media, such as books and articles, and the Internet as my source of information. The result, as can be gathered from the footnotes below, is a hybrid mixture of both. Sometimes the publications I used were available to me in

---

[19] Cf. Gilles Deleuze, *Cinema I: The Movement – Image* (Minneapolis: University of Minnesota Press, 1986).

[20] I would like to thank Kiki Boomgaard and Esther Mulders for their assistance in researching this part of my article. They made working on this piece so much more enjoyable.

[21] http://www.artic.edu/aic/collections/artwork/artist/Giovanni+di+Paolo

print, in other instances I consulted them online. The same was the case with the artwork in question. The references made to websites where the artwork is available, also encourage an interactive reading on the part of the reader. Such a reading is, no doubt, easier with an electronic version of this article, where the links in the footnotes can be directly activated, than in the printed version.

Di Paolo's Paintings of John the Baptist

Giovanni di Paolo lived and worked in Siena, Italy, from about 1403 until 1483. He started working as a miniaturist for the Dominicans but later made larger panels mostly using tempera and gold on wood, the preferred medium in Siena.[22] One of the famous founders of the Sienese school of painting was Duccio (ca. 1255-1319), whose *Maestà* with the Virgin and Christ Child enthroned in Majesty with Angels and Saints is world famous.[23] Di Paolo stood in that tradition, but he was also influenced by other artists: painters, such as Fra Angelico (ca. 1395-1455) and Gentile da Fabriano (ca. 1370-1427) and, as will become clear in what follows, sculptors such as Lorenzo Ghiberti (1378-1455) and his student Donatello (ca.1386-1466). Notwithstanding the fact that Giovanni di Paolo mostly used traditional techniques and the work of other artists for inspiration, as we will see he also made changes to the scenes in question, often in order to enhance their dramatic effect.

As is explained on the website of the Art Institute, the six panels from the John the Baptist collection on display were acquired by the Institute in 1933.[24] They are dated around 1455-60 and include the following scenes: John entering the wilderness; Behold the lamb of God; John visited in prison by two disciples; Salome asking for the head of John; the beheading of John; and the head brought before Herod. The panels were originally part of a larger series of twelve scenes.[25] Most of these other panels are preserved at other musea and are equally accessible online: *The Angel Gabriel Announcing to Zacharias the Birth of a Son* is at the Metropolitan Museum in New York,[26] *The Baptism of Christ* at the Norton Simon Museum of Art in Pasadena,[27] and two further panels, *The Birth of John* and *The Baptist before the Throne of Herod*, are at the Westfälisches Landesmuseum in Münster, Germany.[28] A

---

[22] Timothy Hyman, *Sienese Painting: The Art of the City-Republic (1278-1477)*. (London: Thames & Hudson, 2003), 160-181, and John Pope-Hennessy, *Giovanni di Paolo 1403-1483* (New York: Oxford University Press, 1938).
[23] See: http://www.wga.hu/frames-e.html?/html/d/duccio/index.html.
[24] http://www.artic.edu/aic/collections/artwork/16156?search_no=4&index=0
[25] Hyman, *Sienese Painting*, p.172 n.145.
[26] http://www.metmuseum.org/Collections/search-the-collections/150000025?rpp=20&pg=1&ft=giovanni+di+paolo+%28giovanni+di+paolo+di+grazia%29&pos=11
[27] http://www.nortonsimon.org/collections/highlights.php?period=14H&resultnum=54
[28] http://www.lwl.org/landesmuseum-download/kdm/kdm_Online_Archiv/Mittelalter/Juli%201999%20%28Giovanni%20di%20Paolo,%20Johannestafeln%29.pdf

final panel showing *John Preaching* is part of the Carvallo Collection in Tours (France).[29] Unfortunately, the twelfth panel is missing. A possibility is that it showed John baptizing the multitude.[30] These twelve panels may have been part of a folding altarpiece with two wings, having six panels on each wing,[31] or have served as doors of a niche with a statue of John the Baptist or a reliquary.[32] In the reconstruction of the diptych, the right wing would have included the baptism of Christ and the five scenes related to the arrest and death of John. The four lower panels are clearly paired, insofar as the visit of John in prison and the beheading form one pair and Salome's request for John's head and its presentation to Herod another.

Other work of Giovanni di Paolo that is of interest to us here are four paintings equally related to the life and death of John the Baptist at the National Gallery in London.[33] These smaller paintings were originally part of a predella, a series of small narrative panels at the bottom of a larger altarpiece. The scenes in question include the birth of John, John retiring in the desert, the baptism of Christ and the head of John brought to Herod.[34] These panels are dated around 1454. That is slightly earlier than the larger panels of which they seem to be predecessors. Especially the last panel is of interest to us here, because it also depicts the presentation of John's head to Herod. In what follows I will discuss this scene, first as represented on the predella panel from the National Gallery in London and then on the panel at the Art Institute in Chicago. A comparative analysis of this material is facilitated by their availability on the Internet. We can zoom in on details to a degree hardly ever achieved by printed reproductions of the same material.

The predella panel shows a banquet scene with Herod seated to the left and two other characters sitting at the long end of the table. Herod, draws back, his hands raised when John's head is presented to him on a plate by a soldier, while the other two guests cover their eyes. To the right, we see three other characters: two young men, and a young woman who is dancing. She is standing on the top of her right foot, with her left foot and arm raised and with her right hand lifting up her dress

---

[29] Cf. Léonce Amaudry, 'The Collection of Dr. Carvallo at Paris. Article III: Early Pictures of Various Schools', in *The Burlington Magazine* 6 (1904), 294–312, p. 307.

[30] Thus Meiss and Werner who also present a reconstruction of the panels. Cf. Millard Meiss, 'A New Panel by Giovanni de Paolo from his Altar-piece of the Baptist', in *The Burlington Magazine* nr. 851, vol.116, Feb. 1974, pp. 73–7, p.73, 75. Elke Anna Werner, 'Das Kunstwerk des Monats' (Westfälisches Landesmuseum, Münster, Juli 1999), n.p. (cf. also note 28).

[31] Cf. Helen F. Mackenzie, 'Panels by Giovanni di Paolo of Siena (1403–1483) Showing Scenes from the Life of St. John the Baptist', in *Bulletin of the Art Institute of Chicago* 32 (1938), 106–9, pp. 106–7 and Pope-Hennessy, *Giovanni di Paolo*, 81–3.

[32] Thus Hyman, *Sienese Painting*, p. 172 n. 145.

[33] Accessible online at: http://www.nationalgallery.org.uk/artists/giovanni-di-paolo.

[34] According to Pope-Hennessy the predella originally consisted of five panels. The missing panel would have presented either John Preaching before Herod or his execution. Cf. John Pope-Hennessy, 'Giovanni di Paolo', in *The Metropolitan Museum of Art Bulletin* 46/2 (1988), 6–46, pp. 17–19.

at her back. She does not look at John's head, but at Herod with a slightly amused, maybe even triumphant, smile.

When we compare this panel with the panel at the Art Institute, we first of all notice that the format of the former is smaller. The bottom of the Chicago panel largely corresponds with the scene on the predella. The response of Herod and his guests to the head of John presented by the soldier is the same. The group of three characters with the dancing young woman is almost identical as well, but the girl is no longer smiling and her dress is now olive green instead of pink, the same colour as the cloak Herodias is wearing in the scene where John appears before the throne of Herod.

The most important difference, however, is that there are more characters displayed on the Chicago panel. They are located in the middle part on what looks like a balcony, while the upper part is dominated by the building. One of the effects is that the scene now seems to take place outdoors, in contrast to the more intimate setting of the earlier panel. The additional characters also bring more action to the scene. Sometimes the same character is shown twice, a typical feature of a 'continuous narrative', in which several moments of a story are represented in one single scene. That is the case with the soldier holding the plate with John's head at the very right, who is also presenting the head to Herod. Of course, the most important conflation of two moments from the biblical story is the presentation of John's head and the dancing girl. This is all the more striking since in the Chicago series a painting of the request of Salome (in the logic of the narrative taking place after the dance and Herod's offer, cf. Matthew 14:8; Mark 6:25) and of the beheading of John precede this final scene. The dancing girl therefore appears out of place. So why did Di Paolo include her?

The reason for this can be found in a work from Donatello that represents the same scene and clearly served as a source of inspiration for Di Paolo.[35] It is a bronze relief which probably dates from 1423–5, on the baptismal font in the Baptistery at Siena.[36] To the left we see Herod, his hands raised in horror at the sight of John's head offered to him on a plate by a soldier, a position similar but not identical, as we will see, to the two panels of Di Paolo. On the relief, the soldier is positioned closer to Herod than on the panels and Herod's face expresses horror rather than grief. The group of characters to the right on Donatello's relief: the person at the table who is covering his face and the dancing girl, are positioned in exactly the same way as on Di Paolo's panels. The girl does not look at Herod though, nor at the head, nor is she smiling. She appears rather self-absorbed. The character who *does* look at Herod is seated next to him and extends her hand to the plate. It is Herodias. Interestingly enough she is 'replaced' by Di Paolo with a second guest at

---

[35] Cf. Pope-Hennessy, *Giovanni di Paolo*, 88.
[36] Online at: http://www.wga.hu/frames-e.html?/html/d/donatell/index.html. For a detailed discussion of this work, see Jules Lubbock, *Storytelling in Christian Art from Giotto to Donatello* (New Haven: Yale University Press, 2006), 174–203.

the table who covers his eyes in horror. This clearly changes the dynamic in the picture. Donatello foregrounds the different response of Herod and Herodias to the decapitated head, while Di Paolo rather stresses the tragic character of the scene. Also to be noticed here is that Donatello includes figures in the background, notably someone with the head of John on a platter.[37] Although Di Paolo did not include these figures in his predella painting, probably because the smaller format of the predella imposes restrictions as to what can be represented, they clearly informed his inclusion of the additional characters in the Chicago painting. This difference between the two paintings draws our attention to the role that the materiality of the medium itself plays in the selection of the content represented.

In Bal's terms, Giovanni di Paolo's versions are not simply painted copies or passive recipients of Donatello's bronze reliefs, but rather active interventions in Donatello's work. The same is the case with another scene of Di Paolo which is of interest to us here, more specifically the one with John before the throne of Herod at the museum in Münster.[38] The scene is divided in two by a pillar in the middle. To the left, Herod is sitting on a throne, pointing at John. Next to Herod, Herodias is standing and glancing at Herod. To the right John is looking at Herod and pointing up, while a soldier is holding him captive. Again Di Paolo used a scene here from the font at the baptistery in Siena as a source of inspiration, in this case the bronze relief by Lorenzo Ghiberti showing the exact same scene as here, of John before Herod.[39] Here too we see Herod pointing at John, with Herodias next to him and John held captive to the right. John's right hand is pointing up while his left arm is stretched in the direction of Herod's pointing finger. He is not facing Herod though, as is the case with Di Paolo's version of the scene. Striking in this case is that Di Paolo chose to include Herodias here, while he left her out at the banquet, which raises the question why he included her in one scene and not in the other. I address this issue in what follows.

Di Paolo's interpretation of the banquet scene

As already noted the presentation of the head of John to Herod as painted by Di Paolo is nowhere to be found in the gospel stories, nor is the trial scene before Herod for that matter. However, in light of Culler's observations, both scenes are made possible by the intertextual space of the biblical texts. Thus, the presentation of John before the throne of Herod finds its origin in the logical presupposition, already mentioned earlier, that Herod is called 'king' in Mark and therefore he is

---

[37] See Lubbock, *Storytelling in Christian Art*, 174 and online at: http://www.bluffton.edu/~sullivanm/italy/siena/baptistryfont/0071.jpg.

[38] See reference in note 28.

[39] See http://www.bildindex.de/#|7 and http://www.bluffton.edu/~sullivanm/italy/siena/baptistryfont/0073.jpg. This scene does not occur in the gospels stories, where only John's arrest and imprisonment are mentioned (Mt 14:3; Mk 6:17).

represented on a throne.⁴⁰ Similarly, the presentation of John before the throne and of his head to Herod are both the result of the orders given by Herod to have John arrested and to bring his head, and thus based on the pragmatic presuppositions related to the commands given by Herod.

As we know from the scenes on the baptismal font by Donatello and Ghiberti, Di Paolo did not invent these scenes. In fact, as far as the presentation of the head of John is concerned, the same combination of the dancing girl with the presentation of the head already occurs in the work of Italian artists from the previous century. Two examples are of interest to us here in terms of the similarities and differences with Di Paolo. The first one is a fresco by Giotto in the Peruzzi chapel in Florence dated between 1310 and 1337.⁴¹ Here too the dancing girl is combined with the presentation of the head to Herod. As in the case of Di Paolo, Herodias is absent at the banquet. There is, however, another room to the right, where the girl presents the head to her mother. The second example consists of two works from Giusto de' Menabuoi at the baptistery of the cathedral in Padua, which also dates from the fourteenth century.⁴² It consists of two different representations of this scene: one is a fresco on the wall, the other a painting on a polyptych, dating from the same time as the fresco. Because the scene on the polyptych is better preserved, I will discuss that one first. It is located on the right panel of the polyptych and shows the dancing girl in front of the table at which Herod and his guests are seated. The head of John is presented here to the girl. Herod does not even seem to notice, as he is engaged in a conversation with the guest next to him.⁴³ The scene on the fresco looks slightly different. Here too we see the girl dancing in front of the table with Herod and his guests, but this time the head is presented to Herod, who still does not seem to notice. As in the case of Giotto, here too an additional scene shows the presentation of the head by the girl to Herodias in another room.⁴⁴ From this additional evidence we can conclude that the combination of the dancing girl and the presentation of the head in one scene is fairly traditional.

There is, however, a notable difference as far as the presence or absence of Herodias is concerned. This can easily be explained by the fact that Mark explicitly states that the girl went out (ἐξελθοῦσα) to consult her mother and then came back in (εἰσελθοῦσα) with the response. As noted earlier, this logically presupposes that Herodias is outside the room where the banquet takes place. This in turn explains

---

⁴⁰ Historical accuracy is irrelevant here, as the text creates its own universe. The attribute 'king' in Mark is in fact erroneous. He was a 'tetrarch', as Matthew 14:1 and Luke 3:19 have it.
⁴¹ See http://www.wga.hu/frames-e.html?/html/g/giotto/index.html. Cf. also Lubbock, *Storytelling in Christian Art*, 140–5.
⁴² Cf. Pietro Lievore (ed.), *Padua: Baptistery of the Cathedral. Frescoes by Giusto de' Menabuoi (XIV c.)*. (Padua: Deganello, 1994, 2nd edn.).
⁴³ Cf. Lievore, *Padua*, p. 61, detail on p. 63.
⁴⁴ Cf. Lievore, *Padua*, p. 16 and 29.

the absence of Herodias from the banquet table and her location in a different room in the case of Giotto and Giusto. Matthew is not as clear on that. He only mentions that the girl brought the head to her mother (Mt 14:11).

As already noted, the intertextual space of the biblical texts leaves room for an interpretation in which the head is presented to Herod in some cases, rather than to the girl or her mother. Herod orders a soldier to bring John's head and that is what the soldier does, as stated in Mark 6:28: he 'brought his head on a platter', next he gives it to the girl and the girl gives it to her mother. Matthew uses the passive tense instead: 'the head was brought on a platter and given to the girl' (v.11). Since Herod ordered the head to begin with, it makes sense for the soldier to present it to him first, before giving it to the girl. The biblical stories do not mention the emotional response of Herod at this point in the story, but at an earlier moment, when he grants the girl's request for John's head. At that point Mark notes: 'the king was deeply grieved' (Mk 6:26; Mt 14:9: 'grieved'). This may well have informed Di Paolo's depiction of Herod's response when he sees the head. In that case, it can be understood as a creative reconfiguration of textual elements and thus, in Bal's words, as an instance of visual textuality.

The request for John's head

As we have seen, the combination of the dancing girl with the presentation of John's head to Herod by Giovanni di Paolo is informed by earlier representations, especially the one by Donatello, but Di Paolo made some intriguing changes to the scene, which I think can be explained in view of his larger programme. As noted earlier, the panel with the presentation of John's head clearly matches the one with the request for his head by Salome. Not only is the latter placed on top of the former, but the setting of both scenes and the main characters are also identical. The presence of Salome in both scenes points to the pivotal role she played in turning a feast into a tragedy.

However, we should also take into account that the scene with John before Herod is placed on top of the two banquet scenes. As a result, a certain pattern emerges. In all three cases Herod is positioned at the extreme left end of the painting and in all three a woman appears: Herodias in the first and her daughter in the second and third. The women are visibly linked with each other through the olive green colour of their clothes and the blue ribbon in their hair.

When taking into consideration the images on the baptismal font, we now see how Di Paolo intensifies the scenes in question by making John and Salome face Herod instead of looking away, as is the case in Donatello's and Ghiberti's reliefs, and that he redistributed the elements of Donatello's and Ghiberti's representations over three scenes by reduplicating the banquet scene in order to include the request of the daughter for the head of John. He also changed the dynamic of Donatello's representation by leaving out Herodias and giving her daughter a more active role in asking for the Baptist's head. As a result a clear connection is established between the role of the mother and her daughter, as they both play an instrumental role in the tragic fate of John the Baptist.

Conclusion

In my view, the concepts introduced in the first part of this article generate the following insights with respect to Di Paolo's paintings of John's tragic end. Notwithstanding its limited character, Culler's notion of intertextuality makes it possible to see how particular representations, such as the Baptist before Herod and the presentation of his head to Herod, are creations that emerge from the intertextual space of the biblical texts. Bal's idea of 'visual textuality' and 'preposterous history' in turn help to see the dynamic process at work in and between texts and images. Textual elements such as the dancing girl, the presentation of John's head, and the grieving Herod, for instance, are reconfigured in Di Paolo's work for dramatic effect. Moreover, these representations in turn change our preposterous readings of the biblical texts. Finally, Deleuze and Guattari's concept of the rhizome offers a particular framework for the interactive search for meaning that is never closed, but always open for revision and expansion in different directions. As rhizomatic system par excellence, the Internet enhances one's awareness of the multiple directions in which such a search can set off. It also makes one realize that a linear approach of the relation between texts and images does not do justice to the complex interaction of the two. As we have seen, Di Paolo's work is informed by much more than the biblical texts. It relates to an iconographic tradition, without simply reproducing it. Moreover, his work is just one entry point into time and space that allows us to explore the cultural impact of the figure of John the Baptist, whose story as we discovered, features on frescoes and paintings in churches and baptisteries devoted to John, who was also the patron saint of Florence, and whose name was given to numerous children, including Giovanni di Paolo himself. In this essay I have only been scratching the surface of just one particular fascinating moment in history, but I hope it triggers a search for more.

What Can a Text Do? Reception History as an Ethology of the Biblical Text

Brennan Breed
Columbia Theological Seminary

Introduction: A new generative metaphor

Biblical reception history initiates a perspective shift in biblical scholarship. It offers new and compelling points of view on the nature of biblical texts, the function of contexts, and the concept of meaning. Yet it is difficult to conceive of that which is truly new; the same conventions that help us understand the world as intelligible hinder us from seeing it in a different way. Within the discipline of biblical studies, scholars frequently rely upon a series of iconic narratives and generative metaphors that subtly inform perceptions of source material, practices and goals. As Carol Newsom argues, 'Iconic narratives encode fundamental commitments. . . . These narratives make meaningful – and therefore possible – certain forms of action. . . . they define the horizon of meaningful action within an already given social and moral world'.[1]

When discussing how texts relate to historical contexts, for example, biblical critics often employ metaphors, such as *anchorage*. John Barton explains: 'In reading a text, one needs a sense of its anchorage in a particular period'.[2] And Ehud Ben Zvi, when choosing between potential meanings of a word in Zephaniah, argues that 'those proposals anchored in clearly attested biblical meanings... should be preferred', which implies that some meanings are anchored while others are not.[3] Thus alongside the metaphor of the anchor one often finds the iconic narrative of the unmoored ship that drifts to sea. As John Barton warns, some readers 'detach the Bible from its historical moorings and allow it to float freely in

---

[1] Carol Newsom, *The Book of Job: A Contest of Moral Imaginations* (Oxford: Oxford University Press, 2003), p. 122. Likewise, 'Generative metaphors..."map" situations so that certain decisions or courses of action appear to be the most proper or logical'. Newsom, *Book of Job*, p. 33.
[2] John Barton, *The Nature of Biblical Criticism* (Louisville, KY: Westminster John Knox, 2007), p. 187.
[3] Ehud Ben Zvi, *A Historical-critical Study of the Book of Zephaniah* (BZAW 198; Berlin: Walter de Gruyter, 1991), p. 142.

a timeless realm, thereby making it unable to exist "back there", at the beginning of the tradition, and so witness to the tradition's roots'.[4] The image and narrative of the anchor imply a task for the biblical scholar: put the text back into its true context.

If we are to think in different ways, we must critique current images of thought and conceive of new ones to take their place. Several metaphors have helped me to conceptualize the disruptive potential of reception history. Gilles Deleuze at times fruitfully compared his project to the field of *ethology*, and in this essay I will seek to re-think biblical reception history in these terms.[5] Ethology can be defined as the observation and classification of animal behaviour which emphasizes the range of a species' potential action. It is not interested in the genetic essence of a species, and it does not judge a species' present behaviour with regard to how it has historically behaved. On the contrary, ethology seeks to understand animals by means of *what they actually do*. I will offer examples of an ethological approach to analysing the production and reception history of the book of Daniel, especially chapter 7.

Morality and etiology: Generative metaphors for biblical criticism

Throughout most of the history of modern biblical criticism, biblical scholars have been trying to: (1) discern the proper identity of the original text; and (2) discover the meaning those original texts would have held in their contexts of production. The former task, that of textual criticism, generally produces a *moralizing* discourse that seeks to categorize manuscripts based on their imitation of an ideal, pristine example. Those who do not imitate the ideal are corrupt.[6] The latter task, that of 'higher criticism', generally produces an *etiological* discourse that locates the proper meaning of a text in its context of origin or authorization.[7] The original text and moment of origin have been lost, and must now be found and reunited. This is an iconic narrative of restoration.

---

[4] John Barton, *People of the Book?: The Authority of the Bible in Christianity* (Louisville: Westminster John Knox, 1989), 41. Note also the nautically-themed 'historical moorings' in Barton, *The Nature of Biblical Criticism*, p. 80.

[5] See Gilles Deleuze, *Spinoza: Practical Philosophy* (trans. Robert Hurley; San Francisco: City Light Books, 1988), pp. 17-29, and Gilles Deleuze, *Expressionism in Philosophy: Spinoza* (trans. M. Joughin; Cambridge, MA: MIT, 1990), p. 226.

[6] For example, see Emanuel Tov, *Textual Criticism of the Hebrew Bible* (2nd rev. edn; Minneapolis: Fortress, 2001), p. 177, and P. Kyle McCarter, Jr., *Textual Criticism: Recovering the Text of the Hebrew Bible* (Minneapolis: Fortress Press, 1986), p. 12.

[7] For example, Michael Fox claims that his 'main concern in approaching a text is... to ascertain the meaning of the text, which is to say, the authorial intention'. Michael V. Fox, 'Job 38 and God's Rhetoric', *Semeia* 19 (1981): p. 53.

Yet reception history puts pressure on the constitutive goal of textual criticism – namely, the concept of the 'original' or the 'best' text. Biblical scholars have long known that the matter of textual criticism is complex, but in recent years several textual critics have begun to question the assumption that there ever was an original text.[8] Due to discoveries in the Judaean desert, we now know that several biblical books existed in multiple, irreducible versions in antiquity, and that some textual differences presumed to be later corruptions or recensions are in fact alternative ancient versions, often composed in the 'original' Hebrew.[9] Textual critics are now shifting ever closer to the position that the Bible did not originate from pristine manuscripts, and neither was there one consistent line of authorship or editing that culminated in the communal authorization of a final, authoritative manuscript.[10] Reception historians are in a position to ask some difficult questions about this originary complexity, because if it is true that we study forms of texts and meanings in 'later' periods, then we must ascertain where the boundary lies between the original period and what we should be studying. Upon inspection, it appears that the history of a biblical text is a long process that often has indistinct beginnings, discontinuities and irreducibly different versions of the same text. What is the history of the text, then, but a form of reception history?

Yet if it is 'reception all the way down', what do reception historians offer as a cognitive model for their task that would differ from the typical understandings of biblical criticism? At times reception historians have understood their work as a replication of traditional biblical criticism merely with a different set of texts and contexts – the 'later' ones as opposed to the 'original' ones. One can see this in the common division between the original text/meaning and its reception, as if the two fell neatly into two parts that can be studied separately. For example, according to its series preface, the reception-focused Blackwell Bible Commentary series 'is based upon the premise that how people have interpreted, and been influenced by, a sacred text like the Bible is often as interesting and historically important as what it originally meant.'[11]

---

[8] See Eugene Ulrich, *The Dead Sea Scrolls and the Origins of the Bible* (Grand Rapids, MI: Eerdmans, 1999), pp. 17–33; James E. Bowley and John C. Reeves, 'Rethinking the Concept of "Bible": Some Theses and Proposals', *Henoch* 25 (2003): pp. 3–18.

[9] See Ulrich, *Dead Sea Scrolls*, pp. 34–50, 79–120. In the field of New Testament studies, E .J. Epp critiques the term 'Original Text' but calls for a 'tolerance and acceptance of this very ambiguity' of the term, though keeping the 'earliest attainable text' as the goal of text criticism alongside the description and contextualization of variants; see E. J. Epp, 'It's All About Variants: A Variant-Conscious Approach to New Testament Textual Criticism', *HTR* 100 (2007): p. 287. D. C. Parker pushes further, arguing on the basis of the varying forms of the Lord's Prayer that textual critics must analyze and accept the validity of the whole scope of the 'manuscript continuum'. See D. C. Parker, *The Living Text of the Gospels* (Cambridge: Cambridge University Press, 1997), p. 93

[10] See Gary Martin, *Multiple Originals: New Approaches to Hebrew Bible Textual Criticism* (Atlanta: Society of Biblical Literature, 2010); this is even felt in the field of Septuagintal studies, as seen in Hans Debel, 'Greek "Variant Literary Editions" to the Hebrew Bible?', *JSJ* 41 (2010): pp. 161–90.

[11] Series preface as found in David M. Gunn, *Judges Through the Centuries* (Blackwell Bible Commentaries; Malden, MA: Blackwell, 2005), iv.

And when studying a particular biblical reception, biblical scholars often place the image, music, sermon, or other artifact in its context of production in order to analyse it. For example, Ismo Dunderberg orients the fascinating essay 'Gnostic Interpretations of Genesis' with a discussion of the diversity of second-century CE Judaism and Christianity, as well as the biographical details and general teachings of related individuals such as Valentinus.[12] Through contextualizing these receptions of Genesis in the contexts of their production, we can more clearly understand the communities and individuals associated with the term 'Gnostic'. This is, of course, an extremely helpful exercise, and it often yields very interesting conclusions. But after the contextualization of several artifacts of biblical reception, how should one attempt to understand the larger picture? How can they be compared? What does this tell us about the text itself?

Reception historians often collect texts and meanings in order to perform many of the same moralizing and etiological operations performed by biblical criticism: find interpretations of texts, put them in *their* contexts, and explain *their* original meanings. This is not a terrible thing in itself, but perhaps there are better ways to understand reception history. And perhaps a better way to understand reception history can help us better understand biblical criticism.

Ethology: What can a text do?

My suggestion is that reception historians might helpfully re-conceive of their task in terms of *ethology*. In general, ethology is the study of an animal's behaviour as it relates to a habitat.[13] Ethologists observe how a particular thing acts and how it interacts with its environment(s). Yet there are other potential meanings of the term: John Stuart Mill used the phrase to describe his study of human character as it relates to psychology, and others have meant by it the study of ethics.[14] These meanings are all related, however, as ethics and human psychology also study aspects of human behaviour as situated in a particular environment. For his own purposes, Gilles Deleuze focuses on these overlapping concerns with *action*, as it shifts attention away from transcendent concepts such as nature or essence. In ethological terms, a thing is defined by what it does – or what it *can do* – not by what it should be, or by what it used to look like.

---

[12] Ismo Dunderberg, 'Gnostic Interpretations of Genesis' in *The Oxford Handbook of the Reception History of the Bible* (eds M. Lieb, E. Mason, J. Roberts; Oxford: Oxford University Press, 2011), pp. 383–96.
[13] See P. Lehner, *Handbook of Ethological Methods* (2nd. edn; Cambridge: Cambridge University Press, 1996), pp. 1–16.
[14] On the development of these various meanings, see John Durant, 'Innate Character in Animals and Man: A Perspective on the Origins of Ethology', in *Biology, Medicine and Society 1840–1940* (ed. C. Webster; Cambridge: Cambridge University Press, 1981), p. 160.

As an example of ethological thought, Deleuze offers the biosemiotician Jakob von Uexküll, a forerunner of modern ethology. Uexküll famously describes a tick not by its shape, or its evolutionary origin, or its pattern of DNA, but rather by its *capacities* to find overhanging spaces, to detect the smell of butyric acid, to fall towards heat, and to find hairless spots and bite.[15] The tick is defined by its particular configuration of powers, which are precisely the things that contribute to its survival within its environment.

Gilles Deleuze pushes this concept further by reading Uexküll's ethology through Spinoza's *Ethics*, which urges us to conceive of the world not in static essences, but in terms of dynamic powers, capacities, and potential activities.[16] Deleuze appreciates Spinoza's rebellion against Aristotle's essentialist definition of the human as a 'thinking being' because humans have the capacity to be unthinking as well as thinking. Aristotle's essentialist classification of humans is *moralistic*, as it defines people by what they should, ideally, be doing – rather than what they actually do. In response, Spinoza suggests an ethological definition of the human by asking, 'Of what is a human being capable? What can a human being do?'[17] According to Deleuze, the answer to this question may be found only through repeated experimentation and observation in a variety of distinct contexts.[18] Human beings can do many different things, and moreover the boundaries of human capacities are always in a constant state of flux. People gain and lose capacities over time, and so the definition of 'a human' is also a process of change over time. Ethology asks us to think of things as dynamic processes, not static products.

Deleuze's concept of ethology can also be compared to *etiology*, or the search for a thing's proper origin or cause. In the field of medicine, as Deleuze notes, one may distinguish between symptomatology, the study of the signs exhibited by a particular patient, and etiology, the search for the cause of the symptoms.[19] When a doctor takes careful note of the symptoms of a particular patient, that doctor is noting the effects, or powers, of the illness as it manifests itself in the body of the patient. Symptomatology is thus a sort of ethology, or an observation of the disease's powers within a particular environment.

Biblical scholars are familiar with etiology in a different, but related, sense: namely, stories that purport to narrate the causes and origin of a phenomenon. Some biblical scholars, for example, argue that the book of Esther originated as an origin-story for Purim.[20] Thus, Purim would be somehow explained by its causes

---

[15] Jakob von Uexküll, *A Foray into the Worlds of Animals and Humans: With a Theory of Meaning* (trans. J. O'Neil; Minneapolis: University of Minnesota Press, 2010), pp. 44–53; Deleuze, *Spinoza*, pp. 124–5.
[16] Deleuze, *Spinoza*, 125.
[17] Deleuze, *Expressionism in Philosophy*, p. 226.
[18] Deleuze, *Spinoza*, p. 127.
[19] See Gilles Deleuze, *Desert Islands and Other Texts 1953–1974* (trans. M. Taormina; New York: Semiotext(e), 2004), pp. 133–4.
[20] See Jona Schellekens, 'Accession Days and Holidays: The Origins of the Jewish Festival of Purim', *JBL* 128 (2009): p. 132.

within its moment of historical origin. The problem is that, from detailed text critical studies focusing on the immanent signs of the variant versions of Esther, Carey A. Moore discerned that the Greek Alpha Text of Esther preserved an earlier *Vorlage* that lacked the etiology of Purim.[21] By taking into consideration the presumed 'later' versions of the text, Moore found that the etiology was itself a later addition. Etiologies, it seems, do not always explain the origin. They may also function as retro-jections designed to give a sense of unity and meaning to something that was always-already complex.[22]

Ethology displaces the etiological fascination with origin. It pushes the scholar instead to look at all exemplars of a species in order to chart their particular powers and capacities. Reception history, like ethology, is interested in observing the actual activities and capacities of things as they occur 'in the wild' in all of its diverse processual forms and activities.

Processes generally produce divergence, as we can see in the ongoing process of the development of life on earth.[23] For example, consider the identity of a particular species of mammal such as the domestic dog. There are vast differences between different breeds of dogs, and also differences between individuals of each breed. Moreover, each breed has changed throughout time, and each breed will continue to change in the future. The identity of the species 'domestic dog' is not expressed more truly or fully or pristinely in any particular breed or any specific domestic dog. Neither is the species 'dog' heading towards a perfect *telos* that will finally reveal the true essence of dog-hood. A species is not a static thing whose particular exemplars are judged moralistically according to their degree of deviation from a transcendental model.[24] A species is instead a complex process, an open-ended population, and as such its identity is comprised of the full and irreducible variety of actual dogs.

Likewise, an ethological perspective would define biblical texts by what they actually have looked like in all their variants and translations, by what they have actually done, and by what they are capable of doing in the future, rather than defining them according to an ideal version of what they *should* have done and looked like at one point in their trajectories. If reception historians understand the biblical text as a set of related processes, then we must accept divergence as a normal state of affairs.[25] Whereas biblical criticism tends to think in terms of

---

[21] C. A. Moore, 'A Greek Witness to a Different Text of Esther', ZAW 79 (1967): pp. 351–8.

[22] This does not mean, however, that etiologies are lesser simply because they are later! But it does mean that they cannot explain the text without remainder.

[23] For a discussion of the structure of processes and the importance of divergence, see Manuel DeLanda, *Intensive Science and Virtual Philosophy* (New York: Continuum, 2002), pp. 9–39, especially p. 21.

[24] See DeLanda, *Intensive Science*, pp. 58–62.

[25] For example, an ethological perspective would eschew attempts to characterize the textual history of the Bible with tropes of degradation ('corrupt' versus 'pristine' texts), marginalization ('secondary' texts and readings), pathology and perversion ('deviant' versus 'corrected' texts, or textual 'integrity'). The moral hierarchy of textual criticism is based on an assumption that there is, in the long history of textual production and transmission, a singular moment of purity. Ethology simply accepts deviation and difference as a natural course of affairs, and presumes no universal hierarchy of forms.

morality, asking, 'What text is the best text, and what should one do with it?' or in terms of an *etiology*, asking, 'What did it originally look like, and what did it originally mean?', from the point of view of reception history, biblical scholars can think in terms of *ethology* – that is, 'What can a biblical text do?'

Ethology, context and meaning

Ethology does not merely challenge our ontology of biblical texts. It can also inform a new conception of context, especially as it relates to the problem of textual meaning. From an ethological perspective, contexts and meanings are examples of what Deleuze has called 'problematic fields'.[26] Whereas a simple problem requires one to find a pre-existent correct solution in order to extinguish the question, a problematic field is an open-ended question that allows for many different solutions, so long as they meet the criteria required. As a result, problematic fields cannot be extinguished, and there can be no definitive solution for them.[27] Every possible solution of a problematic field leaves a remainder.

Consider the problematic field of the desert environment of the southwestern United States. Living things successfully inhabit the harsh terrain of the desert, and there are many different kinds of plants and animals that have evolved to thrive in those environments. These different desert-dwelling species face a similar environmental structure that poses similar challenges to all potential inhabitants, including a general lack of water with occasional flash floods, great variations in temperature, a dearth of places to hide from predators, and sandy or rocky soil. We might call this particular assortment of environmental parameters the *structure of the problematic field* that is posed to each desert inhabitant.

The parameters of a given problematic field are certainly real and important, but they are not equally important to all inhabitants. Some inhabitants might construe the temperature variation of the desert as the most crucial element to survival, and other inhabitants might not need to factor temperature variation into their survival strategies. Some species might develop strategies to survive in an environment with little coverage from predators, while this factor might not influence the adaptation of other species. In other words, every specie must construe the problematic field in different ways based on their own particular structure, and as such no construal of the desert is universally applicable. Every construal of a context is contingent, and thus there are bound to be multiple irreducibly different but nevertheless equally valid constraints of any given context.

[26] See Gilles Deleuze, *Difference and Repetition* (trans. Paul Patton; New York: Columbia University Press, 1995), pp. 163–87.
[27] See Deleuze's remarks on the various types of eyes as solutions to the light 'problem', *Difference and Repetition*, p. 211.

Neither are these answers stable over time: they are all provisional and open to change. If the structure of the environment shifts, then the various inhabitant species will face a new constellation of their problematic field, and some will continue to thrive while others will cease being viable solutions in this new context – and so they will vanish from the environment. Likewise, if one transplants an animal from a very different environment, sometimes it will not be able to survive. Yet other species may flourish in that other environment. In the process of transitioning between different environments, an animal may demonstrate capacities that were not evident in its previous environment.

Reception historians can put the concept of *problematic field* to good use within biblical studies. If we conceive of contexts as problematic fields, then a given historical context provides a basic raw structure within which the biblical text can thrive in many divergent and conflicting ways – and there are some things it cannot or will not do in that given context.

The material form of the text, which changes over time, may shift the coordinates of the problematic field and create new potentials. For example, when Augustine hears 'take up and read' (*tolle, lege*), he opens a codex and reads whatever text he happens to see. Augustine then marks the passage with his finger and takes it to his friend, which 'emphasizes the indexical nature of the codex, the way it lends itself to random access and discontinuous reading'.[28] This form of random, and thus mystical and devotional, reading is not entirely compatible with the technology of the scroll. The codex allows for new relations between the reader and the text.

In a similar manner, linguistic shifts can change the semantic potentials of the text. When medieval Latin Christians read of the fruit of the tree of the knowledge of good and evil they often thought of an apple, likely because the Latin word for 'apple' (*mālum*) and 'evil' (*mălum*) are homonyms. This wordplay would not make sense in Hebrew or Greek.

Changes in historical context can also retroactively change the potentials of the text. Several biblical texts, for example, thematize the semantic transformations that the Zion songs undergo after Jerusalem's destruction (cf. Ps 137:3; Lam 2:15). And the problematic field of the Zion songs shifted after the victories of the Hasmoneans, and then changed yet again after the destruction of Jerusalem in 70 CE. But how in particular did they change? This is a job for reception historians, who can trace how the potential capacities of particular biblical texts change through time and space in response to surrounding environments.

---

[28] James Kearney, *The Incarnate Text: Imagining the Book in Reformation England* (Philadelphia: University of Pennsylvania Press, 2009), p. 148.

Ethology and the text of Daniel 7

From a moralistic perspective, one might say that biblical texts tend towards corruption over time: as they are copied, their form deviates from what it *should* be. But from an ethological perspective, one can say that biblical texts simply occur in multiple forms throughout history. That is, they have the capacity to develop different appearances. A particular biblical book can appear simultaneously in multiple, irreducible forms.

The book of Daniel, for example, existed in multiple forms even in the Second Temple Period even as it was in the process of being produced. Ethology thus offers the possibility of studying the book of Daniel as a process in motion. One can analyse the activities of any of the forms available at any of these times, and if one chooses, one can chart the changing capacities of this textual process as it shifts forms and passes through different cultural milieus. Ethology draws no border between 'biblical criticism' and 'reception history', since there never was a time at which the biblical text was ever singular and objectively complete.

From literary analysis, linguistic differences and textual evidence, including the Septuagint (LXX) and *kaige*-Theodotion (θ), it appears that the court stories in chapters 2 to 6 of the book of Daniel circulated independently before the addition of the apocalyptic texts (chapters 7 to 12) and an introductory story (chapter 1).[29] The conflicting versions of chapters 4 to 6 in MT and LXX suggest that *both* versions are secondary, redacted from a now-lost proto-Daniel of uncertain shape and size.[30] To these variant editions of the expanded proto-Daniel, later author-redactors added chapter 7, which is, like most of chapters 2 to 6, written in Aramaic.[31] Other author-redactors at another stage added chapters 8 to 12 and chapter 1, written in an odd, perhaps re-learned, form of biblical Hebrew.[32]

Still later author-redactors added what we now call 'the additions' to LXX, including the Prayer of Azariah, the Song of the Three Jews, Susanna and the Elders, and Bel and the Dragon.[33] Moreover, there is significant variation within each of these forms – that is, the so-called additions to Daniel occur in very different locations in various Greek manuscripts that include them.[34] Even after

---

[29] R. Timothy McLay, 'The Old Greek Translation of Daniel iv–vi and the Formation of the Book of Daniel', *VT* 55 (2005): pp. 318–22. See also John J. Collins, *Daniel: A Commentary on the Book of Daniel* (Hermeneia; Minneapolis: Fortress Press, 1993), pp. 10–11.

[30] Eugene Ulrich, 'The Text of Daniel in the Qumran Scrolls', in *The Book of Daniel: Composition and Reception, vol. 2* (ed. J. Collins and P. Flint; VTSup 83; Leiden: Brill, 2001), p. 582.

[31] See A. van Woude, 'Die Dopplesprachigkeit des Buches Daniel', in *The Book of Daniel in the Light of New Findings* (ed. A. van der Woude; Leuven: Leuven University Press, 1993), pp. 3–12.

[32] For an overview of the various theories of the composition of Daniel, see R. Kratz, 'Reich Gottes und Gesetz im Danielbuch und im werdenden Judentum', in *The Book of Daniel in the Light of New Findings*, pp. 435–79. See also J. Miller, 'The Redaction of Daniel', *JSOT* 52 (1991): pp. 115–24.

[33] See Ulrich, 'The Text of Daniel', p. 582.

[34] See John J. Collins, *Daniel: A Commentary on the Book of Daniel* (Hermeneia; Minneapolis: Fortress Press, 1993), pp. 10–11.

the supposed period of textual stabilization in late antiquity – what some scholars have called the 'Great Divide' – the variant editions, such as LXX and MT, continued to coexist along with their manifold variants.[35] Thus, the entire history of the book of Daniel in the Second Temple Period is one of ongoing transformation and pluriformity. The book of Daniel *is* a pluriform process, not a static object.

Like the rest of the book, the text of Daniel 7 exhibits many differences between LXX, MT, θ and Syriac Peshitta (S) forms.[36] Daniel 7 is a pivotal chapter in which the book shifts from third-person court stories concerning Daniel and his companions to first-person apocalyptic visions that continue until the end of the book. Chapter 7 begins with Daniel relating an account of a vision of four beasts that emerge sequentially from the primordial sea (Dan 7:1–7). Daniel then focuses on one horn of the fourth beast as a meeting of the divine council commences (7:8–10). After the divine 'Ancient of Days' destroys the fourth beast, one 'like a human being' emerges from heaven to rule the world (7:11–14). A divine being then explains that the four beasts are kingdoms, and that the 'holy ones' will possess a final kingdom after being attacked by the 'little horn' (7:11–28).

Some of the textual differences within Daniel 7 have greatly impacted the history of this text's reception, yet have received little attention from biblical scholars because they occurred so 'late' in its textual history.[37] Since later textual differences cannot help to reconstruct the putative original text, they are ignored. Yet these variants can be very powerful.[38]

Interpreters within the Syriac Christian tradition, for example, tend to interpret Daniel 7 in a distinctive manner. Whereas most readers in late antiquity identified the fourth beast-kingdom as Rome, Syriac Christians generally understand it to refer to the Hellenistic empires that derive from the conquests of Alexander the Great.[39] Some scholars assume that this interpretation derives from the writings of Neoplatonic philosopher, noted critic of Christianity and talented philologist Porphyry.[40] Yet in the Syriac Peshitta, the text of Daniel 7:8 includes the name 'Antiochus' to describe the 'little horn'. This likely signifies Antiochus IV, who was notorious for persecuting Palestinian Jews in 167 BCE.[41] Furthermore, in the Syriac Peshitta Daniel 7–8 includes superscriptions that enumerate the four

---

[35] See Shemaryahu Talmon, 'Textual Criticism: The Ancient Versions', in *Text in Context: Essays By Members of the Society for Old Testament Study* (ed. A. D. H. Mayes; Oxford: Oxford University Press, 2000), p. 147.

[36] See the differences noted in Collins, *Daniel*, pp. 274–6.

[37] OG/LXX Daniel, among other books, is beginning to receive more scholarly notice in recent years. See A. Di Leila, 'The Textual History of Septuagint-Daniel and Theodotion-Daniel', in *The Book of Daniel: Composition and Reception*, pp. 586–607.

[38] For example, perhaps OG/LXX has a different Semitic *Vorlage* for chapter 7. See Johan Lust, 'Daniel 7:13 and the Septuagint', *ETL* 54 (1978): 66.

[39] See H. H. Rowley, *Darius the Mede and the Four World Empires in the Book of Daniel: A Historical Study of Contemporary Theories* (Cardiff: University of Wales Press, 1935), pp. 70–85.

[40] See M. Casey, 'Porphyry and the Book of Daniel', *JThSt* 27 (1976), 15–33.

[41] Collins, *Daniel*, p. 275.

kingdoms – it names the Babylonians, Medes, Persians, and lastly the Greeks.[42] It is no wonder, then, why Syriac interpreters were nearly unanimous about the identity of the fourth empire! Many biblical scholars would overlook this significant fact simply because the Peshitta is generally assumed to be a late version, and thus for the most part unimportant for research. But over the years it served as the text for many people, and it continues to serve as the text for some communities today. Thus from the perspective of ethology, minor differences between textual versions, even later additions of marginal worth for textual criticism, are integral to the 'text itself' and worthy of study. Since the book of Daniel exists in a plurality of forms, none of them constitute a universally valid starting point for research. They are simply different answers to different questions.

Ethology and the meaning of Daniel 7

From an etiological perspective, one might argue that the correct meaning of Daniel 7 is anchored in its original context, and it must be read within those constraints. But from an ethological perspective, one can see that this text has exhibited various capacities through its production of many different meanings over time.

Even within its initial context of production, the meaning of this text was complex. To begin, it seems very likely that the text went through stages of redaction. Chapter 7 is written in Aramaic, like most of chapters 2 to 6, and unlike chapters 1 and 8 to 12. Like chapters 8 to 12, Daniel 7 is apocalyptic literature, not a 'court tale' as found in chapters 1 to 6. Yet Daniel 7 is quite unlike the other apocalypses in chapters 8 to 12 because it seems uninterested in the problems in the Jerusalem temple. Instead its concerns seem very closely related to the diasporic elements in chapters 2 to 6, which also focus on divine sovereignty over the course of world history, and especially the question of a kingdom of the righteous.[43] It is quite possible that Daniel 7 was written to be an adaptation of Daniel 2 for a new generation of diasporic Jews, as the basic structure of Daniel 7 recapitulates a four-kingdom schema that is also found in Daniel 2.[44] Later redactors edited the text to reflect the events of 167 BCE, altering the figure of the 'little horn' to symbolize the cosmic evil embodied in Antiochus IV.[45] Whether or not this particular reconstruction of events is accurate, it seems clear that the text of Daniel 7 had meant at least several different things – and had taken several different forms – before any currently existing version was produced.

---

[42] See R. Taylor, *The Peshiṭta of Daniel*, (Leiden: Brill, 1994), p. 324
[43] See C. L. Seow, *Daniel* (Louisville: Westminster John Knox, 2003), p. 8.
[44] See G. Hasel, 'The Four World Empires of Daniel Against Its Near Eastern Environment', *JSOT* 12 (1979): pp. 17–30.
[45] See A. E. Gardner, 'The "Little Horn" of Dan 7:8: Malevolent or Benign?', *Biblica* 93 (2012): pp. 209–22.

Thus the putative 'original' meaning of Daniel 7 was always-already a redeployment of earlier symbolic patterns – and, perhaps surprisingly, even Daniel 2 is an adaptation of an earlier series of three-and-four-kingdom schemas. Though the exact trajectory of transmission is unclear, it appears that Persians developed a three-kingdom periodization of world history in order to legitimate the Persian Empire as the natural successor to Assyria and Babylonia and the culmination of a long process.[46] It is likely that later Greek authors, who were aware of the trope even in the time of Herodotus, added Macedonia or its later Hellenistic empires as a fourth kingdom in order to extend the schema and its legitimacy.[47] Roman historians then added their own empire as a fifth kingdom, reading themselves into the text to understand and promote their own role in the world.[48] Yet this schema was not only used to legitimate empires: it seems that a similar periodization, preserved and updated in the Jewish fourth Sibylline oracle, criticized the Seleucid Empire's culmination of the multiple-kingdom schema as a time of wickedness.[49] It is possible that this form of textual resistance informed Daniel 7's adaptation of the more benign form of the four-kingdom periodization found in Daniel 2.[50]

The author-redactors of Daniel 7 produced this text in order to participate in a long tradition of contemporary reapplications of a traditional multiple-kingdom schema. In other words, even the 'original meaning' of Daniel 7 involves reading motifs and texts out of their original contexts. Structurally, then, the readers and interpretive communities throughout history who have sought to reapply this text to their own context – such as medieval millenialists and modern dispensationalists – participate in the same formal activity that the author-redactors of Daniel used to produce it. Likewise, those biblical critics who locate this text within its putative original context perform a quite different task than the 'original' author-redactors, though they may replicate the same content of the Second Temple author-redactors of Daniel 7. To read Daniel 7 in its context, should one reapply a historical schema to the contemporary world in order to understand one's place in world history? Many readers throughout history have taken this interpretive route, including readers as diverse as Abraham Ibn Ezra and the English Fifth Monarchists.[51] Or should one say that it speaks of Antiochus IV? This is not, as one may assume, merely the conclusion of modern biblical critics: as early as 270 CE, Porphyry offered a very plausible historical-critical reading of Daniel 7, arguing that a

---

[46] Herodotus and Ctesias mention the Persian three-kingdom sequence; see D. Flusser, 'The Four Empires in the Fourth Sibyl and in the Book of Daniel', *Israel Oriental Studies* 2 (1972): p. 154.
[47] Joseph Ward Swain, 'The Theory of the Four Monarchies: Opposition History under the Roman Empire', *Classical Philology* 35 (1940): pp. 7–8.
[48] Swain, 'Theory of the Four Monarchies', p. 2.
[49] Flusser, 'The Four Empires', p. 173.
[50] Flusser, 'The Four Empires', pp. 173–5.
[51] On Ibn Ezra, see H. H. Rowley, *Darius the Mede and the Four World Empires in the Book of Daniel: A Historical Study of Contemporary Theories* (Cardiff: University of Wales Press, 1935), pp. 80–81. On Fifth Monarchists, see B. S. Capp, *The Fifth Monarchy Men: A Study in Seventeenth-Century English Millenarianism* (London: Faber and Faber, 1972).

Palestinian Jew wrote Daniel in 165 BCE.[52] Yet perhaps we do not have to choose between these options. From an ethological perspective both are equally plausible alternatives because the text manifests the capacity to produce both sets of meanings.

Ethological narratives

If one seeks to analyse how a text moves through time – which not all reception historians do – then one must deal with the massive problem of organization and selection. What does one include in a reception historical study? And how does one present the data?

It is important to note that ethologists categorize by *behaviour*, not by genetics, religious affiliation, or location of origin. So instead of grouping readings by general time period into 'medieval' readings and 'modern' readings, or using vast categories such as 'Jewish interpretation', perhaps it would be more fruitful to try to notice similarities in the effect that various readings produce, and then to build narratives out of those sets of readings. Perhaps we should put the emphasis on what texts do; in this way, the text would be the protagonist in this story of its changing capacities.

For example, the overwhelming majority of interpreters of Daniel 7 have understood the fourth kingdom to signify Rome.[53] Yet despite this agreement, not all of these interpretations behave in the same way. For some interpreters, the designation 'Rome' signified the hope that oppressed people might witness divine judgement of their oppressors. The book of 4 Ezra, a pseudepigraphical Jewish apocalypse composed soon after the destruction of the Jerusalem Temple in 70 CE, depicts Rome as an eagle with twelve wings. It explicitly links the eagle to the fourth beast 'in the vision of your brother Daniel' (12:11). As in Daniel 7, God destroys the oppressive kingdom and restores the faithful.[54] Likewise, in the early Christian apocalyptic book of Revelation, John of Patmos redeploys images from throughout Daniel 7 to fashion a new image of the Beast from the sea, symbolizing oppressive Rome (13:1–10). Early Jewish and Christian interpreters generally agreed on this identification, since Rome was problematic for both communities.[55]

---

[52] See John Granger Cook, *The Interpretation of the Old Testament in Greco-Roman Paganism* (Tübingen: Mohr Siebeck, 2004), pp. 187–246.

[53] See Rowley, *Darius the Mede*, pp. 70–91. For a history of Daniel's political use from late antiquity to early modernity, see Klaus Koch, *Europa, Rom und der Kaiser vor dem Hintergrund von zwei Jahrtausenden Rezeption des Buches Daniel* (Göttingen: Vandenhoeck & Ruprecht, 1997).

[54] See Karina Martin Hogan, *Theologies in Conflict in 4 Ezra: Wisdom, Debate, and Apocalyptic Solution* (Leiden: Brill, 2008), pp. 160, 179–85.

[55] See the midrash in *Lev. Rab.* 13:5 and R. Johanan's comments in the Talmud, especially *b. Seb.* 20 and *b. Abod. Zar.* 2b; Also see Irenaeus, *Against Heretics* 5:26 and Hippolytus of Rome, *Commentary on Daniel* 4:5–8.

And for many readers throughout history, the fourth kingdom symbolized their Rome-like oppressors. This includes late antique Jewish Talmudic interpreters (*b. Seb.* 20; *b. Abod. Zar.* 2b), medieval midrashists,[56] early modern Jewish chroniclers,[57] twentieth-century Korean Christians resisting Japanese imperial rule,[58] and recent Nicaraguans resisting the political and military influence of the United States.[59] Thus, one of Daniel 7's capacities is its ability to offer hope for a new political order, whether by revolution or divine intervention.

Yet for other interpreters, the fourth beast's signification of Rome served to justify empire. Careful readers notice that Daniel 1–6 evinces a strong desire for God to convert the foreign monarch, not destroy him (cf. Dan 2:47; 3:29; 4:34–37; 6:26). If readers understand Daniel 7 through the lens of Daniel 1–6 (and perhaps more importantly, if it is politically convenient to do so) then one might understand the fifth kingdom as a conversion of the fourth, not necessarily an eradication. After Constantine's shift to recognizing and privileging Christianity in the Roman Empire, this interpretative potential found ample ground to grow. Eusebius of Caesarea, a noted apologist for Constantine, found exegetical resources in the work of Origen to claim that the fourth kingdom was strong, and perhaps even good.[60] In his third sermon in praise of Constantine and the Holy Sepulchre, Eusebius applied Daniel 7:18 ('the holy ones of the Most High shall receive the kingdom') to the transition of Roman imperial power from Constantine to Constantine's sons.[61] Even after the fall of the Western Roman Empire in the fifth century CE, the belief in the Roman 'fourth monarchy' persisted, and an interpretive struggle ensued to see who might claim continuity with Rome.[62]

This gave rise to the influential medieval concept of *translatio imperii* – the 'transfer of rule' – which continued to shape history in light of Daniel 2 and Daniel 7's four-kingdom schema. For example, Otto Freising, a twelfth-century CE German bishop and chronicler, wrote his chronicle of world history to show that the *translatio imperii* flowed from Rome to Byzantium to the Franks to the Lombards, and then finally the Germans.[63] Otto believed that the Roman Empire would last until the end of the world, and since the world had not ended, then Rome must be continued by other kingdoms. The Byzantine Empire considered

---

[56] See Eliezer Segal, *The Babylonian Esther Midrash: A Critical Commentary, Volume 1: To the End of Esther Chapter 1* (Atlanta: Scholars Press, 1994), p. 144.
[57] See seventeenth-century Egyptian Jewish chronicler Sambari's *Divre Yosef* 77:2–3, cited in Martin Jacobs, 'An Ex-Sabbatean's Remorse? Sambari's Polemics against Islam', *JQR* 97 (2007): p. 356.
[58] See Sangyil Park, *Korean Preaching, Han, and Narrative* (New York: Peter Lang, 2008), p. 22.
[59] See Pablo Richard, 'El pueblo de Dios contra el imperio. Daniel 7 en su contexto literario e histórico', *RIBLA* 7 (1990): pp. 25–46.
[60] See Gerbern S. Oegema, *Early Judaism and Modern Culture: Literature and Theology* (Grand Rapids: Eerdmans, 2011), pp. 162–3.
[61] Oegema, *Early Judaism*, pp. 162–3.
[62] See P. F. Beatrice, 'Pagans and Christians on the Book of Daniel', *StPat* 25 (1993): pp. 34–5.
[63] Otto Freising, *The Two Cities: A Chronicle of Universal History to the Year 1146 A.D.* (trans. C. Mierow; ed. A. Evans, C. Knapp; New York: Columbia University Press, 2002 [1928]), p. 155.

itself contiguous with ancient Rome, but when Constantinople fell in 1453 CE, there was an ideological scramble to claim the Eastern Roman mantle. Nestor Iskander integrated Daniel 2 and 7 into the pseudepigraphical sixteenth-century CE work *Tale of the Taking of Tsargrad*. The work claims that Constantinople had transferred its 'Roman' power to Russia, whose 'Tsars' (*Caesars*) had already begun to interpret an ancient Byzantine legend to predict that they would 'free' Constantinople from Turkish control.[64]

The text of Daniel 7 has exhibited many other capacities and powers, as well. Accusing and validating empires represent only two of them. But perhaps from even this small sample, the potential of an ethological approach to biblical reception history may be evident. Let us discern how readings express powers and capacities of the text. What *can* a text do? Morality and etiology fail us in this endeavour. The task calls for an ethology.

---

[64] See Giovanni Maniscalco Basile, 'Power and Words of Power: Political, Juridical and Religious Vocabulary in Some Ideological Documents in 16th Century Russia', in *Beiträge zur 7. Internationalen Konferenz zur Geschichte des Kiever und des Moskauer Reiches* (Forschungen zur osteuropäischen Geschichte: Historische Veröffentlichungen, Bd. 50; Wiesbaden: Harrassowitz, 1995), pp. 51–79.

8

The End of Biblical Interpretation – the Beginning of Reception History? Reading the Bible in the Spaces of Literature[1]

Samuel Tongue

Introduction

The impetus for this chapter comes from Jacques Berlinerblau's provocative call for the 'end of biblical interpretation' as currently practised and a turn to a secular improvising aesthetic that engages with a fragmentary biblical text. Firstly, I shall offer an overview of some of Berlinerblau's thinking to put this call in context. His ideas about the peculiar intellectual constitution of biblical scholarship on a Bible which is 'a masterpiece of contingencies'[2] leads to his promotion of a secular aesthetic form of interpretation. Placing this move within the wider remit of Timothy Beal's ideas around the 'cultural history of scriptures' enables a deeper analysis of how some of the contentious debates around the legitimacy of so-called 'confessional' or 'non-confessional' biblical interpretation map onto wider questions on religion and secularity. As an example, I shall use a poem by Israeli poet Yehuda Amichai that rewrites the Jacob and the Angel scene from Genesis 32, and ask how far one can necessarily equate the 'aesthetic' with the 'secular' as Berlinerblau contends, or whether such equations become problematic in illuminating ways.

In Philip R. Davies' now classic account of the tensions he perceives in the intellectual make-up of biblical studies (*Whose Bible is it Anyway?* [1995]), some of these approaches to biblical interpretation are so different that they 'imply different definitions of the subject matter, and create two different kinds of discourses on biblical matters, and these discourses are so fundamentally divergent as to require

---

[1] Thanks are due to William John Lyons and Emma England for organizing such provocative and useful discussions around 'reception history', broadly conceived, at the International Society of Biblical Literature Meeting, Universiteit van Amsterdam, 2012. This chapter has benefitted greatly from the ensuing questions and comments and from their guiding editorial hand.
[2] Jacques Berlinerblau, 'The Bible as Literature?,' *Hebrew Studies* 45 (2004): p. 26.

and to imply *separate disciplines*'.³ The approach I am advocating through a more discursive 'cultural history of scriptures', does not attempt to enact another critical separation between religious or secular methods of reading the Bible. Instead, I want to examine how these tensions always inhere within each other and are absolutely key to how biblical studies has imagined its critical project. I will suggest that Berlinerblau's 'end of interpretation' might be a starting point for how 'a cultural history of scriptures' enables us to engage with wider interdisciplinary themes and questions. I will argue that attentiveness to how the terms 'secular', 'religious', 'critical' and 'aesthetic' are deployed puts biblical scholars in a unique position to debate scriptural cultures and contemporary issues around the complex sites of religion in late-modernity.

Biblical scholars: 'Poor birds' in the secular academy

The trajectory of Berlinerblau's work is instructive. In effect, much of his work provides a sociology of biblical studies itself, highlighting many of the foundational elements that are often elided in scholars' own conceptions of what they are doing in their academic work. His progression from initially reconciling himself to the strange 'hybrid ideation' of the religious and the secular/critical (2002) to his later 'heckle mode' (2005), followed by bemoaning religious persuasions as the 'unspeakable in biblical scholarship' (2010), helps place his call for an 'end to interpretation' in context. I shall pick up on a few of the provocative threads in Berlinerblau's thought and examine how the relations between the 'secular', 'religious', 'critical' and 'aesthetic' operate in his thinking.

In his article ' "Poor Bird, Not Knowing Which Way to Fly": Biblical Scholarship's Marginality, Secular Humanism, and the Laudable Occident' (2002), Berlinerblau explores the unique tensions that go to make up the Biblical Studies Guild. On the one hand, critical scholars ought to pursue knowledge 'not by reference to the religious beliefs and the associated interpretive traditions of his or her confessional community but through any number of epistemological frameworks and professional conventions consecrated as legitimate by the secular university'.⁴ On the other hand, and the main source for the contradictions that Berlinerblau sees as inherent to the Guild, the discipline is staffed by 'many professing, or once-professing Christians and Jews'⁵ who 'are studying a body of texts *that is central to these very religious commitments*'.⁶ Able to seemingly move between seminary or

---

³ Philip R. Davies, *Whose Bible Is It Anyway?* (Sheffield: Sheffield Academic Press, 1995), p. 13.
⁴ Jacques Berlinerblau, ' "Poor Bird, Not Knowing Which Way to Fly": Biblical Scholarship's Marginality, Secular Humanism, and the Laudable Occident,' *Biblical Interpretation* 10, no. 3 (2002): p. 280.
⁵ Berlinerblau, 'Poor Bird', p. 279.
⁶ Berlinerblau, 'Poor Bird', p. 279. Emphasis in text.

yeshiva and university department with ease, Berlinerblau contends that if 'we define a secular scholar as one who never had strong religious commitments, or who leaves them totally unexamined, or who rejected them from a very young age, then there are almost no secular biblical scholars'.[7]

Of course, these tensions have a long pedigree. The Higher Criticism of, for example, a Julius Wellhausen or a William Robertson Smith attempted to combine the fruits of critical research with religious conviction. In this sense, according to Berlinerblau 'the field of biblical research is still constituted so that the distinctions radical/conservative, orthodoxy/heterodoxy are undergirded by the type of *doxic* commonalities which prevailed more than a century ago'.[8] I shall explore below how Berlinerblau uses the term *doxic* (taken from sociologist Pierre Bourdieu) and unpack some of the nuances and problems it might invoke for an avowedly *secular* biblical studies. At this point, it refers to the ways in which heterodoxy and orthodoxy share unconscious commonalities and are constituted in relation to one another; in the case of biblical studies, for Berlinerblau, the *doxic* remains the theological cast of both radical and conservative biblical criticism. Uncomfortably coupled with this theological orientation is the demand for 'critical' practice. As such, biblical scholarship is marked by what Berlinerblau calls a 'hybrid ideation' – a hybrid mix of critical reasoning and religious persuasion unique amongst the academic disciplines that operate in the modern secular university. Biblical scholars, he suggests are, in the main, 'poor birds' not knowing which way to fly in the disorientating winds of late modernity.[9] In addition to this, the very text on which a safe perch might be found also begins to crumble away. We thus turn to another of Berlinerblau's socio-hermeneutic elements in the 'end of biblical interpretation'; a critique of the idealized unified Bible itself.

The Bible: Genius redactors or a masterpiece of contingencies?

Berlinerblau notes that business-as-usual in biblical scholarship has been 'making the Bible make sense'[10] through careful study, clarification and translation. But, he argues, this is surely a wilful fudging of the fact that problematic Hebrew and Aramaic texts are often incomprehensible. Secular hermeneutics, by contrast,

> does not amend, touch up, or deodorize problematic Hebrew and Aramaic. Our translations are literal and minimalist. Adding to the artlessness of it all is our insistence on calling attention to irregularities in the text. In the (hypothetical)

---

[7] Berlinerblau, 'Poor Bird', p. 295.
[8] Berlinerblau, 'Poor Bird', p. 296.
[9] Berlinerblau, 'Poor Bird', p. 281. Berlinerblau is quoting 'Saul Bellow's poignant depiction of the soul in modernity' from *Mr. Sammler's Planet* (New York: Penguin), p. 4.
[10] Jacques Berlinerblau, *The Secular Bible: Why Nonbelievers Must Take Religion Seriously* (Cambridge: Cambridge University Press, 2005), p. 74.

Secular Bible Translation (SBT), incomprehensibility would be placed in the foreground; ellipsis points, question marks, parentheses and slashes would occur more frequently than the name of God.[11]

The desire for a meaningful unified text is an ideological offshoot of a theological *doxa*. The hybrid ideation of biblical scholarship means that criticism is meant to lead to *restoration*, a de-cluttered textual opening on authentic and original meanings. However, secular scholars have no reason to posit original texts composed by original authors with a single message. As Berlinerblau imagines it, an 'ideal interpreter, therefore, does not try to understand the original meaning of Scripture. Rather, his or her task is to understand how Scripture has been understood and why it is so difficult to understand. This initiative bears oblique affinities to higher criticism *and* its postmodern nemesis'.[12] As we shall see, this task also bears affinities with a cultural history of scriptures through the ways in which biblical texts become discursive textual elements, generated and regenerated in different cultural contexts and interpreted across different disciplinary boundaries.

With this in mind, Berlinerblau is also wary of the means by which some literary critics have migrated into biblical studies, bringing with them a 'Final-redactor monoauthorism', a designation used to refer to

> those who ascribe an astonishing degree of responsibility for the overall form and contents of biblical texts to one person, allegedly the last person to work over the materials. It is a corollary of this view that one need only scrutinize the final version of the text. By looking exclusively at canonized Scripture, these scholars conveniently bypass the long, complex, compositional history of the Bible (as well as over a century of Higher- and Lower-Critical research).[13]

Singling out Robert Alter's resurrection of the literary-minded author in texts such as *The Art of Biblical Narrative* (1981) for particular opprobrium, Berlinerblau notes that 'if a biblical text seems utterly disjointed, Alter will find its hidden narrative unity. No matter how senseless a given passage seems to be, he will demonstrate its previously unseen coherence. To this we might add another Alterian working premise: *If it's ambiguous it must be artistry!*'[14] Disavowing such a unifying authority (hence, Roland Barthes's famous call for the 'Death of the Author' as an act of textual and writerly liberation) the secular critic must then 'think about how polyauthorism – all that textual meddling, all that copying and

---

[11] Berlinerblau, *Secular Bible*, p. 75.
[12] Berlinerblau, *Secular Bible*, p. 79.
[13] Berlinerblau, 'The Bible as Literature?', p. 12.
[14] Berlinerblau, 'The Bible as Literature?', p. 21.

re-copying, all that gilding and latticing across the centuries – generates ... surfeits of meaning and meanings and meaninglessness in the biblical text'.[15]

The secular exegete can thus liken the Bible to a great city – Rome or Paris – 'built across millennia by countless and assorted specialists ... never coordinated in accordance with any grand overarching blueprint and few of them [working] with any understanding of what the canonized – that is current – version of the city/text would look like'.[16] The 'poor bird' (or hybridized biblical scholar) flaps over the city/text looking for a place to land, perhaps seeing a unity in the 'fountains and boulevards and gardens and bridges and roads' when, in actual fact, the biblical text, like these 'beautiful and enchanting cities' is, according to Berlinerblau, a 'masterpiece of contingencies'.[17]

So far, so secularizing we might say. Critical work on a fragmented bible should proceed as far as is possible without an underlying ideological-theological *doxa*. However, as Berlinerblau hints, the enchantment of the city/text still remains. Without assigning an intentional meaning to an imagined ancient author or restoring 'texts to some pristine state of meaningfulness'[18] secular hermeneutics celebrates 'scholars who engage in self-consciously subjective, artistic, or playfully Midrashic readings' and 'endorses interpretation that self-consciously aspires to achieve the status of a work of art'.[19] It is interesting to note that when Berlinerblau takes Alter to task for his literary readings, he notes that 'Alter's many studies of Scripture have, in fact, been dubbed "pre-critical," "apologetic," "neo-fundamentalist," and "*Midrashic*".[20] The difference seems to be that Berlinerblau disallows Alter's conception of a 'genius-redactor' *behind* the construction of biblical material whilst allowing the secular hermeneut a creative, Midrashic and artistic engagement with a contingent and fragmented text.

For Berlinerblau, the art form of choice that best engages with such a text is jazz. As he writes:

> At its very best, biblical interpretation is a thing of beauty, an art form every bit as exhilarating as skilled jazz improvisation. But improvisers ... rarely assume they have accessed the 'truth' of a melody or discerned what the song's composer was 'really trying to say'. Their interpretations are self-conscious elaborations on, and negotiations with an original.[21]

This is the turn that I argue problematizes Berlinerblau's conception of a secular aesthetic in biblical interpretation. Let me be clear. It is not that one cannot practise

---

[15] Berlinerblau, 'The Bible as Literature?', p. 25.
[16] Berlinerblau, 'The Bible as Literature?', p. 26.
[17] Berlinerblau, 'The Bible as Literature?', p. 26.
[18] Berlinerblau, *Secular Bible*, p. 78.
[19] Berlinerblau, *Secular Bible*, p. 78.
[20] Berlinerblau, 'The Bible as Literature?', p. 10. My emphasis.
[21] Berlinerblau, *Secular Bible*, p. 78.

a secular aesthetic, a blatantly false premise.[22] However, I am interested in the myriad difficulties of how a particular aesthetic can be designated 'secular' or 'religious'. Bringing an improvising aesthetic into the disciplinary citadel of biblical studies is a bold move. The historical and intellectual contingencies that have led to biblical studies as a critical practice mean that its practitioners have an almost congenital fear of 'going too far', perhaps allowing the spectre of uncritical (read *religious*) enthusiasm to stalk the corridors of the Academy.

Yet, invoking the aesthetic as a secularizing medium brings other significant problems in its wake. Although exploring these questions in detail is well beyond the scope of this chapter, for a thinker such as Maurice Blanchot, the 'space' (or domain, or realm) of literature reworks any attempt at conclusive conceptual definition. As he writes, going deeply into poetry one 'meets with the absence of the gods'[23] but, even here, 'the immediacy which common language communicates to us is only veiled distance, the absolutely foreign passing for the habitual, the unfamiliar which we take for customary, thanks to the veil which is language and because we have grown accustomed to words' illusion'.[24] In this realm, a turn to the aesthetic is not a turn to clarification.

If, as we saw above, Berlinerblau argues that the distinctions between radical/conservative and orthodoxy/heterodoxy actually share the same customary *doxic* conceptual ground, what of his supposed dichotomies between secular aesthetics/religious aesthetics or, more broadly, the critical and the aesthetic? What is their common ground? And how do Berlinerblau's own conceptions of *doxic* commonalities question his vision of a secular interpretation built on a jazz aesthetic?

The thinkable and unthinkable (or unspeakable) in Biblical Studies

I want to suggest that Berlinerblau's usage of Pierre Bourdieu's ideas around the *doxic* demonstrates that clearly demarcated dichotomies are difficult to sustain. In

---

[22] As Arthur Bradley and Andrew Tate explain in their introduction to *The New Atheist Novel* '... the New Atheists' desire to create a new *mythos* might also explain why they are so interested in *literature*: what starts out as science-as-novel could almost be said to reach its logical conclusion in the novel-as-science. It is not simply that Dawkins and company have clearly learnt a lot from literature: aesthetics, rhetoric, narrative. At a deeper level, we will see how the New Atheists also hold up the literary as a privileged instance of their idea of a natural, secular experience of beauty, wonder and transcendence. To Christopher Hitchens's jaundiced eyes, for instance, it seems that the novel represents just about the only religion in which it is still possible to believe.' *The New Atheist Novel: Philosophy, Fiction and Polemic after 9/11*, (London: Continuum, 2010), p. 10. Literary aesthetics thus suggest an undecideability between religious and secular definitions; aesthetics in this instance can be used as a 'writing space' to explore the concepts, terms, and narratives at work in both scientific and theological works.

[23] Maurice Blanchot, *The Space of Literature*, trans. Ann Smock (Lincoln: University of Nebraska Press, 1989), p. 38.

[24] Blanchot, *Space of Literature*, p. 41.

his work on a sociology of heresy and orthodoxy, Berlinerblau argues that heresy is defined in terms of its structural position vis-à-vis an orthodoxy that defines its 'other' not by any *inherent* differences but by 'developing in dialectic with heterodoxy'.[25] Orthodoxy is generated by groups or authorities condemning and excluding behaviours, individuals, or groups that are determined as beyond the pale and thus heterodox. One can see here the roots of Berlinerblau's 'heretical' call for an end to biblical interpretation – arguing for a secularizing aesthetic interpretative mode questions the dominant theological paradigms of 'making the bible make sense' in the hybrid ideation of much biblical scholarship.

However, as Berlinerblau admits, positioning heretics 'as intellectuals who dissent from the very orthodoxy to which they once belonged [means that] the heretic is thus an insider by dint of once having performed intellectual activity on behalf of the orthodoxy'.[26] In this sense, the heretic cannot escape the conceptual *doxa* which also constitutes their insider/outsider position. Going further, I argue that the turn to an aesthetic interpretative mode, albeit an important one, comes up against significant limitations. As Bourdieu underlines 'the would-be most radical critique always has the limits that are assigned to it by the objective conditions. Crisis is a necessary condition for a questioning of *doxa* but is not in itself a sufficient condition for the production of a critical discourse'.[27] As such, Berlinerblau's likening of a secular biblical interpretation to a skilled jazz improvisation does not offer a clean break with theo-ideologies but, instead, substitutes a different *doxic* assumption (what '*goes without saying because it comes without saying*'[28]) that begs more questions; the assumption that the 'aesthetic' *a priori* offers inventive creativity, coupling beauty and truth, and pushing the limits of the orthodox business-as-usual of biblical studies. Aesthetic interpretations or elaborations certainly trouble the biblical scholar's mode of production but it is not clear how this is necessarily a secularizing manoeuvre.

Difficulties arise when creative improvisation is too neatly juxtaposed to theo-logic critical discourse. Berlinerblau's choice of jazz as analogy is telling on this point. Jacques Derrida, in conversation with the jazz pianist and composer Ornette Coleman, suggests that 'what we often understand by improvisation is the creation of something new, yet something which doesn't exclude the pre-written framework that makes it possible ... Repetition is already in improvisation ...'.[29] The *doxa* of the thinkable or playable in jazz also exerts its domination over aesthetic production, improvisation being 'a mixture of individual creativity and astute

---

[25] Jacques Berlinerblau, 'Toward a Sociology of Heresy, Orthodoxy, and *Doxa*,' *History of Religions* 40, no. 4 (May 2001): p. 332.
[26] Berlinerblau, 'Toward a Sociology of Heresy', p. 340.
[27] Pierre Bourdieu, *Outline of a Theory of Practice* (Cambridge: Cambridge University Press, 1995), p. 169.
[28] Bourdieu, *Outline*, p. 167.
[29] Jacques Derrida and Ornette Coleman, 'The Other's Language: Jacques Derrida Interviews Ornette Coleman, 23 June 1997,' *Genre* 36 (Summer 2004): pp. 322–3.

participation in a multi-layered dialogue – a dialogue with other players, with the particular musical work, and with the history of jazz performance'.[30] Improvisation is constituted by forms of repetition and participation in a tradition.

It is also important to underline the singularities and contingencies of this form of art. As Sharon D. Welch highlights there are subtle dangers in white intellectuals appropriating African-American musical forms. She emphasizes that 'we must acknowledge the racism that is part of the history and continued struggles of jazz artists'[31] and also remain aware of the tendencies, especially within the context explored here where jazz improvisation is deemed 'other' to scholarly intellectualism, that jazz has been disparaged as 'sensual, ecstatic, and emotional' or romanticized 'for the same "primitive" traits'.[32] Within the field of biblical studies, debates continue to rage over what is deemed 'uncritical' or 'pre-critical' along similar if unspoken lines.[33]

Berlinerblau's attempt at creating a space for a secular aesthetic only makes sense within the discursive traditions of biblical scholarship but, by invoking an idea of the aesthetic, he gestures to discourses outside biblical studies' traditional remit. In an important sense this is also an admission that there can be no 'end to biblical interpretation'; even by turning to the aesthetic, the deeper *doxic* commitment, shared by secular and religious interpreter alike, is that these texts exert an authority, however constituted or imagined, that demands a response. This is not to say that Berlinerblau's call is not a significant or useful move and I will utilize some of his thinking below. However, it is important to note that performing such interpretative improvisation both critiques *and* participates in the battles within biblical studies to

> impose the legitimate mode of thought and expression that is unceasingly waged in the field of the production of symbolic goods [pending] to conceal, not least from the eyes of those involved in it, the contribution it makes to the delimitation of the universe of discourse, that is to say, the universe of the thinkable, and hence to the delimitation of the universe of the unthinkable.[34]

---

[30] Sharon D. Welch, '"Lush Life": Foucault's Analytics of Power and a Jazz Aesthetic', in *The Blackwell Companion to Postmodern Theology*, ed. Graham Ward (Oxford: Blackwell Publishing, 2005), p. 89.

[31] Welch, 'Lush Life', p. 88. To choose one example among many, the pianist, composer and big band leader, Duke Ellington commented during the height of the U.S. civil rights struggles that 'for a long time, social protest and the pride in the Negro [sic] have been the most significant things in what we've done. In that music we have been telling for a long time what it is to be a Negro in this country.' Cf. Nat Hentoff, 'Duke Ellington's Mission,' *Jazz Times* (May 1999).

[32] Welch, 'Lush Life', p. 88.

[33] Cf. the discussions around Ron Hendel's article, 'Farewell to S.B.L: Faith and Reason in Biblical Studies,' *Biblical Archaeology Review* 36, no. 4 (July/August 2010). Similar negative opinions around the place of the uncritical or artistic and aesthetic appropriations of biblical material are expressed by John Van Seters in 'A Response to G. Aichele, P. Miscall and R. Walsh, "An Elephant in the Room: Historical-Critical and Postmodern Interpretations of the Bible,"' *The Journal of Hebrew Scriptures* 9, no. 26 (2009): 2–13.

[34] Bourdieu, *Outline*, p. 170.

Deploying the terms 'secular', 'religious', 'critical' or 'aesthetic' is also an attempt at delimitating the thinkable and unthinkable (or 'unspeakable' as Berlinerblau contends) in the field of biblical studies. I take on board Berlinerblau's analysis of the 'poor birds' in biblical studies and the fragmented, sometimes incomprehensible bible. Rather than jazz however, my argument enters the 'space of literature' which provides an interval or pregnant pause, poised on that fine undecideable point between what is delineated by deploying the 'secular', the 'religious', the 'critical' and the 'aesthetic'. Yehuda Amichai's poetic retelling and appropriation of the Jacob and the Angel story from Genesis 32 raises key questions: How does a poetic interpretation problematize the secular/religious, critical/aesthetic binaries and what might this mean for a rethinking of the *doxa* of biblical studies within the 'cultural history of scriptures'?

The spaces of literature: Doing without names

In thinking these binaries it is important to remember that it is not only the biblical texts that are fragmentary and contingent. The subject as interpreter and writer ('poor birds') also participates in and is constructed from myriad historical contingencies. In my analysis, the poetic retelling functions as a kind of literary performance space, a writing that enacts figurative thought and image but also operates through the always undecideable referential nature of language. A lyric poem such as Amichai's 'Jacob and the Angel' improvises on its references, repeating them differently, allowing words to always mean other than what the author or reader might decide upon. As Theodor Adorno writes, 'the lyric work is always the subjective expression of a social antagonism'.[35] As such, the space of literature is one in which a subject is created by and engages with the *doxic* assumptions of a given social milieu. Adorno goes on:

> For language itself is something double. Through its configurations it assimilates itself completely into subjective impulses; one would almost think it had produced them. But at the same time, language remains the medium of concepts, remains that which establishes an inescapable relationship to the universal and society.[36]

The interpreter of Amichai's lyric poem lives a dual life; she enters the poem's aesthetic space but is aware that the language and concepts used there are also in inescapable relationship with how they are used in social life. Is it possible to decide whether this aesthetic is secular or religious?

---

[35] Theodor W Adorno, 'On Lyric Poetry and Society', in *Notes to Literature*, ed. Rolf Tiedemann (New York: Columbia University Press, 1991), p. 45.
[36] Adorno, 'On Lyric Poetry', p. 43.

In the poem itself, the characters are not named but the title 'Jacob and the Angel' provides the suggestive frame for the whole piece. Jacob's biblical nocturnal struggle is refigured as an erotic encounter; as night passes, the protagonists are brought into the light of the morning after which brings with it a different kind of 'knowing'.[37] The repetition of being held 'that way', especially once we learn that Jacob 'saw her body, / which remained white in the places / the swimsuit had covered yesterday' suggests that this particular poetic 'defeat' is a melancholic metaphor for sex, that the 'hold' which 'brings death' has something of the French, *la petit mort*, but also the seriousness of the struggle within which they find themselves. For the biblical Jacob, the struggle with the 'man' brings a wounding, a breaking and disruption of his own body, but the result of his victory is a blessing in the form of a new name. Instead, the struggling couple in Amichai's poem agree 'to do without names'. However, 'in the first light', this agreement begins to be eroded just as the 'breaking of the day' heralds the biblical Jacob's victory (Gen. 32:26 KJV).

The angel/woman's nakedness and vulnerability begins to undermine the cool foundations of the night-time agreement; then when her name is called suddenly 'from above', the contract is broken. Consigning a name is a powerful act. The Jacob in Amichai's poem wishes knowing and naming to remain separate, uncommitted. During the encounter, they 'know' one another through their bodies (here English biblical translations enable 'knowing' to offer some access to the punning nature of the verb ידע – *yada*). There should be no need for names.

Chana Kronfeld offers a reading of this iconoclastic love poem that demonstrates that the reference to 'hold' and 'defeat' connotes, in children's Hebrew, a kind of childish scuffling, a 'forcing to the mat',[38] confirmed by the calling of the 'angel's' name 'the way you call a little girl from playing in the yard.' *Ma'lach* (מלך), alternatively translated as 'angel' or 'King's messenger', is here, according to Kronfeld, 'anchored in colloquial metaphor ... where it could apply to a woman (in the sense of "a wonderful person") or a child ("a beautiful, peaceful, and pure creature")'.[39] As she goes on to highlight,

> Amichai introduces into the poem the weighty associations of the biblical story of Jacob's struggle with the angel, and with all its national and transcendental implications, in order to describe a one-time erotic encounter [...]. He domesticates and thoroughly demystifies these materials through the ... metonymic frame of child's play. And thus he also effects the sanctification and elevation of both the erotic and the childlike domains.[40]

---

[37] The full poem (translated by Stephen Mitchell) can be found in Yehuda Amichai, 'Jacob and the Angel', in *Selected Poetry of Yehuda Amichai* (New York: Harper & Row, 1986).

[38] *Le-natse'ach* – 'getting the upper hand in a scuffle'. Cf. Chana Kronfeld, *On the Margins of Modernism: Decentring Literary Dynamics* (Berkeley and Oxford: University of California Press, 1996), p. 111.

[39] Kronfeld, *On the Margins*, p. 112.

[40] Kronfeld, *On the Margins*, p. 112.

This double-move between domestication and sanctification and secular and religious spheres provokes tensions inherent in modernist lyric rewriting of 'authoritative' biblical stories, and shows how Amichai's poem is particularly pertinent to the debate with Berlinerblau. Here a biblical text is referenced not only through the content of the poem itself but through the (double) language in which it is written. Sacred biblical Hebrew haunts the blank page onto which contemporary vernacular Hebrew might be written in ways that offer themselves to a poet such as Amichai.[41]

As Ruth Kartun-Blum sees it, modern Hebrew has always been 'doomed to become intertextual'[42] meaning that the 'so-called colloquial register' is burdened 'with various associations and connotations of three thousand years of semantic history.'[43] As she goes on to argue, the Bible

> seems to have fixed Hebrew in an obstinate religious mode; semantic presuppositions, idioms and imagery, all containing religious outlooks, force themselves on the secular poet and place obstacles in the way of the evolving vernacular. Paradoxically, however, the very processes of deconstruction and ironization that poets use to secularize their language often serve to revive the original scriptural energy.[44]

Rewriting, then, is caught in a double-bind. For Amichai, the simultaneous activation of both the biblical canon and an emerging literary canon allows for a punning, ironic recasting of biblical idioms and reception histories.

This dual activation questions Berlinerblau's move to the aesthetic as a necessarily secular one. Amichai's desire to both undermine and shift the connotative functions of the biblical material has led to him being described, on the one hand, as deploying a 'completely secular biblicism, one that does not teem with ... tensions between the mundane and the transcendental [...]'.[45] On the other hand, David Jacobson positions him instead as standing in the long tradition of Jewish reinterpretation of biblical motifs through Midrash and Talmud, noting

---

[41] As Kartun-Blum highlights, 'Twentieth-century Jewish history confronts the Hebrew literary imagination with what seems like an astonishing repetition of the biblical drama. The ingathering of the Jews in the modern state of Israel recalls the biblical exodus from Egypt and, later, the return to Zion of the Babylonian exiles. Israel's War of Independence echoes the conquest of the land by Joshua and the judges. The present-day consolidation of the Jewish State has obvious analogies with the Solomonic Kingdom of Israel. The story of Hagar and Ishmael seems to anticipate the present-day conflict with the Arabs. The revolt of Absalom against David might prefigure the tensions between the founding fathers of Israel and their sons. Moreover, the narrative of the Binding of Isaac has become the metaphor for the most cataclysmic event of the twentieth century, the Holocaust.' *Profane Scriptures: Reflections on the Dialogue with the Bible in Modern Hebrew Poetry*, (Cincinnati: Hebrew Union College Press, 1999), p. 17.
[42] Kartun-Blum, *Profane Scriptures*, p. xi.
[43] Kartun-Blum, *Profane Scriptures*, p. 7.
[44] Kartun-Blum, *Profane Scriptures*, p. 90.
[45] Kartun-Blum, *Profane Scriptures*, p. 49.

that despite the rebellious attitude toward the Jewish tradition that is so prevalent in his writings, Amichai's poetry can be seen as 'a completely legitimate part of the interpretive tradition of past generations'.[46] Amichai seems to write from the insider/outsider status of the heretic, outlined above. As such, his poetry highlights the *doxic* element in the backdrop of debates concerning what constitutes 'legitimate' biblical interpretation: that the Bible, in whichever form 'the biblical' is understood in different societies and cultures, still exerts an authority that demands interpretation.

For my analysis, it is this undecideability that makes Amichai's poetry so important for recasting questions of secularity and religiousness in biblical interpretation. The semiotic reservoir of the biblical and post-biblical writings is where Amichai finds the notes for his poetic improvisations. Using the 'religious' or the 'secular' as orientating points to map out what the poet believes is *less interesting* than reading how he makes meaning with his poetic retelling; in Adorno's words, the poem acts for the reader 'as a philosophical sundial telling the time of history'.[47]

Trying to 'do without names' (like 'secular' or 'religious') is impossible, as Amichai's Jacob discovers in the morning light when a name is called 'from above' and the game is over, seemingly come to a *krisis*, a critical decision. But, in the same moment, a name, as part of a language, cannot, according to Derrida 'be dominated, tamed, instrumentalized, secularized'.[48] Every attempt to 'name' has to cope with the name's ability to always defer its meaning. The conceptualization of the secular or the religious can only bring a reading into a certain alignment for a short time before the 'poor bird' or 'poor angel' has to take flight once more and follow the names around the city/texts. Amichai's poem, then, is a literary interval, a pausing with a biblical motif that is not about exegetical gain per se. The poem situates itself in relation to a mobilized biblical language, a hyper-living textuality that is an end to a theologically unified biblical interpretation in Berlinerblau's sense. I argue, however, that this poem is also a pause at the moment just before 'first light', before it can be decided whether this is a secular or sacred hiatus.

Let me offer a few concluding thoughts as to how this type of biblical poetic retelling and its participation in different *doxa* might feed into Timothy Beal's recasting of 'reception histories' as 'cultural histories of scriptures' and also what this could mean for future interdisciplinary relations between biblical studies and other discourses.

---

[46] David C. Jacobson, *Creator, Are You Listening? Israeli Poets on God and Prayer*, (Bloomington and Indianapolis: Indiana University Press, 2007), p. 43. Jacobson is quoting (and translating) from Admiel Kosman, 'Mayim einam yekholim lahazor biteshuvah: he'arah al megillat Amichai,' *Haaretz*, 20 October 2000.

[47] Adorno, 'On Lyric Poetry,' p. 46.

[48] Jacques Derrida, 'The Eyes of Language: The Abyss and the Volcano', in *Acts of Religion*, ed. Gil Anidjar (New York and London: Routledge, 2002), p. 198.

Calling names from off-stage

Treating Amichai's poem as an act of rewriting opens onto fundamental questions of how the idea of 'the biblical' circulates and is re-imagined across disciplinary borders. Timothy Beal's refiguring of reception history shifts from what he calls 'the common "Adam-and-Eve-through-the-centuries" approach',[49] to one better able to acknowledge that 'The Bible' is not 'a thing but an idea, or rather a constellation of often competing, heterogeneous ideas, more or less related to a wide variety of material biblical things.'[50]

Berlinerblau's ideal biblical interpreter, as we have seen, does not cast Higher- and Lower-criticism's methods aside but, in fact, uses them to explore 'how polyauthorism – all that textual meddling … generates abundances of structure and anti-structure, surfeits of meaning and meanings and meaninglessness in the biblical text.'[51] And yet, even with these important methods in place, exegetical work does not occupy the primary ground in fashioning a creative interpretation. With this in mind, Beal's sense of the 'cultural history of scriptures' is able to overcome the primary/secondary dichotomy between exegesis and reception that Roland Boer highlights as a problem in 'reception history':

> [T]he problem is that reception history assumes that the text is in some way *original*, the pad from which subsequent trajectories launch themselves forth. If 'exegesis' is the primary method appropriate to the originary biblical text, then reception history is secondary. It is a linear straightjacket that preserves the primacy of that strange guild of biblical 'exegetes.'[52]

Instead of this modus operandi, we can conceive of 'biblical texts, the Bible, and the biblical as discursive objects that are continually generated and regenerated within particular cultural contexts in relation to complex genealogies of meaning that are themselves culturally produced.'[53] Amichai's short piece, rather than simply being a secondary part of a 'Jacob and the Angel through-the-centuries' trajectory, becomes a complex literary performance, participating and contributing to 'complex genealogies of meaning' and refusing the hierarchy between exegesis and aesthetic reception *and* secular or religious ultimacy. Beal's harder cultural turn might then herald an appreciation of how biblical studies itself is part of a 'scriptural economy'[54] that casts the mobile yet fragmentary Bible in different roles in

---

[49] Timothy Beal, 'Reception History and Beyond: Toward the Cultural History of Scriptures,' *Biblical Interpretation* 19, no. 4–5 (2011): p. 136.
[50] Beal, 'Reception History and Beyond', p. 368.
[51] Berlinerblau, 'The Bible as Literature?', p. 25.
[52] Roland Boer, 'Against "Reception History"', *The Bible and Interpretation* (May 2011), http://www.bibleinterp.com/opeds/boe358008.shtml.
[53] Beal, 'Reception History and Beyond', p. 371.
[54] For Michel de Certeau, this scriptural economy, in the broadest sense, functions as the 'multiform and murmuring activity of producing a text and producing society as a text.' *The Practice of Everyday Life*, trans. Steven Rendell (Berkeley: University of California Press, 1984), p. 134.

contemporary culture. More searching questions can then be raised, particularly around how the afterlives of 'the biblical' 'trade in various unstable forms of social, cultural, financial, and sacred capital'.[55] Moving away from the priority of exegetical production also shifts the disciplinary constitution of biblical studies. Beal suggests that biblical studies become part of a broader religious studies context, and, as such, a stronger partner in discussions around the dimensions of 'scriptural cultures' more generally.

Contemporary biblical scholars thus move into a unique position. Although Berlinerblau casts the hybrid ideation of theologically inclined interpreters as 'the unspeakable in biblical scholarship',[56] this conflict actually becomes a prime site for studying the religiosecular complex. What does the naming of a particular interpretation as 'religious' or 'secular' achieve? Does the slash between secular/religious become more of a flexible hyphen – secular-religious? As Ward Blanton explores, if it is in biblical studies where, like a voice coming 'from above' comes the stage-direction *'indicate whether you are doing this . . . religiously or secularly'* then our field must be crucial

> for the maintenance of the systematic hegemony of this particular quilting point. After all, to say that we feel the pressure to 'confess' our allegiance, to 'fix' ourselves on the territorial maps that emerge under the auspices of this off-stage voice, is to say (simultaneously) that we could play a potentially subversive role in unhinging the opposition and thus loosening up for rearticulation that complex network of words and things that have found their pre-scripted places under its imperial banner.[57]

Welcoming the end of biblical interpretation and broadening our remit to the study of a cultural history of scriptures allows a deep questioning of the orientating poles of the 'secular' and the 'religious' in critical discourse but also how these terms are played off one another in wider cultural spheres. What I want to suggest is that by perhaps following Berlinerblau's call along the winding, sometimes dangerous, sometimes enchanting streets of the city/text, we might find a poet, artist or jazzman improvising and elaborating on a biblical fragment, risking an aesthetic response that is difficult to define as 'religious' or 'secular', but is a performance in which we all become players, more aware of how the limits of the thinkable and unthinkable encircle what we are able to do with scriptural texts.

---

[55] Beal, 'Reception History and Beyond', p. 366.
[56] Jacques Berlinerblau, 'The Unspeakable in Biblical Scholarship', in *Secularism and Biblical Studies*, ed. Roland Boer (London: Equinox, 2010).
[57] Ward Blanton, 'Neither Religious nor Secular: On Saving the Critic in Biblical Criticism', in *Secularism and Biblical Studies*, ed. Roland Boer (London: Equinox, 2010), p. 154.

9

Reception History of the Bible: Prospects of a New Frontier in African Biblical Studies

Masiiwa Ragies Gunda
Bamberg University, Germany

Introduction

The study of the Bible has always been a central part of education in Zimbabwe from the earliest schools established by missionaries, which were meant to teach the indigenous people how to read the Bible.[1] As Christianity became the dominant religion so the study of the Bible became a dominant presence in the national curriculum. Even when education was subsequently expanded, religious and moral education, essentially meaning the moral of biblical narratives, was developed for primary school children. In secondary schools, students were exposed to the Synoptic Gospels and Acts, while at Advanced Level Divinity students did the Prophets, the Gospels and the Pauline Letters. This dominant presence of the Bible in the Zimbabwean curriculum was meant to accomplish both personal and Christian development of the students.[2] In the University College of Rhodesia and Nyasaland (now University of Zimbabwe), the Department of Theology was introduced from the beginning of the College in 1957, and Robert Craig was appointed as Professor of Theology in 1963.[3] The Department of Theology was later replaced by a Department of Religious Studies, Classics and

---

[1] Chengetai J. M. Zvobgo, *A History of Christian Missions in Zimbabwe 1890-1939* (Gweru: Mambo Press. 1996), 149; Masiiwa R. Gunda, 'Homosexuality and the Bible in Zimbabwe: Contested Ownership and Interpretation of an "Absolute Book"', in Joachim Kuegler and Ulrike Bechmann (eds), *Biblische Religionskritik: Kritik in, an und mit biblischen Texten – Beiträge des IBS 2007 in Vierzehnheiligen* (Münster: LIT Verlag, 2009), 76-94 (78-9).

[2] Godfrey Museka, 'Exorcising the Colonial Jinx: Towards Reconciling Diversity and Pedagogy in Zimbabwe's Religious Education Curriculum', *The Journal of Pan African Studies* 5/1 (2012), 55-68 (56).

[3] Clayton G. Mackenzie, The University of Rhodesia: A Re-appraisal, *Journal of Educational Administration and History* 19/2 (1987), 62-71 (69). David Bloom et al., *Higher Education and Economic Development in Africa*, (Human Development Sector Africa Region, 2006; http://ent.arp.harvard.edu/AfricaHigherEducation/Reports/BloomAndCanning.pdf), 66.

Philosophy in 1980, with the task of teaching all religions professed in Zimbabwe.[4] However, the study of the Christian Bible remained the dominant focus of both departments since that was considered a teaching qualification. Owing to the dominant presence of German scholars in this new Department, the study of the Bible took a thoroughly German face, pursuing ceaselessly a rigid historical-critical approach to the Bible. This approach continues, though it has been somewhat watered down due to new developments in biblical studies in Africa, especially the advent of 'socially engaged biblical scholarship'.[5]

The Bible is a critically important book;[6] even though it was seen as sanctioning the oppression of locals by settler and colonial regimes, the same 'Bible was read at political rallies to inspire people to fight against the settler regime'.[7] The same Bible was also until recently 'the only piece of literature one could find in most homes in Zimbabwe'[8], read 'in times of joy, sorrow and to impart moral lessons on children'[9], it was both a sacred text and an object of strange power.[10] The Bible brought God in people's homes; its presence and words were important. Ordinary people could access God and God's 'thinking' by reading the Bible; hence the populist question: 'is it in the Bible?'[11] It is not clear whether interpretation led to practices or practices led to particular interpretations of the Bible.[12] In the domain of Christian talk, the history of the making of the Bible itself is a non-issue; the Bible is taken in its canonical form. The Bible is taken as the 'alpha and omega' of Christianity, making historical-critical approaches very academic and at odds with Christianity and Christians.

This clear trail of the Bible in Zimbabwe calls for more than the traditional historical-critical, literary or social scientific studies of the Bible. While these approaches remain important, they nonetheless fail to address the issues surrounding the effects and impact of the Bible in the lives of the people in Zimbabwe and other parts of Africa. There is need for a method that does acknowledge that even in the Bible's old age, it remains young enough to be considered relevant by contemporary

---

[4] Jan Platvoet, 'The institutional environment of the study of religions in Africa south of the Sahara' in Michael Pye (ed.), *Marburg Revisited: Institutions and Strategies in the Study of Religion* (Marburg: Diagonal Verlag 1989), 107–26, (113).

[5] Gerald O. West, *The Academy of the Poor: Towards a Dialogical Reading of the Bible* (Pietermaritzburg: Cluster Publications, 2003), x.

[6] I am fully aware that the Bible is a collection of books but the majority of its readers in Zimbabwe understands it and proclaims it to be a book. In essence, the collection of writings we call the Bible has been received in Zimbabwe as a book.

[7] Ndabaningi Sithole, *Obed Mutezo: The Mudzimu, Christian Nationalist* (Nairobi: Oxford University Press, 1970), 118.

[8] Gunda, *The Bible and Homosexuality in Zimbabwe. Bible in Africa Studies 3*. (Bamberg: University of Bamberg Press, 2010), 71

[9] Lovemore Togarasei,. 'Fighting HIV and AIDS with the Bible: Towards HIV and AIDS Biblical criticism' in Ezra Chitando (ed.), *Mainstreaming HIV and AIDS in Theological Education: Experiences and Explorations* (Geneva: WCC Publications, 2008), 71–82 (73).

[10] West, *Academy of the Poor*, vii.

[11] Gunda, *The Bible and Homosexuality*, 257.

[12] Gunda, *The Bible and Homosexuality*, 46.

readers. This desire is behind the rise of reception history as an approach to the study of the Bible. Reception history, therefore, may open up a fruitful collaboration between biblical scholars and Christians as it places emphasis on the users of the Bible or those who have been influenced by the Bible. In this essay, I will begin by defining reception history, highlighting its aims and challenges. I will also attempt a brief application of the approach on the Sodom narrative of Genesis 19.

Reception history: Definition and practice

The exploits of historical-critical, literary and social scientific approaches to the Bible are well documented. Lately, postmodernist and post-colonial approaches (the latter especially in the Third World) have made significant strides in understanding the Bible or appropriating the Bible for profitable use by contemporary societies. While these interactions with the Bible are well known by scholars and students of the Bible, the same cannot be claimed for the documentation of the 'effects' and 'impact' of the Bible in particular communities. This is particularly true in areas dominated by the historical-critical approaches to the Bible, such as in Zimbabwe, where according to Klint '[e]xegetes have traditionally been preoccupied with questions about how the Bible came to be. Or even more typically with the intended meaning (by God or the author) of its different texts.'[13] Klint continues by noting that in all this, 'the ways in which the biblical texts have been actually read and interpreted throughout history have until recently received very little attention.'[14] In Zimbabwe, the 'effects' and 'impact' of the Bible are frequently dealt with unconsciously (sometimes even followed by regret from the scholar for transgressing normal practice), mostly in the process of doing the normal dominant studies of the Bible. In that regard, one could speak of an accidental practice of reception history, as opposed to a systematic reception history.

Reception history did not start as an approach to the study of the Bible. Rather, it developed as an approach to the study of texts, focusing especially on the 'effects' and 'impact' of a text in a given community. The English term reception history comes from two interrelated German concepts '*Rezeptionsgeschichte* and *Wirkungsgeschichte,* respectively "reception history" and "effective, effectual, or impact history"'.[15] Reception history appears like something that has always been done in different communities, yet a systematic interest in the reception history of texts, especially the classics, can be traced back to the 1960s and 1970s. Hans Georg

---

[13] Stefan Klint, 'After Story – a Return to History? Introducing Reception Criticism as an Exegetical Approach', *Studia Theologica – Nordic Journal of Theology* 54/2 (2000), 87–106 (87).
[14] Klint, 'After Story', 87.
[15] Eric Repphun *et al.* 'Editors' Introduction: Beyond Christianity, the Bible, and the Text: Urgent Tasks and New Orientations for Reception History', *Relegere: Studies in Religion and Reception* 1/1 (2011), 1–11 (4).

Gadamer is credited with highlighting what later becomes reception history with his concept of '*Wirkungsgeschichte*' as found in his book *Wahrheit und Methode* (1960).[16] Another leading figure is Hans Robert Jauss whose 'aesthetics of reception', developed in a series of essays in the late 1960s and early 1970s,[17] laid the foundation of what eventually became reception history of texts in general. Central to these two was the placing of emphasis on the relationship between the text and the reader, redirecting the attention of scholars away from an all-important text to a text that is dependent on its readers as much as its readers are dependent on it. From their works, it became possible to seriously consider the effects and impact of the text on its readers and the manner in which the readers have made use of the text. 'Although one may be inclined to insist on the distinction between *Rezeptionsgeschichte* and *Wirkungsgeschichte* such a distinction is largely theoretical because in the world of lived human culture, reception and impact are inseparably bound together',[18] leading Sawyer to define reception history as 'the history of how a text has influenced communities and cultures down the centuries'.[19] In this study, therefore, reception history is taken as the conglomeration of *Rezeptionsgeschichte* and *Wirkungsgeschichte*.

Reception history of the Bible owes much to Gadamer's articulation of the 'classical/classic text'. He points out that 'classical' can refer to an historical period or something more normative, something we have come to regard highly.[20] In attempting to mark out the classic text, it is suggested that it is the work of great thinkers, which gives the impression of being timeless because it continues to appear contemporary to succeeding generations.[21] The impression of timelessness in such works of great thinkers is created by the works' ability to push the context of the lives of the great thinkers into the background in the face of the unique formulations of their ideas. The argument that the classic is not a flat reiteration of the past, but something that in the playing out of differences between it and our current prejudices throws up sparks of light illuminating the present and its possible futures certainly applies to the Bible and how it is viewed in most African societies.[22] It is this claim to uniting the past, present and the future that separates classic texts from ordinary texts. While Gadamer was attacked by his peers for his understanding of classic texts and tradition, I am adopting Allan How's view that the classic text speaks to us authoritatively through tradition; he declares:

---

[16] H-G. Gadamer, *Wahrheit und Methode: Grundzüge einer philosophischen Hermeneutik* (Tübingen: Mohr Verlag, 1960).
[17] Timothy Beal, 'Reception History and Beyond: Toward the Cultural History of Scriptures', *Biblical Interpretation* 19 (2011), 361.
[18] Repphun *et al*, 'Editors' Introduction', 4.
[19] John F. A. Sawyer, *Sacred Language and Sacred Texts* (London: Routledge, 1999), 2.
[20] H-G. Gadamer, *Truth and Method* (2nd revised ed.; translated by J. Weinsheimer and D. G. Marshall, London: Sheed and Ward, 1989), 284–90.
[21] Allan How, ' "That's Classic!" A Gadamerian defence of the classic text in sociology', *The Sociological Review* 46/4 (1998), 828–48 (839–40).
[22] Gadamer, *Truth and Method*, 286.

It certainly may appear timeless in that it seems to address *us* specifically now but as Gadamer rather enigmatically declares, 'this timelessness is a mode of historical being'. By this he means that the truth which classic texts reveal is historical in that it happens *within,* and in a sense is bequeathed by, the ongoing fusion of historical Horizons.[23]

These critical ideas surrounding the classic text are central to the understanding and practice of reception history of the Bible. The idea of the fusion of historical horizons brings to the fore the effects and impact that the classic text bears upon the readers as they appropriate it to their specific historical context. As How argues in agreement with Gadamer, what keeps classic texts relevant and alive is their ability to consistently be different as they encounter different situations.[24] In fact, to prove its classic-ness or classicity, the classic text constantly has to *prove* itself anew by speaking differently to succeeding generations. It has to come alive again to speak meaningfully and to appear contemporary to the prejudices that make up the current horizon to which it addresses itself. Clearly, therefore, like tradition the classic text reveals its continuity with the past not by repeatedly being the same, but by repeatedly becoming different. It is this sameness-in-difference, which is at the heart of the hermeneutic case for the persistence of the classic text.[25] Following Gadamer then, classic texts will remain relevant in different contexts because they constantly make themselves relevant in different situations. The best way of focusing on such classic texts is acknowledging the dual transactions between the text and the reader, the effects and impact of one on the other. This quest clearly separates reception history from the main thrust of the historical-critical approaches to the Bible, which saw universally binding results as critical. Reception history thrives on the differences that exist in the way in which the Bible has been received by different readers.

Reception history of the Bible

The Bible fits neatly into the description of the classical as understood by Gadamer. Further, succeeding generations tussle for the interpretation of this classic text because they all assume it addresses them specifically, echoing John S. Mbiti's claim that 'Africans hear their stories in the Bible.'[26] These observations are not surprising since it is widely acknowledged that '[Christian] communities invariably read the Bible as if it were timeless and addressed to themselves and therefore the historical-critical scrutiny is regarded as being not only unnecessary but intrusive and

---

[23] How, 'That's Classic!', 839.
[24] How, 'That's Classic!', 836–40.
[25] Gadamer, *Truth and Method*, 287.
[26] John S. Mbiti, *Bible and Theology in African Christianity* (Nairobi: Oxford University Press, 1986), 26.

wrongheaded'.[27] According to Agee and Evans, 'reception history is thus best regarded, as an umbrella term for the study of the social employment of religious texts, images, symbols, narratives, words, and physical objects'[28], an 'exploration of particular ways in which the Bible has been received throughout the ages'.[29] Reception history then is the study of the use, influence, and impact of the Bible. It focuses on the many ways in which individuals and communities throughout the centuries have understood and used biblical words, passages, events, characters and books.[30] While the focus is on the reception of the Bible, this is not limited to the text of the Bible only but also to cultural phenomena that show the effects or impact of the Bible in specific communities.

> [T]hose who have read the Bible throughout the centuries have usually read it in light of their own historical, social, and cultural backgrounds. People use these backgrounds, or contexts, as tools to aid them in understanding and applying the Bible.[31]

By noting the importance of the contextual situations of different readers, reception history appreciates that '[d]ifferent readers, different situations, different reasons for reading the text, all yield different readings'.[32] These observations and the attendant question on the reception of the Bible cannot be answered by the philological questions of mainstream historical-critical studies but rather by the reception critic because '[t]he distinct advantage of reception history lies in the particular vantage point it offers for the study of the dynamic interaction between the lives of texts and the societies that receive, read, interpret, and use them'.[33] Timothy Beal argues that 'reception history of the Bible is concerned, most basically, with the history of the reception of biblical texts, stories, images, and characters through the centuries in the form of citation, interpretation, reading, revision, adaptation, and influence.'[34] The question of the origin of the text itself recedes to the background as one focuses on the actual usage of the text. Such usage may or may not rely on the historicity of the text or its claims, especially where such text as the Bible is seen as a vessel for religious faith.

---

[27] Robert P. Carroll, 'The Reader and the Text', in A. D. H. Mayes (ed.), *Text in Context: Essays by Members of the Society for Old Testament Study* (Oxford: Oxford University Press, 2000), 3–34 (19).

[28] James Agee and Walker Evans, *Let Us Now Praise Famous Men: Three Tenant Families* (Boston: Mariner Books. 2001), 10; Robert Morgan, 'Sachkritik in Reception History', *Journal for the Study of the New Testament* 33/2 (2010), 175–90 (176); Repphun *et al.*, 'Editors' Introduction', 5.

[29] R. S. Sugirtharajah, *The Bible and the Third World: Precolonial, Colonial and Postcolonial Encounters* (Cambridge: Cambridge University Press. 2001), 3.

[30] Scott M. Langston, 'The Exodus in American History and Culture'. *Teaching the Bible: An E-Newsletter for Public School Teachers by Society of Biblical Literature* 2010 (available online: www.sbl-site.org/assets/pdfs/TB6_Exodus_SL.pdf, [accessed 13 August 2012], 1–4 (4).

[31] Langston, 'Exodus in American History and Culture', 1.

[32] Carroll, 'The Reader and the Text', 4.

[33] Repphun *et al.*, 'Editors' Introduction', 3.

[34] Beal, 'Reception History and Beyond', 357–72 (359).

The Bible has survived clearly because it is mostly used as a religious document, but reception history does not limit itself to exploring the religious reception, rather:

> It is a wonderful way of exploring the Bible's influence not only in religion, but also in politics, the arts, culture, society, and many other areas. What's more, it provides an excellent opportunity to learn something about a particular individual's or community's own values and culture. Additionally, when a particular passage is studied over time, its changing meanings and uses become apparent.[35]

This is particularly true of post-colonial Africa, where texts and passages have evolved from colonial, nationalists through to post-colonial readings owing to the evolving life of the readers of the Bible. This is easily illustrated by three different scholars touching on three different areas. From an African background, Jeremy Punt contends:

> Political leaders found the Bible to be a superbly useful ally in the establishment and maintenance of Apartheid South Africa during the latter part of the first half of the twentieth century, and in fact referenced biblical texts in their attempts to justify racial segregation.[36]

Such readings were later to be challenged by new readings of the Bible giving rise to different and competing readings, which were largely conditioned by the circumstances of the readers as well as the effects and impact of certain passages of the Bible. A look at the present day United States of America led Scott M. Langston to suggest that:

> There are several benefits in using American history and culture to teach about the exodus. Students can learn how and why different groups responded to significant movements in American history. They can identify and trace various traditions of use, seeing how certain factors shaped these understandings, and then explain modern uses in terms of their historical development.[37]

A final case which points to the multiple manifestations of biblical reception is invoked in an attempt to understand the modern state of Israel.

> A reception-historical approach likewise furnishes the necessary analytical richness for understanding how the founding of the modern state of Israel is not only a consequence of political developments in the nineteenth and twentieth centuries, but is also inseparable from the ways in which particular biblical traditions were appropriated, both ancient Hebrew traditions of a promised land

---

[35] Langston, 'Exodus in American History and Culture', 1.
[36] Jeremy Punt, 'Using the Bible in post-apartheid South Africa: Its influence and impact amidst the gay debate', HTS Theological Studies 62/3, (2006), 885–907 (885).
[37] Langston, 'Exodus in American History and Culture', 4.

for the people of Israel, and more recent Christian dispensationalist readings of biblical texts.[38]

In short, a reception history of the Bible entails a critical study of the manner in which the Bible as a whole, or its parts thereof, has been received by various communities who have treated it as being different from ordinary written works. A systematic reception history of the Bible in Zimbabwe will need to focus on Christian communities, political institutions, and business institutions which have all made use of the Bible dating back to the colonial era. An example of such a study would focus on particular books, narratives or biblical names and practices and how they have been used by different institutions.[39]

Reception history: Assumptions and goals

Reception history assumes that the usage of the Bible is not dependent on its historicity or authenticity,[40] rather it accepts that it affects and is affected by those who read it. With these assumptions, reception history has the potential of mediating the gulf that has developed between believers and biblical scholars in many African communities, where scholars are mostly accused of undermining faith by attempting to correct readings of believers. This is not surprising since in most cases scholars tend to rely on historical reconstructions that are not available to believers while believers 'insist on reading the Bible in conjunction with their own creeds, councils, confessions, and catechisms which determine the meaning of texts',[41] in ways largely seen as irrational by scholars. Further, as Beal observes:

> Insofar as it [reception history] is less interested in discovering meaning *in* biblical texts than it is in how meaning is made *from* biblical texts in different cultural contexts, past and present, it has the potential to bring biblical scholarship into more significant conversation with other fields of academic religious studies.[42]

It is not for the reception historian to determine right readings from false or wrong readings; the reception historian is only interested in articulating the different readings. In doing that the reception historian is searching for the effects

---

[38] Repphun *et al.*, 'Editors' Introduction', 3.
[39] Gunda, 'A Critical Analysis of the Survival and Relevance of Post-Colonial African Initiated (Apostolic) Churches' in L. Togarasei and E. Chitando (eds), *Faith in the City: The Role and Place of Religion in Harare*, (Uppsala: Universitetstryckeriet 2010), 41–62. Gunda, 'The Old Testament and Daily Life: Turning the Bible into a Manual for Practice. The Case of African Initiated "Apostolic" Churches in Zimbabwe' in: Gunda (ed.), *From Text to Practice: The Role of the Bible in Daily Living of African People Today* (Bamberg: University of Bamberg Press 2011), 131–56 (136).
[40] How, 'That's Classic!', 839.
[41] Carroll, 'The Reader and the Text', 20.
[42] Beal, 'Reception History and Beyond', 364.

and impact particular texts, books or even words have had on given specific communities. In this regard, '[m]any reception-historical studies are longitudinal, exploring a particular biblical book, character, or image through the ages (e.g., a reception history of the book of Ruth or the character of Naomi from the earliest to the most recent post-biblical appearances in as many social and cultural works and contexts as can be found)'.[43] Therefore;

> The goal of reception history is not to recover the original meaning of a text or to establish an authoritative reading, or even worse, to redeem a troublesome text – as many biblical scholars are wont to do with the books of Joshua, Ezekiel, or Job – but rather involves examining the readings that have been attached to a given text or object and saying something salient about the social role of that text or object. That some of these readings may be dangerous, destructive, logically incoherent, even morally repellent, does not permit the ethically responsible reception historian to reject them out of hand, or, which is worse, to pretend that they do not follow the grain of the text.[44]

Reception history: Challenges

From the assumptions and goals above, there is a real danger that:

> Reception history will continue to be of limited interest unless it contributes to an understanding of the sheer complexity of the relationships between text and culture. The mere cataloguing of examples of reception can only be superficial unless it is also accompanied by some degree of analysis, not least because the very activity of cataloguing or collection carries with it presuppositions that need to be identified and subjected to critical scrutiny.[45]

This critique is particularly important bearing in mind the suspicions that characterize the relationship between scholars from the 'First World' and those from the proverbial 'Third World'. Reception history must strive for multiplicity of perspectives as opposed to the single perspective mantra of historical-critical approaches of the enlightenment era.

The second challenge of reception history is raised by Timothy Beal who questions the assumption that the Bible exists because 'if there is one thing the material history of Bibles makes extremely clear, it is that there is no such *thing* as the Bible, and there never has been.'[46] While believers emphasize the singularity of the Bible, can there ever be such a thing where there are various authorized versions

---

[43] Beal, 'Reception History and Beyond', 359.
[44] Repphun *et al.*, 'Editors' Introduction', 9.
[45] Repphun *et al.*, 'Editors' Introduction', 2–3.
[46] Beal, 'Reception History and Beyond', 368.

and translations? Are these versions the same thing or are they different? If we are to search for the reception history of 'the Bible' which of the multiple versions are we going to consider? At what point shall we mark as the end point of the production of the Bible and as the starting point of the reception of the produced Bible since there are many versions and canons?[47] This question is particularly important for Christianity in sub-Saharan Africa (excluding the Horn of Africa) because at what point should reception history of the Bible begin there? Can it begin with the early Church when it appears that there was no communion between the early Church and these communities? Can we begin to look that far off when it is apparently clear that these communities did not have any contact with the Bible in any form or size then? Is it then plausible to suggest that reception history of the Bible in most of sub-Saharan African Christian communities can only begin with the advent of western missionaries, who mediated the contact between these African communities and the Bible? This last alternative is apparently the most viable for reception history in societies like contemporary Zimbabwe, where the focus must be on the English Bible(s) and the translations made by the different missionaries for different denominations during the twentieth century.

The third challenge that faces reception history has to do with the definition of Bible. Other approaches have tended to sacralize the 'text' and reception history must be wary of this veneration of the written text. Communities across Africa, which are largely oral communities, may not be relying so much on the written text over generations but rather on interpreted texts. In Zimbabwe, the term reader is used both literally and metaphorically in that it includes the many who are illiterate, but who listen to, retell and remake the Bible.[48] Interpretations made by communities are sometimes privileged more than the text they interpret because it is the interpretations that are easily accessible to the people. It is the interpretation that is regarded as true in the manner in which it casts the text, such that 'the interpreted text can gradually replace the text to be interpreted, in other words, commentary replaces the text.'[49] This process may even challenge the claim to 'closed canons' since the interpretations are a way of adjusting and reshaping the canon itself even if no words or phrases are added to or subtracted from the written text. Indeed, 'when the accepted or traditional way(s) of interpreting the Bible becomes the only authentic interpretation and effectively replaces the Bible, the *interpreted* text eventually constitutes the authority'.[50] In this context, a reception history of the Bible must of necessity focus on the traditions that grow out of the Bible but which over time have ceased to rely on a direct interpretation

---

[47] Beal, 'Reception History and Beyond', 367–8.
[48] West, *Academy of the Poor*, x.
[49] K. C. Boone, *The Bible Tells Them so: The Discourse of Protestant Fundamentalism* (London: SCM, 1989), 78–80.
[50] Punt, 'Using the Bible in post-apartheid South Africa', 894.

of a specific biblical text, such as in the case of sodomy laws in various nation-states, such as Zimbabwe.[51] These laws have remained in Penal Codes on the basis of an interpretation emanating in nineteenth- and twentieth-century Victorian England's Judeo-Christian values. This would also apply in cases to do with gender inequalities where prejudices have become so entrenched through traditional interpretations that the written text itself is no longer consulted. In other words, a reception history of the Bible may also mean a reception history of the interpretations that have replaced the Bible.

Reception history: An example from the Zimbabwean context

First and foremost, in order to avoid simply cataloguing readings and interpretations, I submit that a profitable reception history of the Bible in Zimbabwe and generally in sub-Saharan Africa is better served by a socio-historical analysis of the location of the readers of the text of the Bible and of any stories that were told which came from or were attributed to the Bible. This analytic tool would also raise questions pertaining to the interests of the readers and their intended goals, since readings and interpretations are not merely to understand the text or story but to explain and make sense of contemporary life and experience. All readings therefore betray their social, religious, economic or political role in specific communities. This realization is behind the claim that 'one of the earlier marks of colonial interpretation was the use of the Bible as a vehicle for inculcating European manners',[52] while indigenous reactions later followed. In effect, 'the Bible ... was a cultural weapon which both the colonized and the colonizer employed to enhance their positions'.[53]

As intimated above, a reception history of the Bible in Zimbabwe can only properly begin by considering the contact of indigenous people with the Bible from the period of Gonzalo da Silveira, the Portuguese missionary who is credited with being the first missionary to be within the territory of present day Zimbabwe.[54] At this early stage, focus must be put on the stories that were told by the reading missionaries and why they told such stories to the indigenous people. Until the rise of a reading group among the indigenous Zimbabweans, the Bible was received through stories told by the missionaries and not the text. Since 'texts are largely meaningless unless a hermeneutic is established that opens the way into the texts',[55] even the early indigenous readings may have relied on missionary guidance.

---

[51] Neville Hoad, *African Intimacies: Race, Homosexuality and Globalisation* (Minneapolis: University of Minnesota Press, 2007), xii; Gunda, *The Bible and Homosexuality*, 187.
[52] Sugirtharajah, *Bible and the Third World*, 63.
[53] Sugirtharajah, *Bible and the Third World*, 108.
[54] A. Nicolaides, 'Early Portuguese Imperialism: Using the Jesuits in the Mutapa Empire of Zimbabwe', *International Journal of Peace and Development Studies* Vol. 2/4 (2011), 132–7.
[55] Carroll, 'The Reader and the Text', 3.

Conflicting interpretations would later arise when indigenous people started extracting hermeneutics from their own social, political, religious and economic experiences.

Genesis 19 carries on a narrative that begins in Genesis 18 when Abraham receives three guests in his household and hosts a meal for them. As a consequence of his hospitality to these strangers, two critical things occur: first, Abraham is promised a son to be borne by his elderly wife, Sara. Second, Abraham is informed that the strangers are on a mission to destroy Sodom for its sins. Genesis 19 picks up the narrative when two of the three strangers arrive in Sodom, where they are eventually hosted by an alien resident in the city, Lot. When the men of Sodom try to forcibly 'know' the visitors in Lot's house, Lot begins by offering his daughters to the rowdy men of Sodom, but the offer is rejected. The strangers then strike the men of Sodom with blindness and instruct Lot and his family to escape the city before it is destroyed. To facilitate their escape, they are given an instruction 'not to turn back'. The wife of Lot is accused of disobeying this instruction and thereby transforming into a 'pillar of salt', and the journey continues with Lot and his daughters. That situation forced the daughters to commit incest with their father in order to continue their lineage. This narrative is so complex and rich in subplots that a lot of readings and interpretations are possible. While historical-critical approaches would begin by raising questions of historicity of the narrative, the ordinary Zimbabwean Christian readers do not normally raise such questions. It is what the story teaches that is regarded as critical; in this case, biblical narratives were effectively being used to replace the traditional folklores of 'the hare and the baboon that could speak like human beings, and could even have human girlfriends.'[56] Historicity was therefore never a critical consideration for determining the importance of pedagogical narratives.

From an early age as a child born into a Christian family, even before one could read, one could sing the story of Sodom and Gomorrah. Few knew where exactly in the Bible, this story was; what was important was to know the story and its 'lesson', a lesson that was given in storytelling and song, a story of obedience and disobedience! In this early reception and retelling, even singing, of this story, the focus was on the wife of Lot. She was the example of disobedience and its consequences, while Lot and his daughters were examples of obedience. The song '*mukadzi wa*Lot (the wife of Lot)' was meant to show how it was so easy to obey, yet this woman decided to disobey. We sang:

> The wife of Lot, was told to walk along,
> And not to turn back, but she turned back
> And became a pillar of salt, to this day

---

[56] These occurrences were normal in folklores that we were told when growing up in the rural areas in Zimbabwe. We were fascinated by the tales of the clever Rabbit and the foolish Baboon and we all aspired to be like Rabbit.

She remains a pillar of salt.
We must walk, without turning back
Lest we turn into pillars of salt.[57]

Clearly, this is a reading finding its way back to missionary or colonial readings, especially since missionaries were expected by the colonial regimes to nurture obedient indigenous populations to serve the colonial interests.[58] They viewed 'Africans as children who needed Christian moral values to realize their real human potential'.[59] The focus was therefore directed towards the wife of Lot to teach the hearers the dangers of disobeying God, where God and colonial interests were mostly confused as similar. Obedience to God was obedience to the white man and his institutions. Later on, the same reading would have been found useful to the new indigenous leaders both within the Church and nationally, such that the story continued to be told and retold, to inculcate the sense of obedience in the young and the elderly alike. The continuation of this reading would confirm the idea that 'conformity with the Bantu heritage was taken as a yardstick by which to judge the Bible. Any biblical injunction or regulation which contradicted the Bantu culture was rejected',[60] since obedience to authority is one such heritage, the Sodom story outlived the missionaries and their interests.

While the story of obedience was the popular reading and understanding of the narrative, the colonial regime also brought with them a reading of the narrative which, while not finding its way into the public realm, nonetheless found its way into the Penal Code as the 'sodomy law'. In this law, the wife of Lot does not play any role; rather, the focus is on the 'men of Sodom and their depravity'. Based on an interpretation of the sin of the men of Sodom, the 'sodomy law' assumed that all same-sex practices were abominable to God and hence it criminalized such acts whether consensual or not. In effect, this law criminalized anal penetration, as unnatural. Interestingly, this reading did not easily find its way into the church or home where the wife of Lot held sway, because same-sex sexual practices and relationships were largely unheard of in the public realm. For a long time, this reading remained hidden in the Penal Code, but that changed dramatically in 1995 when through the agency of Robert Mugabe, the President of Zimbabwe, the sodomy interpretation was transposed into the public realm such that the church and the home could no longer ignore it. As this interpretation rose to prominence, the wife of Lot receded into the background. Readers afraid of being politically incorrect[61]

---

[57] A popular song which we sung in Shona in church, school and at home.
[58] Gunda 2009:79; Museka, 'Exorcising the Colonial Jinx', 55–7.
[59] Sugirtharajah, *Bible and the Third World*, 167.
[60] Sugirtharajah, *Bible and the Third World*, 106.
[61] Political incorrectness with regard to homosexuality in Zimbabwe is measured against the position articulated by Mugabe. Voices considered sympathetic to gays and lesbians are vilified for being western stooges and therefore not worthy of being representatives of Zimbabweans. Due to this standard, it is almost impossible for public figures to freely articulate their views on the subject unless they are in agreement with the President.

stayed away from the story. Obedience had been overtaken by the need for the reiteration of heterosexual normativity while maintaining political correctness in an environment where political incorrectness is sometimes met with violent retribution. The world was being divided into the moral Africa or south versus the immoral West or north. Political and economic tensions were reduced to moral blemishes. In this brief analysis, it appears that at each stage the dominant engagement 'with the text overrides any other possible interpretation' without any specific regard to the author's intention.[62]

Conclusion

Reception history of the Bible promises to open up a critical phase in the study of the Bible in Africa, especially because of its insistence that we cannot totally ignore the fact that sub-Saharan Africa has received the Bible through the agency of Western-shaped Christianity. While there is always need to go back to the beginnings as is the argument of the historical-critical approaches that has sometimes come at the expense of studying the actual interaction of Christians and the Bible. The transactions between the Bible and the readers, seen as the effects and impact of one on the other have placed reception history at an advantage for it can begin to access areas that remained grey; areas that were not looked at by either church historians or biblical scholars. Through reception-historical goggles, the history of the Bible in Africa may turn out to be a new gold rush for biblical scholars. It promises to revisit the distant past but even more interesting, the multiplicity of Christianities across the continent of Africa can now be approached from this new perspective. This is particularly important because African Christianity has always claimed to be biblical Christianity.

---

[62] Sugirtharajah, *Bible and the Third World*, 108.

Part Four

Practical Implications, Difficulties and Solutions

10

Unlikely Bedfellows: Lenin, Calvin and Nick Cave

Roland Boer
University of Newcastle, Australia

Why would someone, part of whose training was in biblical scholarship, want or even dare to write books on V. I. Lenin, John Calvin or Nick Cave, among others? In answering that question, I outline three possible reasons and then discuss briefly each of these projects (while trying to avoid the trap of extensive and self-serving navel gazing).[1]

Erotics, the road and intersections

In the beginning are the erotics of knowledge. Deliberately misreading – among others – Plato or Michel de Certeau,[2] I understand such erotics in terms of what gets the juices flowing, what attracts us to a writer, critic, or thinker in the first place. What is it about their work that intrigues and catches our eye? Why does a first glance, a meeting with the words on the page, lead to a desire to meet again, to read further, and get to know this author? Why do I enjoy so much re-reading these texts and thinking about them? Like a love affair, the catch is that as soon as I try to enumerate the reasons – the syntax, the loop of a sentence, the arresting new angle on a problem, the politics and so forth – the actually allure is gone. Or rather, I have missed the point, the intangible element that attracts me in the first place. Of course, some such infatuations last less than a year, if even six months (is that not a common story?), but the ones that intrigue me the most are the long-standing attractions, the ones who do not suddenly appear flat and uninteresting after attracting me so.

---

[1] Mentioning that W. John Lyons first suggested I deal with some of the works I discuss below, in order to indicate where an erstwhile biblical critic may end up, helps me to shift the blame ever so slightly...

[2] Michel de Certeau, *The Practice of Everyday Life* (Berkeley: University of California Press, 1984), 92.

The analogy with lust and love is all too obvious (as my language suggests), but I would suggest it is more than an analogy. Knowledge does have an erotic charge, in and of itself. That it also has its traps, disappointments, broken hearts, betrayals and power struggles goes without saying. Despite, or perhaps because of these pitfalls, I always return. Among these are Lenin, Calvin and Nick Cave, although they are not alone (I would add Alexandra Kollontai, Marx and the Bible). Others simply leave me cold and uninterested. They include Plato, Carl Schmitt and Michel Foucault, no matter how much I may have read them. But a third group annoys me exceedingly, getting under my skin. They would make me angry if that were my wont. Here may be found Terry Eagleton, Giorgio Agamben and Luce Irigaray, although that is by no means an exclusive list. In some respects, this should be the most interesting group of them all, for I do not read them with pleasure, longing to open a volume I read many times before and discovering yet a new insight, a new angle.

A second reason for my attraction is what may be called the lure of the road. No matter how appealing home may be, no matter how much one may wish to stay put and enjoy the rhythms of daily life, the road beckons once again. The pull of faraway and unexplored places lures one on. Even as a student, I was on the road. I had begun my travels in the appealing territory of ancient history, of the Western 'Classics', no matter how constructed and problematic a category that is. From touring far and wide in the realms of Greek, Latin and Sanskrit, I moved on to theology and biblical criticism. Here too I enjoyed the company of the locals, learnt the languages, perhaps in the vain hope that one day I would be able to work in the department of immigration when time machines were in full operation. In the midst of all this I ventured into what was at that time the new territory of Hegel and Marx. Since those times, I have explored literary criticism, cultural criticism, psychoanalysis, music, theology, philosophy, and am now engaged in a full itinerary through economic theory. Some places I visit but once or twice, with little incentive to make any further forays, but to others I long to return and explore further. Marxism, in all its philosophical and political depth, is one such continent, but so also is religion, especially in the perennial question of the relation between the two.[3] Occasionally, one stumbles across a lost but vital manuscript, such as the virtually unknown two-volume work called *Religion and Socialism* by Anatoly Lunacharsky, a Left Bolshevik and Commissar for Enlightenment after the Russian

---

[3] Roland Boer, *Criticism of Heaven: On Marxism and Theology*, Historical Materialism Book Series (Leiden: E. J. Brill, 2007); Roland Boer, *Criticism of Religion: On Marxism and Theology II*, Historical Materialism Book Series (Leiden: Brill, 2009); Roland Boer, *Criticism of Theology: On Marxism and Theology III* (Leiden: Brill, 2011); Roland Boer, *Criticism of Earth: On Marx, Engels and Theology*, Historical Materialism Book Series (Leiden: Brill, 2012); Roland Boer, *In The Vale of Tears: On Marxism and Theology V*, Historical Materialism Book Series (Leiden: Brill, 2014).

Revolution.⁴ As I write, I am making my first forays into Chinese political and philosophical history, with a focus on Mao Zedong and the requisite immersion in the language and local cuisine.

But where and what is home? Some prefer to remain in the known (dis)comforts and security of such a home. But does it really exist? I would suggest that idea of a singular academic discipline is an ideological construct, in which the narrative of its own emergence and effort at singular identity is systematically concealed. For disciplines are really intersections of myriad other disciplines, which themselves operate in the same way. The truth of this situation is revealed by the 'new' disciplines, such as Studies in Religion, or Cultural Studies. While they struggle towards that identity, the various paths at the crossroads are there for all to see: sociology, anthropology, literary criticism, philosophy, and so on, in cultural studies; similarly for Studies in Religion, to which may be added history, political science and psychology (others often join the list). The sneers from 'established' disciplines are as much a sign of the requisite disciplinary chauvinism that comes with the claim to a stable core, as a mark of the buried narrative of their own emergence. In the end, as Wallerstein points out, a discipline is no more than an organization, a journal and an annual conference.⁵ With these institutional forms it polices the shibboleths that give the appearance of unity, not least of which is the designation of 'dilettante' for anyone who ventures beyond the established boundaries.

All of which leads to the third reason for disciplinary restlessness, which is the internal logic of a discipline that leads out from itself. I will take the example of biblical criticism, although that is by no means to prioritize it over any other discipline. If the roads come into the intersection, they also lead out, tempting anyone who is seduced by the lure of the road. In doing so, I do not leave behind me the skills carefully acquired during my sojourn there, but prefer to take them with me, reshape them and deploy them in areas where they may well shed a new angle on debates. I think especially of what may be called biblical commentary: the close reading of a text, attention to its linguistic detail, as well as to its always-already read status within a constellation of interpretations (that is, no pure, unread text exists), and the reality of the complex intersections of exegesis and eisegesis.

I prefer to describe such an approach in terms of five categories: it is intimate, immanent, comparative, historical and constructive. To begin with, this approach is

---

⁴ Anatoly Vasil'evich Lunacharsky, *Religiia i sotsializm: Tom 1* (Moscow: Shilpovnik, 1908); Anatoly Vasil'evich Lunacharsky, *Religiia i sotsializm: Tom 2* (Moscow: Shilpovnik, 1911). After much sleuthing, I and Sergey Kozin are the sole possessors of the only available pdf of this text in the world, written in old Cyrillic, before the language reforms of 1917. A re-publication in Russian and translation into English are planned.
⁵ Immanuel Wallerstein, *The Modern World-System IV: Centrist Liberalism Triumphant, 1789–1914* (Berkeley: University of California Press, 2011), 263.

intimate. By that I mean a careful and patient reading that refuses to rush over texts. Commentary of this type pays attention to the various twists, contradictions, problems and insights of a text. And it does so by working with the texts in their original languages as far as possible. In the process of such commentary, the commentator comes to know the text very closely. The approach is also *immanent*, which means I seek to draw the terms of analysis and critique from the text and thinker in question, deploying their own approach on their texts. Further, it is *comparative*. The approach compares the arguments and positions of one writer in light of the others. In order to avoid overlap with the immanent part of the analysis, this comparative moment is a second step. My approach is also historical, or rather, *genealogical*: the search for and exploration of the various historical paths a tradition of thought has taken. In some cases, it may be the case that such critical work may well establish that such a tradition exists, or at least change the shape it once had. Finally, my approach is *constructive*: I seek to build a coherent body of thought in response to the various contributors to this tradition and thereby renew the debate in the area concerned. The works I will discuss in a moment offer readings of Lenin in relation to theology, of Calvin as a radical, potentially revolutionary theologian, or of Nick Cave's complex interactions with religion. That such work has not really been undertaken before in any of these areas means that I have entertained the small hope that they do indeed engage in some constructive work. But that possibility has been enabled in part by some of the tools and approaches I brought with me on the roads out of that intersection known as biblical criticism.

Lenin, religion, and theology

Apart from the collected works of Marx and Engels, reading my way through the entire works of Lenin was one of the extraordinary experiences of my life. Alongside appreciating him as a revolutionary politician (so much so that the revolution associated with his name constituted the defining historical moment of at least the twentieth century), as a lover of fresh air, an avid cyclist and mountain-hiker, I have come to know him rather well as a writer and editor. When he was asked to fill in his profession, in those preparatory documents for congress delegates, he would simply write, 'literator [litterateur]'.[6] So I decided to read him

---

[6] V. I. Lenin, 'Reregistration Form for Members of the Moscow Organisation of the R.C.P. (B.).' *Collected Works*, Volume 42 (Moscow: Progress, 1960–72 [1920]), 445; V. I. Lenin, Анкета для перерегистрации членов московской организации РКП(б). 17 сентября 1920 г. *Polnoe sobranie sochinenii* [The Complete Collected Works]. 5th edition, Volume 41 (Moskva: Izdatel'stvo politicheskoi literatury, 1958–65 [1920]), 465; V. I. Lenin, 'Questionnaire for Delegates of the Ninth All-Russia Conference of the R.C.P. (Bolsheviks).' *Collected Works*, Volume 42 (Moscow: Progress, 1960–72 [1920]), 449; V. I. Lenin, Личная анкета. Для делегатов Всероссийской партийной конференции РКП большевиков. 20 сентября 1920 г. *Polnoe sobranie sochinenii* [The Complete Collected Works]. 5th edition, Volume 41 (Moskva: Izdatel'stvo politicheskoi literatury, 1958–65 [1920]), 280.

as a writer. A brilliant student, denied any formal university career due to his politics, prison and exile, he managed to forge a life as a writer all the same. The writing, translating, editing and publishing of books, pamphlets, journals and newspapers, would take place in whatever exilic place he and Nadezhda Krupskaya found themselves – Siberia, Germany, Switzerland, England, Poland, and so on. Occasionally, he would comment on the act of writing itself, all done by hand: '12.IV.1902 – I am writing in the train: I apologize for the scribble. If I have time, I shall write again more clearly.'[7] Throughout it all they lived simply indeed, in small quarters, relying on dribbles of money from family, publishing, newspaper subscriptions, or even the infamous 'expropriations'.

The collected works have their own narrative that escapes even the hands of the editors and their extraordinary introductions, full as the latter are of Soviet orthodoxy and not a little twisting as the more intriguing texts by Lenin were brought into line. They begin with the earliest writings from the 1890s by a young man in his early twenties. Full of contest with others on the Left or even the Liberals, partaking in the small, energetic and somewhat idealist revolutionary groups, the productive and not unenjoyable exile to Shushenskoe in Siberia, the long periods of exile to Western Europe, the shuffle from place to place, writing, editing, giving lectures and organizing, organizing, organizing. All the while the much-needed intellectual input to the movement is coupled with the slow spread of the party, its congresses and splits and struggles, the waxing and waning of revolutionary activity, until the crescendos of 1905 and 1917. During these times the writing peaks to an intense production, ideas are reformulated, experiences are assessed, and new plans developed. And then after the October Revolution, the longer texts become rare, while the speeches, telegrams, memos, telephone conversations overflow the long volumes. The desperateness of the multiple post-revolutionary crises shows forth, with hastily written pieces on transport problems, fuel and food shortages, disease, and the ever-present threats on four fronts from 'civil' war[8] – at least until the strokes begin and Lenin takes, under doctor's orders, more and more time away from the pressures. With his death by the thirty-third volume, the supplementary volumes begin, with less coherent collections of political correspondence spread out over the years, supplementary documents and newspaper reports, as well as some volumes of notes on agriculture, imperialism and philosophy. By the thirty-seventh volume a different and very personal correspondence emerges, now with Lenin's family, especially his mother and sisters, and a good number written by Krupskaya herself. We cover the same

---

[7] V. I. Lenin, 'Material for the Preparation of the Programme of the R.S.D.L.P.' *Collected Works*, Volume 6 (Moscow: Progress, 1960–72 [1902]), 71; V. I. Lenin, Материалы к выработке программы РСДРП. Январь–апрель 1902 г. *Polnoe sobranie sochinenii* [The Complete Collected Works]. 5th edition, Volume 6 (Moskva: Izdatel'stvo politicheskoi literatury, 1958–65 [1902]), 253.

[8] The White Armies were financed and equipped, as well as supported by ample troops from the UK, USA, Canada, France and others.

ground again, from the earliest years through to his death, but now with comments on different places, hiking, cycling, health, plans, personal thoughts and greetings. But even here, the habit of using coded texts and code names shows forth (as with the other pre-October correspondence), as does the extensive involvement of women in the party. In these last volumes a noticeable change of editorial direction also appears. Up until the thirty-third volume and Lenin's death, the texts were interspersed with occasional letters and telegrams to Stalin, attempting to indicate how much Stalin was Lenin's natural successor. Yet in the thirty-sixth volume, Lenin's 'Testament' appears, really a collection of letters and notes that were first made public at the famous closed meeting chaired by Khrushchev in 1956. Here are the warnings against the negative sides of Stalin, but also against Trotsky and the possibilities of a split between them (Bukharin and Pyatakov are also assessed rather astutely). By the end of the last volume, more letters critical of Stalin appear, including the famous reprimand for the latter's rudeness to Krupskaya when Lenin was already very ill, while the closer agreements with Trotsky are far more frequent. The open-ended nature of the collection, coupled with Lenin's own concerns about the future of the government leave a curiously unfinished feel, much as Ernst Bloch pointed out regarding any life that ends with so much left undone.

My focus in reading all this material concerned the theological resonances, engagements and reformulations that appear in Lenin's texts. They emerge in unexpected places, arresting moments of discovery and in the contradictory (dialectical) positions he took and then reworked. It may be his love of Gospel parables and sayings, his engagements with marginal Christian socialist groups and with 'God-builders', the encounters with Hegel, the suggestions that a revolution is like a miracle, and even in the veneration that emerged after his death.[9] In each case they provided much food for thought and careful analysis of his texts. The result was a long and detailed study of the multiple and often ambivalent approaches to religion in his texts.

But I also read with an eye for the quirky texts and unexpected moments, the discoveries that make you lift your eyes from the page for a laugh and quick note. Always a tendency of mine in reading texts, watching films, visiting places, engaging with the world, I have found that Roland Barthes related to the world in a similar fashion. He had a propensity to focus on the fragmentary hints and suggestions, the moments in a text – a quirky feature of a sentence, an image evoked or a trigger – that make one pause, look away and follow a train of thought. In thinking about this mode of receiving a text, Barthes spoke in a late and very personal text of a methodological discomfort that continually plagued him: 'the uneasiness of being a subject torn between two languages, one expressive, the

---

[9] Roland Boer, *Lenin, Religion, and Theology* (New York: Palgrave Macmillan, 2013).

other critical.'¹⁰ He goes to say that he had been attracted by the various critical discourses, such as sociology, semiology and psychoanalysis, but that, after a while, he grew weary of them one by one. Whenever they tended to harden and become reductive, he grew unhappy and quietly left them behind. And so he affirms once again an approach that gives him greater pleasure, following a curious hunch, seeing something from an unexpected angle. Nearly always brief, they have the feel of being written first thing in the morning on whatever item has grabbed his attention and triggered some reflection. It is like a photographer whose eye is always on watch for a distinct shot, a unique angle or a quirky feature. Indeed, the expressive and passing insights characteristic of earlier work like *Mythologies* return with rich vigour in later texts such as *The Pleasure of the Text, A Lover's Discourse* and *Camera Lucida*.¹¹ This is what I find myself doing more often than not, so it was reassuring to find that Barthes operated in a similar fashion – and thereby provided a mode of reception that would do well to find a greater role.

In relation to my engagement with Lenin, let me cite a few of the more intriguing examples of such moments. The first concerns Lenin's almost irrepressible optimism, even in the depths of the multiple post-revolutionary crises concerning food, fuel, transport, disease and the 'civil' war: 'There is no such thing as an absolutely hopeless situation.'¹² Another comes from 1922, when the inveterate non-drinker and non-smoker had had enough: 'Warn smokers. No smoking. Strictly. Tea and smoking during the break (in the adjoining room).'¹³ Yet another is a quotation from the irrepressible Engels: 'Each word is like a chamber-pot, and not an empty one at that' (*Jedes Wort – ein Nachttopf und kein leerer*).¹⁴ And, to shift focus slightly, we also stumble across a reference to anal sex. Let me set the scene: in the midst of a detailed demolition of Jean de Sismondi, the French economist,

---

[10] Roland Barthes, *Camera Lucida* (trans. Richard Howard, New York: Vintage 1993 [1980]), 9; Roland Barthes, *La chambre claire: Note sur la photographie*, in *Œuvres complètes, Volume V: 1977–1980* (Paris, Seuil 2002[1980], 794.

[11] Roland Barthes, *The Pleasure of the Text* (trans. Richard Miller, New York: Hill and Wang 1975 [1973]); Roland Barthes, *Le plaisir du texte*, in *Œuvres complètes, Volume IV: 1972–1976* (Paris: Seuil, 2002 [1973]); Roland Barthes, *A Lover's Discourse* (trans. Richard Howard, New York: Farrar, Straus and Giroux, 1978 [1977]); Roland Barthes, *Fragments d'un discours amoureux*, in *Œuvres complètes, Volume V: 1977–1980* (Paris: Seuil, 2002 [1977]); Barthes, *Camera Lucida*; Barthes, *La chamber claire*.

[12] V. I. Lenin, 'The Second Congress of the Communist International, July 19–August 7, 1920.' *Collected Works*, Volume 31 (Moscow: Progress, 1960–72 [1920]), 227; V. I. Lenin, II конгресс Коммунистического Интернационала 19 июля–7 августа 1920. г. *Polnoe sobranie sochinenii* [The Complete Collected Works]. 5th edition, Volume 41 (Moskva: Izdatel'stvo politicheskoi literatury, 1958–65 [1920]), 228.

[13] V. I. Lenin, 'To V.A. Smolyaninov, September 23, 1922.' *Collected Works*, Volume 45 (Moscow: Progress,1960–72 [1922]), 568; V. I. Lenin, В. А. Смольянинову. 23 сентября 1922 г. *Polnoe sobranie sochinenii* [The Complete Collected Works]. 5th edition, Volume 54 (Moskva: Izdatel'stvo politicheskoi literatury, 1958–65 [1922]), 286.

[14] V. I. Lenin, 'Social-Democracy and the Provisional Revolutionary Government.' *Collected Works*, Volume 8 (Moscow: Progress, 1960–72 [1905]), 156; V. I. Lenin, Социал-демократия и временное революционное правительство. 23 и 30 марта (5 и 12 апреля) 1905 г. *Polnoe sobranie sochinenii* [The Complete Collected Works]. 5th edition, Volume 10 (Moskva: Izdatel'stvo politicheskoi literatury, 1958–65 [1905]), 144.

Lenin notes Sismondi's argument that the church is failing in its task of condemning impudent and lusty marriages. According to Sismondi: 'Religious morality should teach people that having produced a family, it is their duty to live no less chastely with their wives than celibates with women who do not belong to them.'[15] Three children and then no more sex, according to Sismondi. Well, says Lenin, we all know how successful the French peasant is at such 'chastity', let alone priests in the church. In fact, as Proudhon argued, 'chastity', or indeed Malthus's 'birth control', is really 'the preaching of the connubial practice of ... a certain unnatural vice.'[16] In this light, it makes one wonder what a 'fist from below' may mean.[17] As a final example, reading some of Lenin's sharper letters is a distinct pleasure, so much so that I compiled what may be called the Lenin letter template, using phrases from such correspondence:

> Dear ...,
>
> I am writing under the fresh impression of your letter, which I have just read. Although you have resented my previous missives, I shall try to be mild and kind.
>
> I know of no task more fatiguing, more thankless and more disgusting than to have to wade through this filth. Yet your senseless twaddle is so exasperating that I am unable to suppress the desire to state my opinion frankly.
>
> You propose that we should collaborate with magniloquent liberal windbags, that we should philander with reaction. Strictly speaking, this proposal is too ludicrous to merit serious consideration, the product of either a charlatan or an absolute blockhead. The only answer can be a bitter laugh. You may couch it in pompous, high-blown phrases, but it is really befouled and spattered with shit. All your talk about freedom and democracy is sheer claptrap, parrot phrases, the product of mean-spirited boors, and your education, culture, and enlightenment are only a species of thoroughgoing prostitution. It is a ridiculous and puerile attempt to be clever.
>
> You either cannot think logically, or you are a liberal hypocrite, wriggling like the devil at mass. May I make one suggestion, as difficult as it may seem: scrape off all this green mold of intellectualist opportunism.
>
> Yours,
> V. Ulianov.

---

[15] V. I. Lenin, 'Draft and Explanation of a Programme for the Social-Democratic Party.' *Collected Works*, Volume 2 (Moscow: Progress, 1960–72 [1895]), 183; V. I. Lenin, Проект и объяснение программы социал-демократической партии. Декабрь, позднее 9 (21), 1895 г.; июнь–июль 1896 г. *Polnoe sobranie sochinenii* [The Complete Collected Works]. 5th edition, Volume 2 (Moskva: Izdatel'stvo politicheskoi literatury, 1958–65 [1895]), 176.

[16] V. I. Lenin, 'Draft and Explanation,' 184; Проект и объяснение, 177.

[17] V. I. Lenin, 'The Reorganisation of the Party.' *Collected Works*, Volume 10 (Moscow: Progress, 1960–72 [1905]), 37; V. I. Lenin, О реорганизации партии. 10–16 (23–29) ноября 1905 г. *Polnoe sobranie sochinenii* [The Complete Collected Works]. 5th edition, Volume 12 (Moskva: Izdatel'stvo politicheskoi literatury, 1958–65 [1905]), 92.

P.S. I cannot share your regret at not having met. After your tricks and your conniving attitude, I do not wish to have anything to do with you except in a purely official way, and only in writing.

One can only dream of writing a letter so. But my own reading has produced a whole series of reconfigurations of what may be called the translatability of politics and theology in a way that counters the tendency of either one to claim absolute status.

Jean Calvin, revolutionary

In some senses, the study of Calvin – timed to appear on the actual day of the celebration of 500 years since his birth (10 July 1509) – came closer to biblical criticism, for Calvin was an astute and careful reader of the Bible.[18] But it was a Calvin with a difference, a Calvin caught between his naturally conservative bent and the clearly radical directions of the many of the texts and doctrinal positions he formulated. So he engages in the 'brawling art which bears the name of speculative theology.'[19]

The study of Calvin was an 'intervention', that is, it sought to shake up some of the basic assumptions about Calvin: that his thought provides the ideological underpinning for capitalism; that he makes sense of the recent neoconservatives (especially in the USA); that he was in favour of reform and not revolution; that he was responsible for a brutal and unforgiving theological system. Instead, I argued that Calvin struggled deeply with the radical and reactionary elements of the Bible and his theological system. I did so through a close reading of his *Institutes of the Christian Religion*.

But the book also reflected my own coming to terms with Calvin, with whom I grew up and whose ideas and legacy frame the world in which I live (my parents were immigrants from the Netherlands and members of the Gereformeerde Kerken, a breakaway group from the Hervormde Kerk). It is well-nigh impossible to brush off such a heritage, although try I did in every possible manner. But it kept returning, so I decided it was best to come to terms with Calvin – not a cordial but frosty acquaintance, like Voltaire's habit of tipping his hat when passing a church so as to keep on good terms with the God he was rejecting, but an intimate and careful coming to terms.

---

[18] Roland Boer, *Political Grace: The Revolutionary Theology of John Calvin* (Louisville: Westminster John Knox, 2009).
[19] Johannes Calvini, *Institutiones Christianae Religionis*, Volume 3 (Ed. P. Barth and G. Niesel. 3 vols, *Opera Selecta*. Monachii in Aedibus: Chr. Kaiser, 1957 [1559]), 22:7–8.

It all began some years ago when, on a whim, I bought my own copy of the *Institutes of the Christian Religion*.[20] Then I found a cheap collection of all his biblical commentaries, translated and published by the Calvin Translation Society in the mid-nineteenth century. I even managed to track down a copy of the *Institutes* in Latin.[21] Soon I began to think much about Calvin. At first they were stray thoughts. Why did he die so early, at fifty-two? The answer seemed obvious: he worked himself to death. One comment brought this home to me like no other. It comes from the 'Epistle to the Reader' prefaced to the last edition of the *Institutes*. Calvin mentions that he suffered from a form of malaria, which he calls the quartan fever (*febre quartana*), through the preceding winter while preparing the final edition ('final' largely because he died before any more could be completed). Did he slow down so that he might recover? Did he take some bed rest and get a decent night's sleep? No, he worked even harder: 'The more the disease pressed upon me the less I spared myself, until I could leave a book behind me.'[22]

Calvin wrote so much in so short a time, all of it by hand. The Protestant work ethic, if it exists? No, Calvin suffered from another affliction: a demanding muse. Søren Kierkegaard was subject to one and died at forty-two. Karl Marx's muse made the same demands, and Marx managed to struggle on to sixty-two, even though he was riddled with ill health for most of it and ceased effective work by his early fifties. Lenin too had the same muse, pushing him, pushing him, until the October Revolution tipped the scales and he had a series of strokes that knocked him over by his early fifties. This muse demands that one write, no matter what the circumstances. Neither a sensitive nor alcoholic muse, this one expects writing no matter what. If you put anything in the way, such as a nonwriting job, hobbies, other people, or relationships, then they will suffer, as will your health and sleep. It is not for nothing that we find the following epigraph in the *Institutes*. It is drawn from Augustine: 'I count myself one of the number of those who by profiting write and by writing profit.'[23]

I asked many other questions as I read. Why did Calvin's system of thought seem so compellingly watertight? What did he see in Augustine, the highly skilled writer and church's theological hit man? Why does he write so well? Why is the *Institutes of the Christian Religion* so thick? And why did it become more and more obvious to me that in some way Calvin and Marx had a lot in common? Why indeed is there a distinct path from Calvin to Marx rather than a high fence? To answer these and other questions I had to write the book. After setting the context in a revolutionary era (with the revolution of Münster and the Peasants under

---

[20] John Calvin, *Institutes of the Christian Religion* (translated by F. L. Battles, The Library of Christian Classics, Louisville, KY: Westminster John Knox, 2006).
[21] Johannes Calvini, *Institutiones Christianae Religionis*.
[22] Johannes Calvini, *Institutiones Christianae Religionis*, 5: 19.
[23] Johannes Calvini, *Institutiones Christianae Religionis*, 7: 8–9.

Thomas Müntzer in the immediate past), the book set out to analyse Calvin's ambivalent doctrine of the Bible, the themes of radical grace, Christian freedom and civil (dis)order.

Through it all, my argument was that Calvin struggles with a theological tension that has long-ranging political implications. It is a tension between radical and conservative elements in his thought, or between the revolutionary and reactionary. Calvin keeps opening up radical possibilities in all manner of theological corners, possibilities that he then sets out carefully to contain in a conservative fashion. In order to illustrate the point, I used the image of the revolutionary cat in the theological bag. Time and again Calvin opens up the mouth of the bag, however small the opening may be, and the cat glimpses daylight and makes a dash for freedom. Each time, Calvin manages to clasp the bag shut again before the cat can break out or even sink a claw or fang into those firm hands wrapped around the mouth of the bag. Calvin may open the bag deliberately or not so deliberately, for sometimes the radical possibility is an unintended consequence of a position he has taken. But every effort to shove the cat back in and tie up the mouth of the bag is definitely intentional. After all, Calvin's default position is a conservative one, and many have read and understood him in precisely this fashion. He would dearly like the world to be so; the problem is that the Bible he reads and the position he espouses are not so neat and tidy. However, by the last chapter of the *Institutes* Calvin does indeed let the revolutionary cat out of the bag. Here it is a conjunction of both his theological position (all of us, rulers included, are fallen creatures and must obey God) and his high view of Scripture (it proceeds from the mouth of God and is not dependent on human beings). Against his better judgement, both make it perfectly clear that believers are not to obey ungodly rulers.

Cave droppings: On love, death and apocalypse

Like the study of Calvin, this was an intimate and personal work, although the reason was quite different.[24] An indispensable feature of my writing is that I must listen to music while doing so, usually the same relatively small selection of music that allows me to enter the intimate space of a very familiar home of thought. With anticipation, a sigh and a deep sense of pleasure, I enter more deeply into that world and as I do so the concerns of the world about me slip into the distance for a while. More than once, that approach has enabled me to deal with difficult periods, providing a blessed relief. But it is also deeply sustaining in all circumstances. Occasionally – to gloss Adorno – I move around the various items of that world, which I envision as a room or shack, but they are deeply familiar and

---

[24] Roland Boer, *Nick Cave: A Study of Love, Death and Apocalypse* (London: Equinox, 2012).

well worn-in: chair, a simple table, a picture, a book or two and a few familiar musicians.

One of those musicians is Nick Cave, a singular, idiosyncratic and brilliant Australian who has not always enjoyed wide acclaim. He is perhaps most well-known as the lead singer of The Bad Seeds, which Chris Bailey, the chain-smoking lead singer of The Saints, once introduced on stage as 'The Best Fucking Band in the Universe.' My study was an effort to understand Cave's appeal, specifically through the lens of his extended biblical and theological engagements. I did so not merely in terms of his written work, the novels and plays and poetry and lyrics that he continues to produce, but also the music itself – even though that division between the lyrical and the musical is a result of the reified and fragmented (that is, capitalist) system in which we live. Above all, I was interested in how Cave reads the Bible, the total depravity of his imaginary world, its apocalyptic patterns, the welcome focus on death, on love, the concern with Christ and the changing nature of the music (specifically in terms of forms of the song) he has produced.

The methodological basis was the music theory of Theodor Adorno and especially Ernst Bloch. I drew heavily from a much-neglected but fascinating opening section of Bloch's *The Spirit of Utopia* called 'The Philosophy of Music.'[25] The key to Bloch's analysis is a sensitivity to the utopian and redemptive possibilities embodied in music, his bold efforts at dialectical reading, his emphasis on the human dimension of music, especially hearing and singing, and above all his realization of the interweaving of religion and music – all of which rendered Bloch's philosophy of music extremely useful for my engagement with Cave. In the text itself, I began with literary analysis, casting aspersions on Cave's written and spoken word as means of controlling interpretation, dealing with his novels, poetry and plays, before passing onto his song lyrics – on the themes of apocalyptic, death, love and Jesus. But even in those thematic considerations, I already broached questions of musical form. Those initial forays led into the last, detailed and long study of the changing forms of the song in three decades of musical production. More specifically, I distinguished between three forms (along with some variants), the anarchic/discordant song, the hymn (and its associated lament) and the dialectical song. As the last form indicates, this was a dialectical analysis, profoundly informed by Bloch's philosophy of music.

What was the outcome of this engagement with musical form and word? Like Beethoven, Willy Nelson and Bob Dylan, to name but a few, Nick Cave seeks an elusive redemption in and through music and literature. And so I traced the different options he has pursued. It might take place, inexplicably, in the midst of

---

[25] Ernst Bloch, *The Spirit of Utopia* (translated by A. A. Nassar. Stanford, CA: Stanford University Press, 2000), 31–164; Ernst Bloch, *Geist der Utopie, Zweite Fassung. Ernst Bloch Werkausgabe*, Volume 3 (Frankfurt am Main: Suhrkamp Verlag, 1985), 49–208. Also published in Ernst Bloch, *Essays on the Philosophy of Music* (translated by P. Palmer. Cambridge: Cambridge University Press, 1985), 1–139; Ernst Bloch, *Zur Philosophie der Musik* (Frankfurt am Main: Suhrkamp, 1974), 7–164.

total depravity, or the grand scale of apocalyptic might provide a glimpse, or death turns out not to be the final word, or the different forms of music in the songs may struggle to achieve a moment of dialectical *Aufhebung*, but the desire for redemption is resolutely persistent.

On the road again

A little earlier I used the metaphor of being on the road in relation to the continual allure of other disciplines, approaches and subject matters. The truth is that I completed each of these three works while literally on the road, or rather at sea or on a long-distance train. Thus, the study of Lenin was finished while I was voyaging on the MV *Finntrader*, a Roro freighter (roll-on, roll-off), on the old Hanseatic League route between Leningrad and Lübeck. The study of Calvin was written while on the MV *Hansa Rendsburg*, a freighter on the Tasman Sea, doing the run between Tauranga, New Zealand and Melbourne. And the work on Nick Cave began on the freighter, MV *La Tour*, which took me half way around the world, from Melbourne to Tilbury via two oceans, five seas and the Panama Canal. Thirty-seven days it took, from late June to the end of July, 2010, travelling in a way that human beings have done for millennia before this strange and brief period of air travel. And I completed the book on the journey home, six months later, on the Trans-Siberian train, crossing from Moscow to Beijing in the midst of a Siberian winter. Biblical criticism leads one on strange and unexpected journeys.

11

Tracing Patmos Through the Centuries

Ian Boxall

Travelling to Patmos

My first visit to the terrestrial island of Patmos occurred in the suitably apocalyptic year 2000. It was an unpredictable journey: I had booked a late-night flight from London to Athens, hoped to find a ferry departing from Piraeus on my arrival in Greece, and had little confidence that I would find suitable accommodation when I finally arrived on Patmos a day later. I travelled with my own image of the Patmos I would find, derived piecemeal from reading the Book of Revelation, classic paintings of John in ecstasy on the island, and the occasional postcard of a beautiful sunset over an idyllic Hellenic landscape. What I discovered when I finally arrived only partly corresponded to the Patmos I had carried with me in my imagination.

I have retraced that journey across the Aegean on several occasions since. But I have also been engaged over the past five years in a parallel journey, to the Patmos of other people's imaginings.[1] My starting-point was the one biblical reference to Patmos, at the beginning of the Book of Revelation. It is a reference which is tantalizingly brief and ambiguous: 'I, John, ... was on the island which is called Patmos on account of the word of God and the testimony of Jesus' (Rev. 1:9). My project was to explore the various avenues which this phrase had opened up to interpreters of the Apocalypse across the centuries. How had Patmos been imagined, within the much broader reception history of the Book of Revelation? What significance had been accorded to John's island, as place, as backdrop to his apocalyptic visions, or as symbol for an alternative way of life made possible by John's visionary book? In what follows, I intend to take a step back and reflect upon that experience of the past five years. I hope that some reflection upon my particular foray into the reception history of the Book of Revelation may contribute to understanding this thing called 'reception history'.

Using the metaphor of a journey to structure my reflections is not without its limitations. In reality it was not one journey, given that it required tapping into the

---

[1] Ian Boxall, *Patmos in the Reception History of the Apocalypse* (Oxford Theology and Religion Monographs; Oxford: OUP, 2013).

divergent journeys of others who had explored the significance of Patmos before me, and encountering their very different 'Patmoses of the imagination'. Nonetheless, the metaphor is a useful one, given my experience of the process as one of exploration and discovery. Like the intrepid visitor to the Aegean Patmos, for whom guidebooks, a good map and a set of ferry timetables are indispensable, my reception-historical exploration required careful preparation, guidance on appropriate directions to take and descriptions of the terrain I could be expected to encounter. As a 'chastened' historical critic[2] learning that I was part of the very historical process I was attempting to investigate, I very soon realized that my historical-critical predecessors had ill prepared me for the voyage. The 'expert' travel guides I had to hand – the critical commentaries of Charles, Swete, or Beale – were not quite up to the task. Were there other possibilities, and other routes to get to my destination, suggested by abandoning the scholarly equivalent of the Lonely Planet or Rough Guide in favour of older or less familiar guidebooks? And where was I to look if I was to find them?

Plotting the journey

My dilemma was a familiar one for those who dive into the deep waters of the reception-historical enterprise. In his discussion of the impact of reception history on New Testament studies, James Crossley identifies three approaches. Some take a theologically-motivated line, which gives priority to classic expositions within specific faith communities. Second, there are those who engage in reception history as a 'corrective', in order to do historical criticism better: asking how earlier receptions might force us to rethink consensus views about original context and meaning. Finally, there is what Crossley calls 'anything goes': keeping the parameters of the search as broad as possible.[3] In my examination of Patmos, rather recklessly perhaps, I opted for the third option. I wanted to encounter as many different receptions of Rev. 1:9 as I could, irrespective of genre, cultural context, or ecclesial commitment (or lack of it). I was keen to examine marginal and maverick interpretations, as well as the mainstream and magisterial: though in the event, even some of the latter provided unexpected surprises.

This 'anything goes' approach may sound all too daunting and unwieldy for someone considering embarking on a reception-historical study themselves. However, I want to offer the budding reception historian some assurance and encouragement. The first thing to acknowledge is that reception history is always provisional, and demands of its practitioners a certain humility and realism. There

---

[2] For the phrase 'chastened historical criticism', see John Barton and John Muddiman, eds., *The Oxford Bible Commentary* (Oxford and New York: OUP, 2001), 1.
[3] James G. Crossley, *Reading the New Testament: Contemporary Approaches* (London and New York: Routledge, 2010), 117–163.

will always be more to uncover, perhaps even tomorrow, which might demand a radical revision of our carefully-crafted conclusions. Markus Bockmuehl uses the metaphor of 'a vast iceberg' which 'lies very largely submerged beneath the waves of history.'[4] Ulrich Luz, meanwhile, reminds us that 'the history of the influence of biblical texts is infinite; the knowledge of every commentator is finite.'[5] We will never have the final word (although the raw material at our disposal is significantly more substantial than that utilized by traditional biblical studies). Our provisional work might, however, be the springboard for better and more detailed reception-historical work by those who come after.

My second reassurance consists in a fairly simple outline of how I went about the task, which proved to be a fruitful yet manageable exercise. The first step was to accumulate relevant material. My starting-point was the small body of scholarly literature on the subject of Patmos, which although not amounting to much in terms of words, did convince me that the subject matter had significant potential.[6] I also made good use of published works on the wider reception history of Revelation, whether across the centuries or in particular periods.[7] Other standard resources, such as *Biblia Patristica*, Migne's *Patrologia Graeca* and *Patrologia Latina*, provided additional leads to be followed up. However, much of the more interesting material was discovered by trial and error, through random key word searches in library catalogues, or Internet bibliographical resources. Given my chosen topic, I was also able to enjoy many a happy hour seeking out visual images of John on Patmos.

But accumulating the material was only the first step. How was I to decide what to include, and to categorize and organize my selection? In terms of selection, I opted to provide examples of different types of interpretation rather than an exhaustive account, which would have risked becoming unwieldy as well as boringly repetitive. As for organization, the principles I adopted were primarily chronological and geographical (although interpretations in visual art were treated separately, given the distinctive issues surrounding visual exegesis). This enabled me to create a narrative framework which, I like to think, gave shape to the material

---

[4] Markus Bockmuehl, 'A Commentator's Approach to the 'Effective History' of Philippians,' *JSNT* 60 (1995), 66.

[5] Ulrich Luz, *Matthew 1-7: A Commentary*, trans. Wilhelm C. Linss (Edinburgh: T. & T. Clark, 1989), 95.

[6] Particularly helpful were Henri Dominique Saffrey, 'Relire l'Apocalypse à Patmos,' *RB* 82 (1975), 385-417; Friedrich Wilhelm Horn, 'Johannes auf Patmos,' in *Studien zur Johannesoffenbarung und ihrer Auslegung. Festschrift für Otto Böcher zum 70. Geburtstag*, ed. Friedrich Wilhelm Horn and Michael Wolter (Neukirchen-Vluyn: Neukirchener Verlag, 2005), 139-159; Eve-Marie Becker, 'Patmos - ein *utopischer* Ort? Apk 1,9-11 in auslegungs- und kulturgeschichtlicher Hinsicht,' *Saeculum* 59/I (2008), 81-106.

[7] E.g. Richard K. Emmerson and Bernard McGinn, eds, *The Apocalypse in the Middle Ages* (Ithaca and London: Cornell University Press, 1992); Arthur W. Wainwright, *Mysterious Apocalypse: Interpreting the Book of Revelation* (Nashville: Abingdon Press, 1993); Judith Kovacs and Christopher Rowland, *Revelation* (Blackwell Bible Commentary; Malden MA, Oxford, and Carlton, Victoria: Blackwell, 2004); Christopher Rowland, 'Imagining the Apocalypse,' *NTS* 51 (2005), 303-27; William John Lyons and Jorunn Økland, eds., *The Way the World Ends? The Apocalypse of John in Culture and Ideology* (Sheffield: Sheffield Phoenix Press, 2009).

without significant distortion of the evidence. It began in the formative early patristic period, before considering the divergent paths taken by Eastern and Western interpreters from about the sixth century onwards. Organizing chronologically and geographically also made it possible to trace potential genealogical relationships between specific interpretations within particular religious traditions. Given the large amount of material discussed, I could not examine the historical and cultural contexts of all interpreters discussed, although I endeavoured to do so for readings which seemed to me particularly unusual or innovative. Finally, a more 'analogical' analysis of the resulting narrative enabled me to juxtapose similar types of interpretation across the centuries, cultures and religious traditions.

Reading closely

Let us return for the moment to the motif of the journey. A wise traveller will undertake exhaustive research in preparation for the trip. She will want to devour every last page of the guidebook, study the map in detail, and ensure that the travel timetables have been accurately interpreted. Similarly, one would expect the New Testament scholar to have engaged in a careful and thoughtful reading of the biblical text. One of the greatest surprises I encountered when I embarked on this enterprise was how much more closely so-called 'pre-critical' interpreters attended to the words of the text than I had been trained to do as a critical scholar. I had been taught to regard Rev. 1:9 as a relatively straightforward text which required little exegetical comment. On the surface, this seems a reasonable presumption. After all, the verse in question occurs in one of the few uncontroversial sections of the Apocalypse, locating the narrator socially and geographically in this world before the heavenly world breaks in at Rev. 4:1.

When I began to slow down, however, and listen to what those alternative voices across the centuries had to say, I began to wonder whether I had really been listening at all. Had I been so keen to ask what 'on account of' might mean (the key exegetical question for most modern commentators on this verse), that I had overlooked other words in this verse, presumably equally carefully chosen by the author? The opening phrase 'I, John ...', after all, might be an important textual marker alerting me to parallels with earlier visionary texts, such as Ezekiel 1 and Daniel 10, where named places become the setting for extraordinary encounters. Had the received scholarly wisdom prevented me from asking about the theological significance of place in a passage such as this?[8] Having been trained to locate

---

[8] Recent theologians who have explored the theology of place include Philip Sheldrake, *Spaces for the Sacred: Place, Memory and Identity* (London: SCM, 2001); John Inge, *A Christian Theology of Place* (Aldershot: Ashgate, 2003); David Brown, *God and Enchantment of Place: Reclaiming Human Experience* (Oxford: OUP, 2004).

Patmos on a map of the Mediterranean world and then to move swiftly on, had I omitted to ask about the significance of the word 'island'? Yet, once I turned to older interpreters, I saw how much had been lost by ignoring the rich biblical associations of the islands with the marginal lands of the Gentiles, not to mention the classical concept of the sacred island (Patmos, after all, was renowned in antiquity as the island of Artemis).

Moreover, how many of my recent scholarly predecessors had paid attention to John's inclusion of the verb to 'call' (καλεῖν), when 'the island of Patmos' would surely have been sufficient? Perhaps even more crucially, why had I failed to notice that the participle καλουμένη was in the passive, potentially a divine passive? In other words, might the text be conveying more than geographical identification at this point? Might it also, perhaps more importantly, be making the claim that *God* has called this island 'Patmos', and that exploration of the name's meaning is not only legitimate but encouraged? When one recalls that Revelation is an apocalypse, and that, as Martha Himmelfarb notes, such writings 'make no distinction between mythic geography and real,'[9] the potential for a more than literal geography becomes compelling. Indeed, it is reinforced by the very similar language of Rev. 11:8 (albeit here καλεῖν is in the indicative rather than a participle), where 'the great city' is 'spiritually called Sodom and Egypt, where also their Lord was crucified.'

All these possibilities, largely forgotten by twentieth- and twenty-first-century commentators,[10] emerged at various points as I embarked on my quest to trace Patmos through the centuries. Nor were these the only options. In the remainder of this paper, I want to reflect upon some of the more surprising examples I encountered on my journey, and some of the unexpected conclusions I was forced to draw as a result. I offer them here as illustrations both of the fruitfulness of reception-historical study, and of its indispensable role in a rounded and textually-grounded biblical criticism.

Patmos as place of exile

I begin with what has become something of an 'assured result' of Revelation scholarship: that John was exiled to Patmos by Roman authorities. John's statement that he was there 'on account of the word of God and the testimony of Jesus' is understood in terms of exile or banishment as a result of preaching. Although

---

[9] Martha Himmelfarb, 'The Temple and the Garden of Eden in Ezekiel, the Book of the Watchers, and the Wisdom of ben Sira,' in *Sacred Places and Profane Spaces: Essays in the Geographics of Judaism, Christianity, and Islam* (Westport, CT: Greenwood Press, 1991), 63–78 (quotation from 63).

[10] One notable exception is Heinrich Kraft, *Die Offenbarung des Johannes* (HNT 16a; Tübingen: J.C.B. Mohr (Paul Siebeck), 1974).

there is the occasional dissenter to this interpretation, it would appear to have solid exegetical grounds. Critical commentators frequently note that it accords better with John's normal usage of the preposition διά with the accusative (to express result rather than purpose) than do alternative readings which have John arrive on Patmos in order to preach or to receive visions.

Second, the exile thesis is the earliest attested interpretation in Revelation's reception history – or at least in that tip of the reception-historical iceberg my research has so far uncovered – and is regularly repeated by interpreters throughout the intervening centuries. It can be found depicted in stained glass and illuminated manuscripts; as part of the story of John's heroic exploits, it is retold in sermons and drama, and survives in popular collections such as Jacobus de Voragine's *Golden Legend*. It is no surprise, therefore, to discover that commentary on this phrase is one of those rare occasions when modern critical scholars engage with Revelation's reception history (although, for the most part, they restrict themselves to the early patristic reception).[11]

However, a closer look at that reception history reveals that things are not so simple. To begin with, a minority of earlier interpreters share the view of the modern dissenters that the Greek διά or the Vulgate's *propter* may be rendered differently, to describe the reason why he went to Patmos. More noticeably, even those who argue for the exile explanation do not necessarily rule out alternatives as mutually exclusive. Thus, to give just one example, the tenth-century Byzantine author Simeon Metaphrastes has John utilize the opportunity of his exile for missionary purposes, converting the islanders to the Christian faith.[12]

Even if one retains the focus on result rather than purpose, other possibilities suggest themselves besides exile. John went to Patmos by divine inspiration, as a consequence of *hearing* God's word and Jesus' own testimony. In other words, God directed him to this island, perhaps to receive the visions he now describes. Alternatively, John found himself on the island because of *studying* God's word: perhaps including those Old Testament prophets who envisaged the conversion of the islands in the last days (e.g. Isa. 66:19 LXX). Or, if he did provoke the wrath of imperial authorities as a consequence of preaching, he could have opted for voluntary flight to Patmos in order to avoid imprisonment. This is precisely the view taken in John Napier's 1593 paraphrase of Rev. 1:9: 'I *Iohn* . . . was fugitiue in only of the yles of the *Sporade*s, called *Pathmos*, for professing the worde of God, and for bearing true testimonie of Christ Iesus.'[13]

---

[11] E.g. Henry Barclay Swete, *The Apocalypse of St John* (London: Macmillan, 1906), 12; R. H. Charles, *A Critical and Exegetical Commentary on the Revelation of St John* (ICC; Edinburgh: T. & T. Clark, 1920), I: 22.

[12] *Symeonis Logothetae, cognomento Metaphrastae, Opera Omnia: PG* 116: 689–92.

[13] John Napier, *A Plaine Discouery of the whole Reuelation of Sainct Iohn* (Edinburgh: Robert Waldegraue, 1593), 72–3.

But there is an even more significant point which the reception history reveals, but which critical commentators such as Swete and Charles seem to have missed. The preference of early patristic authors for the exile interpretation reflects an 'engaged' reading of the biblical text closely related to their own social context. A number of the key patristic players in promoting this theory of exile under Domitian – Tertullian, Origen, Victorinus – do so in situations where Christians were facing persecution from one or other of Domitian's successors.

Tertullian writes against the backdrop of Roman persecution in North Africa at the beginning of the third century. Origen's own father, Leonides, was martyred during the persecution under Septimius Severus. Victorinus' Latin commentary on Revelation was composed in the aftermath of Valerian's persecution, and Victorinus himself would subsequently undergo a martyr's death, under either Numerius or Diocletian. In such contexts, the Apocalypse has quite understandably become a book of consolation for the martyrs.

This formative patristic interpretation had a profound impact on subsequent readers of Revelation. John as victim of imperial persecution becomes the dominant reading. Yet, in rather different times, the heat is taken out of the exile theory, allowing complementary attention to other possibilities. Thus later patristic and medieval readers of Rev. 1:9 also explore the significance of Patmos as place of revelation, including its symbolic potential for the contemplative and monastic life. The centrality of John as beleaguered exile returns with a particular vengeance in early Protestant exegesis. Again, social context plays a key role. Sixteenth-century Protestants find themselves in an analogous situation to that of John – or rather the John of patristic exegetes – facing the ire, not of pagan Rome this time but of papal Rome, the new Babylon.[14] Indeed, a number of them are exiles: the earliest Protestant commentary on the Apocalypse in English, John Bale's *The Image of Bothe Churches* (written in the 1540s), was composed while Bale was an exile in Flanders.

This early patristic and early Protestant reading is a compelling one, which enabled Revelation to speak powerfully in contexts of political oppression and religious controversy. But is it the 'original sense' of the text, as the vast majority of modern critical commentators assert with uncharacteristic confidence?[15] My reception-historical journey has left me wondering. Perhaps the image of John the persecuted exile should be regarded instead as a secondary re-reading for new circumstances (or what Judith Kovacs and Christopher Rowland have called an

---

[14] This anti-papal potential of Revelation is underscored by Cranach's woodcut of Babylon wearing the papal triple tiara, which appeared in Luther's September Testament of 1522. On this see Ian Boxall, 'The Many Faces of Babylon the Great: *Wirkungsgeschichte* and the Interpretation of Revelation 17,' in *Studies in the Book of Revelation*, ed. Steve Moyise (Edinburgh and New York: T. & T. Clark, 2001), 51–68.

[15] For an important challenge to the theory of Domitianic persecution, see Leonard L. Thompson, *The Book of Revelation: Apocalypse and Empire* (New York and Oxford: OUP, 1990).

'actualization', the Apocalypse providing the interpretative lens through which these interpreters have made sense of their situation).[16] John's ambiguous phrase 'on account of the word of God etc.' certainly provides space for the text to speak directly and meaningfully to the Tertullians, Origens and Bales of this world. Reception history reminds us, however, of the intimate interweaving of text and context, as well as opening up other neglected interpretative strands which scholarly preferences might cause us to forget.

Lonely Patmos

Often found in tandem with the exile hypothesis is the image of Patmos as a barren landscape, where John languishes in solitary confinement. John is envisaged as a Robinson Crusoe figure, though without his Man Friday, seated on a rocky, and otherwise deserted, island. Alternatively, he has company, but it is the bitter-sweet company of fellow-prisoners, labouring in the quarries or the mines. Such a view of Patmos has caught the popular imagination, and is reflected in many artistic portrayals of the scene, notably in the West. From Giotto's lone dreamer to Botticelli's solitary figure scribbling his prophecy; from Dürer's woodcut of John voraciously devouring the heavenly book (Rev. 10:10) to Diego Velázquez's youthful visionary experiencing the dark night of the soul: John's Patmos has frequently been imagined as a harsh and lonely environment. Moreover, it is an image reflected in a good number of modern critical commentaries.

Again, the seeds of such an interpretation are relatively early. Victorinus establishes the connection between John's Patmos sojourn and hard labour in the mines, whilst the sixth-century Greek exegete Oecumenius paints a picture of Patmos as a 'small and desolate island.'[17] But they are not the only possibilities (indeed, many of the earliest patristic authors seem decidedly uninterested in the local detail). The popular fifth-century *Acts of John by Prochorus*, which offer a lengthy and detailed narrative of John's years on Patmos, imagine the island as a vast and populous narrative world. Attributed to the Prochorus of Acts 6:5, this early Christian novella has John encounter a significant number of individuals and groups (including Roman officials and pagan priests), and establish a substantial fledgling church from amongst the residents of Patmos. This rather different Eastern picture is also reflected in Byzantine icons of John, where he regularly appears in the company of Prochorus as his disciple and scribe.

---

[16] Kovacs and Rowland, *Revelation*, 7–11.
[17] William C. Weinrich (ed.), *Ancient Christian Texts: Latin Commentaries on Revelation* (Downers Grove: IVP Academic, 2011), p. 13; Oecumenius, *Commentary on the Apocalypse*, trans. John N. Suggitt (The Fathers of the Church; Washington, D.C.: Catholic University of America Press, 2006), p. 48.

A strictly historical approach, despite the impression given by some historical-critical commentators, suggests that the imaginative reconstruction found in the *Prochorus Acts* might be much closer to John's own world than Oecumenius's 'small and desolate island' or the depopulated Patmos of so much Western art. Archaeological and inscriptional evidence reveals Patmos to have had a thriving population large enough to support a gymnasium, and temples to Apollo and Artemis, and historic links with the mainland city of Miletus.[18] This is a far cry from the inherited picture of John the solitary prisoner.

But my reception-historical journey has taught me that this is not all to be said. If the image of a persecuted exile allowed Revelation to speak powerfully to persecuted Christians at various points in Christian history, the perception of the island's solitude and tranquillity was able to serve other purposes in different times. When the monk Christodoulos founded the monastery on Patmos in 1088, for example, the changed circumstances of the island – depopulated in previous centuries due to pirate attacks and subsequently overgrown – made it an ideal location for the contemplative life. Nor was this unique to Orthodox Christianity. The island's remoteness, and the sense that its physical separation from the ordinary world facilitated unhampered access to the heavenly world – a point made by commentators such as Primasius, Beatus and Bede – encouraged figurative interpretations of Patmos as a symbol for monasticism throughout medieval Europe. In making such a claim, medieval monks such as Joachim of Fiore and Geoffrey of Auxerre may have been wide of the mark historically. But can one thereby dismiss their interpretation as a fundamental misreading of Revelation? Or have they tapped into other dimensions of the text, whether the emphasis upon heavenly revelation through contemplation, or the potential invitation (noted above in our close reading of Rev. 1:9) to explore the deeper significance of the name Patmos and its character as an island?

Playing with names and numbers

The latter point brings me to perhaps one of the most puzzling interpretations I encountered on my reception-historical journey. Repeated again and again in medieval Latin commentaries, but utterly unknown to modern critical commentators, it left me bewildered and initially sceptical about its value as exegesis. Reading the authors who proposed it, I knew I had entered a strange and unfamiliar world, for which my roadmap required significant adjustment. This was the world of Friar William of Baskerville and other apocalyptically-inspired characters from Umberto Eco's *The Name of the Rose*, who treated Revelation as a book of mysteries rather than a source for first-century historical reconstruction.

[18] See e.g. Saffrey, 'Relire l'Apocalypse'.

The interpretation in question ran as follows: *Patmos interpretatur fretum.* The Latin is difficult to translate, given the range of possibilities for the noun *fretum*: 'Patmos means raging' or 'swelling', 'strait' (of water), or 'whirlpool'. To this particular historical critic, however 'chastened', such a reading appeared unintelligible. But for readers of the Apocalypse in the Middle Ages, at least amongst the scholarly elite, it seemed to be a popular and an obvious reading of Rev. 1:9. First attested, so far as I can discover, in a seventh- or eighth-century Bodleian manuscript of Primasius's sixth-century commentary, it was regularly cited by commentators from the eighth century onwards (including Ambrose Autpert, Haimo of Auxerre, Joachim of Fiore and Rupert of Deutz), and was incorporated into the highly-popular *Glossa ordinaria*.

But what does it mean? How did the first commentator to offer this interpretation make the link? Was there an etymological connection, as was so often the case in medieval biblical interpretation?[19] None seemed forthcoming, although I considered various possibilities, including a link between *Patmos* and the Greek ποταμός, then translated into Latin (though *flumen* would appear a more obvious choice than *fretum*). In the event I discovered the apocalyptic key to unlock this mystery quite unexpectedly. I was sitting in the Bodleian Library in Oxford doodling on a scrap of paper, in what up to that point had proved a decidedly unproductive library session. I decided to have one more go at a possibility I had unsuccessfully explored several times before: that these medieval exegetes were following a lead provided by Rev. 13:10, which employs gematria in order to find significance in names. Using a different Latin gematrial system (which works straight through the Latin alphabet according an ascending numerical value to each letter, and treating U and V, and I and J as equivalent), I discovered that the words *Patmos* and *fretum* share the numerical value of seventy-nine. This link was confirmed by bringing in other medieval commentaries linking *Patmos* with the Latin word *fervor* ('seething', 'heat' or 'passion'): in the same system, seventy-nine is also the number of *fervor*.

Critical scholars of whatever persuasion might be tempted to dismiss such exegesis as sheer fantasy, the worst kind of unbridled allegorization. Yet if we replace one set of 'prejudices' (in the Gadamerian sense) with another, a more sympathetic conclusion suggests itself. Read in the light of Rev. 13:10, this peculiar exegesis of Rev. 1:9 is not only intelligible but utterly logical. It takes seriously the invitation of the biblical text to 'calculate' the number of names, in order to illuminate the question – arguably a more significant question than where Patmos *is* – of what Patmos *means*. The precise answer given by medieval exegetes may not

---

[19] Marie Anne Mayeski, 'Early Medieval Exegesis: Gregory I to the Twelfth Century', in *A History of Biblical Interpretation. Volume 2: The Medieval through the Reformation Periods*, ed. Alan J. Hauser and Duane Frederick Watson (Grand Rapids and Cambridge: Eerdmans, 2009), 86–112 (quotation from 93).

be the answer a contemporary reader would find convincing. But the question itself, and even the method by which a medieval answer was achieved, is not thereby discredited.

Nor is this the only attempt in the verse's reception history to explore the meaning of the name 'Patmos'. Others too seem to have understood John's phrase 'the island which is called Patmos' as 'the island which *God* has called "Patmos"', thereby inviting consideration of the name's deeper significance. An Amharic commentary, reflecting the Apocalypse interpretation of the Ethiopian Orthodox Church, interprets the name Patmos (or Fǝtmo) as 'place of forgiveness' and 'place of vision', making the extraordinary assertion that Moses, Aaron, Daniel and Jeremiah had seen visions there before John.[20] More surprisingly, perhaps, I discovered that some early modern interpreters – keen though they were to root exegesis in the literal-grammatical sense of the text – were also interested in the meaning of the name. Hence, for example, the Swiss Calvinist Benedict Aretius proposed an etymological link between Patmos and the Greek word πάτος or 'trodden way', the name of John's island thus appropriately describing John's experience as a downtrodden exile.[21] Others saw a link between Patmos and πότμος ('death' or 'fate'), again an appropriate description of John's social context. Most ingenious, perhaps, was the etymological interpretation of the French Jesuit Jean Hardouin (1646–1729), who believed it to be derived from the Hebrew פֶּה, ('face') and טָמֵא ('unclean'). Following Revelation's tendency to treat place-names such as Babylon, Sodom and Armageddon as non-literal, Hardouin suggested that 'Patmos' was an allegorical name for the people of Judah, who according to Isa. 6:5 are a people of 'unclean lips'. As for the medieval *fretum* reading, the oddity of the solution should not blind us to the logic of the method, nor the legitimacy of the question being posed to the text.

Telling John's larger story

A final example from my study of Revelation's reception history reflects a longstanding concern to locate John's island of Patmos, and indeed the whole Apocalypse, within a larger story. It is here that the biblical text has left perhaps its most significant gaps: what happened before John arrived on Patmos, what did he encounter in the days, months or years he spent there, and what happened to him afterwards? One can find hints of an answer in those passing references to Patmos by patristic authors writing about other themes, but the piecemeal nature of the

---

[20] Roger W. Cowley, *The Traditional Interpretation of the Apocalypse of St John in the Ethiopian Orthodox Church* (University of Cambridge Oriental Publications 33; Cambridge: CUP, 1983), p.190.
[21] Benedict Aretius, *Commentarii in omnes Epistolas D. Pauli, et Canonicas, itemque in Apocalypsin D. Ioannis* (Geneva, 1596), 556.

evidence can be very frustrating. Alan Culpepper describes the effect as 'that of viewing slides or stills rather than a motion picture.'[22]

In the various apocryphal Acts and Lives of John, something closer to the motion picture emerges, in which the seer is given a past and a future to provide context for his present. The cultural impact of this evolving biography is immense. It can be felt, for example, in those thirteenth- and fourteenth-century Anglo-Norman Apocalypses which sandwich the biblical text with illustrations from John's life in Ephesus and Rome, and in the Western feast of St John Before the Latin Gate (6 May).

One of the most striking features I encountered in the sustained attempts to describe John's larger story was the relegation of the mainstream interpretation of exile by Rome to a secondary position. Instead, priority was given to the working of divine providence in sending John to Patmos. This theological perspective dominates, for example in the *Acts of John at Rome* (fourth or fifth century), and the above-mentioned *Acts of John by Prochorus*. In the latter, John receives a vision three months before his final arrival on Patmos, in which he is told that his forthcoming exile will be to an island which has need to him, anticipating significant missionary activity there.[23] It is underscored by a typological relationship established in the ensuing narrative between Patmos and Sinai, particularly associated with a scene in which John receives the contents of the Fourth Gospel on a Patmos mountain, accompanied by lightning, thunder and an earthquake.

Similarly, in the *Acts of John at Rome*, Domitian's decision to exile John to Patmos is a reduced sentence, the result of the latter's miraculous activities in the imperial capital. Further, the emperor also relents on his previous decision to have all Christians killed, whilst the overall consequence of his action is to bring John to the place where he is to receive his revelation.

But how legitimate are such elaborate embellishments of the Patmos story? Historical critics may well be concerned with the degree of imaginative gap-filling involved in these narratives, not to mention their problematic assumption of common authorship for the Fourth Gospel and the Book of Revelation. But to get side-tracked into authorial questions may be to miss other important issues. For first, all texts contain gaps and ambiguities, which invite some resolution on the part of the interpreter, and imaginative reconstruction is no less evident in historical-critical analyses of New Testament writings.[24] Moreover, the genre of these apocryphal texts reflects patristic interest in the *historia* of John for imitative and not simply biographical reasons. They are concerned to ask not simply 'What

---

[22] R. Alan Culpepper, *John, the Son of Zebedee: The Life of a Legend* (Edinburgh: T. & T. Clark, 2000), p. 139.

[23] For the text, see Theodor Zahn, *Acta Joannis unter Benutzung von C. v. Tischendorf's Nachlass* (Erlangen: Verlag von Andreas Deichert, 1880), 44.

[24] William John Lyons, 'Hope for a Troubled Discipline? Contributions to New Testament Studies from Reception History,' *JSNT* 33/2 (2010), 207–220.

did Patmos mean for John?' but 'How might the Patmos story impact on our lives?' David Brown's insightful discussion of Christian hagiographical legends has perceptive things to say about what he calls 'truths of the imagination', and how these offer insights into the text, and the significance of the text's protagonist, which complement those offered by the straightforwardly historical.[25]

Yet even if one is interested in addressing 'authorial intention', consideration of the role of providence in the Patmos story need not be out of place. Given the theocentric character of the Apocalypse, structured as it is around visions of the divine throne-room, can we legitimately argue that belief in the guiding hand of God is absent from what the human author intended to convey? Such an assumption may tell us more about historical criticism's tendency to bracket out theological questions than about the concerns of John of Patmos.

What have I learnt?

Having come to the end of this extraordinary journey of discovery, what have I learnt, and how have I been changed by the process? First, the journey has taught me to pay close reading of texts more than mere lip-service. Earlier interpreters were often more careful readers than we are today, squeezing out every last drop of potential from the words on the sacred page. That this was especially the case with the book of mysteries which is the Apocalypse, is a particular challenge to its contemporary interpreters.

Second, I have become much more reticent to dismiss unfamiliar conclusions, and unfamiliar methods of interpretation, simply because they do not conform to the received wisdom of the academy. Indeed, in a number of cases discussed above, earlier receivers of John's text seem to be engaging in the task of historical reconstruction more effectively than their critical successors. But such historical questions are only a part of the exegetical task. My travels have taught me much more clearly, not only where my own questions have come from (and why they might originally have been phrased in the way they were), but also that there are a rich crop of alternative questions, some of which may be better or more appropriate questions to be asking.

In other words, I have come to have a broader appreciation of meaning in biblical texts. Much recent scholarship on my chosen passage has tended to reduce

---

[25] David Brown, *Discipleship and Imagination: Christian Tradition and Truth* (Oxford: OUP, 2000), 353–367.

its meaning to *prolegomena*, such as authorship and geographical location. Why was John on Patmos? Where is the island to be found, and to what use was it put in John's day? Older interpreters were much bolder in asking what Patmos might *mean*, and how that meaning might affect the contemporary reader. They seem to have had an innate sense of the complexity and multivalency of meaning, alongside which the univocal quest of many historical critics can appear impoverished. On any future journeys, my instinct would now be to turn to them for guidance, before plotting my voyage and planning my itinerary. Older maps and tattered travel guides may appear less appealing on the shelf; taken down and dusted off, however, they may reveal hidden gems which will greatly enrich and enliven the ensuing expedition.

12

Digital Humanities and Reception History; or the Joys and Horrors of Databases

Emma England

Digital humanities is concerned with expanding intersections between the humanities and computing through collaboration, open access publishing and open source technology.[1] As well as computational analysis, information retrieval and data visualization, proponents of the digital humanities often suggest new approaches to research and teaching.[2]

This essay introduces digital humanities as used in biblical studies, before presenting one way that biblical scholars, especially those engaged with reception studies, may adopt the approach to produce research that is creative and groundbreaking. Specifically, I present my process of developing a database to answer the seemingly simple question 'How can I usefully record and classify multiple versions of the Genesis flood story retold for children?' In explaining how I answered this question I propose a method for systematically analysing large corpuses of material which retell biblical narratives.

Biblical studies and the digital humanities

The most effective approach to understanding a field as diverse and complex as the digital humanities is to navigate through it, even if only in a rudimentary fashion.

---

[1] I would like to thank the following for their assistance and advice during the database design and data collection process: Prof. dr. Athalya Brenner, Prof. dr. Jan Willem van Henten, Duncan Heyes, Prof. dr. August den Hollander, Tanya Kirk, Prof. dr. Lisa Kuitert, Robert Nieuwenhuijs, and Jill Sheffrin.

[2] More broadly, 'Digital Humanities refers to new modes of scholarship and institutional units for collaborative, transdisciplinary, and computationally engaged research, teaching, and publication. Digital Humanities is less a unified field than an array of convergent practices that explore a universe in which print is no longer the primary medium in which knowledge is produced and disseminated.' Anne Burdick, Johanna Drucker, Peter Lunenfeld, Tod Presner, and Jeffrey Schnapp. *Digital Humanities* (Cambridge, Massachusetts: The MIT Press, 2012), 122, http://mitpress.mit.edu/books/digitalhumanities-0. [All websites throughout this essay were last accessed on 10 December 2012.]

This is particularly easy for digital humanities because most of the core material is available for free and online.[3] Definitions, text books, manifestos, guides, journals, research institutions and projects can all be easily accessed.[4] But what do people who work within the field do and, more specifically, how do biblical scholars work within it? Tara McPherson has suggested three types of research: (a) computing humanities, (b) blogging humanities, and (c) multimodal humanities.[5]

Computing humanities: Within biblical studies computing humanities is the most common type of work undertaken. It focuses on 'building tools, infrastructure, standards and collections,' or what biblical scholars call 'computer assisted research.'[6] It originated as early as 1970, but was still a fledgling field until 1985 when personal computers began to make the research commercially viable.[7] Computer assisted research has primarily been concerned with automating and quantifying textual analysis.[8] An obvious example of this is electronic Bible software (i.e., *Accordance, Bible Works* and *Logos*), which can be used as simple dictionaries and counting mechanisms or as more complex linguistic aids. Electronic resources and archives of primary and secondary sources are also common.[9]

Blogging humanities: The second area of research McPherson suggests is the blogging humanities: 'the production of networked media and peer-to-peer writing.'[10] Within biblical studies this is best illustrated through biblioblogging:

---

[3] Cf. The Alliance of Digital Humanities Organizations, the website of which links to groups, publications, conferences and numerous other resources. http://adho.org/.
[4] Cf. eHumanities Royal Netherlands Academy for Arts and Sciences, http://ehumanities.nl/; UCL Centre for Digital Humanities http://www.ucl.ac.uk/dh/; Susan Schreibman, Ray Siemens, and John Unsworth (eds.). *A Companion to Digital Humanities* (Oxford: Blackwell, 2004), http://www.digitalhumanities.org/companion.; *Digital Humanities Quarterly*, http://www.digitalhumanities.org/dhq/; *The Digital Humanities Manifesto 2.0*, http://www.humanitiesblast.com/manifesto/Manifesto_V2.pdf. An example of how the digital humanities includes new approaches to teaching and open source research is CUNY Academic Commons, an online social academic network: http://commons.gc.cuny.edu/
[5] Tara McPherson, 'Introduction: Media Studies and the Digital Humanities', *Cinema Journal* 48:2 (Winter 2009), 119–23. http://c.ymcdn.com/sites/www.cmstudies.org/resource/resmgr/in_focus_archive/in_focus_48.2.pdf. Cf. Svensson, Patrik. 2010. 'The Landscape of Digital Humanities.' *Digital Humanities Quarterly*. 4.1. http://digitalhumanities.org/dhq/vol/4/1/000080/000080.html
[6] McPherson, 'Introduction,' 119
[7] R. Ferdinand Poswick, 'From Louvain-La-Neuve (1985) to El Escorial in Madrid (2008): 25 Years of AIBI,' in *Computer Assisted Research on the Bible in the 21st Century*, eds. Luis Vegas Montaner, Guadalupe Seijas de los Rios-Zarzosa, and Javier del Barco, 3–11. (Piscataway, NJ: Gorgias Press, 2010): 4. Cf. Mark Hoffman's *Biblical Studies and Technological Tools: From scroll to screen ... codex to computer ...* http://bibleandtech.blogspot.com/.
[8] Luis Vegas Montaner, 'Major Theoretical Issues from Two Decades of Bible and Computer Conferences', in *Computer Assisted Research on the Bible in the 21st Century*, eds. Luis Vegas Montaner, Guadalupe Seijas de los Rios-Zarzosa, and Javier del Barco, 13–23. (Piscataway, NJ: Gorgias Press, 2010).
[9] Cf. *The Electronic Text Corpus of Sumerian Literature* (University of Oxford). http://etcsl.orinst.ox.ac.uk/#; *The Online Critical Pseudepigrapha*. (Society of Biblical Literature and Tyndale). http://ocp.tyndale.ca/.
[10] McPherson, 'Introduction,' 119

blogging devoted to a loosely defined idea of academic biblical studies.[11] Some recent debates in the discipline have taken place initially, if not largely, in the blogosphere.[12] Of specific relevance to this book is what has become irreverently known in some circles as, 'Hurtadogate'. Larry Hurtado, James Crossley and numerous others discussed the 'true' nature of New Testament Studies and the role of reception history alongside/within that discipline.[13] Although the debate was at its most vociferous online, it has continued to influence academic discourse at conferences and in publications.[14]

Multimodal humanities: McPherson's final group of digital humanities research is multimodal humanities, something which utilizes

> scholarly tools, databases, networked writing and peer-to-peer commentary while also leveraging the potential of the visual and aural media that are part of contemporary life... She [the researcher] aims to produce work that reconfigures the relationships among author, reader, and technology while investigating the computer simultaneously as a platform, a medium, and a visualization device. She thinks carefully about the relationship of form to content, expression to idea.[15]

To date, this has been the least developed means of using digital humanities, not only within biblical studies but also more generally. The Open Bible is an example of this kind of work, although it is unclear whether biblical scholars are involved in its production. The website includes complex and interactive visualizations relating to cross-references between biblical books, places and names. More fascinating is the functionality on the website pertaining to appearances of biblical references online. The user can search for a specific verse through Twitter and

---

[11] A history of biblioblogging can be found here: WHAT JUST HAPPENED The rise of 'biblioblogging' in the first decade of the twenty-first century, James R. Davila, University of St. Andrews. 2010 Annual Meeting of the Society of Biblical Literature in Atlanta. http://paleojudaica.blogspot.nl/2010_11_14_archive.html. For discussion of the history, relevance and impact of biblioblogging see four articles from *Bulletin for the Study of Religion 39.3* (2010): Jim West's 'Blogging the Bible: A Short History', pp.3–13; James Frank McGrath's 'Biblioblogging Our Matrix: Exploring the Potential and Perplexities of Academic Blogging', pp.14–25; Robert R. Cargill's 'The Benefit of Blogging for Archaeology', pp.26–36; and James Crossley's 'Biblioblogging, "Religion", and the Manufacturing of Catastrophe', pp. 21–9.

[12] Cf. The controversy following Christopher Rollston's *Huffington Post* article 'The Marginalization of Women: A Biblical Value We Don't Like to Talk About' (31 August 2012, http://www.huffingtonpost.com/christopher-rollston/the-marginalization-of-women-biblical-value-we-dont-like-to-talk-about_b_1833648.html). Donors allegedly threatened to pull funding as a result of the article. Rollston was threatened with disciplinary action. The affair unfolded across the biblioblogging sphere, with almost unanimous approval of Rollston. Paul M. Blower defends his and Rollston's institution, Emmanuel Christian Seminary, in 'Academic Integrity within a Confessional Institution: An "Insider's" Response to Thomas Verenna' (*Biblical Interpretation*, October 2012, http://www.bibleinterp.com/articles/blo368008.shtml). James McGrath posts an update on *Exploring Our Matrix* (October 16, 2012, http://www.patheos.com/blogs/exploringourmatrix/2012/10/support-for-christopher-rollston-update.html).

[13] An analysis of the history of the discussion can be found in James Crossley's article 'An Immodest Proposal for Biblical Studies.' *Relegere: Studies in. Religion and Reception.* 2.1 (2012): 153–77. http://www.relegere.org/index.php/relegere/article/viewFile/515/473.

[14] See the Introduction, James Crossley and Jon Morgan's articles in this volume.

[15] McPherson, 'Introduction', 120.

Facebook.[16] A search [accessed 8 December 2012] for Gen 8:1 generated 18,311 results in 0.69 seconds. Results included lay arguments about biblical historicity, discussions of Bible readings and complex theological discourse, and people participating in Bible quizzes and asking Twitter for the answer. The potential to analyse this data (e.g., to explore biblical literacy in contemporary society), is just one example of what could be done with multimodal analysis.

The potential of the digital humanities has barely been touched upon within biblical studies and it is within this slowly developing environment that I locate my own work on flood stories in children' Bibles. In what follows, I will explain that work and the process of its production and show how it fits into current discussions about reception history.

Reception studies, biblical narratives and databases

How is it possible to record hundreds of versions of the Genesis flood story retold for children so that significant patterns – similarities, generalizations, omissions, and so on – can be uncovered? How can this be done for both words and images? And with an eye to encouraging the expansion of such work, how can this be done so that it is easily reproducible, without extensive technical support or knowledge?[17]

These were the questions I asked myself when I started working, at the University of Amsterdam, on my PhD project 'The Dove, The Rainbow, and The Unicorn: 170 Years of the Genesis Flood Story Retold for Children in Words and Images'. My intention was to analyse the similarities and differences between retellings published in England and the Genesis text, and how these changed between 1837 and 2006. Rather than focusing on one specific element of the narrative, such as the ark or the destruction, I wanted to consider how and with what ideological biases the actors were represented. Critically, I wanted to be able to compare the words and images in the retellings and how they related to each other and to the biblical narrative (Gen 6:1–9:19). It was necessary to find a way to minimize the inevitable subjectivity involved in the research, particularly my own pre-existing assumptions. The solution was a custom-built relational database using Microsoft Access with a custom-made classification system.[18]

---

[16] OpenBible.info: Remix Bible data. http://www.openbible.info/realtime/
[17] The lack of appropriate technical expertise is a major obstacle in the success of digital humanities projects. Without a good awareness of what can be done or without effective communication between relevant experts a project can fail, or be less successful or more expensive than expected. Elizabeth Robar, 'The Hexapla Project: Traditional Scholarship Meets Modern Technology,' in *Computer Assisted Research on the Bible in the 21st Century*, eds. Luis Vegas Montaner, Guadalupe Seijas de los Rios-Zarzosa, and Javier del Barco, 79–96. (Piscataway, NJ: Gorgias Press, 2010).
[18] Microsoft Access is an application for use on all PCs with a Windows Operating System. It is provided as standard with the Microsoft Office Professional package (or higher). No additional costs need to be incurred assuming the researcher has this application and the skills to use it.

The database

A relational database is a management information system based around tables containing carefully labelled data. These tables are connected by relationships to enable searching and filtering along a number of parameters. For example, with my database data can be filtered to show only the material published for a specific target audience between set dates and according to whether or not there are illustrations in black and white and/or colour. Relational databases enable simple and complex searches to be created for further analysis. The database is primarily used to analyse data based upon the classification system I created to analyse the content of the narrative.

A classification system is a way to record material based upon commonalities. The Dewey Decimal System used in many libraries is a common example. It is hierarchical, with divisions and subdivisions. Each book can only have one code. However, an electronic database of all the books in a library will not be restricted to these codes, because each book will also be classified (and, critically, searchable) according to other attributes including author, year, publisher and subject heading. This latter, non-hierarchical, system is what was used to catalogue and record the retellings. It is what is known as a 'facet system' in which many different codes can be applied to each object, including narrative content, type of retelling (i.e., decontextualized, worship) and number of illustrations. A variety of attributes (the technical term for characteristic, property, quality) therefore can be used to search and analyse the data.[19]

The process

Having established what I was going to do, I needed to work out how it was going to be done. This involved a five stage process:

1. Corpus selection
2. Design and pilot
3. Evaluate and finalize
4. Data entry
5. Data analysis

---

[19] For an introduction to Classification Systems see Eric J. Hunter, *Classification Made Simple: An Introduction to Knowledge Organisation and Information Retrieval*. (Farnham: Ashgate, 2009). For a brief introduction to classification systems in the digital humanities see C. M. Sperberg-McQueen, 'Classification and Its Structures,' in *A Companion to Digital Humanities*, eds. Susan Schreibman, Ray Siemens, and John Unsworth, Chapter 14. (Oxford: Blackwell, 2004), http://www.digitalhumanities.org/companion.

Corpus selection

First, a researcher needs to know how much time and technical expertise she has for the project and whether she can borrow or buy some assistance. This will impact upon the type of research that can be done. If only three months are available in which to write an article, cataloguing all retellings ever published on a specific narrative is not going to be possible.[20] Concurrently, an area of focus needs to be chosen, perhaps by publication date/s, language/s, or country/ies. The researcher also needs to know whether or how far she wants to be able to extrapolate and make generalizations about a given topic. If so, she has to be careful about selecting the research material, such as if she wishes to work exclusively with material published from within a specific religious tradition. For the flood project I wanted to be able to make country-wide generalizations covering a long period of publishing history. This meant that the corpus had to be carefully selected.

There are four key elements to corpus selection, although they are unlikely to be established in a linear order: sourcing the material, search parameters, corpus size, and sampling process. Sourcing the material is a key starting place. Due to the fact that I was analysing the content of narratives rather than producing a bibliographic study, which would have focused primarily on the publishing history of the books, the time and space was not available to provide a fully comprehensive catalogue of children's Bibles and flood-story retellings.[21] Nevertheless, an element of bibliographic research was necessary in order to locate the material. This was in part because the cataloguing and collection of published books for children is sporadic and children's Bibles often get overlooked. Children's literature studies rarely discuss Bibles, while the best-known catalogues of English-printed Bibles seldom record children's books.[22] This makes the systematic finding, recording and cataloguing of children's Bibles a daunting task.

I chose to focus on one collection: that of the British Library (BL) in London. For good reason, it is the national library of the United Kingdom and a legal deposit library, and hence a major research library. It is one of the primary collections used

---

[20] In my case I knew that my time, while not unlimited, was not highly pressurized. I would, however, have to do the work myself. I did have the technical support of Robert Nieuwenhuijs. He is a statistician with considerable technical expertise in building databases. He helped me with some of the more complicated elements and troubleshooting.

[21] The only comprehensive bibliographic record of children's Bibles that I am aware of (and even then within limiting defining parameters) is Willem van der Meiden's '*Zoo heerlijk eenvoudig*': *Geschiedenis van de Kinderbijbel in Nederland*. (Hilversum: Verloren, 2009).

[22] T. H. Darlow and H. F. Moule, *Historical Catalogue of the Printed Editions in the Library of the British and Foreign Bible Society In Two Volumes, Vol. 1-English*. (London: The Bible House, 1903); A. S. Herbert, *Historical Catalogue of Printed Editions of The English Bible 1525-1961 Revised and Expanded from the Edition of T. H. Darlow and H. F. Moule, 1903*. (London: The British and Foreign Bible Society, 1968). Furthermore, the *Nineteenth Century Short Title Catalogue 1816-1870* 'Bible' volume (1986) only includes short titles. Thus it does not always indicate when a book is for children. *Nineteenth Century Short Title Catalogue 1816-1870*. ('Bible'). (Newcastle-upon-Tyne: Avero, 1986). http://nstc.chadwyck.com

in historical children's literature research, is easily accessible and has an online catalogue. Inevitably, choosing one library as the focus has its limitations, because of changes in classification, collection and storage protocols.[23] Certain books are not currently stored in the BL even though older variations of the same books are kept. One example particularly relevant for flood retellings is activity books, including colouring books and sticker books. These are not held at the BL irrespective of the content of the book. *My Bible Activity Book* includes stickers, pictures to colour and puzzles.[24] Hence, it is not officially covered under the 'Review of Acquisitions and Retentions Policies' (RARP). This is despite the fact that the stories are more detailed and more complex than many children's books without such activities. In addition to collection guidelines, some books are not held by the library because publishers failed to deposit the book or the book may have been lost.[25]

Having established the source of the material to be researched, the material itself needed to be uncovered. Initial searches undertaken in the catalogue were for the terms 'child? + Bible, any field' and 'Noah's Ark, any field'. Secondary searches, based upon subject headings and tertiary searches, based upon rarer terms in all fields, were also undertaken. These original searches yielded over 1500 results. These search results were not representative of the material sought. The results often overlapped, books were not always accurately recorded, some information recorded had changed over the 170 years, and the subject classification was sometimes (partially) wrong.[26] The books themselves also caused difficulties, with book titles misrepresenting what the book was about, sometimes merely by virtue of historical changes. Victorian titles, for example, are not always clear to today's reader: 'daily texts' refer to small portions of scripture, often in a blank journal.

The results were manually filtered to remove likely inappropriate publications based on the title, place of publication and additional information. Approximately 1000 books remained on the list. At this point in the process, the corpus size and

---

[23] Dust jackets, for example, have not been kept and stored in the same system. The librarian, publication date, acquisition date, the type of publication and other factors all impact upon whether and how the dust jackets of books were stored.

[24] Ronne Randall and Kathryn Jewitt, *My Bible Activity Book*, illus. Rebecca Elliott (Bath: Parragon, 2006). The specific wording of the relevant passage in the RARP is: 'the following are interpreted as out of scope: colouring-in books, dot-to-dot books, cut-out books, fill-in puzzle books, sticky labels books, except where these elements are a small proportion of the overall book' (RARP 3.3.1). Like all classification systems, this is clearly open to the interpretation of the librarian (what is 'small'?), and does not reflect the historical items kept at the library, many of which would not be kept had they been published today.

[25] Examples of books I own but the British Library does not include Arthur S. Maxwell's collection of Hebrew Bible stories *Uncle Arthur's Bible Stories (Vol.1)*. (Watford: The Stanborough Press Ltd, [c.1949]); Wendy Orr's decontextualized retelling *Ark in the Park*, illus. Kerry Millard. (Sevenoaks: Chart Books, 1996); and a movable picture book by an unknown author, *Noah's Ark*, illus. Gill Guile. (Kettering: Bumblebee Books, 2000).

[26] For example, *Bible Stories (Twisted Tales)* is listed as: 'Bible Stories. English' with no 'juvenile' listed, even though the book is clearly aimed at children, and published by the children's publisher Scholastic. Michael Coleman, *Bible Stories (Twisted Tales)*, illus. Michael Tickner. (London: Scholastic Children's Books, 2004).

sampling process had to be considered. Knowing the diversity and quantity of available research material, the aim was to view at least half of the books on the list to ensure there was a thorough overview of the material. A process of stratified sampling, whereby the total sample would be divided into sub-groups according to unifying characteristics, was decided upon. The sub-groups were the decade of publication, and within each group the sampling was undertaken randomly. I had specific research questions and expectations but these needed to be tested not validated. As such it was necessary to be careful in the research methods so as to maintain a balance between answering the questions while still using the data as the driving force of the research.[27]

Design and pilot

When undertaking this kind of research, the researcher will need to design the database for necessity, practicality and feasibility. Everything which needs to be included in the database potentially makes the database more useful, but also more complex to design and more time-consuming to create, pilot, review and use. Each piece of information collected needs to have a clearly defined database field. The specification needs to be as precise as possible to maintain the integrity, searchability and usability of the data.

Here are three examples with their definitions:

- Title – The full title of the retelling. Either book title or, if a story in a book, the section title(s) followed by 'in' and the book title with page numbers. Use capitals for all title words.[28]
- Author – 'Surname, forename' (and title if applicable). Plus named persons: original author, translator but not the designer, series editor, etc. If the author is not named but described add the description, if no name enter 'Anon'. If an unnamed author has been identified add the name in square brackets (i.e., 'A mother [Lucy Wilson]')[29]

---

[27] The order in which different elements of the research process for such a project take place affects the outcome and the database design. In my case the corpus selection and the initial design stages took place at overlapping times, but the database was not designed until the corpus was fully established.

[28] I consciously chose to capitalize all title words in order to maximize consistency within the data collection process. The conventions changed over the 170 years of my research and in different types of publications. There were also differences within books, such as between the front cover and title page. Choosing a standard that would work for all publications proved very difficult. If I were to make the database again, I might choose a different format, perhaps with an 'if, then' formula (i.e., if not front cover, use the title page, if no title page use . . .).

[29] 'Lesson II. Noah's Ark' in *Mamma's Bible Stories For Her Little Boys And Girls: A Series Of Reading Lessons Taken From The Bible And Adapted To The Capacities Of Very Young Children.* (19–25) was written by 'Anon ('Mamma') [Lucy Sarah Wilson]' (London: Griffith, Farran & Co., [c. 1892]). Cf. 'Chapter 4. The Deluge.' in *Bible History For Young Children* (11–14, Vol. 1 of 3) was written by 'Anon ('Dedicated to her own children by a mother')' (Newcastle: F. and W. Dodsworth, 1854). 'Hieroglyphics. No. LX.' in *One Hundred Hieroglyphic Bible Readings For The Young* (33v) was written by 'Anon ('Compiled by the Editors of the 'Children's Friend')' (London: S. W. Partridge & Co., [c. 1869]).

- Format – Measure the first leaf in millimetres (mm) height by width. If not a regular shape book (i.e., cut board books), measure at the longest point and note the shape (i.e., boat)

Knowing the format of the publication can add value to analysis of the content (such as the readability of a retelling), especially when compared with the number of pages and distribution of illustrations and the amount of detail which was included from the flood story.[30] It is this latter element, the (changing) content of the retellings and how they compare to the biblical narrative, however, which is the core purpose of the database. To record this, content was analysed by dividing the Genesis narrative into small narrative units (see Table 12.1). These units needed to be carefully defined to enable clear coding and prevent inferences. If an element from the narrative, such as God sending a wind over the earth (Gen 8:1) was included in the words of a retelling it would be added to the list of included textual elements. If an element from the Genesis narrative were illustrated it would be added to the list of elements visually depicted. In this way each code could represent an element from the Genesis narrative twice for each retelling, once for the words and once for the images.

Table 12.1 Examples of textual/image classification codes

Textual/image classification	Cataloguing instructions
Humanity spread across the earth (6:1)	Any reference to a population increase before the flood
The sons of (the) God/s and daughters of men procreate (6:2)	The interpretation can be Sethite/angels/divine beings, but they must marry or procreate with human beings
Humanity's days are to be 120 years (6:3)	Any reference to the restriction of life motif, in any interpretation, any reference to 120 years should be recorded
Nephilim (6:4)	Any form of Nephilim or giant reference

---

[30] Compare, for example, *When The Purple Waters Came Again* written by Norman C. Habel and illustrated by Jim Roberts (London: Concordia Publishing House, 1971) with 'Noah And The Great Flood' in *Bible Stories: Four Of The Greatest Tales Ever Told* (29–53) by David Borgenicht and illustrated by Peter Malone (London: Running Press, 1994). The former is a very unusual tall narrow size, 306 × 152 mm with only 8 leaves (16 pages). It includes 9 verbal elements of the flood narrative plus 3 verbal additions with, on average, 1 illustration per doublespread. The latter is equally unusual but very small 79 × 64 mm, with 66 leaves (132 pages), although the retelling itself is only 25 pages. There is more than 1 illustration in the retelling, but not one on every doublespread. It is very detailed with 20 verbal elements from the Genesis flood narrative included and 7 verbal additional elements. Just from this information it is possible to conjecture about the potential target audience of the books (larger but fewer pages are more manageable for small hands than tiny books with a lot of pages) and no doubt more.

In addition to recording the elements of the Genesis narrative that were represented in the retellings, a further set of codes were created to record motifs frequently added (or expected to be added) to the retellings, but which were not found in Genesis 6–9 (see Table 12.2).

The creation of such a system is time-consuming and complicated. It is never possible to report all details of a message set. Decisions have to be made based upon researcher requirements and practicalities. For example, I was analysing a large sample and therefore focused on content rather than narratological elements, such as whether or not God spoke directly or indirectly. Even here however, a decision had to be made. For the code 'God commands Noah to build an ark (6:14–16); should this include indirect speech? I decided yes, hence: 'God told Noah exactly how the boat was to be made.'[31] Conversely, narratized discourse nor diegetic summary as God's speech were recorded: 'God caused Noah to make a great ship, an ark.'[32]

With regard to the images there was no time or space to code for close-ups, colour and background. An analysis of this material would be possible if the sample size were smaller or if only one motif were analysed (i.e., the drowning of humanity). Illustrations in the retellings needed as much clarity in the recording as the words. Sometimes, for example, it seemed obvious that the animals were entering the ark because they were lined up in pairs, facing the same direction in a 'queue'. Without the animals at the front of the line clearly entering the ark, however, this could not be classified as 'Animals enter the ark (7:8–9, 14–16)'. The classification system is therefore a record of very specific, explicit events and speeches. Other systems would be framed very differently depending upon the questions being asked.

Table 12.2 Examples of textual/image additions

Textual/image additions	Cataloguing instructions
Noah as preacher/prophet	Noah must be referred to as a preacher or prophet, or acting as such
Noah builds the ark	Noah must be designing/planning/physically building the ark by himself or with others. Reference to others doing that but not Noah should not be included here. 'Noah did all that god commanded him' does not count
The life of Noah on the ark	Any reference to Noah's time, activity, feelings during the flood but only those specifically related to his time on the ark, i.e., feeding the animals, hearing the people trying to enter the ark, seasickness

---

[31] Jenny Robertson, *The Ladybird Bible Storybook*, illus. Alan Parry. (Loughborough: Ladybird Books, 1983), 16.
[32] Philip Turner, *The Bible Story*, illus. Brian Wildsmith. (London: Oxford University Press, 1968), 11.

Once the database is designed, it needs to be piloted. This is essentially a 'practice run' at data entry. It is a way to become more familiar with not only the formatting of the database but also the material and any additional motifs. It gives the researcher extra opportunities to amend her research trajectory. The database will almost certainly not be ready after the first design; requiring numerous updates in order to make it research ready. Documentation pertaining to the database should be produced to ensure clarity in data entry. Ideally, this needs to be created at the beginning design stages and updated throughout the process (saved as different versions so as to keep a historic record of complications, changes and decisions taken).

Evaluate and finalize

Having undertaken a pilot stage, a thorough evaluation is necessary. This includes assessing the content analysis codes, all fields and all specification guidelines. The format of the form used for data entry should also be reviewed (i.e., whether the fields are in the most efficient order). Numerous changes were made before I finalized my database. Two examples offer an indication of the process.

First, 'Retelling Type': The specific type of material the retelling included, (i.e., poem, worship, animal story). Each type had its own set of cataloguing instructions. This information was recorded in a subform so that multiple options were possible (i.e., worship and poem). The types were difficult to establish and changed dramatically. Initially 'traditional' was included as an option (i.e., folk tale or fable). This was removed because it was (a) imprecise, (b) difficult to establish, and (c) very rare. One retelling type added to the subform because of frequency of use was 'Toy/Novelty', as in a book with moving parts in a novelty shape (i.e., lift-the-flap, pop-up, bath time).

Second, 'Textual/Image Classification': God proved the most complex challenge as I attempted to find ways to record his involvement. God's speech was less problematic than establishing when he was visualized. Did he have to be a man with a beard? What about a face in a sun or a shining light? During the piloting stages various attempts at coding possible visualizations were tried, but ultimately they required too great a degree of inference. I eventually decided upon giving God's visualization no additional cataloguing classes and kept the coding as simple as possible. Hence the cataloguing specifications claim that only representations where God is clearly (or at least, with reasonable certainty considering reader interpretations vary) present in the images were to be recorded. Shining lights were not recorded as representations of God; but a sun with a face and hand placing a rainbow in the sky was.

In developing the coding system, four versions of the database were created before it reached its final form. In doing so I ensured that the coding system was appropriate for the material. There were ultimately 88 unique codes for cataloguing the narrative content (each of the 88 codes could be used twice, once for words and once for images) and 25 fields for recording bibliographic and related data.[33] With the finalization of the database, it was time to complete the data entry process.

Data entry

Data had to be recorded in the database accurately and consistently while minimizing subjectivity as much as possible. In this regard the clearer the database specifications and the less ambiguity involved with the fields the more consistent (and more heuristically useful) the data would be. Though there will always be a statistical margin of error because the sample is not 100 per cent, errors caused by the researcher can be minimized with solid planning and preparation.

When quantifiable data is due to guide qualitative analysis, as mine did, and when the research is being guided by specific research questions it is inevitable that, while entering data, particular retellings will spark the researcher's creative process. In such instances (indeed, wherever possible) I purchased a copy of the book. Where this was not possible (due to rarity, unavailability, or cost) as many pages as possible (within copyright) were copied at the library. Photocopies were supported by detailed notes and, in the cases of shorter retellings, the copy-typing of the whole narrative. These notes were not made on the database because the increased subjectivity and lack of 'countable' data involved in the notations would lessen the value of the data as (largely) objective, quantification research. The notes were used during the qualitative analysis process. Were the researcher only interested in quantitative analysis, such note-taking would be less important, if not irrelevant.

From the 1000 potential retellings sourced during the corpus selection stage, I eventually viewed over half of the books, of which around 200 did not include Bible story retellings or were of New Testament stories. Ultimately, 263 flood retellings were added to the database, all of which needed analysing.

Data analysis

Counting appearances was the most basic way of analysing the material, but even this led to 352 unique numbers. With each of the 88 codes used to analyse the narrative up to twice for each retelling, when counting the appearance of each code across all the retellings there were 4 countable figures. As an example, code 26, 'The ark floats on the water (7:17–18)', appears in 43 retellings as an illustration only, in 70 retellings only in the words, in 97 retellings both illustrated and in words, and in 210 retellings in total. Simple data patterns like ordering the codes in

---

[33] A screenshot of the database in action can be found at: https://eeengland.wordpress.com/childrens-bibles/.

frequency of use, adds another layer of calculations while adding other facets including the number of retellings published by specific publishing houses and/or with colour images and/or written in verse adds more complexity. It would be practically impossible to analyse every piece of information that could be garnered from the database. A choice is necessary, one based upon personal research preferences and significant features of the data. The most fundamental counting data is a logical starting place, but only so much of it can be researched for any given project. The fact that Jesus and/or Christ is only referred to in 21 of the 263 retellings, was relegated to a footnote in my PhD thesis, and only then to say how surprised I was it was such a small number.

Even when data is available, as with the representation of Jesus/Christ, a decision needs to be made about the extent to which, and how, that data is represented. At what point, and for what purpose, should visualization be used rather than verbal analysis? When visualization is used, should it be in tables, graphs, or more elaborate formats? This may be determined by audience; a picture may speak a 1000 words, but only if the audience can interpret the picture. The most common chart format used in the thesis was the stacked column chart (see Graph 12.1).

Graph 12.1 presents the number of retellings in which Noah's wife, sons and sons' wives are included in the narrative doing something not explicitly stated in the Hebrew narrative. Noah's sons are most frequently illustrated while performing an action outside of the (floating) ark. This action is usually Noah's sons helping Noah build the ark. Compare this with Noah's wife; she has the highest number of appearances while on the (floating) ark. These images usually represent Noah's wife cooking and cleaning. In contrast, statistics also demonstrate that Noah's wife, sons and sons' wives are all mentioned entering and leaving the ark with about the same frequency, but with a slightly greater number of references to Noah's wife.

Looking at a more complex and specific dataset, the naming of Noah's wife happens in only 28 of the 263 retellings (and all but 4 are as 'Mrs Noah'). Almost half (13) of the 28 are in secular retellings.[34] Similarly, of the 24 secular retellings, over half of them (13) give Noah's wife a name, usually 'Mrs Noah'. Once the process has been gone through to establish this as a dataset, including contemplating that there may be a pattern, it is necessary to explain the data. This is a separate topic, but for example, with this dataset the strong relationship between secular retellings and naming Noah's wife could be a result of authors feeling freer to amend a biblical story. There may be less gender bias, or more consciousness of gender bias. The domesticated wife is still the norm but producers of secular

---

[34] To classify as 'secular' a retelling must not refer to God, the Old and/or New Testament, the Bible, Christianity, or have any paratextual features in which any of these elements can be found, the publisher cannot be Christian (I did not work with Jewish or Islamic retellings). All of these characteristics were recorded on the database as quantifiable data.

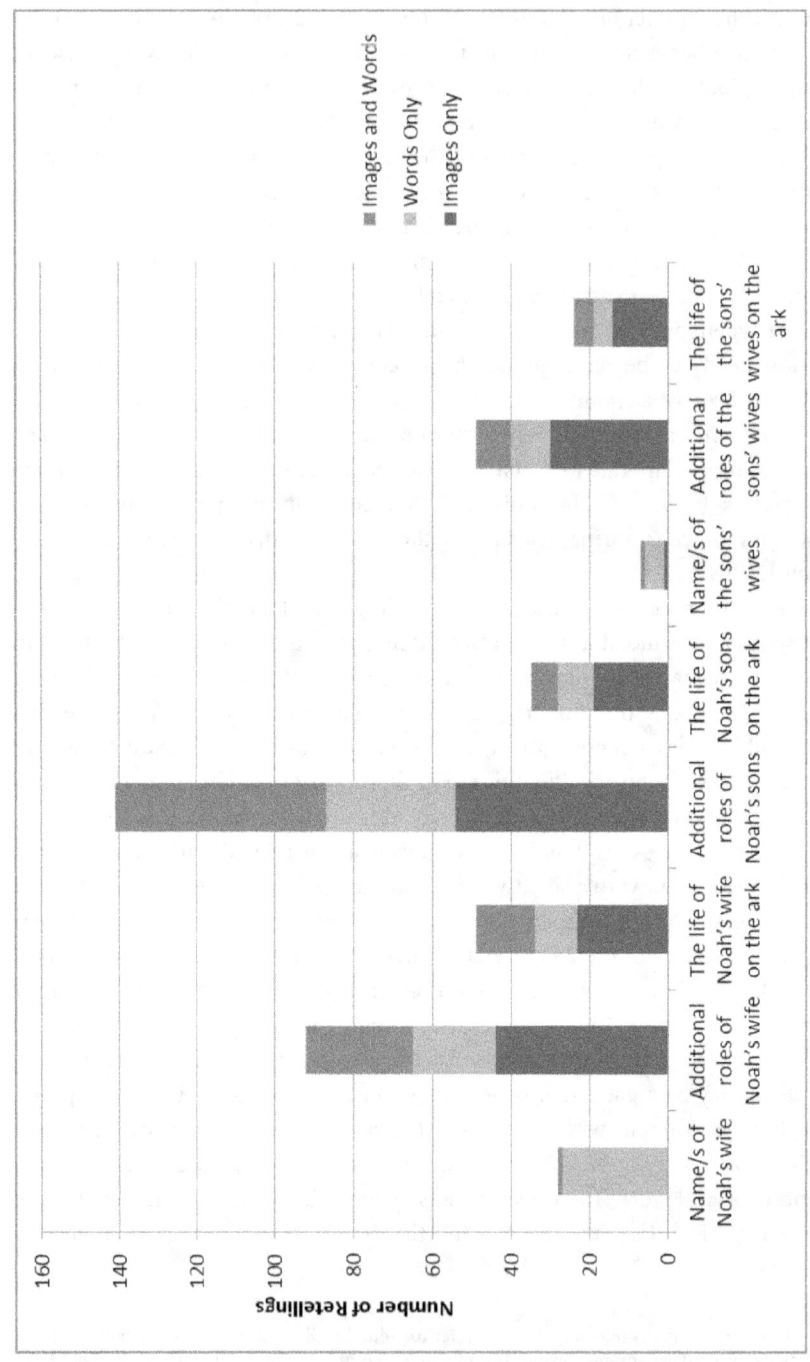

Graph 12.1 Representations of Noah's wife, sons and sons' wives in roles not stated in the Genesis flood narrative

retellings do have a tendency to elevate Noah's wife (in name and character) proportionately more often than overtly religious retellings.

When I started my research of the flood retellings, I expected to uncover representations of normative gender roles, but also that this would be less common in more recent publications. However, using statistical research it was possible to establish that with the increasing prevalence of illustrations, especially since 1970 when they became so significant they began to dominate retellings, the differentiation between men and women increased. In pre-1970 retellings everyone but Noah was generally mentioned to an equal degree, especially in the verbal texts. Since 1970, when the sons or the women were illustrated, the representations almost always followed gender normative patterns.

This finding would have been possible to achieve through conventional methods. However, I would almost certainly have had to focus exclusively on gender representations. So, for example, had I wanted to explore the relationship between the naming of Noah's wife and secular decontextualized retellings without using the database, I would have had to spend a few days going through each of the retellings for this one specific purpose in order to answer a pre-existing question. By recording data in advance, I was able to follow up a specific finding (the number of times Noah's wife was named), to see what other attributes the retellings shared. The depth of the information stored on the database enabled a wide variety of findings to be followed up in this manner. Hence, I was able to analyse the representation of God, the survivors, the wicked, the destroyed, and the animals, as well as additional humans (i.e., children) and entirely fictional beings (i.e., unicorns). Ultimately, the database enabled me to look at small, specific details within the framework of exploring the bigger picture.

Future trajectories

The database proved to be effective at guiding the research in directions I would previously not have believed entirely legitimate.[35] It enabled me to analyse and generalize in a way that could not have been achieved without such a large volume of material. Research into the presence or absence of very specific details over hundreds of texts and across a large time-span was enabled. The results were often surprising and dis/proved my own (and others) preconceived ideas about the material. It was a genuine path of discovery.

---

[35] Of the 263 retellings in the corpus 56 (21 per cent) include talking animals, fictional beings (especially unicorns), or giants (9 before 1900, 10 between 1901 and 1960, 37 since 1970). This is more than all of God's post-flood commands, God remembering Noah, Noah finding favour with God, and numerous other key elements of the Genesis narrative. This helped lead to a major discussion where I considered the retellings through the lens of fantasy literature.

Evaluation of projects, however, can rarely be entirely positive. Not all of the collected information was necessary. The strongest example of largely underutilized material was the subform 'Christian Publisher', in which I marked whether or not each publisher was Christian. This was created because I thought it would be useful. To a point it was (as with the naming of Mrs Noah). However, the data was used so infrequently that it remains questionable whether it was worth collecting. When I planned the database I did not realize that my corpus alone would have 168 different publishers, 116 of which would only be represented by one retelling on the database. Trying to establish the history of all of the publishers and whether they identified themselves as Christian at the time of publication of the retellings was, to be frank, a nightmare of epic proportions. It required hundreds of hours of research, not least because so many of the publishers no longer existed, were small, and/or only existed for a few years.

Nevertheless, this information, and other less utilized data, can still be worthwhile. The database has potential to be used to answer other research questions, as well as be added to with further retellings from the BL or elsewhere. It would also be simple to add retellings in other languages and countries of publication (the language field already distinguishes between British and American English). Were the database placed online with a user-friendly interface it could become open source research useable by anybody, hopefully this will happen. There is little point having so much material available if it is kept secret.

The database as an adaptable tool is also potentially valuable for reception historians working with what can sometimes seem like an insurmountable amount of material. By using a similar method, or by adapting the database, researchers can record, catalogue and analyse large corpuses for the purpose of comparisons between retellings and the hypertext from which they are based. The material could include sermons, songs, novels, television programmes, illuminated manuscripts and biblical commentaries. Data could feed a website for use around the globe, perhaps including a variety of search options and visualization possibilities. This costs money and time. The greatest difficulty with the digital humanities and my methodology is that it is very labour intensive and potentially costly. If we are to take reception history seriously, however, it is time to explore the full breadth of scholarly approaches and find ways to apply them to our texts.

13

Layers of Reception of Jephthah's Daughter (Judges 11) Among the AmaNazaretha: From the Early 1900s to Today

Gerald O. West
University of KwaZulu-Natal

Introduction

My interest in Isaiah Shembe and the community he established in the early 1900s in what is today the KwaZulu-Natal province of South Africa, began with my work with the Ujamaa Centre. At the Centre we read the Bible together with communities of the poor, marginalized and working-class in the late 1980s in the same region. In the early 1900s the region was in a state of considerable socio-political flux, impacted by the Anglo-Zulu War, the Anglo-Boer War, the Bambatha Rebellion and the formation of the Union of South Africa. In the late 1980s the region was torn by conflict between the apartheid state-sponsored Inkatha movement (an ethnically based cultural quasi-political organization) and the United Democratic Front (an umbrella organization with a range of progressive affiliates aligned with the banned African National Congress).

While reading the Bible together as a potential resource for social transformation of our context in the midst of this conflict it became apparent that the Bible was a much more complex artefact than theological and even biblical scholarship acknowledged. In trying to make sense of the role of the Bible in our struggle for liberation I drew deeply on these actual collaborative 'reading' projects, which later became the Ujamaa Centre, but I also read widely in how the Bible 'worked' in other liberation struggles around the world. In my reading I came across two related observations by the African American biblical scholar Vincent Wimbush that were to lead me back in time to Isaiah Shembe.

In trying to understand how African Americans were working with the Bible, Wimbush undertook a hermeneutic history of the Bible among African Americans. In his early work on this he offered two significant observations, namely, that the reception of the Bible by African slaves in America is analytically separable from their reception of Christianity, and that early encounters with the Bible are foundational for subsequent appropriations.[1] Both observations have become useful in my own work with African biblical reception and appropriation. Like Wimbush, I realized that in order to understand how Africans work with the Bible today we need to understand the hermeneutics of how Africans have transacted with the Bible historically in the long conversation and contestation with colonialism.[2]

What makes Isaiah Shembe particularly important in this hermeneutic history is that he is not a product of missionary Christianity; indeed, he is clear in his rejection of both missionary Christianity and in its African kholwa-Christian converts.[3] But he does not reject the Bible; instead, he steals it and redeploys it for the construction of a different kind of 'Christianity',[4] what Joel Cabrita calls a 'theological nationalism', 'a discourse that, to legitimate itself, posited national unity on ideas of virtue, healing, peacefulness, repentance and submission to Jehovah's dictates'.[5] 'Shembe's ministry', she says, 'was preoccupied with both "mourning for [his] scattered nation" [with a particular concern for the plight of African women] and working tirelessly to re-found it upon the new social possibilities exemplified by his Nazaretha communities, some of which endure to this day'.[6]

This essay tracks the reception of a particular biblical text, Judges 11, from the 1900s to today. We begin with my analysis of the appropriation of this text by Isaiah Shembe. Two further receptions are then analysed, each of them a reception of Shembe's reception of this biblical text, one etic (from outside the Nazaretha community), one emic (from within the Nazaretha community). My own reception of these receptions forms a fourth layer of reception.

---

[1] Vincent L. Wimbush, 'The Bible and African Americans: An Outline of an Interpretative History', in *Stony the Road We Trod: African American Biblical Interpretation*, ed. Cain Hope Felder (Minneapolis: Fortress, 1991), 81–97; Vincent L. Wimbush, 'Reading Texts through Worlds, Worlds through Texts', *Semeia* 62 (1993), 129–40.

[2] Gerald O. West, *The Academy of the Poor: Towards a Dialogical Reading of the Bible* (Pietermaritzburg: Cluster Publications, 2003), 82–6; Gerald O. West, 'Early Encounters with the Bible among the BaTlhaping: Historical and Hermeneutical Signs', *Biblical Interpretation* 12 (2004), 251–81.

[3] Joel M. Cabrita, 'A Theological Biography of Isaiah Shembe, C.1870–1935', (University of Cambridge, 2008). 'Amakholwa' was the designation given to early African converts to Christianity. The plural noun is derived from the isiZulu verb 'kholwa' which means 'to believe'.

[4] Irving Hexham and G. C. Oosthuizen, eds, *The Story of Isaiah Shembe: History and Traditions Centered on Ekuphakameni and Mount Nhlangakazi*, Volume 1, Sacred History and Traditions of the Amanazaretha (Lewiston: The Edwin Mellen Press, 1996), 224–8.

[5] Joel Cabrita, 'Isaiah Shembe's Theological Nationalism, 1920s–1935', *Journal of Southern African Studies* 35, no. 3 (2009), 618, 609.

[6] Cabrita, 'Isaiah Shembe's Theological Nationalism', 625. In what follows I will use a related set of designations for the church established by Isaiah Shembe; common to them all is some form of the term 'Nazarite' (English) or 'Nazaretha' (isiZulu).

Jephthah's daughter in the early 1900s

Isaiah Shembe constructed his Christian community, Ibandla lamaNazaretha (the congregation of the Nazarites), using strands from at least three narratives to form a threefold cord or meta-narrative. The first is the narrative of Zulu traditional religion and life, the second narrative is of Shembe's particular context in the early 1900s, and the third is the biblical narrative.[7] From these three strands Shembe forged a neo-indigenous hybrid narrative.

Though Shembe rejected much of missionary Christianity, as I have indicated, he appropriated the missionary-brought Bible. And Judges 11 is a good example of *how* Shembe appropriated biblical narrative, weaving it into the very fabric of the liturgical life of his community.

Remarkably, this biblical text does not have an evident reception history in South Africa prior to this appropriation. The 'liturgy' or 'rule' in which this biblical story is located is preserved in 'The Nazarite Catechism', in the material attributable to the 'Revived Law' of Isaiah Shembe's son, Johannes Galilee Shembe.[8] The written reception,[9] liturgically instituted, is available to us through Isaiah Shembe's successor, Johannes Galilee, who led the church from 1936 until his death in 1977.

'The Rule concerning the maidens of Nazaretha on the Sabbath Day, 27 July, 1933' [the date locates this liturgy under the authority of Isaiah Shembe],[10] begins as follows:

1. This letter confirms the rule for the maidens of amaNazaretha: in the appointed months, they shall always meet in the presence of Jehova, according to the rule.
2. This is an unchanging rule amongst you, maidens of amaNazaretha: On the 25th of every July will be the day of meeting for all the maidens of amaNazaretha under the sun's shadow.
3. Likewise, the 25th of September will always be the great opening dance of the great four-day ceremony for all Nazarite maidens under the sun, in the four compass-points of the world.
5. Blessed are those who keep this rule, and pass this ceremony on to the coming generations, so that they will always follow it.[11]

---

[7] Carol Ann Muller, *Rituals of Fertility and the Sacrifice of Desire: Nazarite Women's Performance in South Africa* (Chicago and London: The University of Chicago Press, 1999), 19.
[8] Robert Papini and Irving Hexham, eds, *The Catechism of the Nazarites and Related Writings*, Volume 4 (Lewiston: The Edwin Mellen Press, 2002), xxxi–xxxvi, 118–20.
[9] For the importance of writing in the formation of this religious community see Elizabeth Gunner, *The Man of Heaven and the Beautiful Ones of God: Writings from Ibandla Lamanazaretha, a South African Church* (Leiden: Brill, 2002), 4–5, 15–17.
[10] Papini and Hexham, eds, *The Catechism of the Nazarites and Related Writings*, 2.
[11] Papini and Hexham, eds, *The Catechism of the Nazarites and Related Writings*, 118.

After the singing of a hymn and further instructions, 'The Nazarite Catechism', within which this liturgy is located, moves on to Shembe's received version of the biblical text:

1. Japhet [Jephthah] made a vow before Jehova, saying: 'If Jehova will give the Ammonites into my hand, then whoever comes forth from my house to meet me, when I return victorious from war, shall be a burnt offering to Jehova from my hand'. And indeed, Jehova gave the Ammonites into the hands of Japhet.
2. Japhet came back to his home at Mizpah. Behold, his daughter came out to meet him with timbrels and with dances. She was his only daughter; besides her he had no other children. When he saw her, he tore his clothes and said: 'Alas, my daughter! You have brought me down, and you cause me great torment. I have opened my mouth to Jehova, and I cannot take back my vow'.
3. His daughter said: 'Father, do to me what you promised to Jehova, for Jehova has given your enemies into your hands. I agree to become an offering to Jehova. But, I ask you to let me alone for two months, that I may go to the mountains and mourn my virginity together with my companions.' (Psalms 38)[12]

The re-membered text of the Judges 11 story follows the isiZulu Bible,[13] though with some significant re-writing.[14] Verse 32a is omitted, recording as it does that 'Jephthah crossed over to the Ammonites to fight against them' (NRSV). What matters is the result, in 32b, which is retained, though with an introductory 'And indeed' to fill in for the missing section. By omitting 32a Shembe's version is more immediate, with no narrative pause between the vow and its fulfilment by God. Similarly, verse 33 is also omitted, in which we read that 'Jephthah inflicted a massive defeat on them from Aroer to the neighbourhood of Minnith, twenty towns, and as far as Abel-keramim. So the Ammonites were subdued before the people of Israel' (NRSV). In appropriating his text Shembe not only emphasizes certain aspects, such as God's immediate response to Jephthah's vow, he also loosens the text from its literary context, the war with the Ammonites.

Shembe's version in this Rule then returns to the biblical text in verses 34 and 35. The third section of Shembe's version has, however, a number of alterations. In verse 36 the biblical text includes Jephthah's daughter saying, 'My father, if you

---

[12] Papini and Hexham, eds, *The Catechism of the Nazarites and Related Writings*, 119–20.
[13] IBaible, *Ibaible Eli Ingcwele* (Cape Town: Bible Society of South Africa, 1893; reprint, 1974). This is the earliest Zulu language translation of the Bible, and remains the preferred translation of the church still today.
[14] I discuss the detail of this re-writing more fully in Gerald O. West, 'The Bible and the Female Body in Ibandla Lamanazaretha: Isaiah Shembe and Jephthah's Daughter,' *Old Testament Essays* 20, no. 2 (2007).

have opened your mouth to the Lord …' (NRSV), but this phrase is omitted in Shembe's version. The conditional clause may have seemed disrespectful (though it need not be read in this way) and so may have been omitted for this reason. More likely, however, is that Shembe chooses to emphasize again the immediacy of response. Just as God responded immediately and affirmatively to Jephthah's vow, so too now Jephthah's daughter responds immediately and affirmatively to her father's vow. As in the omission earlier, so too in this alteration there is a further loosening of the text from its literary context, for the reference to the Ammonites is omitted in Shembe's version of verse 36.

There is also an addition to the biblical text, with Jephthah's daughter saying in Shembe's version, 'I agree to become an offering to Jehova'. The compliance is complete. And it is further emphasized by the ending Shembe chooses. It ends with the words of the virgin daughter, not the words of the narrator, as is the case in the biblical text. The biblical text ends as follows:

> 'Go,' he said and sent her away for two months. So she departed, she and her companions, and bewailed her virginity on the mountains. At the end of two months, she returned to her father, who did with her according to the vow he had made. She had never slept with a man. So there arose an Israelite custom that for four days every year the daughters of Israel would go out to lament the daughter of Jephthah the Gileadite (NRSV).

Her willingness to comply for the sake of her father (and her community) is the final word. Her compliance, removed from the literary context of her death, allows the related emphasis on the two month virginity ritual to be the story's final word. We should note too that Shembe's appropriation of this text includes seclusion of the maidens of Ibandla lamaNazaretha for the full two months claimed by Jephthah's daughter and her companions and not the four days designated by the narrator.

However, although Jephthah's daughter's death and the lament of her companions, 'the daughters of Israel' (verse 40), are not narrated in the Catechism, they are danced and sung in the hymn (referred to here as a Psalm) which immediately follows the narrative, Hymn 38:

1
I shall go alone
Into the valley of sorrow.
Chorus: Give me that strength
Of Japhet's daughter.
2
I too shall go alone
Into my grave.
Chorus

3
I shall lament alone.
Chorus
4
The way of the grave is fearful;
Although all will walk in it, they do not wish to.
Chorus[15]

In 'The Nazarite Catechism' this is the ultimate word, allowing a place for lament and acknowledging the cost of the compliance. Though the amantombazane (young virgin girls) lament their sexual loneliness, they resolutely call out for strength to remain faithful to Jephthah's daughter's example. Within the literary liturgical setting of the Rule, the enemies of Jephthah/Israel/Shembe/Ibandla lamaNazaretha are not given much prominence. What is given prominence is the integral relationship between members of the community, specifically, Shembe, the Nazarite maidens, their parents, the coming generations, the indirectly evoked biblical witness of Moses, David, Jesus and the apostles, the directly cited presence of Jephthah and his daughter, and God. What binds them together (against their enemies, for sure, though this is not foregrounded in the Rule) is immediate and mutual compliance to the Rule.

Within the Rule there are hierarchies of compliance, though these are complex and dynamic. The Rule begins by confirming that it is Shembe's Rule and so Shembe's authority is invoked over the maidens. Immediately, however, the first hymn shifts the maidens' position to a significant position in the hierarchy, for they 'shall fear nothing', for they 'are perfect'. There is a further shift, however, in the second stanza, where the maidens declare their trust in God (and Shembe). The instructions that then follow the hymn grant the parents of the maidens authority over them (under Shembe's direct instruction), but both the parents and Shembe then retreat to the margins as the maidens alone 'dance for Jehova'. The Judges text, partially rewritten by Shembe, establishes a clear line of authority, from Jehovah to Jephthah to his daughter. And yet Jephthah's daughter, like her Nazarite sisters, asserts her agency in declaring that she agrees 'to become an offering to Jehova', and in so doing enables her father to keep his vow to Jehovah. In Shembe's reconstruction and location of the narrative it is this agency of Jephthah's daughter that both enables and maintains the integrity of the community. The final lament, Hymn 38, reveals the cost of such community.

---

[15] Papini and Hexham, eds, *The Catechism of the Nazarites and Related Writings*, 120.

Jephthah's daughter in the early 1990s (an etic reception)

The focus of my work on Shembe (both Isaiah and Johannes Galilee) and their reception of Judges 11 has been historical and hermeneutical, so I have not done research on how this 'liturgy' has been implemented in the years following Isaiah Shembe's death in 1935 and Johannes Galilee's death in 1977. But others have, and so I turn now to another reception of Shembe's reception of Judges 11.

Carol Muller's interest in Judges 11 comes via her primary interest in the performance of religion by, and especially the music of, the amaNazaretha. The performances that are the focus of her book, *Rituals of Fertility and the Sacrifice of Desire: Nazarite Women's Performance in South Africa*, include 'religious song and dance, dream and miracle narratives, and fertility rituals that focus specifically on the female members'.[16] She is particularly interested in the relationship between 'ritual and the sacrifice of desire', examining Nazarite ritual practices and expressive forms 'as one of the means through which to begin to understand the experiences of thousands of black South African women and young girls who have lived through the twentieth century on the margins of a continually changing South African political economy'.[17] Her research was undertaken between 1991–7,[18] immensely important years in the formation of a 'new' democratic South Africa. Muller, as a South African, recognizes that her subjects, like millions of South Africans, were at this time 'filled with an inordinate sense of both hope and disappointment in the possibilities presented by the larger historical moment'.[19]

As a white South African Muller is attentive to post-colonial concerns about the kind of ethnographic research she is doing,[20] part of which includes being overt about the frameworks that inform and shape her research. Her 'reception' of the amaNazaretha reception of Isaiah Shembe's reception of Judges 11 (as represented by his son Johannes Galilee) is framed by her interests, as I have indicated, in the changing face of South Africa's political economy, in general, and in the presence and place of the feminine in this changing political economy, in particular.[21]

For Muller, in order to move the African peoples of KwaZulu-Natal 'into a selective involvement with the emergent industrial economy in the early twentieth century', Isaiah Shembe blended traditional Nguni beliefs and biblical narrative.[22] Shembe's belief in the power of the pure female body, Muller argues, was derived both from traditional Zulu beliefs regarding the power of young female virgins to safeguard the well-being of communities and from the biblical story of Jephthah

---

[16] Muller, *Nazarite Women's Performance in South Africa*, 1.
[17] Muller, *Nazarite Women's Performance in South Africa*, 1–2.
[18] Muller, *Nazarite Women's Performance in South Africa*, 3.
[19] Muller, *Nazarite Women's Performance in South Africa*, 3.
[20] Muller, *Nazarite Women's Performance in South Africa*, 16–19.
[21] Muller, *Nazarite Women's Performance in South Africa*, 263–5.
[22] Muller, *Nazarite Women's Performance in South Africa*, 161.

and his daughter in Judges 11.[23] 'As the story of Jephthah and his daughter demonstrates,' says Muller 'for the Nazarite community to be victorious in its war against racial injustice, the girls are required to offer their virtuous bodies in obedience to the will of the prophet/God'.[24]

Referring to the liturgical ritual discussed above, our first layer of reception of Judges 11, Muller goes on to explain how these young female virgins continue, into the 1990s, to be the central actors in two annual Nazarite rituals that draw on traditional Nguni custom and the biblical narrative of Jephthah's daughter.[25] The first of these rituals derives from the traditional puberty rite held for young girls at the onset of their first menstruation, and is known as the '"girls" conference' or umgonqo (seclusion/confinement). The second rite is also derived from a traditional ritual in which young girls went to meet their lovers, known as the 'girl's camp' or Ntanda (to love/braid).[26]

With respect to the former, Muller argues that Shembe shifted the emphasis of the traditional puberty ritual 'from being simply a rite of passage into full sexuality and the capacity for reproduction, to one that transferred the significance of her newly acquired fertility to the moral and spiritual domain'. In other words, continues Muller, 'a girl's fertility was now harnessed by Shembe for the reproduction of the Nazarite moral and spiritual order'.[27] One of the mechanisms of this appropriation is the biblical narrative of Jephthah's daughter, for Muller recognizes that 'interwoven into the Nazarite construction and exegesis of this rite is the biblical narrative of Jephthah and his daughter'.[28]

Muller's reading/reception of Judges 11 is thus shaped by the reception of this text by the amaNazaretha, which is in turn framed by her understanding of the colonial struggle of Isaiah Shembe. Her account /reception of the biblical text is as follows:

> The story centers on Jephthah, a social misfit because he was born of a prostitute and rejected by the legitimate sons of his father. But he was also an Israelite warrior who was forced into battle with the Ammonites over the issue of land. He made an agreement with God that if the Israelites won the battle, he would sacrifice the first thing that met his eyes on his return home. To his horror, this was his only daughter. She agreed to the sacrifice on one condition, that he give her two months 'to roam the hills and weep with [her] friends' because she would never marry (Judges 11:37). In response, an Israelite custom developed in which young girls entered a period of seclusion to commemorate the daughter of Jephthah.

---

[23] Muller, *Nazarite Women's Performance in South Africa*, 162, 194.
[24] Muller, *Nazarite Women's Performance in South Africa*, 198.
[25] Muller, *Nazarite Women's Performance in South Africa*, 178–9.
[26] Muller, *Nazarite Women's Performance in South Africa*, 179, 189.
[27] Muller, *Nazarite Women's Performance in South Africa*, 179.
[28] Muller, *Nazarite Women's Performance in South Africa*, 179.

Layers of Reception of Jephthah's Daughter 193

The Nazarite girls' ritual performance is thus framed by the metaphor of warfare – though in their case it is not the literal warfare engaged in by the biblical Jephthah. With Isaiah, war is waged instead at the level of morality and spirituality. In this sense, the 'daughters of Isaiah,' like the 'daughter of Jephthah,' have an integral role to play in both the warfare and the victory over the enemy.[29]

Though Muller goes on to analyse the two rituals in detail,[30] she makes little further reference to the appropriation of Judges 11, so it is difficult, from her account, to understand just how the biblical narrative configures the Nazarite ritual. Her description and analysis is also heavily theory-laden, drawing as she does on a range of modern and postmodern social, political and economic theory, which places a markedly etic frame around Nazarite religious ritual, obscuring and obstructing, perhaps, the internal religious logic of the Nazarite appropriation of Judges 11.

Jephthah's daughter after 2010 (an emic reception)

As I have said, I undertake this archaeological work in order to understand the sedimentary layers on which contemporary African biblical interpretation is based. I also encourage my students to do this kind of historical and hermeneutical work, documenting the reception of the Bible in their own communities from their insider, emic, perspectives. One of my students, Nkosinathi Sithole, is a member of the amaNazaretha, being part of the church led until recently by Vimbeni Shembe (a grandson of Isaiah Shembe, who died in 2011). Given his insider status, I asked Sithole to read and comment on my work on Isaiah Shembe's reception of the Bible. What follows is his response to my (and Muller's) work.

He demonstrates a number of differences between my reading of the historical textual tradition, Muller's ethnographic reading, and his understanding of the contemporary liturgical tradition. Whereas both Muller and I (both 'outsiders') have read the historical record as having a communal focus, he discerns a more individual focus in the way the story of Jephthah's daughter is ritualized today. He begins his engagement with my reading by indicating, like Muller, that there are two rituals that 'are linked to and continuous with each other', not only 'because they are for virgin girls', but also because 'both are related to the story of Jephthah's[31] daughter' and so 'they kind of complete each other'.[32] Sithole says in his response to my reading that how he represents these two rituals 'is common knowledge in the

---

[29] Muller, *Nazarite Women's Performance in South Africa*, 180.
[30] Muller, *Nazarite Women's Performance in South Africa*, 180–96.
[31] This is the spelling used in the Nazarite liturgy.
[32] Nkosinathi Sithole, 'Sithole Reading West Reading Shembe Reading Judges 11', (Pietermaritzburg 2008), 1.

Church', but that he has also 'had interviews with virgin girls who take part in these rituals and one married woman, MaNtanzi Mhlongo, who used to stay in Ebuhleni [one of Shembe's sacred places] as a virgin girl'.[33]

The first of these rituals is the iNtanda or oThingweni (long stick) ritual, and it started 'after Shembe had a problem acquiring the land which is now called Ntanda'. 'The story (which is always told at the Ntanda ritual)',[34] says Sithole, goes that Shembe was promised by a Frenchman that he would sell his farm to Shembe. When Shembe went to the farm with the money he was told by a black farmworker that he had 'overheard the whites saying that the farm should not be sold to a black person'. 'Shembe was saddened by this', says Sithole, 'and went back to his congregation', where he 'requested that the girls go to the farm to pray that the church should acquire it'. This the young virgin girls did, and subsequently 'the Frenchman sold the farm to Shembe and Shembe, as a way of thanking God, made a vow that virgin girls would go to worship at Ntanda every July seventh'. 'In this way', continues Sithole, 'Shembe was offering his girls to God even though they were not to be a burnt offering like Jephtah's daughter'.[35]

Sithole's telling of the iNtanda ritual so far resonates with my and Muller's reading of Shembe's use of the Judges 11 story, demonstrating a communal concern, and how virgin girls serve the community by enabling the community to acquire land in a social context in which colonial forces withheld land from blacks.

But Sithole goes on to note in his comments on the iNtanda ritual that '[i]n terms of the actual practice of this ritual, there is not much link with the Jephtah narrative, except for the telling of the text of this story'.[36] Among the activities of the ritual, which is now only one night and a day and not three days, 'the leader, referred to as Mphathi or Anti (aunt) advises them on how to behave as amakhosazane [unmarried women], emphasizing the fact that iNtanda is for virgin girls only. She then tells (or reads to) the girls the story of how the land which is now iNtanda was obtained and also the story of Jephtah and his daughter'.[37]

Judges 11 is, however, a more substantial part of the second ritual, umgonqo, which is 'ideally a two month ritual commencing on the 25th of July to the 25th of September' (appropriating the 'two months' of Judges 11:37), though the constraints of ordinary contemporary life do not make it possible for all participants to be sequestered for the full two months. For '[d]uring this period', says Sithole, 'the girls are supposed to be closeted in their area and must have no contact at all with men'.[38]

---

[33] Sithole, 'Sithole Reading West Reading Shembe Reading Judges 11', 1, note 1.
[34] Muller includes an early account of this story in her book, as one of the sources for these rituals, see Muller, *Nazarite Women's Performance in South Africa*, 191–4.
[35] Sithole, 'Sithole Reading West Reading Shembe Reading Judges 11', 1.
[36] Sithole, 'Sithole Reading West Reading Shembe Reading Judges 11', 1.
[37] Sithole, 'Sithole Reading West Reading Shembe Reading Judges 11', 1.
[38] Sithole, 'Sithole Reading West Reading Shembe Reading Judges 11', 3.

'This ritual', Sithole confirms, still today 'draws on both the biblical narrative of Jephtah and his daughter, and on a traditional rite called umgonqo [an Nguni puberty rite]'. 'It is', says Sithole, 'a commemoration and a lament of the death of Jephtah's daughter', where the ritual 'commences with the reading of the Jephtah text'.[39] But, Sithole argues, the emphasis of these rituals is not lament but 'a celebration of the amakhosazane's virginity', where the story of Jephthah's daughter 'is used to denote the strength she displayed both in keeping her virginity and in accepting death so as to allow her father to keep his promise to God'. And while this is done 'to encourage the girls to also keep their virginity until they are married', 'it is also used to encourage the whole Nazaretha community to have the same strength'. As Sithole says, 'Shembe seems to have valued the kind of bravery displayed by Jephtah's daughter especially'.[40]

But it is at this point in his analysis that Sithole argues for a different emphasis, an argument he develops at length in his PhD thesis *Performance, Power and Agency: Isaiah Shembe's Hymns and the Sacred Dance in the Church of the Nazarites*.[41] The Nazaretha Hymn No. 38, sung by the entire congregation during the umgonqo ritual, has each and every member asking of Jehova, 'Give me the strength/ Of Jephtah's daughter'. Why Shembe valued the bravery of Jephtah's daughter is because, says Sithole, 'Shembe saw being a person of God as something so difficult it required a person to have strength if that person was to hold on to it. The valley of sorrow spoken about in stanza one [of the hymn] refers to the place in the afterlife which is like hell, where those who did not do well on earth will end up'. This idea, Sithole notes, is a regular theme in Shembe's hymns, for example Hymn No. 218 'which also talks about the difficulty of the Shembe laws and the suffering of those who failed to keep those laws'.[42] 'The idea', continues Sithole, 'is that through her religious strength in keeping her virginity and in consenting to be a sacrifice to God, Jephtah's daughter must have made it to heaven, and whoever wants to avoid the valley of sorrow, but instead go straight to heaven, must follow her example in being truthful to their faith'.[43]

Layers of reception

Nkosinathi Sithole suggests a rather different form of revolution here; or perhaps, another form of revolution alongside the more usual form of revolution as resistance to colonial domination. Those of us (see also Muller and Cabrita) who have read

---

[39] Sithole, 'Sithole Reading West Reading Shembe Reading Judges 11', 3.
[40] Sithole, 'Sithole Reading West Reading Shembe Reading Judges 11', 4.
[41] Nkosinathi Sithole, 'Performance, Power and Agency: Isaiah Shembe's Hymns and the Sacred Dance in the Church of the Nazarites', University of KwaZulu-Natal, 2010.
[42] Sithole, 'Sithole Reading West Reading Shembe Reading Judges 11', 4, note 4.
[43] Sithole, 'Sithole Reading West Reading Shembe Reading Judges 11', 4.

this latter form of revolution in Isaiah Shembe's construction of community in the early 1900s are being asked to consider another dimension of his project.

Muller is clear in her ideological appropriation/reception of Isaiah Shembe's reception/appropriation of Judges 11. In his struggle to acquire land, she argues, Shembe called upon his young female followers 'to fulfill certain actions', actions that 'were consistent with traditional Zulu beliefs regarding the power of young female virgins to safeguard the well-being of communities'. 'They were, however', she goes on to argue, 'transferred into a new political frame',[44] a transformation in which Judges 11 plays a part. 'As the story of Jephthah and his daughter demonstrates', she says later, 'for the Nazarite community to be victorious in its war against racial injustice, the girls are required to offer their virtuous bodies in obedience to the will of the prophet/God'.[45]

Indeed, it is common practice for 'outsiders' to the Church of the Nazarites to frame their practice in political and economic terms, as is the case with all those I have cited in this article. But Sithole has asked us to consider another perspective, and he does this by way of a re-reading of an amaNazaretha sacred text.

Sithole queries the English translation of stanza two of Hymn No. 38 (as I have it from Papini and Hexham). Sithole, of course, does not engage this hymn in English. He performs it with other amaNazaretha in isiZulu. He contends that the correct translation is not 'I too shall go alone/ Into my grave', but 'Also, I shall go alone/ into my grave' (Futhi ngongena ngingedwa/ Ethuneni lami), emphasizing the fact that this hymn is about the afterlife and the hardships one is likely to encounter on one's journey'. 'The message put across in Hymn No. 38 is the same as the one in Hymn No. 143, for instance', argues Sithole, 'which points to the difficulty of being a Nazaretha and calls on all who want to join the faith to have religious strength because the Nazaretha way is difficult. According to the speaker in the hymn [and the translation that follows is his], being a Nazaretha is like a slippery rock on which most people cannot manage to walk'.[46]

> Ukukholwa kwethu
> Kulobu buNazaretha
> Kuyidwala elibushelelezi
> Lehlula abaningi.
>
> Wena uyathanda ukusilandela
> Lapha siya khona
> Uboqala uthenge isibindi
> Lapha siya khona.

---

[44] Muller, *Nazarite Women's Performance in South Africa*, 194.
[45] Muller, *Nazarite Women's Performance in South Africa*, 198.
[46] Sithole, 'Sithole Reading West Reading Shembe Reading Judges 11', 4.

[Our faith
In this Nazaretha
It's a slippery rock
It beats many people.

If you like to follow us
Where we are going
You must first buy valour.
Where we are going.]

But, if I may be allowed the final word/reception, is Sithole's reception documenting a shift in the revolutionary project of the amaNazaretha, with the individual heavenly project becoming more of an emphasis in post-colonial South Africa than it was in the days of the colonial struggle? The land Isaiah Shembe acquired and the community he constructed are no longer on the periphery of South African society. Their land is now enclosed within crowded townships, and both Muller and Gunner comment on how Nelson Mandela and other prominent political leaders have drawn the amaNazaretha into the forefront of post-liberation South Africa.[47] New struggles confront them, as they do all South Africans, and HIV is among these challenges.[48]

Given the centrality of healing among almost every form of African Christianity (including the Church of the Nazarites), and the challenge to healing HIV and AIDS pose, there is considerable inter-religious engagement across Christian denominations (and even across religions). It would be strange, in other words, if theological influences from other forms of African Christianity did not find their way into the theological landscape of the amaNazaretha. For example, in the work of the Ujamaa Centre with the Siyaphila support network of people living with HIV and AIDS, a young woman from the Nazarite Church was a regular member of a local support group, among women from a whole range of churches, including Settler Initiated Churches ('mainline' churches), African Initiated Churches, and the newer Pentecostal and Charismatic churches.[49] Furthermore, there is some evidence that in this 'time of AIDS' women join the Nazarite Church because it is a church that allows (under certain conditions) polygamy, in the hope of 'finding a

---

[47] Muller, *Nazarite Women's Performance in South Africa*, 23–4; Gunner, *The Man of Heaven and the Beautiful Ones of God*, 1–4.

[48] Gerald O. West, 'Male and Female Bodies in the Teaching of Isaiah Shembe: Possible Implications for HIV and AIDS,' in *Broken Bodies and Healing Communities: The Challenge of HIV and AIDS in the South African Context*, ed. R. Neville Richardson (Pietermaritzburg: Cluster Publications, 2009).

[49] Gerald O. West and Bongi Zengele, 'The Medicine of God's Word: What People Living with HIV and AIDS Want (and Get) from the Bible,' *Journal of Theology for Southern Africa* 125 (2006).

man who would take them as a second or subsequent wife',[50] and in so doing bring other forms of more individualized and spiritual faith among the amaNazaretha.

Individualized forms of Christian faith are now the norm in South Africa, as they are in most of the African continent.[51] That such forms of Christian faith are now the norm is a new phenomenon in South Africa, for we have always had a robustly contested Christian terrain.[52] So does Sithole's response to my reception of Shembe's reception of Judges 11 reflect some contextual (and 'normative') reconfiguration of the (politicized) faith tradition of Ibandla lamaNazaretha? Or have we outsiders misunderstood the emphasis of this movement from the outset, imagining a more socio-political religious formation than Sithole's religio-cultural insider understanding of the Nazarite Church? Only further layers of reception will tell.

---

[50] Mark Hunter, *Love in the Time of AIDS: Inequality, Gender, and Rights in South Africa* (Pietermaritzburg: University of KwaZulu-Natal Press, 2010), 152. I thank Beverley Haddad for bringing this example to my attention.

[51] Paul Gifford, 'Trajectories in African Christianity', *International Journal for the Study of the Christian Church* 8, no. 4 (2008).

[52] The Kairos theologians, *Challenge to the Church: The Kairos Document: A Theological Comment on the Political Crisis in South Africa* (Braamfontein: The Kairos theologians, 1985); Gerald O. West, 'Jesus, Jacob Zuma, and the New Jerusalem: Religion in the Public Realm between Polokwane and the Presidency', *Journal for the Study of Religion* 23, no. 1&2 (2010).

Part Five

Bible, Reception and Popular Music

14

The Story of Leonard Cohen's 'Who by Fire', a Prayer in the Cairo Genizah, Babylonian Astrology and Related Rabbinical Texts[1]

Helen R. Jacobus
University College London

Introduction

In this essay, I trace the textual background, ancient ideas and influences behind the song 'Who by Fire', a well-known composition by the Jewish Canadian poet and singer-songwriter, Leonard Cohen. It is a standard number in his live repertoire and in his album compilations.[2] The song's lyrics consist of a mixture of verbatim and modern rewording of the second section of *Unetaneh toqef*, a Hebrew liturgy recited in the synagogue on the Jewish New Year – Rosh Hashanah, and the Day of Atonement – Yom Kippur, ten days later, that describes various rewards and unusual fatal punishments to be meted out according to the outcome of divine judgement. The part of *Unetaneh toqef* on which Cohen's song is based opens with the verse: 'On Rosh Hashanah it is written and on Yom Kippur it is sealed.' This is a reference to one's forthcoming fate in the coming year.

The first section of the synagogue prayer is quite different.[3] Unless otherwise specified all references to *Unetaneh toqef* refer to the second part, that which

---

[1] My thanks to Ben Outhwaite, Head of the Genizah Research Unit, Cambridge, for re-dating the Cairo Genizah manuscript and for assistance with the problematic first line of the text at my request, and to Francesca Rochberg for kindly sending me her unpublished paper on the Babylonian concept of divine law. I am also grateful to Pennina Barnett for her feedback on the final draft of this article.

[2] Cohen's albums which contain 'Who by Fire' include: *New Skin for the Old Ceremony* (Columbia, 1974), *The Best of Leonard Cohen* (Columbia, 1975), *So Long, Marianne* (Columbia, 1989), *Cohen Live* (Sony, 1994), *The Essential Leonard Cohen* (Columbia, 2002), *MOJO Presents: An Introduction to Leonard Cohen. 23 Classic Songs* (Sony, 2003), *Live in London* (2009). The song was covered by the band The House of Love on the tribute album *I'm Your Fan* (EastWest Record, UK; Sony, France; Atlantic Records, US; 1991).

[3] Idelsohn summarizes the first section of *Unetaneh toqef* as describing 'the procedure of Judgment and the stir it occasions among the hosts on high.' A. Z. Idelsohn, *Jewish Liturgy and Its Development*, New York: Dover Publications [replication of 1st edition 1932, New York: Henry Holt], 220. The 'procedure' includes God writing in the Book of Remembrance, sealing it, and considering the souls of all mankind, the angels trembling in awe and mustering for the Day of Judgement, and the sounding of the trumpet of judgement, the *shofar*, a ram's horn.

contains the words in the title of Cohen's song, 'Who by Fire'. The song's title is taken from a hemistich in the synagogue liturgy, who will die by fire, one way amongst several possible ways that a person's natural life can be curtailed. The synagogue liturgy infers that everyone has a destiny and it closes with a verse exclaiming that the 'evil decree' can be bypassed by practising 'repentance [*teshuvah*], prayer [*tefillah*] and charity [or righteousness, *tzdaqah*].'

This essay follows the path from Cohen's text back through 1,000 years of history: the *Unetaneh toqef* as it is read in synagogues today, the eleventh-century Cairo Genizah version of the prayer in a water-damaged Hebrew manuscript rediscovered in this research and presented in a preliminary translation for the first time, a Babylonian astrological tablet, Hebrew Bible texts and related rabbinical writings. Cohen's song, in which each stanza is written in the style of the synagogue prayer, may be regarded through a telescope of history, taking into account historical discussions about how one can control one's destiny.

This study begins with Cohen's own intellectual and musical interpretations of his version of the prayer as he has performed it for more than 35 years.

Unetaneh toqef in Cohen's words

'Who by Fire' first appeared on Cohen's 1974 album, *New Skin for the Old Ceremony*, in the form of a duet with Janis Ian. The lyrics begin with 'And who by fire, who by water,' strongly alluding to the forms of dying, fate and judgement recited in the synagogue prayer, using an intriguing mixture of rural and traditional, with urban and modern imagery.

The composition consists of four verses of three couplets each, the fourth verse repeating the lyrics of the first. The first five lines in each verse take the form of parallel, contrasting statements, such as, 'Who in the night-time, who in the day-time,' echoing contrasting forms of parallelism in Hebrew poetry. They are prefixed by the interrogative phrase 'Who by . . .' or 'Who in . . .' As Ratcliffe notes, no verb follows the roll-call of the destinies of different souls.[4] The sixth and final line – a question – in each verse contains the only verb in each stanza: 'And who shall I say is calling?' It is an unexpected rhetorical device, not in the synagogue prayer, and it is disconnected structurally from the preceding lines, yet on a mystical and thematic level it fits them perfectly.[5]

In a video interview accompanying a performance of 'Who by Fire', Cohen explains that he based his composition on the contemporary synagogue

---

[4] M. Ratcliffe, *Leonard Cohen: The Music and the Mystique* (London: Omnibus, 2012), 31.

[5] For copyright reasons we are unable to provide the lyrics. Readers may use a search via a licensed provider, to find the lyrics using key words, such as 'Who by Fire.' One such licensed website is, http://www.metrolyrics.com/ [accessed 24 January 2014].

prayer and that he changed the central idea of Judgement.⁶ The interview is as follows:

> Leonard Cohen: That song derives very directly from a Hebrew prayer that is sung on the Day of Atonement or the evening of the Day of Atonement, *Mi Bamayim, Mi Baherev* (מי במים מי בחרב)'Who by fire, Who by sword, Who by water' [sic].⁷ According to the tradition, the Book of Life is opened and in it is inscribed all those who will live and all those who will die for the following year. And in that prayer is catalogued all the various ways in which you can ... [he pauses] quit this vale of tears.
> The melody, if not actually stolen, is certainly derived from the melody that I heard in the synagogue as a boy. But, of course, the conclusion of the song, as *I* [Cohen's emphasis] write it is somewhat different: 'Who shall I say is calling?'
> [There is longer pause].
> Interviewer: Who is calling?
> Leonard Cohen: Well, that is, that is, that is what makes the song into a prayer. For me, in my terms, who is it, or what is it that determines who will live and who will die.

The musical arrangement of Cohen's 'Who by Fire', has developed in various ways over 35 years. Some of the videoed performances are different from the range of musical arrangements on the live and studio albums (there are now hundreds of performances available to watch or listen to on YouTube, many having been filmed at his concerts and uploaded by fans). The original version was musically unusual enough to be commented on by several biographers and musical journalists. Tim Footman describes the 1974 musical arrangement with Janis Ian, as hinting at 'Hasidic melancholy'.⁸ The song's ending is abrupt, possibly in keeping with the musical depiction of the one who is 'calling'. Whatever the reason, the effect impressed the music writer Ratcliffe sufficiently to remark:

> (I am not aware of any other instance of a song ending in a bass solo. If it is as unique as my experience suggests, then it is a marvellous bit of musical originality dropped casually into the set).⁹

Ratcliffe reports that the arranger of 'Who by Fire', Tony Palmer, thought that it was

---

⁶ The URL on www.youtube.com: *Leonard Cohen-Who By Fire with interview (1979)* http://www.youtube.com/watch?v=elbG-SFJM8w (uploaded on 21 March 2009 by 'messalina79'). [Accessed 12 September 2013]. The source of the video, with French sub-titles, is not given in the metadata.
⁷ Cohen does not translate 'Who by fire' (*Mi Ba'esh*) into Hebrew.
⁸ Tim Footman, *Leonard Cohen. Hallelujah. A New Biography* (New Malden, Surrey: Chrome Dreams, 2009), 97.
⁹ Ratcliffe, *Leonard Cohen. The Music and the Mystique*, 77.

one of his [Cohen's] most profound songs ... The first time you hear it, you're struck by the power of the imagery ... the simplicity of the music ...

Describing it as a 'haunting, eerie hymn-like song' Ratcliffe explains that it

> ... did in fact owe its origins to the eleventh century Jewish prayer known as *Unetanneh Toqef* or *Unesanneh* [Ashkenazi pronunciation] *Toqef* but Cohen rarely spoke of the background to his songs and the musicians and producer responded to them purely as music.[10]

Stephen Scobie remarks that the dominant string arrangement in the original recording reflects the song's spirit of deep anticipation:

> 'Who by Fire' is a brilliantly unsettling *memento mori*. The verses simply list possible ways of dying. The ominous mood is marvellously sustained by the backing vocals and the jerky strings arrangement.[11]

Dorman and Rawlins intuit that Cohen is articulating a revision of the Jewish theme of divine judgement:

> 'Who by Fire,' based on a prayer recited at the sacred time of atonement, when reconciliation is effected, echoes the response-to-the-voice that repeatedly finds expression in later work. But the context to the original prayer is one of judgement; a call to self-examination. There can be no reconciliation without that, is the inference.[12]

In contrast to the emphasis on arrangements with stringed instruments in different versions of 'Who by Fire', Cohen's only jazz and blues-style rendition of his prayer (to my knowledge), took place on an American jazz and eclectic music show, 'Night Music'.[13] He was accompanied by the world famous saxophonist Sonny Rollins, other session jazz musicians, and harmonizing male backing singers (highly unusual for Cohen) in addition to his then-regular female backing singers. The prominent wind instrumentals produced a very different type of lead-in, appearing to riff on the sound of the blowing of the *shofar*, part of the ritual for Rosh Hashanah.

Rollins completes the song on his saxophone with a solo that also appears to follow the pattern of the *shofar*. These notes are the *tekia*, a long stretched sound; *shevarim*, three broken notes; and *tĕrua*, nine staccato notes, then the repetition of

---

[10] Ratcliffe, *Leonard Cohen. The Music and the Mystique*, 119. His assertion that the prayer can be sourced in an eleventh-century text is supported in this essay (he does not give a source for his information).

[11] Stephen Scobie, *Leonard Cohen* (Vancouver: Douglas and McIntyre, 1978), 167.

[12] Loranne S. Dorman and Clive L. Rawlins, *Leonard Cohen, Prophet of the Heart* (London: Omnibus, 1990), 277.

[13] TV show 'Night Music', 13 February 1989, 'Who by Fire', featuring Sonny Rollins on You Tube www.youtube.com (Leonard Cohen/ Sonny Rollins–Who By Fire–Night Music, uploaded 24 April 2011). The recording is not on an album.

the *tekia*.¹⁴ This sound sequence has little to do with any recognizable jazz rhythm or musical harmony. The saxophone solo contrasts with the original ending, on a bass, ending abruptly, but it retains the challenging idea of the End of Life by concluding on what must surely be the lowest possible notes on a saxophone.

The visual presentation of the 'Night Music' performance is also memorable. The camera begins on a close-up of Rollins and slowly pulls out during the instrumental introduction to reveal the other musicians and Cohen who, against convention, has his back three-quarters profile to the audience, facing Rollins, who is behind him. After singing the lyrics to 'Who by Fire', enhanced by counter harmonies, blues-style and accompaniments by a male vocalist, Cohen turns around a full 180 degrees. He presents his back to the camera completely and watches Rollins's *shofar*-sax finale, as if facing the *bimah*. Ratcliffe comments that Cohen is 'visibly moved' and that he observes Rollins's solo 'with obvious reverence'.¹⁵

Various transmissions

In his biography of Cohen, *Various Positions* (the book title comes from Cohen's 1984 album of the same name), Nadel describes Cohen's Orthodox Jewish background and his connection with rabbis and Judaic scholars on both sides of his family.¹⁶ Intellectually and spiritually, Simmons informs us in the biography, *I'm Your Man* (named after the title-track of Cohen's 1988 album) that Cohen leans towards Jewish mysticism and the Kabbalah.¹⁷ Cohen's deep Judaic knowledge is probably reflected in a hermeneutical aspect of the lyrics in 'Who by Fire'; in particular, Cohen's verse: 'Who by high ordeal, who by common trial,' may be an allusion to line 10 in the second section of the *Unetaneh toqef*. It is best to see this in its surrounding context, and so here is the relevant part of the liturgy, as experienced in today's synagogue service.¹⁸

Unetaneh toqef

1. On Rosh Hashanah it is inscribed,
2. And on the Day of the Fast of Kippur it is sealed.
3. How many will pass over and how many will be created,
4. Who will live and who will die,
5. Who will reach the end of his days and who shall not reach the end of his days,

---

[14] See Idelsohn, *Jewish Liturgy*, 211–12, for the technical description of the blowing of the *shofar*.
[15] Ratcliffe, *Leonard Cohen. The Music and the Mystique*, 217.
[16] Ira B. Nadel, *Various Positions: A Life of Leonard Cohen* (New York: Random House, 1996), 7, 9, 10, 11–14, 19, 213–4.
[17] Sylvie Simmons, *I'm Your Man: The Life of Leonard Cohen* (London: Jonathan Cape, 2012), 438–440.
[18] My modified translation from Scherman, *Artscroll Machzor*, 532–3. The arrangement of verses is mine to illustrate the poetry.

6. Who by water and who by fire,
7. Who by sword and who by beast,
8. Who by famine and who by thirst
9. Who by earthquake and who by plague,
10. Who by strangulation and who by stoning.
11. Who will rest and who will wander,
12. Who will have quiet and who will be savaged,
13. Who will be undisturbed and who shall be tormented,
14. Who will be poor and who will be enriched,
15. Who will be brought low and who will be exalted,
16. But repentance, and prayer and charity avert the evil decree[19]

The stich, 'Who by strangulation and who by stoning.' מי בחניקה ומי בסקילה, may be an allusion to the four methods of capital punishment for biblical sins or crimes, described in the Mishneh (*Sanhedrin* 45a and 52a, 52b) and codified by Maimonides (1135–1204) in his *Mishneh Torah* (*Sanhedrin*: chapter 15): stoning, *Seqilah*; burning, *Serefah*; beheading, *Hereg*; and strangulation, *Heneq*.[20] It is possible that for the author of line 10, the hemistichs 6b and 7b – 'Who by Fire,' *Mi Ba'esh* and 'Who by Sword,' *Mi Baherev* – refer to rabbinical methods of execution. Such an interpretation might be in keeping with the prayer for atonement that includes advice on how to avoid a terrible punishment.

It would be fair to say that most modern congregants would not know that the inclusion of strangulation referred to a rabbinical method of biblical capital punishment. To worshippers without advanced knowledge of the Talmud, the verse seems incongruous. The language of verse 10 is not poetic, but legalistic and somewhat obscure – stoning is mentioned in the Bible,[21] and therefore, understood, but strangulation is not. It is not an absolute given that 'death by fire' and 'death by sword' refer to capital punishments; in fact, those manners of death are not specific. Furthermore, the technical legal terminology for capital punishment by burning: pouring molten lead down a person's throat, and being put to the sword: decapitation,[22] are not used in the liturgy. The poetry states *Mi Ba'esh*, 'Who By Fire,' not *Mi Baserefah*, 'Who By the Burning Punishment.'

---

[19] See also Rabbi Joel M. Hoffman (Trans), 'Behind the Translation,' in *Who By Fire, Who By Water—Un'taneh tokef*. Edited by Lawrence A. Hoffman (Woodstock, Vermont: Jewish Lights, 2010), 33–48.
[20] Irene Marker Rosenberg and Yale L. Rosenberg, 'Of God's Mercy and the Four Biblical Methods of Capital Punishment: Stoning, Burning, Beheading and Strangulation,' *Tulane Law Review* 78 (2003): 1169–1212 (esp. 1169–1204).
[21] Deut: 22:20, 24.
[22] The mishnaic methods for the four methods of execution are given as: stoning in tractate *Sanhedrin* (45a); burning: *Sanhedrin* (52a); decapitation and strangulation: *Sanhedrin* 52b; Fred Rosner (ed. and trans) *Maimonides' Commentary on the Mishnah: Tractate Sanhedrin* (New York: Sepher Hermon Press, 1981).

I would argue that Cohen's verse 'Who by high ordeal, who by common trial' is exegeting and poeticizing 'Who by strangulation and who by stoning,' since he is working closely with the synagogue text. His verse, referring to different types of earthly judgement, may suggest that Cohen has understood that the synagogue prayer contains a reference to rabbinical capital punishment. If so, it is possible that Cohen translated the line to keep the Hebrew poetic parallelism and the prayer's abbreviated, repetitive literary form in order to faithfully render the liturgy's meaning.

The history of the history

Until the 1950s there was an accepted tradition that the *Unetaneh toqef* was an early medieval liturgical poem that had been either composed or introduced into the Rosh Hashanah service by a Rabbi Amnon of Mainz who was martyred in the eleventh century. Rabbi Amnon is said to have appeared in a dream to a well-known medieval rabbi telling him to disseminate the prayer in the diaspora as his memorial.[23] In Scherman's account Rabbi Amnon intended the prayer to be said at the Rosh Hashanah service and it was included in the Yom Kippur service in most communities at a later date. Some modern *machzorim* (the prayer book used for services on Rosh Hashanah and Yom Kippur) repeat this tradition.[24] The current dominant view, however, is that the prayer originated in Palestine in the Byzantine period and that Rabbi Amnon is a legend.[25]

The story of Rabbi Amnon was reassessed in the late 1950s following the information from Dr M. Zulay, of the Hebrew University in Jerusalem, that the

---

[23] The story is contained in the *Sefer Or Zarua*, a work by Rabbi Isaac ben Moses of Vienna (1180–1250) who said he took it from a manuscript written by Rabbi Ephraim of Bonn (1132–1197) who stated that the story came from Kalonymous of Mainz (c.1000) who said that *Unetaneh Toqef* had been revealed to him in a dream by Rabbi Amnon of Mainz and that he should spread it to dispersed Jews. E. Werner, *The Sacred Bridge: The interdependence of liturgy and music in synagogue and church in the first millennium* (London: Dobson, 1959), 252–253. E. G. L. Schrijver, 'Some Light on the Amsterdam and London manuscripts of Isaac Ben Moses of Vienna's Or Zarua', *Bulletin of the John Rylands University Library* 75:3 (1993): 53–82. See, Ivan G. Marcus, 'A Pious Community and Doubt: Jewish Martyrdom among Northern European Jewry and the Story of Rabbi Amnon of Mainz,' in *Essays in Hebrew Literature in Honour of Avraham Holtz* (ed. Zvia Ben-Yosef Ginor; New York: Jewish Theological Seminary of America, 2003), 21–46 (at 35–37). See, the article by Rabbi Prof. David Golinkin, President of the Schechter Institutes, 'Do Repentence, Prayer and Tzedakah Avert the Severe Decree?' in The Schechter Institutes's online newsletter, *Insight Israel* 6 (2005), Appendix A: http://www.schechter.edu/insightisrael.aspx?id=19.

[24] Scherman, *Artscroll Machzor*, 530.

[25] Lawrence A. Hoffman, 'Un'taneh Tokef as Poetry and Legend,' in *Who By Fire, Who By Water*, ed. Hoffman, 13–24; and idem (trans), 'The Legend of Rabbi Amnon,' 26–8. Cf. Menahem Schmelzer, 'Penitence, Prayer and (Charity?),' in *Minḥah le-Naḥum: Biblical and Other Studies Presented to Nahum M. Sarna in Honour of his 70th Birthday* (eds. Marc Brettler and Michael Fishbane; Sheffield: Sheffield Academic Press, 1993), 291–9 (at 291).

prayer was in a manuscript from the Cairo Genizah and that it probably dates back to the eighth century.[26] The reliability of this date, which is much earlier than most other manuscripts in the Genizah, seems questionable. Dr Zulay's opinion on the age of the manuscript has now been re-evaluated by Dr Ben Outhwaite, Head of the Genizah Research Unit at Cambridge University. At my request Dr Outhwaite kindly looked at the digitized manuscript on the Friedberg Genizah Project website and considered there was no reason to date the manuscript to an unusually early period. He also found that the handwriting style was Syro-Palestinian, not European:

> ...it's a Syro-Palestinian hand of the 11th c., I would say: not particularly early, but very much Classical Genizah Period. Also it's on paper, so a date before the end of the 10th c. would have to have extraordinary justification.[27]

The manuscript has, therefore, very probably been unrealistically dated to the late eighth century,[28] instead of the eleventh century, the period into which most of the medieval Jewish archive from the Cairo Genizah falls. As it is written in a Syro-Palestinian hand, there is no primary source evidence of its having eleventh-century European origins to support the story of Rabbi Amnon.

Below is my translation of the second section of the prayer *Unetaneh toqef* from the Cairo Genizah, that is, the section that contains the 'who by fire' *piyyut*; the text is in the British Library's Oriental manuscripts collection and online.[29] It is the first translation of this segment of the prayer.[30] The square brackets in the translation indicate letters or words that are water damaged on the page (the text is written in ink which has washed away in patches). The line by line arrangement, below,

---

[26] *The Complete Artscroll Machzor*. Co-edited by M. Zlotowitz and A. Gold (Translation. N. Scherman) (Brooklyn: Mesorah 1998), Heb. and trans.: 530–3 (opening verse: 530–1); the 'Who By Fire' section, is at 532–3. The 10 days between the Jewish New Year on the first day of the seventh month (1 Tishri) and Yom Kippur (10 Tishri) are known as the Days of Awe.

[27] Private communication with Dr Ben Outhwaite, 30 April 2013.

[28] Dated by Eric Werner or M. Zulay (unclear) in a communication to Werner from Zulay cited in Werner, *The Sacred Bridge*, 253; accepted Golinkin, 'Do Repentence, Prayer and Tzedakah Avert the Severe Decree?' §2 online, op. cit.

[29] British Library, MS shelfmark: Or 5557 G fols. 67b–68b. The manuscript is digitized and online in the Friedberg Genizah Project [www.Genizah.org]. Page 1 of the prayer begins three-quarters down the page on London, British Library Or. 5557G.67 (FGP shelfmark C253223, frg 1 v). The extant 'Who By Fire' section is at London, British Library Or. 5557G.68 (FGP shelfmark C253225, frg 1 v).

[30] Some verses in the first section of *Unetaneh toqef* were translated by Werner, *Sacred Bridge*, 254. Werner's study focuses only on this part of the liturgy. It is unclear in his book if the given folio numbers (Or 5557 G fols. 67b–68b) included the remainder of the prayer, or constituted the first section only. Further, it was not stated whether the second section existed at all in the Genizah manuscript (it could have been added at another time or in a different version), and if so, how close it was to the prayer used in the synagogue today. Seeing the 'Who By Fire' section – 'who by water, who by fire' is perfectly clear in Hebrew letters undamaged by water – was beyond my expectation. It was surprising and felt quite thrilling to actually see the iconic words of Cohen's song, in Hebrew, 1000 years old.

reproduces the lay-out of the remaining 1,000-year-old text. The commentary that follows this translation indicates the text's reception history. The shorter length of the Genizah version probably indicates that it is older than the version currently recited from the High Holy Days prayer book.

Unetaneh toqef (source: Cairo Genizah)
[On Rosh Hashanah it is inscribed]

1. And on Yom Kippur it is sealed. How many [will pa]ss over.
2. And how many will be created.[*vacat*] Who will live;
3. And who will die. Who will reach the end of his days. Who shall not
4. Reach the end of his days. Who by water. Who by fire.
5. Who by sword. Who by beast. Who by earthquake.
6. [Who by pla]gue. [Who will re]st. [Who will w]ander.
7. [Who will have] qu[iet]. Who will be savaged. Who will be undisturbed.
8. Who [shall be torment]ed. [Who will be] exalted. Who will be brought low.
9. [Who will be po]or. [Who will] become enriched. But repentance,
10. [and prayer and charity avert] the evil decree

In Table 14.1, the translations of the two texts are placed side by side so that the comparisons between them are easier to see (the additional lines in the synagogue version are in bold).

It is evident that the Genizah version differs, but not drastically, from the surviving synagogue version of the 'who by fire' pericope. Before comparing the textual differences, I shall first note some important points in the material text that are relevant to our understanding of the poem in the Cairo Genizah manuscript.

Table 14.1 *Unetaneh toqef* synagogue and Genizah versions compared

Synagogue version verse by verse	Genizah text line by line on the page
1. On Rosh Hashanah it is inscribed	[On Rosh Hashanah it is inscribed] (overleaf)
2. And on the Day of the Fast of Kippur it is sealed.	1. And on Yom Kippur it is sealed. How many [will pa]ss over.
3. How many will pass over and how many will be created	2. And how many will be created. [*vacat*] Who will live;
4. Who will live and who will die,	3. And who will die. Who will reach the end of his days. Who shall not
5. Who will reach the end of his days and who shall not reach the end of his days	4. Reach the end of his days. Who by water. Who by fire.
6. Who by water and who by fire,	5. Who by sword. Who by beast. Who by earthquake.

(*Continued*)

Table 14.1 (Continued)

Synagogue version verse by verse	Genizah text line by line on the page
7. Who by sword and who by beast	6. [Who by pla]gue. [Who will re]st. [Who will w]ander.
8. Who by famine and who by thirst	7. [Who will have] qu[iet]. Who will be savaged. Who will be undisturbed.
9. Who by earthquake and who by plague	8. Who [shall be torment]ed. [Who will be] exalted. Who will be brought low.
10. Who by strangulation and who by stoning	9. [Who will be po]or. [Who will] become enriched. But repentance,
11. Who will rest and who will wander	10. [and prayer and charity avert] the evil decree
12. Who will have quiet and who will be savaged	
13. Who will be undisturbed and who shall be tormented	
14. Who will be poor and who will be enriched	
15. Who will be brought low and who will be exalted	
16. But repentance, and prayer and charity avert the evil decree	

Material description and textual commentary

The folio on which the *piyyut* is written is part of a codex: page 68 verso (marked on the manuscript as 68b), that is, the right-hand sheet.[31] As can be seen on the online digitized copy, there are a number of small lacunae in addition to the large tear from the middle to the bottom of the page. Despite ink bleeding through the sheet, the damaged words can be discerned enough to be partially reconstructed and compared with the synagogue version of *Unetaneh toqef*. Aside from the lacunae, some letters in line 1 are unclear.[32] Most notably, it is unlikely that a *piyyut* would begin with a preposition. It is therefore probable that 'And on Yom Kippur it is sealed' is the second half of the verse. However, much of the lower section of the page is missing and so we cannot be sure what the first half of the verse would be. Based on comparisons with the prayer in current usage, we can, however, conjecture

---

[31] In codices written in right-to-left scripts such as Hebrew the verso is on the right and the recto is on the left, the opposite of verso-recto in left-to-right handwriting.

[32] The *pe* in Yom Kippur looks like a *tav* due some rubbing; the *kap* in כמה ('how many') looks like a *bet* because of the scribe's unclear handwriting; finally the *yud ayin* of [ע]בורון] ('will pass over') the last word on the line is missing. I thank Dr Ben Outhwaite for his restoration of this word and for his advice on the other two letters.

that the verse begins with 'On Rosh Hashanah it is inscribed' at the bottom of the previous page, that is, overleaf on the recto.[33] A large part of the lower section of the page is now missing.

The punctuation of the poem creates the rhythm. There is a point in the middle of each space between every hemistich and a double point like our colon (:) after 'Who will live'. This phrase is preceded by a larger-than-average word space, as if indicating a pause. Due to the care taken in apparently giving directions for this section to be chanted or recited aloud, such as the colon-like marks, it is unlikely that the scribe accidentally missed out the two additional lines that appear in today's *Unetaneh toqef*.

The section of the Genizah *Unetaneh toqef*, upon which Cohen's 'Who by Fire' is based, is divided into three sections of four verses each, with each verse consisting of parallels, some of which are alliterative. Section A, lines 1–5, opens with the judgement motif for Rosh Hashanah and Yom Kippur and lists synonyms for living and dying. Section B, lines 6–10, describes contrasting pairs of methods of dying; section C, lines 11–15, lists opposing qualities of life.

Given the 1,000 years of transmission history between the Genizah text and the version known today, the two recensions are very close. The verse 'who by famine, who by thirst' in line 8 of today's *Unetaneh toqef* that is absent from the Genizah text is an addition that completes the symmetrical tripartite structure of the poem. It may have been added later, perhaps at the same time as the verse on capital punishment to even up the number of paired verses, or because it is based on a different tradition.

The verses that are absent from the Genizah's *Unetaneh toqef* (not due to damage) are: 'Who by hunger and who by thirst,' found in line 8 of today's *Unetaneh toqef* and, as discussed above, 'Who by strangulation and who by stoning' (line 10). The Genizah *Unetaneh toqef*, has 'Who will be exalted and who will be brought low' (line 8) instead of line 15 in today's *Unetaneh toqef*, 'Who will be brought low and who will be exalted.' The received version we know today places this verse after 'Who will be poor and who will become enriched,' whereas in the Genizah text it precedes it, so that 'Who will be poor and who will become rich' finalizes the list of fates or judgements. The re-ordering of the verses (assuming the Genizah text is the more original) is open to further analysis.

Repentance, prayer and charity

The final admonition of both versions of *Unetaneh toqef* states the three ways of overcoming one's predestined fate: 'repentance, prayer and charity.' This formula

---

[33] See Friedberg Genizah Project (FPG) online, London, British Library Or. 5557G. 68 recto. (FGP shelfmark, C253224. frg 1r)

emanates from a lesson in the Jerusalem Talmud [*Yerushalemi*], tractate *Ta'anit* 2:1. III 5, which is attributed to 'Rabbi Eleazar'.[34] It is part of his commentary on 2 Chron 7:14:

> If my people who are called by my name humble themselves, pray, seek my face, and turn from their wicked ways, then I will hear from heaven, and will forgive their sin and heal their land.

In the Babylonian Talmud,[35] tractates *Shabbat* 156a and *Shabbat* 156b,[36] there are linked narratives that conclude with the statement that charitable deeds can overturn a fated decree of death, in each tractate, from a venomous snake. In both stories, astrologers' predictions that the subject of either passage would die from a snake bite were averted by the individuals themselves acting from free will. One, a woman (Rabbi Akiva's daughter), and one an unnamed man, performed charitable acts just before the snake that had been destined to kill each of them was due to bite them fatally. (The astrologer predicted that the unnamed man would return from the journey where he was destined to meet the snake, if he was an Israelite.)

The message of R. Eleazar is repeated in the medieval rabbinical commentary on Genesis, *Midrash Rabba* 44:12.[37] This citation repeats the order in the Jerusalem Talmud ('prayer, charity, repentance', not that of *Unetaneh toqef*: 'repentance, prayer and charity'). The hermeneutical context here is to provide the influence of astrology, specifically citing Jer 10.2 ('Do not ... be terrified by signs in the heavens'). The locus of the midrashic discourse is Abram's statement that he could not have children because it was his planetary fate: *Midrash Rabba* 44:10–12 (esp. 44:10):

> R. Samuel b. Isaac commented: [Abraham said:] My planetary fate oppresses me and declares: Abram and Sarai cannot beget a child. Said the Holy One, blessed be He, to him: 'Let it be even as thy words: Abram and Sarai cannot beget but Abraham and Sarah can beget.' (See Footnote)

> (Footnote): By changing your names I will free you from your planetary fate.[38]

---

[34] Jacob Neusner, *Theological Dictionary of Rabbinic Judaism. Part One. Principal Theological Categories. Studies in Judaism* (Lanham, MD, 2005), 135; Golinkin, 'Do Repentence, Prayer and Tzedakah Avert the Severe Decree?' §3.#4.

[35] For further background on the Jerusalem Talmud, see S. Stern, 'The Talmud Yerushalmi,' in eds., P. S. Alexander and M. Goodman, *Rabbinic Texts and the History of Late-Roman Palestine*. (Proceedings of the British Academy 165. London: British Academy, 2010), 143–64.

[36] *Soncino Babylonian Talmud*. 18 vols (v. Shabbat) (ed. I. Epstein; London: Soncino, 1961).

[37] (Translation). *Midrash Rabba. Genesis in Two Volumes*. Translated by Rabbi Dr H. Freedman and Maurice Simon. 10 vols. (London: Soncino Press), 368 fourth paragraph. Hebrew: *Bereschit Rabba*, 44:12 (ed. Theodor Albeck, 1912), page 434.

[38] *Midrash Rabba*, (English) op. cit, 367–9; *Bereschit Rabba* (Heb), op.cit, 432–4. For online hyperlinks, see note above. Babylonian Talmud, tractate *Nedarim* 32a. It describes how Abram has gazed at the constellation that rules his destiny and seen that he is not fated to have children but God tells him that Israel is not subject to planetary influences.

The solution to overcoming Abram's negative planetary influence, according to *Midrash Rabba*, was that God changed his name to Abraham, 'meaning father of a multitude'.[39] The sages in *Midrash Rabba* conclude that Jews can overcome their astrological fate through prayer, charity, repentance, fasting, changing one's name, and also moving place (the interpretation of Gen 12:1 is that God tells Abram to leave Haran) in order to change his pre-determined destiny.

This example of intertextuality between the Bible, astrology, both Talmuds, Rabbi Eleazar, Genesis Rabba and the final verse of the Genizah *Unetaneh toqef* illustrates the complexity of reception. It is possible to look more closely at one of these items, astrology, to get an idea of depth as well as breadth.

A Babylonian horoscope handbook and related rabbinical writings

One of the most noticeable aspects of *Unetaneh toqef* is that there is a similarity with sections of a late Babylonian astrological tablet (AO 6483), from around 300–150 BCE.[40] The cuneiform tablet, translated and edited by Abraham Sachs, appears to be the equivalent of an instruction book for astrologers, explaining how a particular astrological method works, and how to use it in practice. This Babylonian divination guide contains an explanation, near the beginning, of how to subdivide each of the 12 signs of the zodiac into 12 zodiac signs again over 30 days of the month in order to fine-tune a horoscope (AO 6483 obv. 8–20).[41] Sachs coined the term for this system of sub-divisions in the zodiac, the 'micro-zodiac'.[42]

There then follows a brief prediction of the kind of life or death for the subject of a horoscope when a celestial body, that is, a planet or the sun and moon is in one of the zodiacal sub-divisions.[43] The predictions are listed in an orderly sequence of the signs of the zodiac from 'the place' of Aries (the first sign of the zodiac) to 'the place' of Pisces (the last sign of the zodiac) within the lunar month of 30 days (obv. lines 22–6). For ease of reference this will be referred to as Section A.

---

[39] *Midrash Rabba*, op. cit, 393, n. 5.
[40] A. Sachs, 'Babylonian Horoscopes,' *Journal of Cuneiform Studies* 6 (1952): 65–75, translations, 68, 70, Tablet no. TCL VI No. 14 (AO 6483) obv: lines 22–25; rev: lines 29–38.
[41] The text describes a 360-day zodiac calendar: the months have 30 days each of which is assigned to one sign of the zodiac, as the moon goes through each sign of the zodiac in a month, every 2½ days it changes sign (AO 6483 obv. 10–12) (trans, Sachs, 'Babylonian horoscopes,' 68). The mathematics is schematic, and Sachs refers to each of the portions as 'synthetic astrological' points (Sachs, 'Babylonian horoscopes,' 73); he explains the system and includes comparative information from Hellenistic astrology (Sachs, 'Babylonian horoscopes,' 71–3).
[42] Sachs, 'Babylonian horoscopes,' 72. I studied this section of the tablet for my PhD dissertation on zodiac calendars in the Dead Sea Scrolls and their reception (PhD, Manchester, UK, 2011) and was struck by the similarity between the sections on astrological predictions and *Unetaneh toqef* 2.
[43] Sachs, 'Babylonian horoscopes,' 73.

AO 6483 lines 22–5 obv. (Section A)

22. The place of Aries: death of his family. The place of Taurus: death in battle. The place of Gemini: death in prison.
23. The place of Cancer: death in the ocean; longevity. The place of Leo: he will grow old, he will be wealthy; secondly, the capture of his personal enemy. The place/ he will grow old/ he will be wealthy; secondly, the capture of his personal enemy. The place of Virgo: he will be wealthy; anger.
24. The place of Libra: wealthy; anger; good days; he will die at the age of? 40? years (?) The place of Scorpius: death by rage (is?) his death by fate. The place of Sagittarius: death in the ocean.
25. The place of Capricorn: he will be poor[44] he will be hysterical (?), he will grow sick and die. The place of Aquarius: (at the age of?) 40 (?) years (?), he will have (?) sons; death by water. The place of Pisces: (at the age of?) 40 (?) years (?), he will die; distant days ...

Section A intersects with *Unetaneh toqef* with respect to:

- 'death by water,' (line 25, 'in the place of Aquarius'); possibly 'death in the ocean,' as a synonym (lines 23, 24, Cancer, Sagittarius)
- 'he will be wealthy,' (lines 23: Leo. Virgo. Line 24: Libra); 'he will be poor' (line 25, Capricorn 1)
- 'Death in battle' (line 22, Taurus) is similar to 'Who by sword.'
- 'Death by fate' recalls 'who will die at the end of his days' interpreted in the *Artscroll Machzor* as 'who will die at his predestined time,' as noted above.
- If 'death in prison' (Line 22, Gemini) means a capital punishment it may be an early echo of 'Who by strangulation and stoning' in *Unetaneh toqef*. If that is the case then the author of that variant may have been Judaizing this prediction.

The tablet includes further sections stating brief predictions for the subject of the horoscope when certain planets are rising and setting, and, finally, when specific stars in constellations are rising (rev. 29–38),[45] known as *ziqpu* stars; when their culminations are used to measure the hours.[46] Like the section above, these lines contain predictions that are relevant to our discussion, here called Section B.

---

[44] Compare the 4Q186 Zodiacal Physionomy in the Dead Sea Scrolls in which 'he will be poor' is associated with the subject's connection with the sign of Taurus. See 4QZodiacal Physionomy frg 1 col. 11 line 9, M. Popović, '4Q186. 4QZodiacal Physiognomy. A Full Edition' in *The Mermaid and the Partridge. Essay on the Copenhagen Conference on Revision Texts from Cave 4* (Studies on the Texts of the Deserts of Judah 96; Leiden: Brill, 2011), 235.

[45] Sachs, 'Babylonian horoscopes,' translation, 70–71.

[46] Sachs, 'Babylonian horoscopes,' 74; Francesca Rochberg, *The Heavenly Writing: Divination, Horoscopy, and Astronomy in Mesopotamian Culture* (Cambridge: Cambridge University Press, 2004), 6.

AO 6483 lines 29–38 rev. (Section B)

29. [If? a? child? born? When α bootis comes forth, he will ...]. When ε bootis comes forth, he will not [have?] a son.
30. [When β coronae borealis comes forth, he will ...] When β herculis comes forth, death (caused) by a crane (?)
31. [When ζ herculis comes forth, he will ...] When μ herculis comes forth, he will be poor.
32. [When α lyrae comes forth, he will ...] When δ cygni comes forth, he will have the itch (variant: he will be deaf).
33. [When α cygni comes forth, he will ...] When η pegasi comes forth, (he will die) the death of his fate.
34. [When α andromedae comes forth, he will ... When the constellation around ν andro]medae comes forth, death (caused) by a snake.
35. [When γ andromedae comes forth, he will ... When β per]sei comes forth, death by we[apon (?)].
36. [When ε persei comes forth, he will ... When α aurigae] comes forth, he will be rich; death by a we[apon (?)]
37. [When τ aurigae comes forth, he will ... When α geminorum] comes forth, death in pri[son (?)]
38. [When β geminorum comes forth, he will ... When ι canceri] comes forth, death by a weapon [...]

Section B intersects with *Unetaneh toqef* in a similar manner to Section A: 'He will be poor,' 'he will be rich,' 'death by weapon' '(he will die) the death of his fate,' and 'death in prison.'

In addition there are parallels with other Jewish texts. The prediction, 'he will not [have?] a son' (line 29) appears to foreshadow the midrash that Abram saw that he would not have a son by gazing at his constellation that ruled his destiny (b. *Ned* 32a), telling God that his planetary fate oppressed him in this regard (*Midrash Rabba* 44:10).

'Death by snake' (line 34) is an astrological prediction that seems to be echoed in the Babylonian Talmud, tractates *Shabbat* 156a and *Shabbat* 156b, as noted above. It appears to have been a known culturally transmitted malevolent prediction. The pericopae on the emphasis on doing genuine charitable deeds (having a good heart) to dispel a malevolent astrological destiny in b. *Shabbat* 156a and *Shabbat* 156b also intersects with the three acts that 'nullify the harsh decree ... prayer, charity and repentance' in the Jerusalem Talmud (*y. Ta'an* III.5). This statement is apparently, in turn, echoed in the *Unetaneh toqef* in the final line: 'But repentance, prayer and charity avert the evil decree.'

I argue that this sequence of textual interconnections suggests that the *Unetaneh toqef* is influenced by astrological definitions of fate and destiny from Babylonian horoscope manuals and that these have been absorbed into Jewish culture and debated in rabbinical texts. The sages of late antiquity, like their modern counterparts, probably felt uncomfortable about the idea that one's life was entirely pre-determined by the stars. Interestingly, the Jerusalem and Babylonian Talmud passages on astrology discussed in this essay, as well as the *Unetaneh toqef*, are not putting forward an argument in favour of free will and against the idea that astrological determinism does not exist. Instead, they are advocating that Jews perform intercessionary actions to thwart any possible negative destiny that is written in the stars, or that people should move to a different country to change their predestined fate. Finally, God can intervene to change a name, thereby also manipulating the person's fated bad luck.

Questions of 'reception history'

By being inspired by Leonard Cohen's 'Who by Fire' and the second section of *Unetaneh toqef*, I have been able to uncover a hitherto untranslated version of *Unetaneh toqef* and a likely connection to astrological texts. The synagogue prayer ends with the verse that originates from the Jerusalem Talmud, reflecting a belief in astrological predestination amongst the sages in Palestine. Interestingly, Schmelzer states:

> To counteract these forces, the rabbis urge the individual to resort to three things [repentance, prayer and charity], which for sure, will act as an antidote to ill fate destined by astrology or predicted by dreams.[47]

It appears to be taken for granted by some scholars, therefore, that there was a linkage between one's journey through life and the stars. There is a wide cultural and temporal gap between the astrological predictions of the Babylonian tablet A06453 and what looks like a poeticized, yet similar, wording of that which fate may have in store for us all expounded in the second part of *Unetaneh toqef*. The synagogue liturgy that possibly originated from a copy of the text in the Cairo Genizah may have been influenced and mediated by rabbinical commentaries. Its concise question, 'Who by water, who by fire?' has also travelled far and wide: it muses that there is divine judgement and also fate in some form, but that one's destiny is ultimately in one's own hands.

Cohen's version of the prayer may mirror a similar process 1000 years forwards in time from the eleventh century. In Cohen's 'Who by Fire', the medieval literary construction has been transformed and set within a completely different time, place and culture to that of the medieval Jewish community in Egypt. The cosmology of antiquity discussed in rabbinical literature, reformulated in liturgical

---

[47] Schmelzer, 'Penitence, Prayer and (Charity?),' 292.

poetry, and transformed into contemporary lyrics in the 'haunting' music performed by some of the world's top musicians, has been preserved outside of time. Cohen took a poetic theme: destiny, divine judgement, or self-determination, from the liturgy of the Jewish New Year and the Day of Atonement and created a modern 'prayer', as he himself describes his song.

What this study has done is to open up new vistas of exploration. The origins of the prayer are unknown, though it comes with its own chronologically linear background narrative, that of Rabbi Amnon, a historical account that is said to have been related in a dream by one rabbi and recorded by another. The handed-on narrative about the process of the legend's reception spanning 300 years was written down by yet another rabbi. It is not improbable that the author of the legend, whoever wrote it, was aware of the *piyyut*, a copy of which lay in the Cairo Genizah for 900 years before being found and eventually stored in the British Library.

Possibly, in a parallel transmission, in another span of time, a variant of the Genizah liturgy found its way into the High Holy Days prayer-books of the Jewish diaspora, and inspired Leonard Cohen to write one of his most mystical, musically enchanting songs. A clue to the origins of this text from medieval Cairo remains to be uncovered.

15

'Time to cut him down to size?' A Critical Examination of Depeche Mode's Alternative 'John of Patmos'[1]

William John Lyons
University of Bristol

Actualizations of the Apocalypse, or the good, the bad and the downright ugly

Stalin's 'Great Terror' of 1937-9 is, I want to suggest, a concrete manifestation of an ideology derived – in small part at least – from the Apocalypse of John. The necessity of excluding those with the beast's mark (Rev. 19.20-21), those not in the 'book of life' (20.15), and the 'cowardly, the faithless, the polluted, [the] murderers, fornicators, sorcerers, idolaters, and all liars' (21.8) from the 'New Jerusalem' completely (Rev. 21), is mirrored in the destruction of the bourgeois envisaged by Karl Marx and Friedrich Engels in *The Communist Manifesto* (1848), and incompletely realized a century later by the murderous purges of Stalin's NKVD.[2]

---

[1] Grateful thanks are here offered to those who commented on drafts of this essay, to Genevieve Liveley, Emma England and Simon Woodman, and to those who offered questions and feedback on readings of the paper at the SBL meeting in Atlanta in November 2010 and the Bible and Deception conference in Bristol in December 2010. The idiosyncrasies and foibles that doubtless remain are mine alone.

[2] Cf. e.g., S. S. Montefiore, *Stalin: 1979-1939* (London: Phoenix, 2004), pp. 199-304; and M. Burleigh, *Sacred Causes: Religion and Politics from the European Dictators to Al Qaeda* (London: Harper Press, 2006), pp. 75-89. This connection is not as reaching as at first it may seem. Jorunn Økland argues that Marx and Engels found inspiration in the book of Revelation, writing the Manifesto as they did during a time of apocalyptic fervour in Europe that culminated in the widely heralded non-return of Christ in 1844 ('The Spectre Revealed and Made Manifest: The Book of Revelation in the Writings of Karl Marx and Friedrich Engels', in W. J. Lyons & J. Økland (eds), *The Way the World Ends? The Apocalypse of John in Culture and Ideology* (Sheffield: Sheffield Phoenix Press, 2009), pp. 267-88 (p. 267, 284). Additionally, Eric Hobsbawm notes that Marx and Engels' realization of a classless future for the proletariat was not based upon Marxian economic analysis, but rather upon 'a philosophical – indeed, an eschatological – argument about human nature and destiny' (*The Communist Manifesto: A Modern Edition* (Verso Books, 1998), p. 22).

Readers could perhaps be forgiven for now being rather puzzled. Why does an essay about a song written by Martin L. Gore, chief lyricist for the generally apolitical band, Depeche Mode, begin with Stalin, Marx and Engels? The answer is to do with the main issue under consideration in this essay, the notion of *actualization* as it is described in Judith L. Kovacs and Christopher Rowland's *Revelation* commentary. Set in opposition to a once-for-all-time 'decoding' strategy, they define 'actualization' as being in one of two related forms:

> In one form the imagery of the Apocalypse is juxtaposed with the interpreter's own circumstances, whether personal or social, so as to allow the images to inform understanding of contemporary persons and events and to serve as a guide for action.... [The second form] is the appropriation by visionaries, where the words of the Apocalypse either offer the opportunity to 'see again' things similar to what had appeared to John or prompt new visions related to it.[3]

Not all actualizations are seen as valid, however. Kovacs and Rowland note that some have led to imitation of the violence described in the book; these are incompatible with 'the gospel', they argue, being at odds with 'the pattern of Jesus' life, death and resurrection'.[4] For Rowland and Kovacs, actualizations appear to divide into two types: positive 'Christ-centred' ones and negative 'other-centred' ones. It seems likely that for them the book of Revelation is itself a prime example of the former, being perhaps the definitive Christ-centred actualization of the apocalyptic traditions of texts such as Daniel and Ezekiel.[5]

Heikki Räisänen, however, has noted, in response to Kovacs and Rowland's assertion that violence is at odds with Jesus, that the rider on the white horse in Rev. 19.11-21, the 'word of God', 'brings righteousness and embodies it by *making war* (v. 11)';[6] this 'Jesus' figure does not mitigate violence, but is rather a causal agent of it. Indeed the martial view of Revelation's Jesus has usually predominated, certainly during Christendom and on occasions more recently. Remember the January 2010 story about Trijicon's sniper scopes, used in Afghanistan and Iraq by

---

[3] Judith L. Kovacs and Christopher Rowland, *Revelation* (Oxford: Blackwell, 2005), pp. 9–10.
[4] Kovacs and Rowland, *Revelation*, pp. 248–9.
[5] For example, in response to Økland, Rowland (siding with Fredric Jameson) denies the Apocalypse a utopian vision because it is too bound up with present power struggles. It is clear to me that actualizations are being rendered acceptable by the presence of – something like – Rowland's own radical Jesus. 'The Interdisciplinary Colloquium on the Book of Revelation and Effective History', in W. J. Lyons & J. Økland (eds), *The Way the World Ends? The Apocalypse of John in Culture and Ideology* (Sheffield: Sheffield Phoenix Press, 2009), pp. 289–304 (p. 301); Cf. also e.g., his *Radical Christianity: A Reading of Recovery* (Cambridge: Polity, 1988); with M. Corner, *Liberating Exegesis: The Challenge of Liberation Theology to Biblical Studies* (Louisville, KY: Westminster/John Knox Press, 2002); and his edited volume, *The Cambridge Companion to Liberation Theology* (Cambridge: Cambridge University Press, 1999).
[6] Heikki Räisänen, 'Revelation, Violence, and War: Glimpses of a Dark Side', in W. J. Lyons & J. Økland (eds), *The Way the World Ends? The Apocalypse of John in Culture and Ideology* (Sheffield: Sheffield Phoenix Press, 2009), pp. 151–85 (p. 153) – his emphasis.

the US and its allies, and engraved with, among other New Testament texts (e.g., Jn 8.12; 2 Cor. 4.6), apparently Rev. 21.23: 'The city does not need the sun or the moon to shine on it, for the glory of God gives it light, and the Lamb is its lamp'![7]

Though one might be tempted to consider the purges of mid-twentieth-century Stalinism a competitor for the title of Kovacs and Rowland's 'definitive other-centred actualization', its echoing of the Apocalypse's ideology of exclusion, with an idealized and purified proletariat in place of Jesus and the saints, is more in line with the violent 'Jesus' of Rev. 19.11-21 and the 'New Jerusalem' than liberal scholarship might wish. Actualizing an eschatological purge in the present ultimately failed for Stalin, but I submit that, as an appropriation of the ideology of the Apocalypse, such an action has much to commend it; think WWJ[Rev.19]D? What Would the Jesus of Rev. 19.11-21 Do? Especially with a sniper rifle![8]

In the discussion that follows, I want to consider two musical responses to the Apocalypse and ask about their status as actualizations of that text. The first, examined briefly, is the traditional gospel call and response song, 'John the Revelator', first recorded by Blind Willie Johnson in 1930, and then with major variants by, among numerous others, Son House, Beck, John Mellencamp, Nick Cave, R.E.M., and The Blues Brothers; Son House's version is the focus here. The second, examined in considerably more detail, is Martin Gore's 'John the Revelator', a song that echoes aspects of the traditional song's structure and was written for Depeche Mode's 2005 album, *Playing the Angel*. It was performed to nearly three million people at 124 gigs during a nine-month tour of Europe and North America in 2005–6, and was released in the UK on 3 July 2006 as the fourth single from the album, a double A-side with 'Lilian'. It has since been covered by bands, Komor Kommando and – with a female vocalist – Caustic. In contrast to the traditional song, it is usually understood as an outright rejection of the ideology of the Apocalypse, describing as it does the eponymous John as both a liar and a thief; one critical Christian video response posted on YouTube describes the song as 'a bitter and outspoken attack on the apostle John [sic] and his apocalyptic message'.[9] The conclusion to this essay will argue, however, that that is far too simplistic a response to the nature of the relationship between the Depeche Mode song and the book of Revelation.

---

[7] See, e.g., http://www.huffingtonpost.com/2010/01/21/trijicon-will-remove-secr_n_432349.html [accessed 16 July 2013]. On the use of Rev. 21.23 on the RXnn scope, see http://criminalbrief.com/?p=10785#codes [accessed 16 July 2013].

[8] One T-shirt manufacturer – Zazzle – produced clothing bearing an image of a sniper with a headband and cigarette with the words 'Jesus saves, sniper Jesus kills' underneath the image (e.g., https://www.facebook.com/177354875635285/photos/pb.177354875635285.-2207520000.1421660447./177357508968355/?type=1&theater [accessed 19 January 2015]. Many other such images of the sniper Jesus can also now be found online (e.g., http://www.motivelab.com/wp-content/postimages/who-would-jesus-shoot.jpg; and http://www.deviantart.com/morelikethis/152891448?view_mode=2 [both accessed 16 July 2013].

[9] http://www.youtube.com/watch?v=QOD-P0em0Os [accessed 16 July 2013].

Son House's version of the traditional 'John the Revelator'[10]

Eddie James 'Son' House was born near Lyon in the state of Mississippi in 1902 and died in Detroit, Michigan in 1988. Early localized fame became more widespread during the 'blues revival' in the 1960s, the period when his recording of 'John the Revelator' was made.[11] His rendition consists of three verses, interspersed with a chorus of call ('Who's that writin'?') and response ('John the Revelator'), sung twice between each verse. Of the three verses, one focuses on the Fall and Adam's shame, the second on Jesus' ineffectual request to the three apostles to watch as he prays in Gethsemane, and the third on the appearance of the risen Christ on Easter morning and his instruction to the women to tell his disciples to go to Galilee. The earliest recording by Blind Willie Johnson in 1930 contains *none* of these verses, but does include the following verse in a similar vein: 'Well, Moses to Moses, watchin' the flock/Saw the bush where they had to stop/God told Moses, "Pull off your shoes"/Out of the flock, well you I choose'.[12] Johnson's version has been sung more recently by Nick Cave.[13]

Despite its lack of coverage of the Bible per se, of biblical themes in general, or of Kovacs and Rowland's radical Christian edge, there seems little difficulty in seeing the song as, in the words of our Christian critic of Depeche Mode, 'true traditional gospel'; it is, as he puts it, 'in harmony with the Bible'.[14] Even the involvement of a singer as heterodox as Cave does not manage to put the traditional song out of sync with 'biblical religion'.[15]

Depeche Mode's version of 'John the Revelator'

The band's background

Depeche Mode emerged in the early eighties as a youthful synth band whose founder members, Andrew Fletcher, Martin Gore, Dave Gahan and Vince Clarke (soon to depart for pop success elsewhere), all hailed from the Essex town of Basildon, just outside London. As teenagers, Clarke, Fletcher and Gore were involved in a local church, St Paul's Methodist Church;[16] Gahan, from the other

---

[10] To hear House's recording, visit http://www.youtube.com/watch?v=uGBoP70A7Q0 [accessed 16 July 2013].
[11] http://www.msbluestrail.org/_webapp_1300060/Son_House [accessed 16 July 2013].
[12] http://www.youtube.com/watch?v=5hucTDV1Fvo [accessed 16 July 2013].
[13] http://www.youtube.com/watch?v=uPmacnYVb6A [accessed 16 July 2013].
[14] http://www.youtube.com/watch?v=QOD-P0em0Os [accessed 16 July 2013].
[15] Cf. R. Boer, 'Jesus of the Moon: Nick Cave's Christology', in P. Culbertson and E. M. Wainwright, *The Bible in/and Popular Culture: A Creative Encounter* (Atlanta: SBL, 2010), pp. 127–39; and his volume, *Nick Cave: A Study of Love, Death and Apocalypse* (London: Equinox, 2012).
[16] J. Miller, *Stripped: Depeche Mode* (Updated edition; London: Omnibus Press, 2008), pp. 13, 16.

side of Basildon, was the exception, bad boy more than church goer.[17] Clarke and Fletcher were members of the Boys Brigade, attended Greenbelt – described by Fletcher as a 'massive Christian Rock festival' – and tried public preaching.[18] Their earliest forays into music also occurred in that setting.[19]

Though their church involvement had diminished by the end of their teens – with Fletcher attributing this to boredom[20] – 'church' ideas have remained a prominent part of their lives. Albums like *Songs of Faith and Devotion* (1993) and *Playing the Angel* (2005) and songs like 'Blasphemous Rumours' (1984), 'Personal Jesus' (1989), 'Sacred' (1989), 'Death's Door' (1991), 'Judas' (1993), 'Home' (1997), 'Sinner in me' (2005), 'Martyr' (2006) and 'Jezebel' (2009) give some idea of the continuing high level of God-talk in their songbook.[21] Asked about his top ten lyrical themes in 1990, Gore replied: 'Relationships, domination, lust, love, good, evil, incest, sin, religion, immorality.'[22] As he put it in another interview: 'Religion's one of the themes that crops up a lot in my songs. I think I have got this fascination with religion, and I think that's inherent in everything – from the feel of the music to touching on things in lyrics.'[23] In fact it has proved so prominent a theme that Gore was even able to say of the song 'Home' on the band's 1997 album *Ultra*, that 'I think it's got quite a spiritual feel, but religion is probably touched on less on this album that it has been in the past... I think I've overdone religion.'[24] The content

---

[17] Miller, *Stripped*, p. 31.
[18] Miller, *Stripped*, p. 13.
[19] Miller, *Stripped*, pp. 13–14.
[20] Miller, *Stripped*, p. 199.
[21] On a personal level, Fletcher, an occasional sufferer from depression, refers in one interview to two minister friends, describing himself as saying to one of them: ' "You know what the Bible says – I'm going to be spewed out of God's mouth when I die!" I'm worse than a non-believer, because a person who believes and then doesn't is supposedly going to be spewed out of God's mouth' (Miller, *Stripped*, p. 290).

Following his drug-induced heart attack in 1996, Gahan wrote of heroin: 'I believe heroin is the devil because it takes your soul away. I think if there is a God there, he chooses to leave you and let you get on with it and that's what it feels like. You're this walking shell. I couldn't even look at myself in the mirror. I do a lot of praying. I don't pray for forgiveness but what I do is get on my knees and I thank God for keeping me sober another day. I pray to the ceiling in the hope that somebody's listening. But you know what? I feel a lot better doing it.' (Steve Malins, *Depeche Mode: Black Celebration: A Biography* [London: Andre Deutsch, 2006], p. 238).

Malins attributes Gahan's god-talk here perhaps to the religious underpinnings of AA and rehab (*Depeche Mode*, p. 238). According to biographer, Trevor Baker, Gahan, the only original non-church goer, converted to Greek Orthodox Christianity in 1999 in order to marry his third wife Jennifer in a Greek Orthodox church (*Dave Gahan: Depeche Mode & the Second Coming* [Church Stretton, Shropshire: Independent Music Press, 2009], p. 158).

The details of Gore's personal beliefs will occupy us in the section 'Martin Gore' and 'John the Revelator' below.
[22] Miller, *Stripped*, p. 309.
[23] Miller, *Stripped*, p. 290.
[24] Malins, *Depeche Mode*, p. 242. For journalist Stephen Dalton, however, 'an enduring curiosity about spirituality still runs through [Gore's] blasphemous beats and devotional lyrics' (*Uncut*, May 2001; quoted in *Stripped*, p. 16).

of *Playing the Angel* suggests that Gore's conclusion about *Ultra* did not restrict him for too long, however.[25]

The critical nature of Gore's take on religion has not been uncontroversial, even within the group itself. His song 'Blasphemous Rumours' (1984) is described by André Boße and Dennis Plauk, as a 'heißblütiger Abgesang auf Gottesbild konservativer Christen' (a 'passionate [lit. hot-blooded] farewell to the image of God of conservative Christians').[26] It is about a girl who survives a suicide bid and finds Jesus but then dies in a car crash, and harks back to Gore's experience of childhood church services where people were seemingly prayed for until they died:[27] 'I don't want to start any blasphemous rumours / But I think that God's got a sick sense of humour / And when I die I expect to find Him laughing' runs the chorus.[28] Fletcher has said that he was quite offended on first hearing it.[29]

Gore's 'Personal Jesus' (1989) was written in response to Priscilla Presley's book, *Elvis & Me*,[30] and refers to people's unhealthy tendency to make partners into often domineering Jesus-figures.[31] Though found offensive by many, this song illustrates another significant feature of Gore's song-writing, its deliberate ambiguity. As Fletcher puts it:

> Martin doesn't get around the table and say, 'Listen lads, this is what this one's about.' He never explains the lyrics at all... I've heard about ten different interpretations of 'Personal Jesus' and that's what Martin really likes.[32]

In the promotional DVD that accompanies *Playing the Angel*, the group discuss the album's title, a lyric taken from its last track, 'The Darkest Star':

---

[25] Gore has been Depeche Mode's song-writer for most of their existence. Since 2005, however, Gahan has also written songs for the band's albums. On *Playing the Angel*, Gahan supplied three songs – 'Suffer well', 'I want it all', and 'Nothing's impossible' – with Gore writing the rest (Miller, *Stripped*, p. 538).

[26] André Boße and Dennis Plauk, *Insight–Martin Gore und Depeche Mode: Ein Porträt* (Hannibal Verlag GmbH, 2010), p. 186.

[27] Miller, *Stripped*, p. 199. In Malins' *Depeche Mode: Black Celebration*, Gore is quoted as follows: 'I was going to Church a lot at the time, not because I believed in it, but because there was nothing else to do on a Sunday... I found the service very hard to take seriously. The whole set-up is quite handy, but I am not sure that is what God intended. Particularly a part of the service called the Prayer List, when the preacher rattles off the names of those sick and about to die. The person at the top of the list was guaranteed to die, but still everyone went right ahead thanking God for carrying out his will. It just seemed so strange to me, so ridiculous and so removed from real experience' (p. 90).

[28] http://www.lyricsfreak.com/d/depeche+mode/blasphemous+rumours_20039337.html [accessed 16 July 2013]. The capitalized H ('Him') is reproduced on the Depeche Mode website (http:// http:// archives.depechemode.com/lyrics/blasphemousrumours.html [accessed 16 July 2013]), and in Gore's book, *Lays* (Nantes: Editions Normant, 2009), an apparently official version of some of his lyrics.

[29] Miller, *Stripped*, p. 199.

[30] Priscilla Presley, *Elvis & Me* (London: Century, 1985).

[31] Miller, *Stripped*, p. 290.

[32] Miller, *Stripped*, p. 290.

Fletcher: I think it means, you know, it has meanings on various levels and that's why we like it. We've always quite liked, mm, sort of a bit of ambiguity. Ambiguity...

Gahan: That means we can't explains what it means. [*laughter from all three*]³³

The fact that Gore rarely discusses the origins and meanings of his songs – the two just mentioned are atypical – means that details about his inspiration for and intention in writing 'John the Revelator' are absent; we are told it was written and recorded in six hours, but precious little else.³⁴ Without his explicit commentary, the song has been described in various ways: as an 'even handed critique of organised religion, damning the fundamental intensity of prophets' (Andy Gill, *The Independent*);³⁵ as a discussion of how 'certain groups (or individuals) appropriate God for their own means' (Scott C. Smith, Blogcritics);³⁶ as an 'old blues/gospel standard [re-wired] into an anti-preacher lyric' (Steve Malins);³⁷ and as 'what Personal Jesus would sound like on LSD' (reviewer CF, Amazon).³⁸ Critical consensus about its meaning there clearly is not!

The protagonist's 'John the Revelator'³⁹

Depeche Mode's 'John the Revelator' song owes much to the traditional gospel song, using both its title and its call and response structure to good effect. The potential trap posed to any lyricist – that no-one ever really hears the words – is largely avoided by the mechanism of wrapping the theme within a highly repetitive structure. Ostensibly a hostile protagonist is calling 'John the Revelator' out as a liar, a point that is rammed home by a booming and repeated chorus-line punctuated by rhythmic electronic 'claps': 'Seven lies, multiplied by seven, multiplied by seven again'. In the two opening sections, John is described as 'a smooth operator', who needs to be 'cut... down to size'; after all, the chorus adds, 'all he ever gives us is pain... He should bow his head in shame'. The unrepentant John is to be set on high and permitted to 'tell his book of lies', which may or may not be the same as his being placed on the stand to offer his 'alibis'. His text, with its 'seven angels' and their 'seven trumpets' is to be rejected, 'sent home on the morning train'.

---

³³ Mute Records, 2005.
³⁴ Miller, *Stripped*, p. 542.
³⁵ Andy Gill, *The Independent*, October 14, 2005, p. 27; quoted in *Stripped*, p. 561.
³⁶ http://blogcritics.org/music/article/cd-review-depeche-mode-playing-the/ [accessed 16 July 2013].
³⁷ Malins, *Depeche Mode*, p. 291.
³⁸ http://www.amazon.com/Playing-Angel-Depeche-Mode/dp/B000B2YQX4 [accessed 16 July 2013].
³⁹ If readers of this essay have not heard Gore's 'John the Revelator' before, now is the time to log on and listen; what follows assumes familiarity with its music and lyrics. A Google search or a search on YouTube for the 'band' and the 'song name' will throw up a variety of suitable performances of 'John the Revelator'. A word of warning, however; cover versions are best avoided!

Here is the song's crux. John's crime, as it is perceived by the protagonist, is not that he is a liar per se, but rather that he has become a thief by virtue of his lies: 'By claiming God as his holy right / He's stealing a God from the Israelites / Stealing a God from a Muslim, too.' By simultaneously breaking the eighth and ninth commandments, John obtained his deity fraudulently *and* then fashioned that deity in his own exclusivist and idolatrous image; an image whose principal gift to the world has been 'pain'. On its back cover, the *Playing the Angel* album is itself described as 'pain and suffering in different tempos'; each of the songs on the album can thus be seen by listeners as testifying in its own way to the impact of John's deceitful theology.

This focus on exclusivism means that the song is not a wholesale indictment of organized religion. Nor is it a simple indictment of the 'liars' and 'thieves' who break the eighth and ninth commandments. It is instead an explicitly theistic critique – 'There is only one God through and through' – which is aimed at a specific individual, the theologically exclusivist 'John the Revelator'. His fundamental crime was to annex Gods from Israelite and Muslim as if that were 'his holy right'. It is for that offence that he is to be put on the stand, deposed, and exiled. The almost mechanistic opening synth beat, the musical disruption heralded by the dissonant instrumental interlude between the chorus repetitions, and Gahan's raw vocals over the whole, render the apocalyptic tones of the lyrics perfectly; John's world of pain is about to end with his public expulsion and, with the creation of a *new* 'New Jerusalem', the protagonist's hoped-for inclusivistic theological world is set to begin.

From the perspective of the song's protagonist then, the Apocalypse can hardly be what Brian Blount describes it as, a 'call to non-violent arms against any and every human person or people who would position themselves as lord over the destinies of others';[40] John the Revelator (= John of Patmos!) has done exactly that! His text was not written 'to be read in constant intertextual relationship with the Old Testament' as Richard Bauckham would have it;[41] it was instead written in order to 'rebrand' the Jewish Scriptures for a very different audience. It is therefore nonsensical to describe Revelation, as Larry Helyer and Richard Wagner do in their book, *Revelation for Dummies*, as a 'natural follow-up to the Old Testament books of Daniel, Ezekiel, and Zechariah'.[42] The redistribution of the glory of Ezekiel's Temple to John's heavenly city – noted uncritically by Old Testament in the New Testament specialist, Steve Moyise[43] – is not evidence for John Sweet's

---

[40] Brian Blount, *Revelation: A Commentary* (Louisville, KY: Westminster John Knox, 2009), p. xi.
[41] Richard Bauckham, *The Climax of Prophecy: Studies on the Book of Revelation* (New edn; T&T Clark International: London, 1998), p. xi.
[42] Larry Helyer and Richard Wagner, *Revelation for Dummies* (Hoboken, NJ: John Wiley & Sons, 2008), p. 38.
[43] Steve Moyise, *The Old Testament in the Book of Revelation* (Sheffield: Sheffield Academic Press, 1995), p. 81.

effusive three-fold conclusion about John's attitude to the Old Testament book: that (a) he 'had a creative grasp of a "diffuse and obscure book" '; that (b) he 'clarified and concentrated its message'; and that (c) he 'enlarged its vision'.[44] Instead what it shows us is that John did not care very much about the one thing that Ezekiel held most dear (cf. Ezek. 40-48).

Contrary to these biblical scholars' assumptions of his probity, the song's protagonist would instead argue that John of Patmos is not so much the authoritative mediator of Ezekiel's words as the 'Big Brother' who is trying to control a distinctive voice once heard unmediated. Our liar-cum-thief is an oppressive tyrant who gags his victims and then speaks eternally for them while they silently scream in their canonical cages. When our Christian critic plaintively asks what the author of the Apocalypse did to deserve this song, here is the protagonist's answer. Liar, thief, vicious tyrant – it's time to cut him down to size!

'Martin Gore' and 'John the Revelator'

So far I have tried to be careful to talk only of the views of the protagonist of the song when discussing its content and meaning, and not of the views of Gore himself. One legitimate way to extend our understanding of the song's meaning further, however, would be to view it against the backdrop of its writer's attitude to God and religion as far as it can be ascertained through his admittedly limited public comments, to see the song through the eyes of a construct public persona carefully marked out with single quotation marks as 'Martin Gore'.

As we have seen, this 'Gore' has long been fascinated by religious themes and has not hesitated to weave them into his songs whenever and wherever 'he' can. But these expressions of interest do not have to indicate any kind of personal theistic belief at all, not even of the open-ended and vague kind of theism that the song's protagonist offers to us. Publically, 'he' has sometimes explicitly mentioned his atheism.[45] This is perhaps not the whole story, however. God has often been mentioned both by 'Gore' 'him'-self and by others in connection with 'him'. Perhaps the most repeated story is this one, told by Dave Gahan.

> It was in Chile, the same night as the Kurt Cobain thing happened [Cobain's body was discovered on 8 April 1994; Depeche Mode performed in Santiago, Chile on Sunday, 10 April].[46] It was very late and we'd been drinking a lot. Whether Martin was drunk, I don't know if he can even remember it but it sticks in my mind anyway. He said to me that he feels like he gets his songs... like something from God and he thought that he was losing it because he was

---

[44] John Sweet, *Revelation* (London: SCM Press, 1990), pp. 39-40.
[45] Miller, *Stripped*, p. 16.
[46] http://archives.depechemode.com/past_tours/summertour94/dates.html [accessed 16 July 2013].

drinking and stuff. For some reason, he thought he had to channel that work through me, and I was his voice, kind of thing, which I thought was the most beautiful thing he had ever said to me, I mean we were both in one of those I love you modes, but it really stuck in my mind like maybe I really am supposed to deliver some kind of message, you know.[47]

The kind of God language attributed to 'Gore' in Gahan's anecdote also appears elsewhere in 'his' public utterances. In one particularly illuminating comment placed alongside the release of 1990 album, *Violator*, by group biographer, Steve Malins, 'Gore' says:

> I do believe in some sort of power even though I haven't really had any particular experience myself. I am still searching. I really like the idea of belief but I've never found something to believe in. The only Godlike things I know are sex and love. In my eyes God is sex personified, by the same token love is too. Both have something that's longer than a moment. Love and sex last forever and therefore bring some sort of reason for our being. Therefore it is no surprise that I write about God, sex and love all the time. As far as I am concerned they're the biggest mystery of this planet.[48]

The impression given by 'Gore' here is that belief in the God of traditional theism has always been beyond 'him' ('I haven't really had any particular experience myself... still searching... I've never found something to believe in'), but 'his' equation of sex and love with the deity does in fact offer a distinctive and radically alternative theism in which to believe. 'His' God is 'sex-like' and 'love-like', with an infinite horizon of existence that puts this particular deity on a different plain of reality from all that is mundane and transitory. Mystery of mysteries, these three elements – love, sex and God – are seen as the all-encompassing and all-surpassing realities at the centre of the world that we know and are, it would seem, the principal focus of 'Gore' and his creative activities.

Following 'his' move to Santa Barbara California at the end of the nineties, 'Gore' was able to relate to God, presumably similarly-defined, in a more positive frame of mind: 'I wake up every day and I see sunshine and I see amazing mountain views, and I do feel a bit more in touch with God, whatever God is.'[49] For Malins, this sense of ease is seen as evidence that Depeche Mode were slipping into 'middle age' at the time: 'They've embraced this natural process on *Exciter* [2001], with Gore allowing a less tortured spirituality to float, hushed and barely spoken into the new material.'[50] *Playing the Angel* in 2005 suggests, however, that the 'pain' and 'suffering' aspect of 'his' spirituality has not passed away just yet.

---

[47] Malins, *Depeche Mode*, pp. 205–06: (cf. T. Baker, *Dave Gahan*, p. 151).
[48] Malins, *Depeche Mode*, p. 182.
[49] Malins, *Depeche Mode*, p. 265.
[50] Malins, *Depeche Mode*, p. 265.

Though the beliefs of 'Martin Gore' – the single quotation marks, remember, signifying the inevitable gap between the man and this account of his public persona – are not those of orthodox Christianity, there are clearly deep theistic echoes in 'his' few public utterances on the topic and, as we have already seen, within many of 'his' songs. The protagonist of 'John the Revelator' offers us a similarly vague theistic belief system; '[t]here is only God through and through'. It is not so hard then to interpret this particular song through the lens of the public persona of a theistic 'Martin Gore'. Nor is it so hard to see why a theistic belief founded on an identification of the deity with sex and love and their 'attributes' would find the more hard-nosed deity of 'John the Revelator' problematic, even obnoxious. This protest is not against religion per se, but only against that exclusivist theistic form of it.

The song's advocacy of inclusiveness would, I suggest, also leave a substantial gap between it and exclusivist forms of Judaism and Islam. 'Gore' and his protagonist are apologists for neither one. Since they are not explicitly trying to redeem and resurrect Ezekiel's deity, however, it seems likely that their real objection to the Apocalypse must instead be to its attempt to forestall the arising of any deity but its own; the charge of pre-emptively stealing a God from the Muslims is much more relevant than the charge of stealing one from the Israelites.

The religion of preference for 'Gore' is a contemporary theism in the universalizing mode of a John Hick; it is only the claim to exclusive access that ultimately proves heretical. Since some forms of inclusive Christian theistic religion do envisage a wide-open-armed Jesus at their forefront, we might even imagine that 'Gore' and his protagonist could – given the right Jesus, a 'Personal Jesus' – be viewed as offering an acute theistic critique from within a certain 'Christian' circle; the exclusionary John may well be out, but the welcoming Jesus may well be in. Do the echoes of a youthful church background stretch that far, I wonder? No matter, the theism of 'Gore' allows a perfectly adequate reading of the song as an inclusivist theistic critique of John's deity and religion; 'he should hang his head in shame!'

Conclusion – A positive actualization?

One common scholarly attitude towards popular culture's use of biblical themes is to attempt to explain, to clarify and to finesse. Perhaps in this case we should listen first, however. Should biblical scholars really continue to characterize John of Patmos' use of Ezekiel, for example, with the language of harmony and fulfilment? Or should we perhaps try to think rather more seriously about the implications of the song's depiction of John as the stealer of Ezekiel's religious identity?

Returning to Kovacs and Rowland's notion of positive actualization, I want to close by asking whether the song has to be understood as a rejection of the ideology of the Apocalypse. There is obviously no way that the song can be simply put alongside the traditional 'John the Revelator' and described as 'true traditional gospel'.[51] But just as Stalin's 'Great Terror' and Marx and Engels' *Communist Manifesto* can both be seen as positively actualizing a strand of biblical ideology – the violence and exclusivism of the utopian 'New Jerusalem' – in service to the needs of their political projects, it also seems quite feasible to try to identify a similar strand-based commonality between the book of Revelation and Depeche Mode's 'John the Revelator'. I want to suggest that one of the ideological moves made by the song echoes an important move made by John of Patmos as he is depicted by 'Martin Gore': in service to an exclusivist theological agenda, John of Patmos positively actualized Ezekiel *et al.* by subordinating their religious beliefs to the dominant ideals that were exemplified by his Jesus, his 'Personal Jesus'. In his turn, and in service to a rousing populist call for an alternative 'inclusivist' theistic faith, 'Martin Gore' and his protagonist should be understood as having positively actualized John's implicit ideology of 'fair usage' for his religious sources (i.e. his underhand, deceitful assimilation of their content); they have utilized the methodology of deception and theft that underlies the Apocalypse's creation to construct a stridently competitive religious tract which presents the Gospel according to 'Gore'.

With his tract now firmly in circulation in various guises within popular culture, the questions that now come to mind are these: how many already believe in the religion/spirituality now explicitly on offer from 'Martin Gore' and Depeche Mode, and who will now choose to accept his words and believe in the future? God, love and sex – there are worse creeds in which to believe, are there not? Are there any takers?

---

[51] http://www.youtube.com/watch?v=QOD-P0em0Os [accessed 16 July 2013].

16

'God', 'God Part II' and 'God Part III': Exploring the Anxiety of Influence in John Lennon, U2 and Larry Norman

Michael J. Gilmour
Providence University College (Canada)

Nostalgia, Harold Bloom and the inevitable precursors of rock and roll

I never tire of Don McLean's 1971 song 'American Pie', that nostalgic, cryptic and whimsical romp through post-1959 rock music history, which is to say the years following the plane crash claiming Buddy Holly, Ritchie Valens and The Big Bopper. Nowhere else do we find the spiritual capacity of popular music so eloquently expressed, and the blurring of the lines between religion and the arts more flagrant and heartfelt than this tribute to the three men McLean admires most, 'Father, Son, and Holy Ghost'. This song also offers a curious glimpse into a dynamic of artistic creativity easily overlooked by those of us fascinated by the reception of the Bible in literature, music, painting and other cultural artifacts.

Literary critic Harold Bloom argues that successful poets are those 'with the persistence to wrestle with their strong precursors, even to the death.'[1] Poets choose their vocation because some earlier writer grips their imagination but their relationship with that predecessor is ambivalent, analogous to what Freud observes in the Oedipal relation of son to father.

According to Bloom, there is a mix of admiration, hate and envy because strong poets need to be autonomous and original, and they fear the earlier writer's

---

[1] Harold Bloom, *The Anxiety of Influence: A Theory of Poetry* (2nd edn; New York: Oxford University Press, 1997 [1973]), 5. On Bloom's various contributions to literary theory, see the chapters in *The Salt Companion to Harold Bloom*, ed. Graham Allen and Roy Sellars (Cambridge: Salt, 2007). On the anxiety of influence specifically, see especially R. Clifton Spargo, 'Toward an Ethics of Literary Revisionism' (66-119) and T. J. Cribb, 'Anxieties of Influence in the Theatre of Memory: Harold Bloom, Marlowe and *Henry V*' (170-82). Also helpful for locating Bloom's views on influence in relation to alternative perspectives is Graham Allen's *Intertextuality* (The New Critical Idiom) (London and New York: Routledge, 2000), esp. 133-44.

pre-emption of their own imaginative space. Locked in an Oedipal rivalry with his castrating precursor,[2] the poet resists by rewriting, revising and recasting the precursor poem, thus clearing space for his own imaginative work. As this language suggests, Bloom finds in Freud a conceptual frame of reference and indeed, he insists Freud's 'mythology of the mind has survived his supposed science, and his metaphors are impossible to evade.'[3] With respect to poetic influences, Bloom argues, 'creative freedom can be evasion but not flight. There must be agon [conflict], a struggle for supremacy, or at least for holding off imaginative death.' Art is 'a contest for the foremost place' and when '[t]hreatened by the prospect of imaginative death, of being entirely possessed by a precursor, [poets] suffer a distinctively literary form of crisis. A strong poet seeks not simply to vanquish the rival but to assert the integrity of his or her own writing self.'[4] As Terry Eagleton puts it, Bloom reads literary history 'as an heroic battle of giants or [a] mighty psychic drama' a form of Romantic individualism 'fiercely at odds with the skeptical, anti-humanist *ethos* of a deconstructive age.'[5]

Don McLean's 'American Pie' alludes not only to the holy trinity of songwriters mentioned above, but also – many speculate – a predictable who's-who of musical luminaries of the intervening years between the plane crash and the song's release, including Bob Dylan, the Byrds, the Rolling Stones, the Beatles and Janis Joplin. Now consider McLean's quasi-religious reverence for these and other artists who inspired him to become a singer-songwriter in the first place. How could he possibly hope to write anything original and free of the contaminating influence of Holly's 'That'll Be the Day', Dylan's 'Blowing in the Wind', or the Stones' 'Jumpin'

---

[2] Bloom's Freudian reading of literary history introduces an androcentric and patriarchal vocabulary but not all feminist readers find this wholly objectionable. Sandra M. Gilbert and Susan Gubar, for instance, point out that 'Western literary history *is* overwhelmingly male – or, more accurately, patriarchal – and Bloom analyzes and explains this fact, while other theorists have ignored it' (*The Madwoman in the Attic: The Woman Writer and the Nineteenth-Century Literary Imagination* [New Haven and London: Yale University Press, 1979], 47, italics original). Bloom's construct is useful to them because it identifies and defines 'the patriarchal psychosexual context' of much Western literature and helps distinguish the anxieties of female and male writers. The female writer must 'confront precursors who are almost exclusively male', who 'incarnate patriarchal authority' and 'enclose her in definitions of her persona and her potential which, by reducing her to extreme stereotypes... drastically conflict with her own sense of her self' (48). The female poet thus experiences 'an even more primary "anxiety of authorship" – a radical fear that she cannot create, that because she can never become a "precursor" the act of writing will isolate or destroy her' (48–9; for their full discussion of Bloom, 46–53). For another example of a Bloomian analysis of poetry from a feminist perspective, see Michael J. Gilmour, 'Confronting Colonial Religion and the Anxiety of Influence in Louise Bernice Halfe's *Blue Marrow*', in *Feminist Theology with a Canadian Accent: Canadian Perspectives of Contextual Feminist Theology*, ed. Mary Ann Beavis, with Elaine Guillemin and Barbara Pell (Ottawa: Novalis, 2008), 371–85.

[3] Harold Bloom, *Genius: A Mosaic of One Hundred Exemplary Minds* (New York: Warner, 2002), 178; cf. also 162–3, 177–84.

[4] Harold Bloom, *The Anatomy of Influence: Literature as a Way of Life* (New Haven and London: Yale University Press, 2011), 6–8.

[5] Terry Eagleton, *Literary Theory: An Introduction*, Anniversary Edition (Minneapolis: University of Minnesota Press, 2008), 159.

Jack Flash'? To think of this in light of Harold Bloom's theory, writers who follow great writers are necessarily competitive. There may be affection, even love for the great precursors but poets are only as good as their ability to push aside artistic influences, to carve out a creative space that allows them to claim autonomy and articulate their unique genius. Notice that McLean does not actually name any musicians in 'American Pie'. Instead he offers a surreal landscape populated by ambiguous characters. Is this evidence of his creative anxiety, as if naming the pantheon of his musical gods is a threat to his aspirations to join their number? After all, his own claim to musical greatness is contingent, requiring evasion of earlier masters: 'A long time ago / I can still remember how / That music used to make me smile / And I knew *if I had my chance* / That I could make those people dance / And maybe they'd be happy for a while.' The very existence of Buddy Holly's album *The 'Chirping' Crickets* (1957) or the Rolling Stones' *Beggars Banquet* (1968) threatens to assign McLean to musical oblivion unless he is successful in his Oedipal rivalry with those and other castrating precursors.

Anxiety among the 'Gods'

The trilogy of God songs listed in my title nicely illustrates ways that Harold Bloom's theory helps us think about the reception of the Bible and religious discourse in the arts. U2 and Larry Norman explicitly identify their God songs as responses to John Lennon's precursor, the high point of his 1970 debut solo album *John Lennon/Plastic Ono Band*, and we find in both later tributes to that song evidence of artistic conflict and competition. Both U2 and Larry Norman write and sing in the enormous shadow of the inescapable precursor that is the Beatles and John Lennon. Like Don McLean, they must find ways to distinguish themselves, thus proving lyrically they are autonomous and original geniuses while simultaneously celebrating Lennon's greatness. They too want their chance, to make the people dance.

U2 and Norman both show affection for Lennon and this is consistent with Bloom's notion of influence, which he defines simply 'as *literary love, tempered by defense*. The defenses vary from poet to poet. But the overwhelming presence of love is vital to understanding how great literature works.'[6] U2 opens their 1988 album *Rattle and Hum*, which includes 'God Part II', with a live performance of the Beatles' 'Helter Skelter', and they dedicate 'God Part II' to Lennon. For his part, Larry Norman praises his influential predecessor but also betrays an artistic anxiety, prefacing a live performance of 'God Part III' by saying, 'This is... a song

---

[6] Bloom, *Anatomy of Influence*, 8 – his italics.

John Lennon wrote. He wrote a song called "God", and I heard it and I really liked it. So I wrote it too. And I changed the words. And the tune. And the chords.'[7]

Despite a general family resemblance, Lennon's 'God', U2's 'God Part II' and Larry Norman's 'God Part III' are very different from one another, particularly with respect to their theological orientation. John Lennon's distrust of religion is well known. He imagines a world with no heaven, and in *John Lennon/Plastic Ono Band* he sings, 'There ain't no Jesus gonna come / from the sky' ('I Found Out'), he likens Jesus and Paul to junkies pushing cocaine ('I Found Out'), and with a nice conspiratorial touch, he fears a system that keeps people 'doped with religion' ('Working Class Hero'). Believers think they are 'so clever and classless and free' but to Lennon, they are 'still fucking peasants / as far as I can see.' In the song 'God', he adds bluntly, 'I don't believe in Bible', 'I don't believe in Jesus', nor do I believe in 'I-ching', 'tarot', 'Buddha', 'Mantra', 'Gita', or 'Yoga'.[8]

If Lennon is openly critical of religion, sweeping it away without distinction or explanation, Bono's lyrical engagements with the Bible and religion in 'God Part II' are much subtler.[9] Like Lennon, lyricist Bono lists items he refuses to believe, beginning with the line, 'Don't believe the devil [sic] I don't believe the book / But the truth is not the same without the lies he made up.'[10] On one level, this song refers to Albert Goldman (here, 'the devil') and his book *The Lives of John Lennon* (about which, see below) but there is a religious dimension to 'God Part II' that is unmistakable, especially given U2's persistent exploration of spirituality and their explicit conversation here with Lennon's concerns in 'God'. U2's song does not reject religion or its claims, avoids overly simplistic conclusions, and suggests willingness to live with paradox and ambiguity. U2's music often includes religious content but it is a highly creative, restless and wondering relationship with religious mysteries. They look for the baby Jesus under the trash and would take bread and wine if there were a church they could receive in, but their articulation of sacred themes is often playful and always incomplete, as if they never quite find what they are looking for.

Fewer know Larry Norman's music but his work represents a seminal contribution to the Christian rock movement of the late 1960s and early 1970s.[11]

---

[7] Taken from a 2000 performance posted on YouTube [accessed June 2012]. Norman offers an appreciative nod to U2 as well, sending out 'Love To... Bono And The Edge' in his album's acknowledgments. Though not as widely known as Lennon or U2, various general market artists including 'three-fourths of U2 (Bono, The Edge, and Larry Mullen Jr.) have... cited Norman as a prominent influence' (Mark Allan Powell, *Encyclopedia of Contemporary Christian Music* [Peabody, Mass.: Hendrickson, 2002], 633).

[8] Lyrics taken from the *John Lennon/Plastic One Band* liner notes (2010 EMI re-release).

[9] He does talk openly about his spirituality in other venues, as in the various interviews included in *Bono in Conversation with Michka Assayas* (New York: Riverhead, 2005).

[10] *Rattle and Hum* liner notes, here and throughout. This reference to the devil seems to anticipate his on-stage, *Screwtape*-like mockery of the devil during the Zoo TV tour of the early 1990s when he wore face paint and devil horns as part of his Mr. Mephisto persona.

[11] See e.g., Powell's entry on Norman in *Contemporary Christian Music*, 632–41.

I am again oversimplifying but whereas Lennon tends to reject religion outright and U2 sings about its mysterious ways and at least partial unknowability, Larry Norman represents a Christian conservatism both confident of its rightness and critical of those failing to embrace a particular definition of orthodoxy. His God song lacks Lennon's cynicism about spiritual realities and U2's playfulness, and states clearly 'I'm gonna walk the streets of gold' (cf. Rev 21:21).[12] He opens with the assertion 'I don't believe in beatles,' taken directly from Lennon's God song, as if stressing the danger of putting too much faith in (secular?) celebrities, and also uses U2's phrase '[i] don't believe the devil.' However, Norman's 'God Part III' is unambiguously confessional and a departure theologically from the earlier two God songs. Seven times Norman asserts 'i believe in God,' thus departing from U2's less specific phrase 'I believe in love,' and he rejects Lennon's view that 'God is a concept / By which we measure our pain,' which is to say a human construction. Norman also embraces a very specific understanding of orthodoxy when he informs listeners, 'i don't believe the papacy when fallible lies are told,' and announces his rejection of evolution. Both concerns suggest he is a product of late-twentieth-century American fundamentalism. If Lennon is *critical* of religion and Bono *creative* in his writing about it, Norman is *confessional*.

To illustrate further how these songs resemble and differ from one another, and betray a form of Bloomian poetic anxiety, I turn briefly to two lyrical themes present in all three songs. The first concerns the divergent ways these artists understand the very idea of the God so central to each song (see Table 16.1).

For Lennon, God is a psychosocial phenomenon ('a concept / By which we measure our pain'). This recalls lines from the same album cited earlier ('I Found Out' and 'Working Class Hero') that equate religion with the false comforts provided by drugs. Lennon subsumes all religion and all religious experience without distinction under that catch-all concept called 'God,' and blurs sacred texts, practices and beliefs with human celebrity and the accolades afforded to them, whether rock stars (Elvis, Zimmerman, Beatles) or politicians (Hitler, Kennedy). This may explain why U2, rather unexpectedly, does not use the term 'God' at all in the song, apart from the title. Lyricist Bono refuses to group all religion together or mingle sacred language with reverence for renowned individuals.

Table 16.1

John Lennon, 'God'	U2, 'God Part II'	Larry Norman, 'God Part III'
'God is a concept'; 'I don't believe in Jesus'; etc.	'Don't believe the devil'; 'I believe in love'; etc.	'i believe in God'

[12] Taken from the *Stranded in Babylon* liner notes, here and throughout.

U2's God song offers instead a far more nuanced understanding of the Divine, which includes a theological particularity absent from Lennon's lyrics. Though subtle, Bono grounds 'God Part II' quite deliberately in Christian biblical tradition by substituting Lennon's term 'God' with the term 'love'. In doing so, he alludes to 1 John 4:7–8:

> ... let us love one another, because love is from God; everyone who loves is born of God and knows God. Whoever does not love does not know God, for God is love. God's love was revealed among us in this way: God sent his only Son into the world so that we might live through him.

This is a fascinating twist on Lennon's God song. Bono's repeated use of the phrase 'I believe in love' affirms and celebrates Lennon and his oft-repeated mantra that love is the answer to all the world's problems, as we hear, for instance, in his solo composition 'Mind Games' (*Mind Games*, 1973), or the earlier Beatles' song 'All You Need is Love' (1967; written with Paul McCartney). Bono deftly embraces this most familiar Lennon-ism while deftly rejecting and misreading his theological assumptions. Lennon tells the world to love one another but so does the New Testament, which for Bono is a critical oversight by his singer-songwriter predecessor.

Bono suggests on the one hand that Lennon is absolutely right. Quite unintentionally, the ex-Beatle aligns himself with the very God he rejects because according to 1 John, everyone who loves is born of God. Lennon is also absolutely wrong according to Bono because he fails to recognize a theological detail imbedded in this biblical language. Whereas Lennon declares, 'There ain't no Jesus gonna come / from the sky' ('I Found Out') and 'I don't believe in Jesus' ('God'), Bono's allusion to 1 John recalls the central place of Jesus in Christian thought: God sent the Son 'into the world so that we might live through him'. U2's 'God Part II' is both homage to Lennon and a significant departure from his religious views.

Larry Norman's 'God Part III' does not include the same subtlety or affection for Lennon we find in Bono's lyrics. Norman begins his song not with a statement about religion, like Lennon and U2, but instead with the words 'i don't believe in beatles, i don't believe in rock', taking the first phrase directly from Lennon's song. The liner notes to Norman's *Stranded in Babylon* describe 'God Part III' as a 'response to John's song', which suggests something far less affectionate than U2's note that their song is 'for John Lennon'. Unlike U2's generous affirmation of the truth imbedded in Lennon's emphasis on love, Norman's direct confrontation with Lennon, the Beatles and rock more generally suggests there is no truth to be found in music; 'you can easily hit number one with a bullet', he says, 'and totally miss the heart'. Bono disagrees, finding truth in Lennon, even if he is misguided in certain particulars.

Norman's opening phrase creates greater distance between 'God Part III' and the Lennon precursor than we find in U2's God song. Bono does not name the

Beatles or Lennon explicitly, nor is there any veiled criticism of their music. Instead, there is an unambiguous lyrical nod to Lennon in the phrase 'Instant karma's gonna get him,' referring to his single 'Instant Karma! (We All Shine On)' (1970). Furthermore, as the inclusion of the name '[Albert] Goldman' in the song makes clear, Bono directs this judgemental citation at the author of the unauthorized 1988 biography *The Lives of John Lennon*. This book is a highly critical account of the former Beatle, one Bono clearly rejects. The ambiguous 'Don't believe' that begins the stanza is either the singer's declaration (as if to say, *I* refuse to believe Goldman, and that Lennon is anything less than great) or an imperative demanding audiences ignore Goldman (don't *you* believe Lennon is anything less than great).

My second illustration of the anxiety-motivated, push-and-pull dynamics of these three God songs emerges in their respective remarks about rock music (see Table 16.2).

Larry Norman follows Lennon in the somewhat ironic rejection of music as something worthy of our trust. For his part, Bono resists the blunt language of Lennon's list of rejected things and he is far more ambivalent. I suspect we should hear the second half of the fourth stanza in U2's song ('Don't believe that Rock 'n' Roll...') in light of the commentary provided in the fifth ('Don't believe in the sixties...'). That is to say, the singer does not want to see music treated as a museum piece, left in the 1960s as it were, as though irrelevant for the concerns of later generations and impotent to inspire change in the contemporary world. Bono refuses to eulogize the music of the past, as Don McLean does in 'American Pie', and as John Lennon does in 'God'. Lennon does not believe in Elvis, Dylan, or the Beatles anymore, but Bono does, because 'Late last night', which is to say, in the present, he 'Heard a singer on the radio... [who] says he's gonna kick the darkness / Till it bleeds daylight' (alluding here to Bruce Cockburn's song 'Lovers in a Dangerous Time', *Stealing Fire*, 1984).[13] Music can change the world, turn darkness to light, fight for justice, feed the hungry, and so on. Of course Bono of all people

Table 16.2

John Lennon, 'God'	U2, 'God Part II'	Larry Norman, 'God Part III'
'I don't believe in Elvis... Zimmerman... Beatles... The dream is over'	'Don't believe that Rock 'n' Roll / Can really change the world... Don't believe in the sixties / The golden age of pop'	'i don't believe in beatles, I don't believe in rock... i don't believe... in the gospel chart'

---

[13] For theological perspectives on Bruce Cockburn's music, see Brian J. Walsh, *Kicking at the Darkness: Bruce Cockburn and the Christian Imagination* (Grand Rapids: Baker, 2011).

believes this emphatically but music is useless if it remains locked in time, in some past golden age of pop.

Lennon sings the heart-wrenching words 'I was the Dreamweaver /...I was the Walrus / But now I'm John /...The dream is over,' thus indicating that whatever he and the Beatles represented is now finished. The music of the 1960s is dead and irrelevant and can accomplish nothing more. Larry Norman accepts this, placing the phrase 'i don't believe in beatles' conspicuously and emphatically at the beginning of the song, and later asserting that music has no power to help 'the masses [who] stay unfed.' Bono disagrees. Rock and roll is indeed a force for change if it remains a vital, living resource and not a museum piece. This is true not only of more recent, active performers like Bruce Cockburn and U2 itself, but also those musicians representing the 'golden age of pop', including the Beatles, Bob Dylan, Billie Holiday, B. B. King, Elvis Presley and Jimi Hendrix, all of them featured in *Rattle and Hum* in one form or another, not to mention Martin Luther King, Jr. whose timeless message from the 1960s also informs that album. Those voices continue to speak, but so also do the musicians of subsequent generations. Even within *Rattle and Hum* (both the album and film), U2 confronts issues of their own day, including apartheid in South Africa, racism in America and religious violence in Ireland.

Anxiety and reception

Obviously, we find artistic engagements with the Bible and religious ideas throughout the arts. I suggest we need to take into account the dynamic of artistic anxiety described by Harold Bloom and illustrated in the poetic and theological struggles occurring in these songs. I realize I am slumming here in the 'low arts' of popular culture but what is true of the poets examined by Bloom is true of artists working in other media. Bono and Norman do not simply throw biblical and religious language into their songs. They are not just singer-songwriters, they are singer-songwriters who are anxious to find their own voices and escape Lennon's overwhelming influence, which threatens to doom their efforts at creative composition to oblivion. This anxiety of influence shapes their reception of the Bible. This dynamic also repeats among all artists anxious to carve out an imaginative space for their unique craft, and to the extent that the Bible is present in that process, scholars concerned with reception must remember the sacred text is an innocent bystander caught between warring factions, or to borrow Eagleton's colourful phrase again, a text caught up in 'an heroic battle of giants or [a] mighty psychic drama'. What we observe as biblical reception in strong art is an anxiety-induced misreading of biblical tradition as mediated by strong precursors.

Long before I read Harold Bloom's ideas about poets and anxiety, I heard Bono sing 'The Fly' from 1991's *Achtung Baby*: 'Every artist is a cannibal, every poet is a thief; / All kill their inspiration and sing about the grief.' The idea of artists stealing from their muse, and then struggling with that poetic parent sounds remarkably like Bloom. I doubt Bono has read Bloom but for a brief moment in this song, high and low art meet, and literary criticism sounds a lot like rock and roll.

High, Low and In-between: Reception History and the Sociology of Religion and Popular Music

Ibrahim Abraham

Introduction

The recent sale of an annotated Bible belonging to Elvis Presley for almost $100,000 – at the same auction in which a pair of the King's very own soiled underwear failed to find a home, no less – is one example of the ongoing relationship between scripture and popular music.[1] This essay focuses on a different relationship, on the increasing turn to the study of popular music – primarily rock, pop, country and the spaces between – by biblical scholars engaged deliberately or otherwise in what has come to be called reception history. My specific concern in this essay will be to open up a dialogue between the reception history of the Bible in popular music and certain methodological and theoretical debates ongoing within the sociology of religion, the sociology of popular music and the social sciences more generally. Rather than seeking to catalogue or review the reception history of popular music in its entirety, my focus will be on a handful of outstanding examples of the emerging sub-subdiscipline which, because of their thoroughness and erudition, open themselves up for critique or counter-reading from the perspectives of different scholarly paradigms to show how the reception history of popular music might advance beyond its current methodological and theoretical foci.

This essay is based on the belief that there is much that the reception history of popular music is doing very well; that it is making innovative use of scripture in popular music to offer interesting arguments about the ways in which scripture is used and consumed in contemporary culture. Opportunities exist to go beyond its current limitations, however. On my reading, these limitations are framed by three interrelated problems or prejudices; the privileging of the production of popular music over its consumption; the privileging of subjective scholarly readings and

---

[1] Cass Jones, 'Elvis Presley's Bible Sells for £59,000' *The Guardian* (London), 8 September 2012.

journalistic or fan biographies of songwriters over engagement with the lives of listeners in secularizing societies; and, the tendency to approach popular music in an ironically conservative academic manner, as a literary text like scripture that rewards scholars with a truer and deeper meaning upon close reading and historical reconstruction. The failure to move beyond the theoretical and methodological limits of biblical studies and literary theory that one might have imagined would have accompanied the move beyond biblical literature, limits the potential of reception history.

My arguments in this essay are also based on the assumption that reception history is concerned with investigating and articulating changes in the use and status of scripture in particular and, more speculatively perhaps, elucidating the historical and social specificities of changes in religious culture more generally. Based on this supposition I will suggest that theories and methodologies from the sociology of religion and the sociology of popular music indicate that there are, first, better uses to be made of the current data being analysed – which consists almost exclusively of song lyrics – and, secondly, that there are better sources and types of data than this which are currently not being pursued. I will deal with this question of methodology in the second substantive section of this essay. First, however, I will focus on a particular understanding from within the sociology of religion, secularization, that can be used to analyse scriptural references in popular music in a different way than they currently are, as well as helping to explain and untangle certain underlying issues concerning scripture in popular music only vaguely alluded to within existing studies.

Popular music's secular public

Although a much abused term given a variety of meanings by scholars in different disciplines, within sociology secularization refers to an emergent process through which religion loses its social force and becomes one more differentiated social sphere, in the process losing the ability to regulate other differentiated social spheres like popular music.[2] This standard secularization thesis does not argue that religious or spiritual sentiments are absent in secularized societies, since fundamentalisms and eclectic esoteric beliefs are partly consequences of religious institutions losing their ability to regulate individual and collective behaviour and belief. Nor does the thesis argue that religious institutions are not relevant public actors, simply that if they do want to be taken seriously in political debates they are obliged to engage with the political through secular argument and deliberation

---

[2] See generally: David Martin, *A General Theory of Secularization*, Oxford: Blackwell, 1978; Bryan R. Wilson, *Religion in Sociological Perspective*, Oxford: Oxford University Press, 1982; Steve Bruce, *Secularization*, Oxford: Oxford University Press, 2011.

rather than relying on religious – especially scriptural – authority. For example, when the Church of England recently took issue with proposals to alter restrictions on Sunday trading, their public complaint was not that God or the Bible demands the Sabbath be kept holy, but that such reforms would negatively impact small businesses, family leisure time and abrogate a hungover nation's right to a lie-in on Sunday morning.[3] Even amongst social scientists who remain convinced of religion's political vitality in late modernity, and even amongst various 'post-secular' discontents, the idea of scripture having some vital social force or public moral authority is rejected. However the authority of scripture may animate the sentiments of religious actors in public life, the invocation of scriptural authority or political debate over its interpretation is a rarity in public life in Western Europe and most of its settler colonies.

While most reception history of popular music acknowledges, on some level, the marginal appreciation of scripture in extant studies or amongst fans of the artist in question, this is in part a celebration of the novelty of the work in question. It is much like religion scholars prefacing their studies of imminent religion or popular culture *as* religion with some caricatured sketch of the secularization paradigm, all the better to revel in the joy of discovery when finding faith in a football stadium or *Star Trek* convention. Several studies are particularly pertinent here in drawing out the secular nature of popular music in terms of its audience and in terms of the constitutive organizational principles of the various genres and subgenres of popular music which are, in fact, partly policed by audiences themselves.[4] James Crossley's socially-engaged study of the changing nature of scriptural references in Manchester's indie rock scene between the mid-1970s and mid-1990s,[5] Deane Galbraith's exhaustive study of 'hidden' biblical references in the lyrics of U2,[6] and Roland Boer's work on the Christology of the music of Nick Cave,[7] all draw out certain core features of secularizing societies and cultures, but neglect some of the more fundamental issues at work here which go to the heart of the project and problems of the reception history of popular music.

Galbraith's study is exemplary for its scholarly detective work, which makes the broader problems of this kind of reception history all the more obvious in the sense that if work of the calibre of Galbraith's, Crossley's and Boer's is getting something 'wrong', or missing something out, we can safely say there are structural

---

[3] Martin Beckford, 'Church Warns against Sunday Trading Laws Being Relaxed by the Back Door'. *Daily Telegraph* (London), 18 March 2012.
[4] Simon Frith, *Performing Rites: Evaluating Popular Music*, Oxford: Oxford University Press, 1996, pp. 75–95.
[5] James Crossley, 'For EveryManc a Religion: Biblical and Religious Language in the Manchester Music Scene, 1976–1994', *Biblical Interpretation* vol. 19, no. 2, 2011, pp. 151–80.
[6] Deane Galbraith, 'Drawing Our Fish in the Sand: Secret Biblical Allusions in the Music of U2', *Biblical Interpretation* vol. 19, no. 2, 2011, pp. 181–222.
[7] Roland Boer, 'Jesus of the Moon: Nick Cave's Christology', in Philip Culbertson and Elaine M. Wainwright, eds, *The Bible in/and Popular Culture*, Atlanta: SBL, 2010, pp. 127–39.

issues affecting how the reception history of popular music is being carried out in general. Galbraith illustrates the distance between the recognition of the secular public of popular music on the one hand and the type of analysis carried out within reception history on the other hand, in what can be read as something of an immanent critique of the reception history of popular music. He insists firstly that the fact U2's lyrics are 'saturated with biblical allusions… is so obvious it barely requires stating' and then points out that this is hardly the case for non-Christians commenting on U2's work who are not only ignorant of scriptural references, but sometimes reject the notion of a religiosity within the songs altogether.[8] Moreover, the 'mainstream listeners' who are unlikely to identify the religious references in U2's music,[9] whom Galbraith mentions and then sets aside, are fundamental social actors and fundamental to understanding the status of the Bible in late modernity.

Rather than engage with these issues in a way that acknowledges the decreased social significance of scripture in the contemporary cultures in question, Galbraith makes two moves that downplay this reality. Firstly, focussing on a small group of obsessive U2 fan-scholars who do take an interest in biblical references in the lyrics, actual or speculative and, secondly, the notion of religious references being deliberately obscured in the manner of early Christian communities. These fan-scholars must be a welcome resource because their work mirrors that of biblical scholars, carefully dissecting what they treat as literary texts in search of a deeper meaning, or at least a different one, hardly considered by non-experts.[10] Such an approach to popular music is not representative or even very common; it in fact revives the long dead dichotomy between typically male, middle-class and middle-aged 'collectors' of 'rock', who appreciate the music on a much deeper level than the typically younger, female 'consumers' of 'pop'.[11] Nor is the argument that through the double-coding of lyrics 'U2 follows a deliberate strategy of obscuring their beliefs from the full view of some sections of the public and the mainstream media'[12] entirely convincing. How can one be hiding what very few would recognize or question in the first place? Moreover, why? Acknowledge the reality of rock music's secular public and its lack of concern with the vagaries of Charismatic Christian doctrine or biblical authority, and the conspiracy theory falls apart.

The kind of sociological reading that I am suggesting can help the reception history of popular music move beyond its current foci would suggest that U2's music is primarily consumed according to the genre norms of commercial rock 'n' roll; a secular cultural sphere emphasizing creative self-expression in which the

---

[8] Galbraith, pp. 183–5.
[9] Galbraith, p. 186.
[10] Galbraith, pp. 213–16, 221–2.
[11] See generally, Lisa A. Lewis, ed., *The Adoring Audience: Fan Culture and Popular Media*, London: Routledge, 1992.
[12] Galbraith, p. 187.

precise meaning of lyrics is only of interest to a minority, and the fidelity of those lyrics with received scriptural or ecclesiastic authority of interest to an even smaller minority. The success of U2 that Galbraith alludes to is itself an example of a secularized culture;[13] it is true that U2's commercial success came in spite and not because of their religious beliefs, but the nature of these religious beliefs in secular cultures is not by their mere existence or utterance grounds for any profound social conflict, being largely private concerns that do not get in the way of enjoying the band's contribution to a secular genre. Few are concerned with stand-up comedian Russell Brand's Krishna Consciousness so long as he continues to make passable jokes about clitorises. Ironically enough, the only genre of popular music that routinely shows the kind of obsession with the meaning of lyrics that reception history scholars do is contemporary Christian music; a genre almost uniquely lacking in any strict musicological rules but strictly constructed around behavioural and ideological ones.[14] It is not only a genre deliberately disavowed by U2 – along with many other Christian artists in the mainstream commercial music industry[15] – but also a genre all but ignored within the reception history of popular music, since buying biblical studies some contemporary credibility by engaging secular culture seems to me the *sine qua non* of the subdiscipline.

James Crossley's study of the Manchester music scene is similarly amenable to a sociological counter-reading. While it is at times historical criticism in the guise of familiar popular music biography, asking what events in the life of Joy Division's Ian Curtis may have influenced the tragic biblical imagery in the lyrics he wrote,[16] far more valuable is Crossley's use of the lyrics of a later generation of bands, Happy Mondays and the Stone Roses, as documents revealing social changes in late modern Britain. His emphasis is on Manchester's passage from industrial workhouse, to post-industrial wasteland, and finally the neo-liberal reinvention of the city on the back of the experience economy; the celebrated centre of culture and hedonism called 'Madchester' in which the days of existential angst are forgotten and an ecstasy-fuelled rave in an abandoned warehouse is a much better way to spend a Saturday night than hanging yourself in the kitchen.[17] The lyrics of the Stone Roses, by vocalist and later solo artist Ian Brown, who identifies with and articulates a 'universalistic spirituality', belief in a 'higher force' and the use of drugs for spiritual experiences,[18] illustrate the turn to a less doctrinal and more

---

[13] Galbraith, pp. 191–3.
[14] Jay R. Howard and John M. Streck, *Apostles of Rock: The Splintered World of Contemporary Christian Music*, Lexington: University Press of Kentucky, 1999, pp. 7–21.
[15] The fragmentary nature of music industry marketing, as well as the self-policing of fans, means that separating music into genres separates listeners by demographics – including religion. Reebee Garofalo, 'How Autonomous is Relative: Popular Music, the Social Formation and Cultural Struggle', *Popular Music* vol. 6, no. 1, 1987, pp. 77–92.
[16] Crossley, pp. 157–69.
[17] Crossley, pp. 168–77.
[18] Crossley, p. 179.

personalized religiosity that is becoming increasingly dominant in Western Europe and its settler colonies in late modernity; 'I am the resurrection and I am the light / I couldn't ever bring myself / To hate you as I'd like.' Such lyrics are representative of individualistic expressions of belief that are increasingly eclectic through the decreasing regulatory authority of religious institutions, and are above all pragmatic and therapeutic in nature.[19] Similarly, orthodox religion is replaced by sheer hedonism in Happy Mondays' lyrics in which God becomes a benevolent drug dealer.[20] While some scholars of religion, using rather subjective criteria, seek to argue that the experiences of excess inherent in club culture are shamanic or revelatory and therefore worthy of being classified as religious,[21] others such as Steve Bruce suggest that such category creep is problematic insofar as it obfuscates fundamental changes in social life in Western Europe such that 'young people are more likely to find ecstasy in a dance hall than a church or invest more of their energy and wealth in following a football team than worshipping God.'[22]

In this spirit, Crossley makes the important argument that the tradition of Irish immigration and Catholicism in Manchester may have made bands from this city more biblically literate than their peers; 'the Irish Catholic background partly explains why the bands and singers could draw upon such imagery and language'.[23] Indeed, Andrew Greeley speculates about a Catholic 'subculture' in late modern Britain that has been 'protected from the decline of religion in the larger society' through traditional family-facilitated religious practices.[24] This emphasis on cultural defence, on religion as a part of or proxy for one's ethnic identity, could indeed explain this scriptural literacy, but we can take this issue further and suggest that the difficulties in maintaining the social force of religion through cultural defence in the context of a society as diverse and mobile as Britain's also explain why the artists in question demonstrate mere awareness of and interest in scripture rather than any commitment to its authority, let alone the authority of the institutions through which they first encountered it.[25] The number of Roman Catholics attending church in England declined by 45% between 1979 and 2005,[26] placing the Madchester generation, mostly born in the 1960s, at the soggy end of

---

[19] Steve Bruce and David Voas, 'The Spiritual Revolution: Another False Dawn for the Sacred', in Kieran Flanagan and Peter C. Jupp (eds) *A Sociology of Spirituality*. Farnham: Ashgate, 2007, pp. 43–62.
[20] Crossley, pp. 172–3.
[21] See generally, Marcus Moberg, 'Religion in Popular Music or Popular Music as Religion?', *Popular Music & Society* vol. 35, no. 1, 2012, pp. 113–30.
[22] Bruce, *Secularization*, p. 81.
[23] Crossley, p. 178.
[24] Andrew Greeley, 'Unsecular Europe: The Persistence of Religion', in Detlaf Pollack & Daniel V. A. Olson (eds) *The Role of Religion in Modern Societies*, London: Routledge, 2008, pp. 141–62, at pp. 155–8.
[25] Bruce, *Secularization*, pp. 49–52.
[26] Peter Brierley, *Painting with Numbers: An Introduction to Church Statistics*, London: Christian Research, 2005, pp. 21–7.

the Catholic cultural cigarette. So it is disappointing that the question Crossley raises as to '[w]hether audiences in Manchester (and beyond) would have picked up on the consistent use of religious and biblical imagery and language by the Manchester bands' is set aside as 'a moot point'.[27] Admittedly it is hardly the most urgent of history's unanswered questions, but it is the kind of question that the reception history of popular music needs to ask if it wants to move beyond its current foci, since such a question goes to the core of understanding how popular music functions, and how scripture functions in secular societies like contemporary Britain.

Much the same counter-reading can be made of Boer's analysis of the Christology of songwriter Nick Cave. It is an idiosyncratic Christology, and a vaguely eroticized one, constituting an Enlightenment 'heresy' in Boer's reading.[28] A sociological reading would suggest something else, however. There is no shortage of sensuous songs about Jesus; even Charles Wesley self-censored some of his own hymns because of their erotic undertones.[29] As is the case with Ian Brown's spiritual utterances, moreover, there is nothing scandalous about Cave's unusual Christology in the late modern era in countries such as the UK or Australia in which churches, with rare exceptions, are unable to police the beliefs of their own congregations, let alone anyone else. Social teachings are routinely flouted by believers, ignored or mocked by everyone else, and various 'Eastern' and esoteric religious beliefs are not uncommon amongst even active Christians.[30] The same socio-historical process that allows for creative use of the Bible prevents these creative uses having any great cultural resonance. Since it has so little social force in Western Europe and most of its settler colonies, unless these banal 'heresies' are printed on the side of a bus, not even the multicultural mandarins making their living by being vicariously offended are likely to notice. Similarly, the Marxism underlabouring Boer's analysis raises its head at the most inappropriate time to castigate Cave for the 'underlying ideology of the private individual' dwelling in his songs.[31] Since rock 'n' roll has never been a form of creative self-expression much given to democratic centralism or communitarian hand wringing,[32] criticizing a rock 'n' roll singer for being too individualistic is like criticizing a biblical prophet for being too judgemental. There are certain assessments one can make about or within a particular genre piece that make more or less sense and are more or less convincing within the confines of

---

[27] Crossley, p. 178.
[28] Boer, pp. 136-7.
[29] For an overview of these issues in historical and contemporary contexts, see, John McCormack, *Listen, Jesus, They're Playing our Song: A Sociological Study of Worship Music in Melbourne's Megachurches*, PhD dissertation, Melbourne: Monash University, 2009.
[30] Steve Bruce, *God is Dead: Secularization in the West*, Oxford: Blackwell, 2002, pp. 118-39.
[31] Boer, pp. 136-7.
[32] Rehan Hyder, *Brimful of Asia: Negotiating Ethnicity on the UK Music Scene*, Aldershot: Ashgate, 2004, pp. 114-22.

cultural history; secular rock as heretical or inappropriately individualistic certainly falls amongst the less convincing ones.

Methodological departures

The second substantive argument I want to make about the ways in which a dialogue between the sociology of religion and popular music can enhance the reception history of popular music has to do with the particular methodologies employed. The primary units of study are songs, typically furnished with journalistic commentaries or biographies. These songs end up being treated as primarily literary objects, with a few nods towards the music. Timothy Beal makes a similar point in his general critique of reception history for conceiving of scripture 'primarily, if not exclusively, in terms of literary content' without due regard for 'the materiality and mediality of scriptures themselves' and how this informs the process of production and consumption of scripture through human interactions.[33] This is a criticism also advanced by Crossley, who pushes reception history beyond mere 'listings or comparisons' towards more sophisticated socio-cultural analysis.[34] While endorsing these broad criticisms, I would suggest that to conceive of popular music primarily, if not exclusively, in terms of literary content is even more problematic than to do so with scripture. This is therefore one area wherein certain theologians – such as Tex Sample[35] – have the edge over biblical scholars, being far more concerned with how popular music works in the everyday lives of laity.

Within the reception history of popular music, musicological analysis, or a kind of musicological semiotics, is hardly engaged in, for some of the same reason that Lee Marshall argues it is often resisted by sociologists of popular music; there is usually a lack of training, and in any case the suspicion – although not necessarily correct – is that we cannot engage with the language of music without falling into a subjective idealism.[36] Many scholars of popular music from biblical and religion studies are wont to do this in any case, but it does not help that at the other extreme lies the equally troubling realm of neuropsychology with its potential to unlock a fixed relationship between sound and stimuli. Chris Kennett, for one, rejects

---

[33] Timothy Beal, 'Reception History and Beyond: Toward the Cultural History of Scripture', *Biblical Interpretation* vol. 19, nos. 4–5, 2011, pp. 357–72, at pp. 355–6.
[34] Crossley, p. 180.
[35] Tex Sample, *White Soul: Country Music, the Church and Working Americans*, Nashville: Abingdon Press, 1996; Tex Sample, *Blue Collar Resistance and the Politics of Jesus*, Nashville: Abingdon Press, 2006; Tex Sample, ' "Help Me Make it Through the Night": Narrating Class and Country Music in the Theology of Paul', in Philip Culbertson and Elaine M. Wainwright, eds, *The Bible in/and Popular Culture*, Atlanta: SBL, 2010, pp. 111–25.
[36] Lee Marshall, 'The Sociology of Popular Music, Interdisciplinarity and Aesthetic Autonomy', *British Journal of Sociology* vol. 62, no. 2, 2011, pp. 154–74.

anything approaching this paradigm on the basis that he has experienced no meaningful limits on the interpretations or associations offered in response to an instrumental fragment.[37] Similar findings are related by W. John Lyons in his analysis of the uses YouTube's postmodern consumer-producers, amongst others, have found for Johnny Cash's apocalyptic track 'The Man Comes Around'; from enlivening home movies and amateur sport, to providing a soundtrack to the Kennedy assassination and the 9/11 attacks, there are no clear biographical, cultural, or political determinates.[38] The inherent problem in attempting to define these determinates is evident in one of the few examples of the reception history of popular music that does genuinely seek methodological innovation through a musicological opening, Boer's analysis of change in music, or the different 'organization of noise', that characterizes shifts in Nick Cave's song writing. The recourse to pop biography in explaining the chaotic sound of early Cave, linked to German reunification and Cave's father's death, shows how speculative and subjective this approach can actually be; while the latter event was traumatic for Cave, the former was presumably traumatic for Boer.[39]

A similar problem of subjectivity within the reception history of popular music, this time focussing on its preferred data source, song lyrics, is evident in Jay Twomey's study of Johnny Cash in a Pauline perspective; he is reflexively aware that within the more openly religious music the reception history of popular music engages with, such as certain work by Johnny Cash, 'as with love or travelling songs, so with gospels, perhaps: the distinction between biblically-informed language and non-religious lyrics is often hard to maintain.'[40] This analysis also reveals the inherent limitations of the reception history of popular music undertaken as a form of qualitative data dredging. Knowing a songwriter's religious proclivities or picking up on a familiar religious phrase or allusion then gives one licence to proceed to pan through the back catalogue and build an argument based on intriguing possibilities. This is something Twomey could be accused of engaging in himself, despite his critical awareness of the difficulties of the data he is working with, when referring to certain Johnny Cash lyrics as being *potentially Pauline* for their focus on travel, desire and so forth.[41] Lyrics that contradict this, or simply have nothing to do with religious or biblical tropes, and more closely adhere to what Tex Sample identifies as the populist traditionalist ideological genre norms of

---

[37] Chris Kennett, 'Is Anyone Listening?' in Allan Moore (ed.) *Analyzing Popular Music*, Cambridge: Cambridge University Press, 2003, pp. 196–217, at pp. 198–204.

[38] William John Lyons, 'The Apocalypse According to Johnny Cash: Examining the "Effect" of the Book of Revelation on a Contemporary Apocalyptic Writer', in William John Lyons and Jorunn Økland (eds), *The Way the World Ends? The Apocalypse of John in Culture and Ideology*, Sheffield: Sheffield Phoenix Press, 2009, pp. 95–122, at pp. 109–18.

[39] Boer, pp. 128–31.

[40] Jay Twomey, 'The Biblical Man in Black: Paul in Johnny Cash / Johnny Cash in Paul', *Biblical Interpretation* vol. 19, no. 2, 2011, pp. 223–52, at p. 240.

[41] Twomey, p. 242.

country music, emphasizing freedom from modern institutional constraints,[42] can then be read as a *repudiation* of the Pauline and folded into the argument accordingly. My point is not that Twomey is doing anything wrong as such, but simply to illustrate that subjective readings and speculative listenings will be an almost inevitable feature of the reception history of popular music based on this kind of close reading of lyrics.

Conversely, the analysis of popular music has focussed for some time on the body and the social production of identity and affect, subsequently rendering the notion of popular music as a vehicle for the communication of ideas via the vocalized or printed lyrics of a poetic genius reductive or naive.[43] Yet there remains some significant debate about just what kind of cultural process and product popular music is and how it can and cannot be studied. The main antagonists here have been musicology and cultural studies, engendering the question of the extent to which contemporary popular music is sufficiently distinct from other forms of music or from other cultural artifacts of capitalist late modernity to warrant some innovative and independent means of analysis, or whether contemporary popular music can be analysed in much the same way as, say, atonal art music or parliamentary speeches.[44]

In any case, there is a recognition that the analysis of popular music must go beyond the 'readings' of individual scholars if it is going to argue convincingly about significant aspects of social life. As Chris Kennett points out, 'listening to the same music in different situations, with different purposes and with different intensity, will affect the analytical meanings which may arise from the experience.'[45] So for scholars to consume *REO Speedwagon: All The Hits* as they might consume the Dead Sea Scrolls, with the same professional obligation, focus, and the same desired outcome of peer-reviewed publication, is likely to produce an interpretation of songs thoroughly alien to the processes of interpretation engaged in by most other consumers in most other contexts. As Tex Sample would no doubt remind us, if you are listening to Johnny Cash while sitting at a table at work it is more likely being piped in to the warehouse where you are sexing chickens than part of your attempt to gain tenure in a religion department. Such methodology or limited ambition is unproblematic, of course, if one is satisfied to restrict the task of reception history to the question of how professional biblical scholars and clerics, a 'homogeneous group of codal experts, all of whom are giving the music their full, undivided attention,'[46] encounter the biblical text used by a songwriter within and alongside non-biblical media. If, however, one believes that reception history

---

[42] Sample, *White Soul*, 120–7; Sample, *Blue Collar Resistance*, pp. 31–48.
[43] Dai Griffiths, 'From Lyric to Anti-Lyric: Analyzing the Words in Pop Songs', in Allan Moore (ed.) *Analyzing Popular Music*, Cambridge: Cambridge University Press, 2003, pp. 39–51.
[44] Marshall.
[45] Kennett, p. 197.
[46] Kennett, p. 208.

should move beyond these contexts, then at the very least a high degree of methodological reflexivity is required of those producing the hitherto normative analysis of popular music within reception history. As it stands, current practice seems to mirror the probably apocryphal story of Theodor Adorno – the 'pessimist aristocrat'[47] whose influence over the study of popular music has thankfully long subsided – whose preferred method of consuming music was alleged to have been sitting alone in his office and reading the sheet music.

So the study of popular music in the social sciences has increasingly focussed on its consumption by non-scholars and non-experts, seeking some measure of empirically verifiable data. A methodological naturalism almost wholly distinct from standard approaches in the reception history of popular music has become the norm, even if it is sometimes still carried out by 'fan researchers' in the social sciences who may have more in common with the Professor of Patristics or Lecturer in Akkadian publishing the odd article about their favourite rapper than they would care to admit.[48] Daniel Cavicci's ethnographic study of Bruce Springsteen fans is amongst the best work in this field.[49] He clearly identifies how much the literary content of lyrics can mean to fans to the point that one research participant confesses that she thinks and speaks 'in Springsteen'; 'sometimes the words I say rhyme too much... they're not regular speech.'[50] Other fans are less concerned with the lyrics than the music, however. Even then, for some it is technical ability, while for others the sheer 'energy' allures. Some fans become fixated upon the music by default because they simply cannot understand Bruce's 'garbled' vocals.[51] This is a recurrent issue in this area of the study of music that genuinely demands some serious reflection unless we are all going to focus our efforts on studying rock's most perspicuous singer, Roger McGuinn, or assume that everyone takes the time to study lyrics. Indeed, Galbraith picks up on this in analysing lyrics obscured by guitars on U2's track 'Sunday Bloody Sunday', but insisting that it is part of a deliberate strategy of hiding the band's religiosity[52] rather than entertaining more mundane explanations such as the fact that a single rock 'n' roll song can contain the same internal contradictions and multiple concerns as its genre. Moreover, Cavicci can find no consensus on the meaning of lyrics amongst fans; two people may find the same song intensely significant, but

---

[47] Jacques Attali, *Noise: The Political Economy of Music*, Minneapolis: University of Minnesota Press, 1985, p. 45.
[48] Andy Bennett, 'The Use of "Insider" Knowledge in Ethnographic Research on Contemporary Youth Music Scenes', in Andy Bennett, Mark Cieslik and Steven Miles (eds) *Researching Youth*, Basingstoke: Palgrave Macmillan, 2003, pp. 186–99.
[49] Daniel Cavicci, *Tramps Like Us: Music and Meaning Among Springsteen Fans*, New York: Oxford University Press, 1998.
[50] Cavicci, p. 109.
[51] Cavicci, pp. 110–16.
[52] Galbraith, pp. 196–7.

for very different reasons based on completely different analyses of the same track.[53]

What is needed within the reception history of popular music is an appreciation of the long agreed upon assessment within sociology that genres of popular music, while with a few exceptions being resolutely secular forms, are also internally contradictory forms; rock music combines the new and sentimental, the conformist and rebellious, the rawly self-expressive and the commercially calculated.[54] Moreover, genres of popular music mediate their own ideological content.[55] This latter point is picked up on by Eric Repphun in critiquing the notion that biblical studies needs to engage hip hop aesthetics to develop a radical anti-imperialist politics; one cannot simply insist upon an authentic experimental and counter-hegemonic hip hop by ignoring its commercialized and standardized misogynistic incarnations or claiming they are somehow incidental or erroneous innovations.[56] That may work in theology, but not in secular analysis of popular music – and this is despite the fact that many of its core texts fall within the genre of self-consciously revolutionary theory.[57]

Conclusion

To put this argument in a way so as not to offend or unnerve, at its current early stage of development the reception history of popular music is a collection of studies by biblical scholars using the theories and methodologies designed for or applied to the analysis of sacred literature, seeking to understand and analyse cultural products and processes that are neither sacred nor literary. As Repphun says, biblical studies appears 'blithely ignorant' of scholarship from other disciplines produced over many decades.[58] The studies I have looked at in this essay have all managed to break out of that academic ghetto, but with Boer and Crossley it appears to be a search for theories that are politically agreeable rather than methodologically current or appropriate. At the very least such work requires the reflexivity to acknowledge awareness of later liberal degradations of a discipline, even if they are being consciously avoided, much as one would expect a media studies scholar working on the Bible and citing no one after Bultmann to explain themselves. It seems clear from this essay's overview of some of the finest work in this sub-subdiscipline that, absent such reflexive acknowledgments, just like

---

[53] Cavicci, pp. 112–13.
[54] Richard Middleton, *Studying popular music*, Milton Keynes: Open University Press, 1990, p. 139.
[55] Frith, p. 35.
[56] Eric Repphun, 'Review of Philip Culbertson and Elaine M. Wainwright, eds., *The Bible in/and Popular Culture*', *The Bible and Critical Theory*, vol. 8, no. 1, 2012, pp. 95–7, at p. 96.
[57] Dai Griffiths, 'The High Analysis of Low Music' *Music Analysis*, vol. 18, no. 3, 1999, pp. 389–435.
[58] Repphun, p. 97.

European Maoists of the 1960s whose translations were a move or two behind the intrigues of Mao's court, the reception history of popular music has found itself accidently caught in an acid house ketamine hole by trying to toe a certain political line. I can only imagine this is why Crossley invokes the Marxist subcultural studies of Birmingham's Centre for Contemporary Cultural Studies, despite the fact that two paradigms emerged in repudiation of the Birmingham School's class-focussed structuralism to study the very genres of popular music and culture Crossley is concerned with, clubculture theory and neo-tribal theory,[59] both committed to the belief that the consumers of popular music are better able to understand and narrate the meanings of their own haircuts and bathroom stall encounters than Antonio Gramsci or Louis Althusser.[60]

These fundamental questions of methodology will have to be confronted by the reception history of popular music in order to develop approaches more suited to the precise types of cultural data being analysed. As this essay has intended to make clear, however, the sub-subdiscipline is an emergent one, and while certain advances in the studies of popular music have been made in the social sciences, there are many open debates within which the reception history of the Bible in popular music can seek inclusion. Finally, any thorough history of the reception of the Bible in popular music will, sooner or later, have to deal with the disavowed subjects this essay has alluded to – Crossley's 'moot point' and Galbraith's 'mainstream listeners'[61] – whose secularized subjectivity poses, on the one hand, an obvious challenge to biblical studies, but on the other hand, an opportunity to make inroads into understanding the changing social significance of the Bible in contemporary culture.

---

[59] See generally, Steve Redhead, et al. (eds) *The Clubcultures Reader*, Oxford: Blackwell, 1998; Andy Bennett, 'Sub-Cultures or Neo-Tribes?' *Sociology*, vol. 33, no. 3, 1999, pp. 599–617.

[60] See generally, David Muggleton and Rupert Weinzierl (eds) *The Post-Subcultures Reader*, Oxford: Berg, 2003; Andy Bennett, 'The Post-Subcultural Turn: Some Reflections 10 Years On', *Journal of Youth Studies*, vol. 14, no. 5, 2011, pp. 493–506.

[61] Crossley, p. 178; Galbraith, p. 186.

Bibliography

Adorno, T. W., 'On Lyric Poetry and Society,' in *Notes to Literature*, ed. Rolf Tiedemann (New York: Columbia University Press, 1991).

Agee, J., and W. Evans, *Let Us Now Praise Famous Men: Three Tenant Families* (Boston: Mariner Books, 2001).

Aichele, G., P. Miscall, and R. Walsh, 'An Elephant in the Room: Historical-Critical and Postmodern Interpretations of the Bible,' *Journal of Biblical Literature* 128 (2009), 383–404.

Allen, G., *Intertextuality* (The New Critical Idiom) (London and New York: Routledge, 2000).

Allen, G., and R. Sellars (eds), *The Salt Companion to Harold Bloom* (Cambridge: Salt, 2007).

Allen, R. C., 'From Exhibition to Reception: Reflections on the Audience in Film History,' *Screen*, Vol. 31 (1990).

Amaudry, L., 'The Collection of Dr. Carvallo at Paris. Article III: Early Pictures of Various Schools,' *The Burlington Magazine* 6 (1904), 294–312.

Amichai, Y., 'Jacob and the Angel,' in *Selected Poetry of Yehuda Amichai* (New York: Harper & Row, 1986).

Anderson, P., *The Origins of Postmodernity* (London and New York: Verso, 1998).

Anon, 'Chapter 4. The Deluge,' in *Bible History For Young Children* (11–14, Vol. 1 of 3) (Newcastle: F. and W. Dodsworth, 1854).

Anon, 'Hieroglyphics. No. LX.' in *One Hundred Hieroglyphic Bible Readings For The Young* (London: S.W.Partridge & Co., [c. 1869]).

Anon ('Mamma') [Lucy Sarah Wilson], 'Lesson II. Noah's Ark,' in *Mamma's Bible Stories For Her Little Boys And Girls: A Series Of Reading Lessons Taken From The Bible And Adapted To The Capacities Of Very Young Children* (London: Griffith, Farran & Co., [c. 1892]), 19–25.

Aston, M., *The King's Bedpost: Reformation and Iconography in a Tudor Group Portrait* (Cambridge: Cambridge University Press, 1993).

Attali, J., *Noise: The Political Economy of Music* (Minneapolis: University of Minnesota Press, 1985).

Attridge, H. W., and M. E. Fassler, *Psalms in Community: Jewish and Christian Textual, Liturgical and Artistic Traditions* (Atlanta: SBL, 2003).

Avalos, H., *The End of Biblical Studies* (Amherst, NY: Prometheus Books, 2007).

Badiou, A., *Saint Paul: The Foundation of Universalism* (trans. Ray Brassier; Stanford: Stanford University Press, 2003).

Baker, T., *Dave Gahan: Depeche Mode & the Second Coming* (Church Stretton, Shropshire: Independent Music Press, 2009).

Bal, M., *Quoting Caravaggio. Contemporary Art, Preposterous History* (Chicago: University of Chicago Press, 1999).

Bal, M., *Loving Yusuf: Conceptual Travels from Present to Past* (Chicago: The University of Chicago Press, 2008).

Barr, J., *History and Ideology in the Old Testament* (Oxford: Oxford University Press, 2000).

Barthes, R., *The Pleasure of the Text* (trans. R. Miller; New York: Hill and Wang, 1975 [1973]).
Barthes, R., *A Lover's Discourse* (trans. R. Howard; New York: Farrar, Straus and Giroux, 1978 [1977]).
Barthes, R., *Camera Lucida* (trans. R. Howard; New York: Vintage 1993 [1980]).
Barthes, R., 'Fragments d'un discours amoureux', in *Œuvres complètes, Volume V: 1977–1980* (Paris: Seuil, 2002 [1977]).
Barthes, R., 'La chambre claire: Note sur la photographie', in *Œuvres complètes, Volume V: 1977–1980* (Paris, Seuil 2002[1980]).
Barthes, R., 'Le plaisir du texte', in *Œuvres complètes, Volume IV: 1972–1976* (Paris: Seuil, 2002 [1973]).
Barton, J., *People of the Book?: The Authority of the Bible in Christianity* (Louisville: Westminster John Knox, 1989).
Barton J. (ed.), *The Cambridge Companion to Biblical Interpretation* (Cambridge: Cambridge University Press 1998).
Barton, J., *The Nature of Biblical Criticism* (Louisville, KY and London: Westminster John Knox, 2007).
Barton, J., and J. Muddiman (eds), *The Oxford Bible Commentary* (Oxford and New York: Oxford University Press, 2001).
Basile, G. M., 'Power and Words of Power: Political, Juridical and Religious Vocabulary in Some Ideological Documents in 16th Century Russia', in *Beiträge zur 7. Internationalen Konferenz zur Geschichte des Kiever und des Moskauer Reiches* (Forschungen zur osteuropäischen Geschichte: Historische Veröffentlichungen, Bd. 50; Wiesbaden: Harrassowitz, 1995), 51–79.
Bauckham, R., *The Climax of Prophecy: Studies on the Book of Revelation* (New edn; T&T Clark International: London, 1998).
BBC, 'Schools get King James Bible to mark 400th anniversary', *BBC News* (15 May 2012). http://www.bbc.co.uk/news/education-18073996.
Beal, T., 'Reception History and Beyond: Toward the Cultural History of Scriptures', *Biblical Interpretation* 19 (2011), 357–72.
Beatrice, P. F., 'Pagans and Christians on the Book of Daniel', *StPat* 25 (1993), 27–45.
Becker, E.-M., 'Patmos – ein *utopischer* Ort? Apk 1,9–11' in auslegungs- und kulturgeschichtlicher Hinsicht', *Saeculum* 59/I (2008), 81–106.
Beckford, M., 'Church warns against Sunday trading laws being relaxed by the back door'. *Daily Telegraph* (London), 18 March 2012.
Begg, C. T., *Flavius Josephus: Judean Antiquities 5–7* (Leiden: Brill, 2005).
Begg, C. T., and P. Spilsbury, *Judean Antiquities 8–10* (Leiden: Brill, 2005).
Berlinerblau, J., 'Toward a Sociology of Heresy, Orthodoxy, and Doxa', *History of Religions* 40, no. 4 (2001), 327–51.
Berlinerblau, J., '"Poor Bird, Not Knowing Which Way to Fly": Biblical Scholarship's Marginality, Secular Humanism, and the Laudable Occident', *Biblical Interpretation* 10, no. 3 (2002), 267–304.
Berlinerblau, J., 'The Bible as Literature?', *Hebrew Studies* 45 (2004), 9–26.
Berlinerblau, J., *The Secular Bible: Why Nonbelievers Must Take Religion Seriously* (Cambridge: Cambridge University Press, 2005).
Berlinerblau, J., *Thumpin' It: The Use and Abuse of the Bible in Today's Presidential Politics* (Louisville: Westminster John Knox, 2008).
Berlinerblau, J., 'The Unspeakable in Biblical Scholarship', in *Secularism and Biblical Studies*, ed. Roland Boer (London: Equinox, 2010), 20–24.
Bennett, A., 'Sub-Cultures or Neo-Tribes?', *Sociology* 33 (1999), 599–617.

Bennett, A., 'The Use of "Insider" Knowledge in Ethnographic Research on Contemporary Youth Music Scenes', in A. Bennett, M. Cieslik and S. Miles (eds), *Researching Youth* (Basingstoke: Palgrave Macmillan, 2003), 186–99.

Bennett, A., 'The Post-Subcultural Turn: Some Reflections 10 Years On', *Journal of Youth Studies* 14 (2011), 493–506.

Ben Zvi, E., *A Historical-critical Study of the Book of Zephaniah* (BZAW 198; Berlin: Walter de Gruyter, 1991).

Blanchot, M., *The Space of Literature* (trans. Ann Smock; Lincoln: University of Nebraska Press, 1989).

Blanton, W., 'Neither Religious nor Secular: On Saving the Critic in Biblical Criticism', in *Secularism and Biblical Studies*, ed. Roland Boer (London: Equinox, 2010), 154.

Bloch, E., *Zur Philosophie der Musik* (Frankfurt am Main: Suhrkamp, 1974).

Bloch, E., *Essays on the Philosophy of Music* (trans. P. Palmer; Cambridge: Cambridge University Press, 1985).

Bloch, E., *Geist der Utopie, Zweite Fassung. Ernst Bloch Werkausgabe*, Volume 3 (Frankfurt am Main: Suhrkamp Verlag, 1985).

Bloch, E., *The Spirit of Utopia* (trans. A. A. Nassar; Stanford, CA: Stanford University Press, 2000).

Bloom, D., et al., *Higher Education and Economic Development in Africa*, (Human Development Sector Africa Region, 2006; http://ent.arp.harvard.edu/AfricaHigherEducation/Reports/BloomAndCanning.pdf), 66.

Bloom, H., *The Anatomy of Influence: Literature as a Way of Life* (New Haven and London: Yale University Press, 2011).

Bloom, H., *The Anxiety of Influence: A Theory of Poetry* (2nd edn; New York: Oxford University Press, 1997).

Bloom, H., *Genius: A Mosaic of One Hundred Exemplary Minds* (New York: Warner, 2002).

Blount, B., *Revelation: A Commentary* (Louisville, KY: Westminster John Knox, 2009).

Blower, P. M., 'Academic Integrity within a Confessional Institution: An "Insider's" Response to Thomas Verenna' *The Bible and Interpretation* (October 2012), http://www.bibleinterp.com/articles/blo368008.shtml.

Bockmuehl, M., 'A Commentator's Approach to the "Effective History" of Philippians', *Journal for the Study of the New Testament* 60 (1995), 57–88.

Boer, R., *Criticism of Heaven: On Marxism and Theology* (Historical Materialism; Leiden: E. J. Brill, 2007).

Boer, R., *Criticism of Religion: On Marxism and Theology II* (Historical Materialism; Leiden: Brill, 2009).

Boer, R., *Political Grace: The Revolutionary Theology of John Calvin* (Louisville: Westminster John Knox, 2009).

Boer, R., 'Jesus of the Moon: Nick Cave's Christology', in P. Culbertson and E. M. Wainwright (eds), *The Bible in/and Popular Culture* (Atlanta: SBL, 2010) 127–39.

Boer, R., 'The Closing of Larry Hurtado's Mind', http://stalinsmoustache.wordpress.com/2011/09/09/the-closing-of-larry-hurtados-mind/.

Boer, R., 'Against "Reception History"', *The Bible and Interpretation* (May, 2011), http://www.bibleinterp.com/opeds/boe358008.shtml.

Boer, R., *Criticism of Theology: On Marxism and Theology III* (Leiden: Brill, 2011).

Boer, R., *Criticism of Earth: On Marx, Engels and Theology* (Historical Materialism; Leiden: Brill, 2012).

Boer, R., *Nick Cave: A Study of Love, Death and Apocalypse* (London: Equinox, 2012).

Boer, R., *Lenin, Religion, and Theology* (New York: Palgrave Macmillan, 2013).

Boer, R., *In the Vale of Tears: On Marxism and Theology V* (Historical Materialism; Leiden: Brill, in press).
Boer R., and F. Segovia (eds), *The Future of the Biblical Past: Envisioning Biblical Studies on a Global Key* (Atlanta, GA.: Society of Biblical Literature, 2012).
Boitani, P., *The Bible and its Rewritings* (trans. Anita Weston; Oxford: Oxford University Press, 1999).
Bono and Michka Assayas. *Bono in Conversation with Michka Assayas* (New York: Riverhead, 2005).
Boone, K. C., *The Bible tells them so: The Discourse of Protestant Fundamentalism*. London: SCM, 1989).
Borges, J. L., *Selected Non-Fictions* (ed. Eliot Weinberger, trans. Esther Allen; New York: Penguin, 1999).
Bourdieu, P., *Outline of a Theory of Practice* (Cambridge: Cambridge University Press, 1995).
Borgenicht, D., 'Noah And The Great Flood', in *Bible Stories: Four Of The Greatest Tales Ever Told* (illustrated by P. Malone; London: Running Press, 1994), 29–53.
Boße A., and D. Plauk *Insight – Martin Gore und Depeche Mode: Ein Porträt* (Hannibal Verlag GmbH, 2010).
Bowley, J. E., and J. C. Reeves, 'Rethinking the Concept of "Bible": Some Theses and Proposals', *Henoch* 25 (2003), 3–18.
Boxall, I., 'The Many Faces of Babylon the Great: *Wirkungsgeschichte* and the Interpretation of Revelation 17', in S. Moyise (ed.), *Studies in the Book of Revelation* (Edinburgh and New York: T. & T. Clark, 2001), 51–68.
Boxall, I., *Patmos in the Reception History of the Apocalypse* (Oxford: Oxford University Press, 2013).
Bradley, A., and A. Tate, *The New Atheist Novel: Philosophy, Fiction and Polemic after 9/11* (London: Continuum, 2010).
Brady, C., 'How many languages does it take to get to the center?', http://targuman.org/blog/2011/09/06/how-many-languages-does-it-take-to-get-to-the-center/.
Bramley, S., and B. Rheims, *INRI* (New York: Monacelli Press, 1999).
Brierley, P., *Painting with Numbers: An Introduction to Church Statistics* (London: Christian Research, 2005), 21–7.
Brown, D., *Discipleship and Imagination: Christian Tradition and Truth* (Oxford: Oxford University Press, 2000).
Brown, D., *God and Enchantment of Place: Reclaiming Human Experience* (Oxford: Oxford University Press, 2004).
Brown, W., 'American Nightmare: Neoconservatism, Neoliberalism, and De-democratization', *Political Theory* 34 (2006), 690–714.
Bruce, S., *God is Dead: Secularization in the West* (Oxford: Blackwell, 2002).
Bruce, S., *Secularization* (Oxford: Oxford University Press, 2011).
Bruce, S., and D. Voas, 'The Spiritual Revolution: Another False Dawn for the Sacred', in K. Flanagan and P. C. Jupp (eds) *A Sociology of Spirituality* (Farnham: Ashgate, 2007), 43–62.
Burdick, A., J. Drucker, P. Lunenfeld, T. Presner and J. Schnapp, *Digital Humanities* (Cambridge, MA: The MIT Press, 2012).
Burleigh, M., *Sacred Causes: Religion and Politics from the European Dictators to Al Qaeda* (London: Harper Press, 2006).
BW16, 'The Victorian Straight-Jacket of "Subjective" Empiricism in British New Testament Studies', http://bwsixteen.wordpress.com/2011/09/04/the-victorian-straight-jacket-of-subjective empiricism-in-british-new-testament-studies/.

BW16, 'An Objective Queer Marxist Rejoinder to Larry Hurtado's Hegemonic Essentialisms', http://bwsixteen.wordpress.com/2011/09/05/an-objective-queer-marxist-rejoinder-to-larry-hurtados-hegemonic-essentialisms/.
Byron, J., *Cain and Abel in Text and Tradition: Jewish and Christian Interpretations of the First Sibling Rivalry* (Leiden: Brill, 2011).
Cabrita, J., 'Isaiah Shembe's Theological Nationalism, 1920s–1935', *Journal of Southern African Studies* 35, no. 3 (2009), 609–25.
Cabrita, J. M., 'A Theological Biography of Isaiah Shembe, c.1870–1935.' (University of Cambridge, 2008).
Callaway, M. C., 'What's the use of Reception History?', http://bbibcomm.net/files/callaway2004.pdf.
Calvini, J., *Institutiones Christianae Religionis*, Volume 3 (Eds P. Barth and G. Niesel. 3 vols, *Opera Selecta*. Monachii in Aedibus: Chr. Kaiser, 1957 [1559]), 22:7–8.
Calvin, J., *Institutes of the Christian Religion* (trans. F. L. Battles, The Library of Christian Classics; Louisville, KY: Westminster John Knox, 2006).
Cambridge Idioms Dictionary (Cambridge University Press, 2nd edn, 2006).
Cameron, D. 'Prime Minister's King James Bible Speech (December 16)', *Number 10 Downing Street* (2011), http://www.number10.gov.uk/news/king-james-bible/.
Capp, B. S., *The Fifth Monarchy Men: A Study in Seventeenth-Century English Millenarianism* (London: Faber and Faber, 1972).
Cargill, R. R., 'The Benefit of Blogging for Archaeology', *Bulletin for the Study of Religion* 39 (2010), 26–36.
Carr, E. H., *What Is History?* (Cambridge: Cambridge University Press, 1961).
Carroll, R. P., 'The Reader and the Text', in A. D. H. Mayes (ed.), *Text in Context: Essays by Members of the Society for Old Testament Study* (Oxford: Oxford University Press, 2000), 3–34.
Carruthers, J., *Esther through the Centuries* (Oxford: Wiley-Blackwell, 2007).
Casey, M., 'Porphyry and the Book of Daniel', *JThSt* 27 (1976), 15–33.
Cavicci, D., *Tramps Like Us: Music and Meaning Among Springsteen Fans* (New York: Oxford University Press, 1998).
Certeau, M. de, *The Practice of Everyday Life* (Berkeley: University of California Press, 1984).
Charles, R. H., *A Critical and Exegetical Commentary on the Revelation of St John* (ICC; Edinburgh: T. & T. Clark, 1920).
Christianson, E. S., *Ecclesiastes through the Centuries* (Oxford: Wiley-Blackwell, 2006).
Coleman, M., *Bible Stories (Twisted Tales)* (illus. Michael Tickner; London: Scholastic Children's Books, 2004).
Collins, J. J., *Daniel: A Commentary on the Book of Daniel* (Hermeneia; Minneapolis: Fortress Press, 1993).
Collins, J. J., *The Bible After Babel: Historical Criticism in a Postmodern Age* (Grand Rapids, MI: Wm. B. Eerdmans, 2005).
Cook, J. G., *The Interpretation of the Old Testament in Greco-Roman Paganism* (Tübingen: Mohr Siebeck, 2004).
Cowley, R. W., *The Traditional Interpretation of the Apocalypse of St John in the Ethiopian Orthodox Church* (University of Cambridge Oriental Publications 33; Cambridge: Cambridge University Press, 1983).
Cox, J. E. (ed.), *Miscellaneous Writings and Letters of Thomas Cranmer, Archbishop of Canterbury, Martyr, 1556* (Parker Society; Cambridge: Cambridge University Press, 1846).

Cranmer, T., 'v. Of good woorkes,' in *Certayne Sermons, or homelies, appoynted by the kynges Maiestie, to be declared and redde, by all persones, Vicars, or Curates, euery Sondaye in their churches, where they haue Cure* (London: Printed by Richard Grafton, July 31, 1547).

Crossley, J. G., *Reading the New Testament: Contemporary Approaches* (London and New York: Routledge, 2010).

Crossley, J. G., 'Biblioblogging, "Religion", and the Manufacturing of Catastrophe', *Bulletin for the Study of Religion* 39 (2010), 21–9.

Crossley, J. G., 'Languages, Humanities and a New Testament PhD', *Sheffield Biblical Studies* (7 September 2011), http://sheffieldbiblicalstudies.wordpress.com/2011/09/07/languages-humanities-ntphd/.

Crossley, J. G., 'More on Widening the Definition of NT Studies', *Sheffield Biblical Studies* (8 September 2011), http://sheffieldbiblicalstudies.wordpress.com/2011/09/08/more-on-widening-the-definition-of-nt-studies/.

Crossley, J. G., 'An Immodest Proposal for Biblical Studies', *Relegere* (2011), 95–116.

Crossley, J. G., 'For Every Manc a Religion: Biblical and Religious Language in the Manchester Music Scene, 1976–1994', *Biblical Interpretation* 19 (2011), 151–80.

Crossley, J. G., *Jesus in an Age of Neoliberalism: Quests, Scholarship, Ideology* (Sheffield: Equinox, 2012).

Crossley J. G. and J. Harrison, 'The Mediation of the Distinction of "Religion" and "Politics" by the UK Press on the Occasion of Pope Benedict XVI's State Visit to the UK (2010)', (forthcoming).

Crystal, D., *Begat: The King James Bible and the English Language* (Oxford: Oxford University Press, 2010).

Culler, J., *The Pursuit of Signs. Semiotics, Literature, Deconstruction* (London: Routledge, 2001).

Culpepper, R. A., *John, the Son of Zebedee: The Life of a Legend* (Edinburgh: T. & T. Clark, 2000).

Daniell, D., *The Bible in English: Its History and Influence* (New Haven: Yale University Press, 2003).

Dalton, S., 'Depeche Mode: Retrospective and Interview', *Uncut*, May 2001.

Darlow, T. H., and H. F. Moule, *Historical Catalogue of the Printed Editions in the Library of the British and Foreign Bible Society In Two Volumes, Vol. 1 – English*. (London: The Bible House, 1903).

Davies, E., *The Dissenting Reader: Feminist Approaches to the Hebrew Bible* (Aldershot and Burlington, VT: Ashgate, 2003).

Davies, P. R., *Whose Bible Is It Anyway?* (Sheffield: Sheffield Academic Press, 1995).

Dawkins, R., *The God Delusion* (London: Bantham Press, 2006).

Dawkins, R. 'Why I want all our children to read the King James Bible', *Observer* (May 19, 2012).

Debel, H., 'Greek "Variant Literary Editions" to the Hebrew Bible?', *JSJ* 41 (2010), 161–90.

De Certeau, M., *The Practice of Everyday Life* (trans. Steven Rendell; Berkeley: University of California Press, 1984).

DeLanda, M., *Intensive Science and Virtual Philosophy* (New York: Continuum, 2002).

Deleuze, G., *Cinema I: The Movement – Image* (Minneapolis: University of Minnesota Press, 1986).

Deleuze, G., *Spinoza: Practical Philosophy* (trans. Robert Hurley; San Francisco: City Light Books, 1988).

Deleuze, G., *Expressionism in Philosophy: Spinoza* (trans. M. Joughin; Cambridge, MA: MIT, 1990).
Deleuze, G., *Difference and Repetition* (trans. Paul Patton; New York: Columbia University Press, 1995).
Deleuze, G., *Desert Islands and Other Texts 1953–1974* (trans. M. Taormina; New York: Semiotext(e), 2004).
Deleuze, G., and F. Guattari, *A Thousand Plateaus. Capitalism and Schizophrenia* (London: Continuum, 2004).
Derrida, J., 'The Eyes of Language: The Abyss and the Volcano', in *Acts of Religion*, ed. Gil Anidjar (New York and London: Routledge, 2002), 191–226.
Derrida, J., and O. Coleman, 'The Other's Language: Jacques Derrida Interviews Ornette Coleman, 23 June 1997', *Genre* 36 (Summer 2004), 322–3.
Di Leila, A. 'The Textual History of Septuagint-Daniel and Theodotion-Daniel', in J.J. Collins and P.W. Flint (eds), *The Book of Daniel: Composition and Reception* (Leiden: Brill, 2001), 586–607.
Dorman L. S. and C. L. Rawlins, *Leonard Cohen, Prophet of the Heart* (London: Omnibus, 1990).
Duffy, E., *The Voices of Morebath: Reformation and Rebellion in an English Village* (New Haven: Yale University Press, 2001).
Duffy, E., *The Stripping of the Altars: Traditional Religion in England c. 1400–c. 1580* (2nd edn; New Haven and London: Yale University Press, 2005).
Dunderberg, I., 'Gnostic Interpretations of Genesis', in M. Lieb, E. Mason, J. Roberts (eds), *The Oxford Handbook of the Reception History of the Bible* (Oxford: Oxford University, 2011), 385–96.
Dunson, J. and E. Raim (eds), *Anthology of American Folk Music* (New York: Oak Publications, 1973; also available at http://towerofbabel.com/sections/music/troubadours/anthology/anthologypage73.jpg.
Durant, J., 'Innate Character in Animals and Man: A Perspective on the Origins of Ethology', in C. Webster (ed.), *Biology, Medicine and Society 1840–1940* (Cambridge: Cambridge University Press, 1981), 157–92.
Eagleton, T., *The Illusions of Postmodernism* (Oxford: Blackwell, 1996).
Eagleton, T., *Literary Theory: An Introduction* (Anniversary Edition; Minneapolis: University of Minnesota Press, 2008).
Edwards, K., *Ad Men and Eve: The Bible and Advertising* (Sheffield: Sheffield Phoenix Press, Forthcoming).
Edwards, K., *The Messiah Wears Prada: Functions of Christ-imagery in Contemporary Popular Culture* (Sheffield: Sheffield Phoenix Press, 2012).
Elliot, T. S., 'Tradition and the Individual Talent', in *The Sacred Wood: Essays on Poetry and Criticism* (1920). Available online at http://www.bartleby.com/index.html.
Emmerson, R. K. and B. McGinn (eds), *The Apocalypse in the Middle Ages* (Ithaca and London: Cornell University Press, 1992).
Epp, E. J., 'It's All About Variants: A Variant-Conscious Approach to New Testament Textual Criticism', *HTR* 100 (2007), 275–308.
Exum, J. C., *Retellings: The Bible in Literature, Music, Art and Film* (Leiden: Brill Academic Publishers 2007).
Feldman, L., *Flavius Josephus: Judean Antiquities 1–4* (Leiden: Brill, 2004).
Fish, S. E., *Is There a Text in this Class? The Authority of Interpretive Communities* (Cambridge, MA: Harvard University Press, 1980).
Fisher, A., *Radical Frontiers in the Spaghetti Western: Politics, Violence and Popular Italian Cinema* (London and New York: I.B. Tauris, 2011), 193–201.

Flusser, D., 'The Four Empires in the Fourth Sibyl and in the Book of Daniel', *Israel Oriental Studies* 2 (1972), 148–75.
Footman, T., *Leonard Cohen. Hallelujah. A New Biography* (New Malden, Surrey: Chrome Dreams, 2009).
Forster, E. M., *Maurice* (ed. P. N. Furbank; introduction and notes by D. Leavitt; London: Penguin, 2005; 1st edn, London: Edward Arnold, 1971).
Fox, M. V., 'Job 38 and God's Rhetoric', *Semeia* 19 (1981), 53–61.
Foxe, J., *Actes and Monuments*, 1570 edition, 9:1521–1522; 1576 edition, 9:1281–1282; 1583 edition, 9:1318–1319. See *The Unabridged Acts and Monuments online* or *TAMO* (HRI Online Publications, Sheffield, 2011). Available from: http://www.johnfoxe.org [accessed 1 December 2012].
Freising, O., *The Two Cities: A Chronicle of Universal History to the Year 1146 A.D.* (trans. C. Mierow; eds A. Evans, C. Knapp; New York: Columbia University, 2002 [1928]).
Freund, E., *The Return of the Reader: Reader-Response Criticism* (London & New York, NY: Methuen, 1987).
Frith, S., *Performing Rites: Evaluating Popular Music* (Oxford: Oxford University Press, 1996).
Frost, D., *Making the Liturgical Psalter. The Morpeth Lectures 1980* (Bramcote, Notts: Grove Books, 1981).
Gadamer, H-G., *Wahrheit und Methode: Grundzüge einer philosophischen Hermeneutik* (Tübingen: Mohr Verlag, 1960).
Gadamer, H-G., *Truth and Method* (second revised edition, trans. J. Weinsheimer and D. G. Marshall; London: Sheed and Ward, 1989).
Galbraith, D., 'Drawing Our Fish in the Sand: Secret Biblical Allusions in the Music of U2', *Biblical Interpretation* 19 (2011), 181–222.
Gardner, A. E., 'The "Little Horn" of Dan 7:8: Malevolent or Benign?', *Biblica* 93 (2012), 209–22.
Garofalo, R., 'How Autonomous is Relative: Popular Music, the Social Formation and Cultural Struggle', *Popular Music* 6 (1987), 77–92.
George, K., 'Cornish', in M. J. Ball and J. Fife (eds), *The Celtic Languages* (London: Routledge, 1993), 410–68.
Gillingham, S., *Psalms through the Centuries, Volume One* (Oxford: Wiley-Blackwell 2008).
Gillingham, S., 'The Reception of Psalm 137 in Jewish and Christian Traditions', in Susan Gillingham (ed.), *Conflict and Convergence. Proceedings of the Oxford Conference on Jewish and Christian Approaches to the Psalms* (Oxford: Oxford University Press, 2012), 64–82.
Gillingham, S., 'Seeing and Hearing Psalm 137', in Kristinn Ólason, et al. (eds), *Mótun menningar. Shaping Culture. FS Gunnlaugur A. Jónsson* (Reykjavík: Hið íslenska Bókmenntafélag 2012), 91–108.
Gilmour, M. J., 'Confronting Colonial Religion and the Anxiety of Influence in Louise Bernice Halfe's *Blue Marrow*', in *Feminist Theology with a Canadian Accent: Canadian Perspectives of Contextual Feminist Theology*, ed. Mary Ann Beavis, with Elaine Guillemin and Barbara Pell (Ottawa: Novalis, 2008), 371–85.
Goodman, B., 'Assured Lament: U2 sing the Psalms', *Relegere* 2/1 (2012) (http://www.relegere.org/index.php/relegere/article/view/483).
Greeley, A., 'Unsecular Europe: The Persistence of Religion', in D. Pollack and D. V. A. Olson (eds), *The Role of Religion in Modern Societies*, London: Routledge, 2008), 141–62.
Griffiths, D., 'The High Analysis of Low Music', *Music Analysis* 18 (1999), 389–435.

Griffiths, D., 'From Lyric to Anti-Lyric: Analyzing the Words in Pop Songs', in A. Moore (ed.), *Analyzing Popular Music* (Cambridge: Cambridge University Press, 2003), 39–51.
Gifford, P., 'Trajectories in African Christianity', *International Journal for the Study of the Christian Church* 8, no. 4 (2008), 275–89.
Golinkin, D., 'Do Repentence, Prayer and Tzedakah Avert the Severe Decree?', in The Schechter Institutes's online newsletter, Insight *Israel* 6 (2005), Appendix A: http://www.schechter.edu/insightisrael.aspx?id=19.
Gore, M. L., *Lays* (Nantes: Editions Normant, 2009).
Gunda, Masiiwa R., 'The Old Testament and Daily Life: Turning the Bible into a Manual for Practice. The Case of African Initiated "Apostolic" Churches in Zimbabwe', in Gunda (ed.), *From Text to Practice: The Role of the Bible in Daily Living of African People Today* (Bamberg: University of Bamberg Press, 2011), 131–56.
Gunda, Masiiwa R., 'Homosexuality and the Bible in Zimbabwe: Contested Ownership and Interpretation of an "Absolute Book"', in Joachim Kuegler and Ulrike Bechmann (eds), *Biblische Religionskritik: Kritik in, an und mit biblischen Texten – Beiträge des IBS 2007 in Vierzehnheiligen* (Münster: LIT Verlag, 2009) 76–94.
Gunda, Masiiwa R., 'A Critical Analysis of the Survival and Relevance of Post-Colonial African Initiated (Apostolic) Churches', in L. Togarasei and E. Chitando (eds), *Faith in the City: The Role and Place of Religion in Harare* (Uppsala: Universitetstryckeriet, 2010), 41–62.
Gunda, Masiiwa R., *The Bible and Homosexuality in Zimbabwe. Bible in Africa Studies 3*. (Bamberg: University of Bamberg Press, 2010).
Gunn, D. M., *Judges Through the Centuries* (Blackwell Bible Commentaries; Malden, MA: Blackwell, 2004).
Gunner, E., *The Man of Heaven and the Beautiful Ones of God: Writings from Ibandla Lamanazaretha, a South African Church* (Leiden: Brill, 2002).
Habel, N. C., *When The Purple Waters Came Again* (illustrated by Jim Roberts; London: Concordia Publishing House, 1971).
Hall, S., 'Encoding/decoding', in S. Hall, et al. (eds), *Culture, Media, Language: Working Papers in Cultural Studies, 1972–79* (London: Hutchinson, 1980), 128–38.
Harding, J. E., 'David and Jonathan between Athens and Jerusalem', *Relegere: Studies in Religion and Reception* 1 (2011), 37–92.
Harding, J. E., *The Love of David and Jonathan: Ideology, Text, Reception* (BibleWorld; Sheffield: Equinox Publishing, 2013).
Harvey, D., *The Condition of Postmodernity* (Oxford: Blackwell, 1989).
Harvey, D., *A Brief History of Neoliberalism* (Oxford: Oxford University Press, 2005).
Hasel, G., 'The Four World Empires of Daniel Against Its Near Eastern Environment', *JSOT* 12 (1979), 17–30.
Hauser A. J., and D. F. Watson (eds), *A History of Biblical Interpretation. Volume 1. The Ancient Period*, (Grand Rapids, MI: William B. Eerdmans Publishing Company, 2003).
Hauser A. J., and D. F. Watson (eds), *A History of Biblical Interpretation. Volume 2, The Medieval through Reformation Periods* (Grand Rapids, MI: William B. Eerdmans Publishing Company, 2009).
Heidegger, M., *Being and Time* (trans. Maquarrie and Robinson; Oxford: Blackwell, 1962).
Helyer, L., and R. Wagner, *Revelation for Dummies* (Hoboken, NJ: John Wiley & Sons, 2008).
Hendel R., 'Farewell to S.B.L: Faith and Reason in Biblical Studies', *Biblical Archaeology Review* 36, no. 4 (July/August 2010), 28–29.
Hentoff, H., 'Duke Ellington's Mission', *Jazz Times* (May 1999), 218.

Herbert, A. S., *Historical Catalogue of Printed Editions of The English Bible 1525–1961 Revised and Expanded from the Edition of T. H. Darlow and H. F. Moule, 1903* (London: The British and Foreign Bible Society, 1968).

Hexham, I., and G. C. Oosthuizen (eds), *The Story of Isaiah Shembe: History and Traditions Centered on Ekuphakameni and Mount Nhlangakazi*. Volume 1, Sacred History and Traditions of the Amanazaretha. (Lewiston: The Edwin Mellen Press, 1996), 224–8.

Himmelfarb, M., 'The Temple and the Garden of Eden in Ezekiel, the Book of the Watchers, and the Wisdom of Ben Sira', in J. Scott and P. Simpson-Housley (eds), *Sacred Places and Profane Spaces: Essays in the Geographies of Judaism, Christianity, and Islam* (Westport, CT: Greenwood Press, 1991), 63–78.

Hoad, N., *African Intimacies: Race, Homosexuality and Globalisation* (Minneapolis: University of Minnesota Press, 2007).

Hobsbawm, E., *The Communist Manifesto: A Modern Edition* (Verso Books, 1998).

Hogan, K. M., *Theologies in Conflict in 4 Ezra: Wisdom, Debate, and Apocalyptic Solution* (Leiden: Brill, 2008).

Hoffman, L. A., 'Un'taneh Tokef as Poetry and Legend,' in L. A. Hoffman (ed.), *Who By Fire, Who By Water* (Woodstock, Vermont: Jewish Lights, 2010), 13–24.

Hoffman L. A., 'The Legend of Rabbi Amnon', in L. A. Hoffman (ed.), *Who By Fire, Who By Water* (Woodstock, Vermont: Jewish Lights, 2010), 26–8.

Hoffman, J. M., (trans.), 'Behind the Translation', in L. A. Hoffman (ed.), *Who By Fire, Who By Water – Un'taneh tokef* (Woodstock, VT: Jewish Lights, 2010), 33–48.

Holub, R. C., *Reception Theory: A Critical Introduction* (London & New York, NY: Methuen, 1984).

Horn, F. W., 'Johannes auf Patmos', in *Studien zur Johannesoffenbarung und ihrer Auslegung. Festschrift für Otto Böcher zum 70. Geburtstag*, ed. Friedrich Wilhelm Horn and Michael Wolter (Neukirchen-Vluyn: Neukirchener Verlag, 2005), 139–59.

How, A., ' "That's Classic!" A Gadamerian defence of the classic text in sociology', *The Sociological Review* (1998), 828–48.

Howard, J. R., and J. M. Streck, *Apostles of Rock: The Splintered World of Contemporary Christian Music* (Lexington: University Press of Kentucky, 1999).

Hoy, D., *The Critical Circle: Literature, History, and Philosophical Hermeneutics* (Berkley, CA: University of California Press, 1978).

Hunter, E. J., *Classification Made Simple: An Introduction to Knowledge Organisation and Information Retrieval* (Farnham: Ashgate, 2009).

Hunter, M., *Love in the Time of AIDS: Inequality, Gender, and Rights in South Africa* (Pietermaritzburg: University of KwaZulu-Natal Press, 2010).

Hurtado, L. W., 'New Testament Studies at the Turn of the Millennium: Questions for the Discipline', *Scottish Journal of Theology* 52 (1999), 158–78.

Hurtado, L. W., 'Tools of the Trade,' *Larry Hurtado's Blog* (4 September 2011), (http://larryhurtado.wordpress.com/2011/09/04/tools-of-the-trade/).

Hurtado, L. W., 'Tools of the Trade . . . Encore', *Larry Hurtado's Blog* (5 September 2011), (http://larryhurtado.wordpress.com/2011/09/05/tools-of-the-trade-encore/).

Hurtado, L. W., 'Languages, Theories, Approaches', *Larry Hurtado's Blog* (8 September 2011), (http://larryhurtado.wordpress.com/2011/09/08/languages-theories-approaches/).

Hurtado, L. W., 'The UK PhD: Structure and Pressures', (http://larryhurtado.wordpress.com/2011/09/10/the-uk-phd-structure-and-pressures/).

Hurtado, L. W., 'NT Research Languages: Encore', (http://larryhurtado.wordpress.com/2011/09/27/nt-research-languages-encore/).

Hurtado, L. W., 'On Diversity, Competence and Coherence in New Testament Studies: A Modest Response to Crossley's "Immodest Proposal"', *Relegere* 2 (2012), 353–64.
Hyder, R., *Brimful of Asia: Negotiating Ethnicity on the UK Music Scene* (Aldershot: Ashgate, 2004).
Hyman, T., *Sienese Painting: The Art of the City-Republic (1278–1477)* (London: Thames & Hudson, 2003).
IBaible. *Ibaible Eli Ingcwele* (Cape Town: Bible Society of South Africa, 1893. Reprint, 1974).
Idelsohn, A. Z., *Jewish Liturgy and Its Development* (New York: Dover Publications [replication of 1st edition 1932, New York: Henry Holt]).
Inge, J., *A Christian Theology of Place* (Aldershot: Ashgate, 2003).
Iser, W., *The Act of Reading: A Theory of Aesthetic Response* (Baltimore, MD: Johns Hopkins University Press, 1978).
Jacobs, M., 'An Ex-Sabbatean's Remorse? Sambari's Polemics against Islam', *JQR* 97 (2007), 347–78.
Jacobson, D. C., *Creator, Are You Listening? Israeli Poets on God and Prayer* (Bloomington and Indianapolis: Indiana University Press, 2007).
Jameson, F., *The Political Unconscious: Narrative as a Socially Symbolic Act* (Ithaca: Cornell University Press, 1981).
Jameson, F., *Postmodernism, or, The Cultural Logic of Late Capitalism* (London and New York, 1991).
Jauss, H. R., *Towards An Aesthetic of Reception* (trans. Bahti; Minneapolis: University of Minnesota Press, 1982).
Jones, C., 'Elvis Presley's Bible Sells for £59,000', *The Guardian* (London), 8 September 2012.
Kairos, the theologians. *Challenge to the Church: The Kairos Document: A Theological Comment on the Political Crisis in South Africa* (Braamfontein: The Kairos theologians, 1985).
Karton-Blum, R., *Profane Scriptures: Reflections on the Dialogue with the Bible in Modern Hebrew Poetry* (Cincinnati: Hebrew Union College Press, 1999).
Kearney, J., *The Incarnate Text: Imagining the Book in Reformation England* (Philadelphia: University of Pennsylvania Press, 2009).
Kennett, C., 'Is Anyone Listening?', in A. Moore (ed.), *Analyzing Popular Music* (Cambridge: Cambridge University Press, 2003), 196–217.
Kitchen, K. A., and P. J. N. Lawrence, *Treaty, Law and Covenant in the Ancient Near East* (3 vols; Wiesbaden: Harrassowitz Verlag, 2012).
Klancher, N. 'A Genealogy of Reception History', *Biblical Interpretation* 21 (2013), 99–129.
Klein, N., *The Shock Doctrine: The Rise of Disaster Capitalism* (London: Allen Lane, 2007).
Klint, S., 2000. 'After Story – a Return to History? Introducing Reception Criticism as an Exegetical Approach', *Studia Theologica – Nordic Journal of Theology* 54/2, 87–106.
Knight D. A., and A.-J. Levine, *The Meaning of the Bible: What the Jewish Scriptures and Christian Old Testament can teach us* (New York: HarperCollins, 2011).
Koch, K., *Europa, Rom und der Kaiser vor dem Hintergrund von zwei Jahrtausenden Rezeption des Buches Daniel* (Göttingen: Vandenhoeck & Ruprecht, 1997).
Kosman, A., 'Mayim einam yekholim lahazor biteshuvah: he'arah al megillat Amichai,' *Haaretz* 20 October 2000.
Kovacs, J., and C. Rowland, *Revelation* (Blackwell Bible Commentary; Malden MA, Oxford, and Carlton, Victoria: Blackwell, 2004).

Kraft, H., *Die Offenbarung des Johannes* (HNT 16a; Tübingen: J. C. B. Mohr (Paul Siebeck), 1974).
Kratz, R., 'Reich Gottes und Gesetz im Danielbuch und im werdenden Judentum', in A. van der Woude (ed.), *The Book of Daniel in the Light of New Findings* (Leuven: Leuven University Press, 1993), 435–79.
Kreitzer, L. J., *The Old Testament in Fiction and Film: On Reversing the Hermeneutical Flow* (Sheffield: Sheffield Academic Press, 1993).
Kreitzer, L. J., *The New Testament in Fiction and Film: On Reversing the Hermeneutical Flow* (Sheffield: Sheffield Academic Press, 1993).
Kreitzer, L. J., *Pauline Images in Fiction and Film: On Reversing the Hermeneutical Flow* (Sheffield: Sheffield Academic Press, 1999).
Kreitzer, L. J., *Gospel Images in Fiction and Film: On Reversing the Hermeneutical Flow* (New York, NY: Continuum, 2002).
Kronfeld, C., *On the Margins of Modernism: Decentring Literary Dynamics* (Berkeley and Oxford: University of California Press, 1996).
Lang, B., *Joseph in Egypt: A Cultural Icon from Grotius to Goethe* (New Haven: Yale University Press, 2009).
Langston, S. M., 'The Exodus in American History and Culture', *Teaching the Bible: An E-Newsletter for Public school teachers by Society of Biblical Literature* (2010) available online www.sbl-site.org/assets/pdfs/TB6_Exodus_SL.pdf [accessed 13 August 2012].
Lawson, D., 'Pope Benedict . . . an apology', *Independent* (21 September 2010), http://www.independent.co.uk/opinion/commentators/dominic-lawson/dominic-lawson-pope-benedict-an-apology-2084788.html.
Lehner, P., *Handbook of Ethological Methods* (2nd edn; Cambridge: Cambridge University, 1996).
Lenin, V. I., Проект и объяснение программы социал-демократической партии. Декабрь, позднее 9 (21), 1895 г.; июнь–июль 1896 г. *Polnoe sobranie sochinenii* [The Complete Collected Works]. 5th edition, Volume 2 (Moskva: Izdatel'stvo politicheskoi literatury, 1958–65 [1895]).
Lenin, V. I., Материалы к выработке программы РСДРП. Январь–апрель 1902 г. *Polnoe sobranie sochinenii* [The Complete Collected Works]. 5th edition, Volume 6 (Moskva: Izdatel'stvo politicheskoi literatury, 1958–65 [1902]).
Lenin, V. I., Социал-демократия и временное революционное правительство. 23 и 30 марта (5 и 12 апреля) 1905 г. *Polnoe sobranie sochinenii* [The Complete Collected Works]. 5th edition, Volume 10 (Moskva: Izdatel'stvo politicheskoi literatury, 1958–65 [1905]).
Lenin, V. I., О реорганизации партии. 10–16 (23–29) ноября 1905 г. *Polnoe sobranie sochinenii* [The Complete Collected Works]. 5th edition, Volume 12 (Moskva: Izdatel'stvo politicheskoi literatury, 1958–65 [1905]).
Lenin, V. I., Анкета для перерегистрации членов московской организации РКП(б). 17 сентября 1920 г. *Polnoe sobranie sochinenii* [The Complete Collected Works]. 5th edition, Volume 41 (Moskva: Izdatel'stvo politicheskoi literatury, 1958–65 [1920]).
Lenin, V. I., Личная анкета. Для делегатов Всероссийской партийной конференции РКП большевиков. 20 сентября 1920 г. *Polnoe sobranie sochinenii* [The Complete Collected Works]. 5th edition, Volume 41 (Moskva: Izdatel'stvo politicheskoi literatury, 1958–65 [1920]).
Lenin, V. I., II конгресс Коммунистического Интернационала 19 июля–7 августа 1920. г. *Polnoe sobranie sochinenii* [The Complete Collected Works]. 5th edition, Volume 41 (Moskva: Izdatel'stvo politicheskoi literatury, 1958–65 [1920]).

Lenin, V. I., В. А. Смольянинову. 23 сентября 1922 г. *Polnoe sobranie sochinenii* [The Complete Collected Works]. 5th edition, Volume 54 (Moskva: Izdatel'stvo politicheskoi literatury, 1958-65 [1922]).
Lenin, V. I., 'Draft and Explanation of a Programme for the Social-Democratic Party', *Collected Works*, Volume 2 (Moscow: Progress, 1960-72 [1895]).
Lenin, V. I., 'Material for the Preparation of the Programme of the R.S.D.L.P.', *Collected Works*, Volume 6 (Moscow: Progress, 1960-72 [1902]).
Lenin, V. I., 'Social-Democracy and the Provisional Revolutionary Government', *Collected Works*, Volume 8 (Moscow: Progress, 1960-72 [1905]).
Lenin, V. I., 'The Reorganisation of the Party', *Collected Works*, Volume 10 (Moscow: Progress, 1960-72 [1905]).
Lenin, V. I., 'The Second Congress of the Communist International, July 19-August 7, 1920', *Collected Works*, Volume 31 (Moscow: Progress, 1960-72 [1920]).
Lenin, V. I., 'Reregistration Form for Members of the Moscow Organisation of the R.C.P. (B.)', *Collected Works*, Volume 42 (Moscow: Progress, 1960-72 [1920]).
Lenin, V. I., 'Questionnaire for Delegates of the Ninth All-Russia Conference of the R.C.P. (Bolsheviks)', *Collected Works*, Volume 42 (Moscow: Progress, 1960-72 [1920]).
Lenin, V. I., 'To V.A. Smolyaninov, September 23, 1922', *Collected Works*, Volume 45 (Moscow: Progress, 1960-72 [1922]).
Lievore, P. (ed.), *Padua: Baptistery of the Cathedral. Frescoes by Giusto de' Menabuoi (XIV c.)*. (2nd edn; Padua: Deganello, 1994).
Lewis, L. A. (ed.), *The Adoring Audience: Fan Culture and Popular Media* (London: Routledge, 1992).
Lubbock, J., *Storytelling in Christian Art from Giotto to Donatello* (New Haven: Yale University Press, 2006).
Lunacharsky, A. V., *Religiia i Socializm: Tom 1* (Moscow: Shilovnik, 1908).
Lunacharsky, A. V., *Religiia i Socializm: Tom 2* (Moscow: Shilovnik, 1911).
Lust, J., 'Daniel 7:13 and the Septuagint', *ETL* 54 (1978), 62-9.
Luz, U., *Matthew 1-7: A Commentary* (trans. Wilhelm C. Linss; Edinburgh: T. & T. Clark, 1989).
Lyons, W. J., 'The Apocalypse According to Johnny Cash: Examining the "Effect" of the Book of Revelation on a Contemporary Apocalyptic Writer', in W. J. Lyons and J. Økland (eds), *The Way the World Ends? The Apocalypse of John in Culture and Ideology* (Sheffield: Sheffield Phoenix Press, 2009), 95-122.
Lyons, W. J., 'Hope for a Troubled Discipline? Contributions to New Testament Studies from Reception History', *Journal for the Study of the New Testament* 33 (2010), 207-20.
Lyons, W. J., and J. Økland (eds), *The Way the World Ends? The Apocalypse of John in Culture and Ideology* (Sheffield: Sheffield Phoenix Press, 2009).
Malins, S., *Depeche Mode: Black Celebration: A Biography* (London: Andre Deutsch, 2006).
Mein A., and P. Joyce (eds), *After Ezekiel: Essays on the Reception of a Difficult Prophet* (London and New York: T & T Clark International, 2010).
Miller, J., *Stripped: Depeche Mode* (Updated edition; London: Omnibus Press, 2008).
Montefiore, S. S., *Stalin: 1979-1939* (London: Phoenix, 2004).
Moyise, S., *The Old Testament in the Book of Revelation* (Sheffield: Sheffield Academic Press, 1995).
MacCulloch, D., *Tudor Church Militant: Edward VI and the Protestant Reformation* (London: Penguin, 1999).
Mack, B., *Christian Mentality: The Entanglements of Power, Violence, and Fear* (London: Equinox, 2011).

Mackenzie, C. G., 'The University of Rhodesia: A Re-appraisal', *Journal of Educational Administration and History* 19/2 (1987), 62–71.

Mackenzie, H. F., 'Panels by Giovanni di Paolo of Siena (1403–1483) Showing Scenes from the Life of St. John the Baptist', in *Bulletin of the Art Institute of Chicago* 32 (1938).

Marcus, I. G., 'A Pious Community and Doubt: Jewish Martyrdom among Northern European Jewry and the Story of Rabbi Amnon of Mainz', in *Essays in Hebrew Literature in Honour of Avraham Holtz* (ed. Zvia Ben-Yosef Ginor; New York: Jewish Theological Seminary of America, 2003), 21–46.

Marshall, L., 'The Sociology of Popular Music, Interdisciplinarity and Aesthetic Autonomy', *British Journal of Sociology* 62 (2011), 154–74.

Martin, C., *Masking Hegemony: A Genealogy of Liberalism, Religion and the Private Sphere* (London and Oakville: Equinox, 2010).

Martin, D., *A General Theory of Secularization* (Oxford: Blackwell, 1978).

Martin, G., *Multiple Originals: New Approaches to Hebrew Bible Textual Criticism* (Atlanta: Society of Biblical Literature, 2010).

Maxwell, A. S., *Uncle Arthur's Bible Stories (Vol.1)* (Watford: The Stanborough Press Ltd, [c.1949]).

Mayeski, M. A., 'Early Medieval Exegesis: Gregory I to the Twelfth Century', in A. J. Hauser and D. F. Watson (eds), *A History of Biblical Interpretation. Volume 2: The Medieval through the Reformation Periods* (Grand Rapids and Cambridge: Eerdmans, 2009), 86–112.

Mbiti, J. S., *Bible and Theology in African Christianity* (Nairobi: Oxford University Press, 1986).

McCarter, P. K., *I Samuel: A New Translation with Introduction and Commentary* (AB 8; New York: Doubleday, 1980).

McCarter, P. K., *II Samuel: A New Translation with Introduction and Commentary* (AB 9; New York: Doubleday, 1984).

McCarter, P. K., *Textual Criticism: Recovering the Text of the Hebrew Bible* (Minneapolis: Fortress Press, 1986).

McCormack, J., *Listen, Jesus, They're Playing our Song: A Sociological Study of Worship Music in Melbourne's Megachurches* (PhD dissertation, Melbourne: Monash University, 2009).

McCutcheon, R. T., *Religion and the Domestication of Dissent: or, How to live in a less than perfect nation* (London & Oakville: Equinox, 2005).

McGrath J. F., 'Biblioblogging Our Matrix: Exploring the Potential and Perplexities of Academic Blogging', *Bulletin for the Study of Religion* 39 (2010), 14–25.

McGrath, J., 'Essential Languages for New Testament Study?', http://www.patheos.com/blogs/exploringourmatrix/2011/09/essential-languages-and-tools-for-new-testament-study.html.

McLay, R. T., 'The Old Greek Translation of Daniel iv-vi and the Formation of the Book of Daniel', *VT* 55 (2005), 318–22.

McPherson, T., 'Introduction: Media Studies and the Digital Humanities', *Cinema Journal* 48 (2009), 119–23.

Meiden, W. van der, *'Zoo heerlijk eenvoudig': Geschiedenis van de Kinderbijbel in Nederland* (Hilversum: Verloren, 2009).

Meiss, M., 'A New Panel by Giovanni de Paolo from his Altar-piece of the Baptist', in *The Burlington Magazine* 851, vol. 116, Feb. 1974.

Middleton, R., *Studying popular music* (Milton Keynes: Open University Press, 1990).

Miller, J., 'The Redaction of Daniel', *JSOT* 52 (1991), 115–24.

Midrash Rabba. Genesis in Two Volumes (trans. Rabbi Dr H. Freedman and Maurice Simon, 10 vols; London: Soncino Press).

Mirowski, P., and D. Plehwe (eds), *The Road from Mont Pelerin: The Making of the Neoliberal Thought Collective* (Cambridge, MA: Harvard University Press, 2009).

Moberg, M., 'Religion in Popular Music or Popular Music as Religion?', *Popular Music & Society* 35 (2012), 113–30.

Moberly, R. W. L., *The Theology of the Book of Genesis* (Cambridge: Cambridge University Press, 2009).

Montaner, L. V., 'Major Theoretical Issues from Two Decades of Bible and Computer Conferences', in L. V. Montaner, G. S. de los Rios-Zarzosa, and J. del Barco (eds), *Computer Assisted Research on the Bible in the 21st Century* (Piscataway, NJ: Gorgias Press, 2010), 3–11.

Moore, C. A., 'A Greek Witness to a Different Text of Esther', *ZAW* 79 (1967), 351–8.

Moore, S. D., and Y. Sherwood, *The Invention of the Biblical Scholar: A Critical Manifesto* (Minneapolis: Fortress, 2011).

Morgan, R., 'Sachkritik in Reception History', *Journal for the Study of the New Testament* 33/2, (2010), 175–90.

Morris, P., and D. Sawyer (eds), *A Walk in the Garden. Biblical, Iconographical and Literary Images of Eden* (Sheffield: JSOT Press, 1992).

Muggleton, D., and R. Weinzierl (eds), *The Post-Subcultures Reader* (Oxford: Berg, 2003).

Muller, C. A., *Rituals of Fertility and the Sacrifice of Desire: Nazarite Women's Performance in South Africa* (Chicago and London: The University of Chicago Press, 1999).

Murdoch, B., *Cornish Literature* (Cambridge: D. S. Brewer, 1993).

Museka, G., 'Exorcising the Colonial Jinx: Towards reconciling Diversity and Pedagogy in Zimbabwe's Religious Education Curriculum', *The Journal of Pan African Studies* 5/1 (2012), 55–68.

Nadel, I. B., *Various Positions: A Life of Leonard Cohen* (New York: Random House, 1996).

Napier, J., *A Plaine Discouery of the whole Reuelation of Sainct Iohn* (Edinburgh: Robert Waldegraue, 1593).

Neusner, J., *Theological Dictionary of Rabbinic Judaism. Part One. Principal Theological Categories. Studies in Judaism* (Lanham, MD, 2005).

Newsom, C., *The Book of Job: A Contest of Moral Imaginations* (Oxford: Oxford University Press, 2003).

Nicolaides A., 'Early Portuguese Imperialism: Using the Jesuits in the Mutapa Empire of Zimbabwe', *International Journal of Peace and Development Studies* Vol. 2/4, (2011) 132–7.

Norris, R. A. (trans.), *Gregory of Nyssa: Homilies on the Song of Songs* (Writings from the Greco-Roman World 13; Atlanta, GA: Society of Biblical Literature, 2012).

Oegema, G. S., *Early Judaism and Modern Culture: Literature and Theology* (Grand Rapids: Eerdmans, 2011).

O'Kane, M., and J. Morgan-Guy (eds), *Biblical Art from Wales* (Sheffield: Sheffield Phoenix Press, 2010).

Oecumenius, *Commentary on the Apocalypse* (trans. John N. Suggitt; The Fathers of the Church; Washington, DC: Catholic University of America Press, 2006).

Økland, J., 'The Spectre Revealed and Made Manifest: The Book of Revelation in the Writings of Karl Marx and Friedrich Engels', in W. J. Lyons & J. Økland (eds), *The Way the World Ends? The Apocalypse of John in Culture and Ideology* (Sheffield: Sheffield Phoenix Press, 2009), 267–88.

Orr, W., *Ark in the Park* (illus. Kerry Millard; Sevenoaks: Chart Books, 1996).

Papini, R. and Irving Hexham (eds), *The Catechism of the Nazarites and Related Writings* Volume 4. (Lewiston: The Edwin Mellen Press, 2002).
Parker, D. C., *The Living Text of the Gospels* (Cambridge: Cambridge University Press, 1997).
Parker, P., 'Preposterous Events', *Shakespeare Quarterly* 43 (1992), 186–213.
Patte, D. M., *The Global Bible Commentary* (Nashville, TN: Abingdon Press, 2004).
Platvoet, J., 'The institutional environment of the study of religions in Africa south of the Sahara', in Michael Pye (ed.), *Marburg Revisited: Institutions and Strategies in the Study of Religion* (Marburg: Diagnoal Verlag, 1989), 107–26.
Plehwe, D., B. J. A. Walpen and G. Neunhoffer (eds), *Neoliberal Hegemony: A Global Critique* (London: Routledge, 2007).
Pope-Hennessy, J., *Giovanni di Paolo 1403–1483* (New York: Oxford University Press, 1938).
Pope-Hennessy, J., 'Giovanni di Paolo,' in *The Metropolitan Museum of Art Bulletin* 46/2 (1988), 6–46.
Popović, M., '4Q186. 4QZodiacal Physiognomy. A Full Edition', in G. J. Brooke and J. Høgenhaven (eds), *The Mermaid and the Partridge: Essays from the Copenhagen Conference on Revising Texts from Cave Four* (Studies on the Texts of the Desert of Judah 96; Leiden: Brill, 2011), 221–58.
Poswick, R. F., 'From Louvain-La-Neuve (1985) to El Escorial in Madrid (2008): 25 Years of AIBI', in L.V. Montaner, G. S. de los Rios-Zarzosa, and J. del Barco (eds), *Computer Assisted Research on the Bible in the 21st Century* (Piscataway, NJ: Gorgias Press, 2010), 3–11.
Powell, M. A., *Encyclopedia of Contemporary Christian Music* (Peabody, MS: Hendrickson, 2002).
Presley, P., *Elvis & Me* (London: Century, 1985).
Punt, J., 'Using the Bible in post-apartheid South Africa: Its influence and impact amidst the gay debate', *HTS Theological Studies 62/3* (2006), 885–907.
Pyper, H. S., *An Unsuitable Book: The Bible as Scandalous Text* (Sheffield: Sheffield Phoenix Press, 2006).
Pyper, H. S., *The Unchained Bible: Cultural Appropriations of Biblical Texts* (T&T Clark, 2012).
Pyper, H. S., 'Wrestling the Bible', *SBL Forum* (July 2006), http://sbl-site.org/Article.aspx?ArticleID=569.
Räisänen, H., 'Revelation, Violence, and War: Glimpses of a Dark Side', in W. J. Lyons and J. Økland (eds), *The Way the World Ends? The Apocalypse of John in Culture and Ideology* (Sheffield: Sheffield Phoenix Press, 2009), 151–85.
Randall, R., and K. Jewitt, *My Bible Activity Book* (illus. R. Elliott; Bath: Parragon, 2006).
Ratcliffe, M., *Leonard Cohen: The Music and the Mystique* (London: Omnibus, 2012).
Redhead, S., et al. (eds), *The Clubcultures Reader* (Oxford: Blackwell, 1998).
Repphun, E. et al. 'Editors' Introduction; Beyond Christianity, the Bible, and the Text: Urgent Tasks and New Orientations for Reception History'. *Relegere: Studies in Religion and Reception 1/1*, (2011) 1–11.
Repphun, E., 'Review of Philip Culbertson and Elaine M. Wainwright, eds, *The Bible in/and Popular Culture*', *The Bible and Critical Theory* 8 (2012), 95–7.
Reventlow, H. G., *Epochen der Bibelauslegung* (Bände 1–4) (München: Verlag C.H. Beck oHG, 1990–2001), trans. Leo G. Perdue and James O. Duke, *History of Biblical Interpretation* (4 Volumes) (Atlanta, GA: SBL 2009–10).
Richard, P., 'El pueblo de Dios contra el imperio. Daniel 7 en su contexto literario e histórico', *RIBLA* 7 (1990), 25–46.

Ricoeur, P., *The Conflicts of Interpretation: Essays in Hermeneutics* (trans. Domingo et al.; Evanston, IL: Northwestern University Press, 1974).
Robar, E., 'The Hexapla Project: Traditional Scholarship Meets Modern Technology', in L. V. Montaner, G. S. de los Rios-Zarzosa, and J. del Barco (eds), *Computer Assisted Research on the Bible in the 21st Century* (Piscataway, NJ: Gorgias Press, 2010).
Roberts, J., 'Introduction' in Michael Lieb et al. (eds), *The Oxford Handbook of the Reception History of the Bible* (Oxford: Oxford University Press, 2011), 1–8.
Robertson, J., *The Ladybird Bible Storybook* (illus. A. Parry; Loughborough: Ladybird Books, 1983).
Rochberg, F., *The Heavenly Writing: Divination, Horoscopy, and Astronomy in Mesopotamian Culture* (Cambridge: Cambridge University Press, 2004).
Rollston, C. 'The Marginalization of Women: A Biblical Value We Don't Like to Talk About', 31 August 2012, http://www.huffingtonpost.com/christopher-rollston/the-marginalization-of-women-biblical-value-we-dont-like-to-talk-about_b_1833648.html.
Rooke, D., *Handel's Israelite Oratorio Libretti: Sacred Drama and Biblical Exegesis* (Oxford: Oxford University Press, 2012).
Rosen, A., 'True Lights. Seeing the Psalms through Chagall's Church Windows', in Susan Gillingham (ed.), *Conflict and Convergence. Proceedings of the Oxford Conference on Jewish and Christian Approaches to the Psalms* (Oxford: Oxford University Press, 2013).
Rosenberg, I. M., and Y. L. Rosenberg, 'Of God's Mercy and the Four Biblical Methods of Capital Punishment: Stoning, Burning, Beheading and Strangulation', *Tulane Law Review* 78 (2003), 1169–1212.
Rosner F., (ed. and trans.) *Maimonides' Commentary on the Mishnah: Tractate Sanhedrin* (New York: Sepher Hermon Press, 1981).
Rowland, C., *Radical Christianity: A Reading of Recovery* (Cambridge: Polity, 1988).
Rowland, C., 'Imagining the Apocalypse', *NTS* 51 (2005), 303–27.
Rowland, C. (ed.), *The Cambridge Companion to Liberation Theology* (2nd edn; Cambridge: Cambridge University Press, 2007).
Rowland, C., 'The Interdisciplinary Colloquium on the Book of Revelation and Effective History', in W. J. Lyons and J. Økland (eds), *The Way the World Ends? The Apocalypse of John in Culture and Ideology* (Sheffield: Sheffield Phoenix Press, 2009), 289–304.
Rowland, C., *Blake and the Bible* (New Haven: Yale University Press, 2011).
Rowland, C. and M. Corner, *Liberating Exegesis: The Challenge of Liberation Theology to Biblical Studies* (Louisville, KY: Westminster John Knox Press, 2002).
Rowland, C., and J. Roberts, *The Bible for Sinners. Interpretation in the Present Time* (London: SPCK, 2008).
Rowley, H. H., *Darius the Mede and the Four World Empires in the Book of Daniel: A Historical Study of Contemporary Theories* (Cardiff: University of Wales, 1935).
Sachs, A., 'Babylonian Horoscopes', *Journal of Cuneiform Studies* 6 (1952), 65–75.
Saebø, M. (ed.), *Hebrew Bible Old Testament. The History of Its Interpretation*, I/1: *Antiquity*, (Göttingen, Vandenhoeck & Ruprecht, 1996); I/2: *The Middle Ages* (Göttingen, Vandenhoeck & Ruprecht, 2000); II: *From the Renaissance to the Enlightenment* (Göttingen, Vandenhoeck & Ruprecht, 2008).
Saffrey, H. D., 'Relire l'Apocalypse à Patmos', *RB* 82 (1975), 385–417.
Sample, T., *White Soul: Country Music, the Church and Working Americans* (Nashville: Abingdon Press, 1996).
Sample, T., *Blue Collar Resistance and the Politics of Jesus* (Nashville: Abingdon Press, 2006).

Sample, T., '"Help Me Make it Through the Night": Narrating Class and Country Music in the Theology of Paul', in P. Culbertson and E. M. Wainwright, eds, *The Bible in/and Popular Culture* (Atlanta, GA: SBL, 2010), 111–25.

Sangyil Park, *Korean Preaching, Han, and Narrative* (New York: Peter Lang, 2008).

Sawyer, J. F. A., *The Fifth Gospel: Isaiah in the History of Christianity* (Cambridge: Cambridge University Press, 1996).

Sawyer, J. F. A., *Sacred Language and Sacred Texts* (London: Routledge, 1999).

Sawyer, J. F. A, *A Concise Dictionary of the Bible and its Reception* (Louisville, KY: Westminster John Knox Press, 2009).

Schellekens, J., 'Accession Days and Holidays: The Origins of the Jewish Festival of Purim', *JBL* 128 (2009), 115–34.

Schmelzer, M., 'Penitence, Prayer and (Charity?)', in M. Brettler and M. Fishbane (eds), *Minhiiiah le-Nahiiium: Biblical and Other Studies Presented to Nahum M. Sarna in Honour of his 70th Birthday* (Sheffield: Sheffield Academic Press, 1993), 291–9.

Schreibman, S., R. Siemens, and J. Unsworth (eds), *A Companion to Digital Humanities* (Oxford: Blackwell, 2004).

Schrijver, E. G. L., 'Some light on the Amsterdam and London manuscripts of Isaac Ben Moses of Vienna's Or Zarua', *Bulletin of the John Rylands University Library* 75 (1993), 53–82.

Scobie, S., *Leonard Cohen* (Vancouver: Douglas and McIntyre, 1978).

Segal, E., *The Babylonian Esther Midrash: A Critical Commentary, Volume 1: To the End of Esther Chapter 1* (Atlanta: Scholars Press, 1994).

Seow, C. L., *Daniel* (Louisville: Westminster John Knox, 2003).

Seraphim Rose, *Genesis, Creation, and Early Man: The Orthodox Christian Vision* (2nd edn; ed. Hieromonk Damascene; Platina, CA: St Herman of Alaska Brotherhood, 2011).

Sheehan, J., *The Enlightenment Bible: Translation, Scholarship, Culture* (Princeton, NJ: Princeton University Press, 2004).

Sheldrake, P., *Spaces for the Sacred: Place, Memory and Identity* (London: SCM, 2001).

Sherwood, Y., *A Biblical Text and Its Afterlives: The Survival of Jonah in Western Culture* (Cambridge: Cambridge University Press, 2000).

Sherwood, Y., 'Bush's Bible as a Liberal Bible (Strange though that Might Seem)', *Postscripts* 2 (2006), 47–58.

Simmons, S., *I'm Your Man: The Life of Leonard Cohen* (London: Jonathan Cape, 2012).

Simpson, J., *Burning to Read: English Fundamentalism and its Reformation Opponents* (Cambridge, MA: Belknap, 2007).

Sithole, N., *Obed Mutezo: The Mudzimu, Christian Nationalist* (Nairobi: Oxford University Press, 1970).

Sithole, N., 'Sithole Reading West Reading Shembe Reading Judges 11', Pietermaritzburg, 2008 (Unpublished paper).

Sithole, N., 'Performance, Power and Agency: Isaiah Shembe's Hymns and the Sacred Dance in the Church of the Nazarites', University of KwaZulu-Natal, 2010 (Unpublished PhD thesis).

Smith, D., 'This Isn't Kindergarten', http://www.telecomtally.com/this-isnt-kindergarten/.

Smith, D., 'The Backyard Of Biblical Studies', http://www.telecomtally.com/the-backyard-of-biblical-studies/.

Soncino Babylonian Talmud. 18 vols (v. Shabbat) (ed. I. Epstein; London: Soncino, 1961).

Sperberg-McQueen, C. M., 'Classification and Its Structures', in S. Schreibman, R. Siemens, and J. Unsworth (eds), *A Companion to Digital Humanities* (Oxford: Blackwell, 2004), http://www.digitalhumanities.org/companion.

Staiger, J., *Interpreting Films: Studies in the Historical Reception of American Cinema* (Princeton, NJ: Princeton University Press, 1992).
Stern, S., 'The Talmud Yerushalmi', in P. S. Alexander and M. Goodman (eds), *Rabbinic Texts and the History of Late-Roman Palestine*. (Proceedings of the British Academy 165. London: British Academy, 2010), 143-64.
Stocker, M., *Judith, Sexual Warrior: Women and Power in Western Culture* (New Haven: Yale University Press, 1998).
Sugirtharajah, R. S., 'Loitering with Intent: Biblical Texts in Public Places', *Bib. Interpretation* 11 (2001), 567-78.
Sugirtharajah, R. S., *The Bible and the Third World: Precolonial, Colonial and Postcolonial Encounters* (Cambridge: Cambridge University Press, 2001).
Suleiman, S. R., and I. Crosman (eds), *The Reader in the Text: Essay on Audience and Interpretation* (Princeton, NJ: Princeton University Press, 1980).
Swain, J. W., 'The Theory of the Four Monarchies: Opposition History under the Roman Empire', *Classical Philology* 35 (1940), 1-21.
Sweet, J., *Revelation* (London: SCM Press, 1990).
Swete, H. B., *The Apocalypse of St John* (London: Macmillan, 1906).
Svensson, P., 'The Landscape of Digital Humanities', *Digital Humanities Quarterly*. 4.1. (2010), http://digitalhumanities.org/dhq/vol/4/1/000080/000080.html.
Talmon, S., 'Textual Criticism: The Ancient Versions', in A. D. H. Mayes (ed.), *Text in Context: Essays By Members of the Society for Old Testament Study* (Oxford: Oxford University Press, 2000), 141-70.
Taylor, R., *The Peshiṭta of Daniel* (Leiden: Brill, 1994).
Thiselton, A. C., *Hermeneutics: An Introduction* (Grand Rapids, MI: Eerdmans, 2009).
Thiselton, A., *1 & 2 Thessalonians: Through the Centuries* (Blackwell Bible Commentaries; Oxford: Wiley-Blackwell, 2011).
Thompson, L. L., *The Book of Revelation: Apocalypse and Empire* (New York and Oxford: Oxford University Press, 1990).
Thompson, M. P., 'Reception Theory and the Interpretation of Historical Meaning', *History and Theory*, Vol. 32, No. 3, (1993).
Togarasei, L., 'Fighting HIV and AIDS with the Bible: Towards HIV and AIDS Biblical Criticism', in Ezra Chitando (ed.), *Mainstreaming HIV and AIDS in Theological Education: Experiences and Explorations* (Geneva: WCC Publications 2008), 71-82.
Tompkins, J. P. (ed.), *Reader-Response Criticism: From Formalism to Post-Structuralism* (Baltimore, MD: Johns Hopkins University Press, 1980).
Tov, E., *Textual Criticism of the Hebrew Bible* (2nd rev. edn; Minneapolis: Fortress, 2001).
Turner, P., *The Bible Story* (illus. Brian Wildsmith; London: Oxford University Press, 1968).
Twomey, J., 'The Biblical Man in Black: Paul in Johnny Cash / Johnny Cash in Paul', *Biblical Interpretation* 19 (2011), 223-52.
Uexküll, J. von *A Foray Into the Worlds of Animals and Humans: With a Theory of Meaning* (trans. J. O'Neil; Minneapolis: University of Minnesota Press, 2010).
Ulrich, E., *The Dead Sea Scrolls and the Origins of the Bible* (Grand Rapids, MI: Eerdmans, 1999).
Ulrich, E., 'The Text of Daniel in the Qumran Scrolls', in J. Collins and P. Flint (eds), *The Book of Daniel: Composition and Reception, vol. 2* (VTSup 83; Leiden: Brill, 2001), 573-85.
Unknown, *Noah's Ark* (illus. Gill Guile; Kettering: Bumblebee Books, 2000).

Van Seters, J., 'A Response To G. Aichele, P. Miscall and R. Walsh, "An Elephant In The Room: Historical-Critical And The Postmodern Interpretations Of The Bible"', *Journal of Hebrew Studies* 9: 26, (2009), http://www.jhsonline.org/Articles/article_128.pdf [accessed 7 January 2013].

Wainwright, A. W., *Mysterious Apocalypse: Interpreting the Book of Revelation* (Nashville: Abingdon Press, 1993).

Wallerstein, I., *The Modern World-System IV: Centrist Liberalism Triumphant, 1789-1914* (Berkeley: University of California Press, 2011).

Walsh, B. J., *Kicking at the Darkness: Bruce Cockburn and the Christian Imagination* (Grand Rapids: Baker, 2011).

Walton, S., 'What Is Progress in New Testament Studies?', *Exp. Tim.* 124 (2013), 209-26.

Ware, R., *The Second Part of Foxes and Firebrands: or, a Specimen of the Danger and Harmony of Popery and Separation* (Dublin: Printed by Jos. Ray, for Jos. Howes, to be sold by Awnsham Churchill, 1682), 2-9.

Weinrich, W. C. (ed.), *Ancient Christian Texts: Latin Commentaries on Revelation* (Downers Grove: IVP Academic, 2011).

Welch, S. D., ' "Lush Life": Foucault's Analytics of Power and a Jazz Aesthetic,' in *The Blackwell Companion to Postmodern Theology*, ed. Graham Ward (Oxford: Blackwell Publishing, 2005), 79-104.

Werner, E., *The Sacred Bridge: The interdependence of liturgy and music in synagogue and church in the first millennium* (London: Dobson, 1959).

Werner, E. A., 'das Kunstwerk des Monats' (Westfälisches Landesmuseum, Münster, Juli 1999), n.p.

West, G. O., *The Academy of the Poor: Towards a Dialogical Reading of the Bible* (Pietermaritzburg: Cluster Publications, 2003).

West, G. O., 'Early Encounters with the Bible among the BaTlhaping: Historical and Hermeneutical Signs', *Biblical Interpretation* 12 (2004), 251-81.

West, G. O., 'The Bible and the Female Body in Ibandla Lamanazaretha: Isaiah Shembe and Jephthah's Daughter', *Old Testament Essays* 20, no. 2 (2007), 489-509.

West, G. O., 'Male and Female Bodies in the Teaching of Isaiah Shembe: Possible Implications for HIV and AIDS', in *Broken Bodies and Healing Communities: The Challenge of HIV and AIDS in the South African Context*, ed. R. Neville Richardson (Pietermaritzburg: Cluster Publications, 2009), 39-60.

West, G. O., 'Jesus, Jacob Zuma, and the New Jerusalem: Religion in the Public Realm between Polokwane and the Presidency', *Journal for the Study of Religion* 23, no. 1&2 (2010), 43-70.

West, G. O. and Bongi Zengele, 'The Medicine of God's Word: What People Living with HIV and AIDS Want (and Get) from the Bible', *Journal of Theology for Southern Africa* 125 (2006), 51-63.

West, J., 'Blogging the Bible: A Short History', *Bulletin for the Study of Religion* 39 (2010), 3-13.

West, J., 'What Languages Must One Know in order to be Competent in the Field of Biblical Studies?', http://zwingliusredivivus.wordpress.com/2011/09/06/what-languages-must-one-know-in-order-to-be-competent-in-the-field-of-biblical-studies/.White, H., 'Interpretation in History', *New Literary History*, Vol. 4, No. 2, (1973).

White, H., *Metahistory: The Historical Imagination in Nineteenth-Century Europe* (Baltimore, MD: Johns Hopkins University Press, 1973).

White, J., 'Students must now choose between learning and earning,' *New Statesman*, 5 June 2011, http://www.newstatesman.com/education/2011/06/students-university-learning [accessed April 9, 2013].

Wilson, B. R., *Religion in Sociological Perspective* (Oxford: Oxford University Press, 1982).
Wimbush, V. L., 'The Bible and African Americans: An Outline of an Interpretative History', in Cain Hope Felder (ed.), *Stony the Road We Trod: African American Biblical Interpretation* (Minneapolis: Fortress, 1991), 81–97.
Wimbush, V. L., 'Reading Texts through Worlds, Worlds through Texts', *Semeia* 62 (1993), 129–40.
Witherington, B., 'The Pretenders and the Contenders – NT Studies Doctoral Students', http://www.patheos.com/blogs/bibleandculture/2011/09/04/the-pretenders-and-the-contenders-nt-studies-doctoral-students/.
Woude, A. S. van der, 'Die Dopplesprachigkeit des Buches Daniel', in A. S. van der Woude (ed.), *The Book of Daniel in the Light of New Findings* (Leuven: Leuven University Press, 1993), 3–12.
Zahn, T., *Acta Joannis unter Benutzung von C. v. Tischendorf's Nachlass* (Erlangen: Verlag von Andreas Deichert, 1880).
Žižek, S., *The Sublime Object of Ideology* (London and New York: Verso, 1989).
Žižek, S., *The Puppet and the Dwarf: The Perverse Core of Christianity* (Cambridge, MA: MIT Press, 2003).
Zlotowitz, M., and A. Gold (eds), *The Complete Artscroll Machzor* (trans. N. Scherman; Brooklyn: Mesorah 1998).
Zvobgo, C. J. M., *A History of Christian Missions in Zimbabwe 1890–1939* (Gweru: Mambo Press. 1996).

Index

Abraham 126, 212-13, 215
Abram, *see* Abraham
Academy 18-19, 28-9, 31, 34, 36, 39, 75, 112, 116, 167
Adorno, Theodor 119, 122, 151-2, 251, 256
Aesthetic, -ism 8, 9, 23, 111-12, 115-19, 121, 123-4, 128, 248, 252
Aichele, George 32, 46, 64-6, 70, 118, 255
Africa 9, 11, 125, 126, 128-9, 131-2, 134-5, 137-8, 161, 185-8, 191-4, 196-8, 238
AmaNazaretha 185, 187-93, 196-8
America 20, 25, 45, 47, 49-50, 54, 56, 62, 101, 108, 118, 130-1, 184-5, 204, 221, 231-3, 235, 237-8, 248
Amichai, Yehuda 9, 111, 119-23
Amnon of Mainz, Rabbi 207-8, 217
Anachronism, -tic 68, 73
Anal sex 147-8
Anxiety of influence 12, 231-3, 235, 237-8
Apocalyptic, -ism 56, 103-5, 107, 152-3, 155 163-4, 219-21, 226, 249
Aristotle 99
Audience 5, 6, 35, 54, 58, 62, 68, 173, 177, 181, 205, 226, 237, 243-4, 247
Astrology 11, 201, 212-13, 216

Babylonian astrological tablet (AO 6483) 11, 12, 202, 213-14, 216
Bal, Mieke 4, 8, 80, 83
Baptist, John the 8, 9, 80-2, 86-9, 93
Barr, James 65
Barthes, Roland 114, 146-7
Beal, Timothy 9, 47, 79-80, 111, 122-4, 128, 130, 132-4, 248
Behaviour 9, 11, 96, 98, 107, 117, 242, 245
Berlinerblau, Jacques 9, 49, 111-19, 121-4
Bible
    Children's Bible 10, 169, 172, 174-6, 180

Commentaries on Bible 22, 26-7, 29, 37, 38, 63, 75, 97, 150, 156, 161-5, 184, 212, 216, 220
Cultural Bible 49, 51-2, 56
Enlightenment Bible 51
Fragmentary Bible 111, 115, 119, 123-4
King James Bible 49-50, 51, 53
Liberal Bible 8, 49-52, 56
Neoliberal Bible 45, 52-8
Radical nature of Bible 149, 151
Biblical criticism 29, 34-5, 39, 66, 96-8, 100, 103, 113, 142-4, 149, 153, 159
Biblical Literacy 4, 172, 246
Biblioblogging 170-1
Bloch, Ernst 146, 152
Bloom, Harold 12, 231-3, 235, 238-9
Boer, Roland 3, 10, 24, 32, 34, 47, 70, 123, 124, 141-2, 146, 149, 151, 222, 243, 247, 249, 252
Branch Davidian 75

Cairo Genizah 11, 201-2, 208-11, 213, 216-17
Calvin, Jean 10, 141-2, 144, 149-51, 153
Cameron, David 49, 54
Canon 10, 18-19, 71, 114-15, 121, 126, 134, 227
Canonization 48
Capitalist, -ism 49, 51, 53-5, 58, 149, 152, 250
Cash, Johnny 35, 56, 57, 249-50
Cave, Nick 10, 141-2, 144, 151-3, 214, 221-2, 243, 247, 249
Christendom 48, 220
Chronology, -ical 19, 24, 48, 83, 157-8, 217
Cinema 24-5, 28, 33, 45, 56, 58, 71, 76, 85-6, 146, 203, 238
Classic text 128-9
Close reading 12, 75, 81, 143, 149, 158, 163, 167

Cohen, Leonard 11, 201–2, 203–5, 207–8, 211, 216–17
Coherence, -t/incoherence, -t 7, 8, 24, 28, 32, 33, 34, 35, 36, 37, 46, 47, 114, 133, 144–5
Collaborative, -ion 6–8, 27–9, 39, 44, 74, 127, 148, 169, 185
Colonialism 11, 34, 186
Community, -ies 4, 9, 11, 13, 25–6, 28–9, 31, 42, 52, 68, 98, 105–7, 112, 127–35, 156, 185–7, 189–97, 207, 216, 244
Competence 28, 34–5, 38, 69
Computing Humanities 170
Conservative, -ism 3–4, 12, 61, 68, 72–3, 113, 116, 149, 151, 224, 235, 242
Consumption 12, 79, 241, 248, 251
Corpus, -es 10–11, 21, 169, 173–6, 180, 183–4
Cranmer, Thomas 42–3
Crossley, James 7, 32–4, 43, 45–6, 50, 53, 56, 58, 70–1, 156, 171, 243, 245–8, 252–3
Culler, Jonathan 8, 80–5, 90, 93
Cultural capital 53, 56–7
Cultural history 4, 19–20, 26, 79, 111–12, 114, 119, 123–4, 248
Cultural Studies 6, 31, 45, 46, 74, 143, 250, 253

Daniel, Book of 9, 96, 103–9, 158, 220, 226
Database 10–11, 27, 169, 171–4, 176, 179–81, 183–4
Davies, Eryl 74
Davies, Philip R 111–12
Death 41, 44, 57, 86, 88, 114, 120, 145, 146, 150–3, 161, 165, 187, 189, 191, 195, 206, 213–15, 220, 223, 231–2, 249
Decaffeinated Bible 49, 51
Deleuze, Gilles 8, 9, 80, 82, 84–6, 93, 96, 98–9, 101
Depeche Mode 12, 35, 219–25, 227–8, 230
Dialectics 75–6, 117, 146, 152–3
Digital Humanities 10, 169, 170–2, 184
Doxa (Bourdieu) 114–15, 117, 119, 122

Engels, Friedrich 144, 147, 219–20, 230
Erotics of reading 10, 141

Eschatology 219, 221
Esther, Book of 36, 82, 99–100
Ethology 98–101
Etiology 99–100
Evangelical 18, 42–3, 56–8
Exclusivism, -tic 226, 229–30
Exile 20, 121, 145, 159–63, 165–6, 226
Expert, -ise 6, 26, 33, 38, 48, 61, 156, 172, 174, 244, 250–1
Ezekiel, Book of 12, 133, 158, 220, 226–7, 229–30

Faith 12, 31, 48, 107, 130, 132, 156, 160, 190, 195–8, 207, 219, 230, 235, 243
Feminist, -ism 18, 72, 74, 232
Film, see Cinema
Fletcher, Andrew 222–5
Forster, EM 40–1

Gadamar, Hans-Georg 4, 23, 75, 128–9, 164
Gahan, Dave 222–8
Galbraith, Dean 56, 243–5, 251
Gatekeepers 8, 69, 74
Geography, -ical 157–9, 168
Gillingham, Susan 7, 76
Gore, Martin 12, 220–4, 227–30
Gove, Michael 51
Guattari, Felix 8, 80, 82, 84–6, 93

Heresy, -tic 51, 73, 117, 122, 229, 247–8
Hermeneutics 11, 23, 24, 37, 62–3, 65, 73, 75–6, 80, 113, 115, 128–9, 135–6, 185–6, 191, 193, 205, 212
Hermeneutics of suspicion 65
Herod 81–2, 84, 86–93
Heterodox 113, 116–17, 222
Historical criticism 6, 7–8, 18, 20, 22, 34–5, 38–9, 46–8, 59, 63–9, 71–6, 95, 106, 126–7, 129–30, 133, 136, 138, 156, 163–4, 166–8, 245
Homosexual, -ity 41–2, 137
House, Son 221–2
Hurtado, Larry 32–6, 38, 40, 43, 46, 69, 70–1, 74, 171
Hurtadogate 69, 171
Hybrid 86, 112–15, 117, 124, 187

Iconography, ical 22, 83–5, 93
Identity 7, 12, 31, 32, 36, 54, 96, 100, 105, 143, 229, 246, 250
Imagine, -ary, -ative, -ion 11–12, 37, 43, 68, 73, 76, 112, 114–15, 118, 121, 123, 152, 155–6, 162–3, 166–7, 198, 229, 231–2, 234, 238, 242, 253
Improvise, -ation 111, 115–19, 122, 124
Individual, -ism 3, 6, 7, 10, 11, 13, 19–20, 25–8, 39, 53, 72, 98, 100, 117, 130–1, 162, 193, 197–8, 212, 216, 225–6, 232, 235, 242, 246–8, 250
Intertextuality 8, 12, 80–2, 84–5, 93, 213
Intrinsic qualities 36
Islam, *see* Muslim

Jauss, Hans Robert 4, 23, 128
Jephthah's daughter 11, 185, 187–95
John the Revelator (Depeche Mode) 12, 221–2, 225–7, 229–30
John the Revelator (Son House) 221–2
Josiah 32, 42
Judaism 34, 36, 39, 48, 98, 229
Judges, Book of 185–6, 187–8, 190–4, 196, 198

Koresh, David 75

Language, -s 6, 12, 17, 21, 33–4, 38–9, 43, 49, 51–2, 55–8, 67–72, 74, 116, 119, 121–2, 142–4, 146, 159, 174, 184, 206, 228–9, 232, 235–8, 243, 246–9
Lenin, Vladimir 10, 141–2, 144–8, 150, 153
Lennon, John 12, 231, 233–8
Letter template 148
Liturgy, -ical 11, 21, 28, 43, 187–8, 190–3, 201–2, 205–8, 216–17
Love 17, 31, 41, 50, 120, 141–2, 144, 146–7, 151–2, 192, 223, 228, 233–6, 249
Lyons, William John 8, 12, 35, 38–9, 56, 62–8, 74–6, 111, 141, 219, 249–50
Lyricist 12, 201, 220, 225, 232, 234–6, 238, 242, 247, 249, 250
Lyrics, -ists 12, 56, 119, 121–2, 152, 201–2, 205, 217, 223–6, 233–7, 242–6, 249, 251

Maimonides 206
Manuscript 24, 28, 37–8, 55, 96–7, 103, 142, 160, 164, 184, 201–2, 207–10
Marx, Karl 150, 219
Marxist, -ism 142, 247, 253
Metaphor 7, 9, 10, 17, 63, 95, 96, 120, 121, 134, 153, 155–7, 193, 232
Method, -ology 5–8, 10, 18–20, 22, 23–4, 28, 31–2, 34, 36, 40, 48, 61–8, 70, 73–6, 98, 112, 123, 126, 128–9, 146, 152, 165, 167, 169, 176, 183–4, 206, 211, 213, 222, 230, 241–2, 248–51, 253
Miracle, -ulous 146, 166, 191
Miscall, Peter 64
Missionary, ies 11, 135, 137, 160, 166, 186–7
Morality 96, 101, 109, 148, 193, 223,
Muller, Carol 11, 191–7
Multicultural, -ism 51, 247
Multimodal Humanities 170–2
Music, 9, 17, 21, 24, 25, 28, 35, 39, 55–7, 76, 84–5, 98, 118, 142, 151–3, 191, 202–3, 205, 217, 221, 223, 226, 231–4, 236–8, 241–3
  Christian Contemporary Music 56, 236–7, 245
  Manchester Music 243, 245–7
  Popular Music 7, 11–12, 5557, 152–3, 199, 202, 204–5, 217, 221, 223, 226, 231–4, 236–8, 241–53
Musicology 245, 248–9
Muslim 39, 52, 181, 226, 229,
Myth 47, 64–6, 83, 116, 147, 159, 232

Neoliberal, -ism 45, 52–8
Norman, Larry 12, 231, 233–6, 238

Oxford Bible Commentary, The 75

Painting 9, 84, 85, 87–93, 155
Patmos 10, 12, 107, 155–7, 159–68, 227, 229–30
Patristic 48, 157–8, 160–2, 165–6, 251
Planetary fate (Talmud) 212–13, 215
Poet, -ic, -ry 9, 12, 18, 20, 21, 71, 111, 116, 119–22, 124, 152, 202, 205–7, 216–17, 231–3, 235, 238, 250
Poetic Retelling 119, 122

Postcolonial, -ism 71, 127, 131–2, 191, 197
Postmodern, -ism 32, 34, 46, 49, 54–5, 57–8, 64–7, 69, 72–3, 75, 114, 127, 193, 249
Pragmatism, -ic 4, 18, 23, 25, 46, 81, 91, 246
Prayer 11, 12, 21, 43, 97, 103, 201–4, 206–13, 215–17, 224
Pre-posterous history 8, 80
Problematic Field 9, 101–2
Production 12, 47, 79, 80, 83, 88, 96, 98, 105, 117–18, 124, 134, 145, 152, 170–2, 192, 241, 248, 250
Protestant, -ism 4, 21, 48, 50, 150, 161
Psalms, Book of 7, 19–25, 27–9, 188–9

Qualitative analysis 10, 180
Quantitative analysis 10, 180, 249

Räisäsnen, Heikki 220
Reader-response criticism 20, 62
Redemption 152–3
Retelling 9, 119, 122, 136, 172–81, 183–4
Revelation, Book of 12, 35–6, 42, 51, 56, 107, 155, 157, 159–63, 165–6, 220–1, 226, 230
Rezeptionsgeschichte 4, 23, 35, 42, 127–8
Rhizome 84–6, 93
Rhizomorphous systems 8, 80, 84–6
Roberts, Jonathan 23–4, 26
Rollins, Sonny 204–5
Roman Catholicism 21, 43, 50, 246–7
Rosh Hashanah (Jewish New Year) 11, 201, 204–5, 207, 209, 211
Rowland, Christopher 20, 22, 23, 25, 48, 161, 220–2, 229

Sachs, Abraham 213
Salome 84, 87–9, 92
Sample, Tex 248–50
Sarai/Sarah 212
Sawyer, John 22–4, 26–7, 128
Secular Bible Translation (SBT) 114
Secularization 242–8
Selection, -vity 11, 25, 28, 63, 90, 107, 151, 157, 173–4, 176, 180, 191
Sex 41–2, 49, 51, 120, 137–8, 147–8, 190, 192, 228–30
Shembe, Isaiah 11, 185–98
Sismondi, Jean de 147–8

Sithole, Nkosinathi 193–8
Sociology 12, 26, 31, 33, 112–13, 117, 128, 143, 147, 241, 242, 244–7, 251–3
Sodom and Gomorrah 9, 41, 127, 136–7, 159, 165
Song 10–12, 22, 37, 56, 57, 102, 103, 115, 136, 137, 152–3, 184, 191, 201–4, 208, 217, 220–7, 229–38, 242, 244, 247–51
Songwriter, *see* Lyricist
Spinoza, Baruch 99
Spiritual 50, 159, 192–3, 198, 205, 223, 228, 230–1, 234–5, 242, 245–7
Stalin, Josef 146, 219–20, 230
Subculture 56, 246
Subjective, -ity 7, 12, 25–6, 37, 115, 119, 172, 180, 241, 246, 248–50, 253
Sugirtharajah, RS 52–3
Synagogue 11, 18, 29, 48, 201–2, 207–10, 216

Talmud 11, 107, 121, 206, 212–13, 216
Twomey, Jay 249–50

U2 243–5, 251
Uexküll, Jakob von 99
Undertaker, The (WWE) 57–8
Unetaneh toqef 11–12, 201–2, 204–5, 207–16

Van Seters, John 64–6, 68–9, 73–4, 118
Vulgate 160

Waco 75–6
West, -ern 25, 33–5, 37, 43, 49, 52, 53, 58, 70, 85, 108, 134, 137–8, 142, 145, 158, 162–3, 166, 232, 243, 246–7
Who by fire (Leonard Cohen) 11, 201–9, 211, 216
Wirkungsgeschichte 4, 20, 23, 25, 42, 127–8
Wissenschaftlich 66, 74–5

Yom Kippur (Day of Atonement) 11, 201, 205, 207–11

Zimbabwe 9, 125–7, 132, 134–7
Žižek, Slavoj 51–2
Zulay, M 207–8

www.ingramcontent.com/pod-product-compliance
Lightning Source LLC
Chambersburg PA
CBHW072127290426
44111CB00012B/1813